BLACK LEGACY PRESS™
WWW.BLACKLEGACYPRESS.ORG

SLAVE NARRATIVES

VOLUME I
ALABAMA NARRATIVES

By
United States.
Work Projects Administration

Copyright © 2024 by BLACKLEGACYPRESS.ORG

All rights reserved. No part of this publication may be reproduced or transmitted in any form or by any means electronic or mechanical, including information storage and retrieval systems without permission in writing from the publisher, except for student research using the appropriate citations.

ISBN: 978-1-63652-196-1

SLAVE NARRATIVES

A Folk History of Slavery in the United States. From Interviews with Former Slaves

**UNITED STATES.
WORK PROJECTS ADMINISTRATION**

TYPEWRITTEN RECORDS PREPARED BY
THE FEDERAL WRITERS' PROJECT
1936-1938
ASSEMBLED BY
THE LIBRARY OF CONGRESS PROJECT
WORK PROJECTS ADMINISTRATION
FOR THE DISTRICT OF COLUMBIA
SPONSORED BY THE LIBRARY OF
CONGRESS

WASHINGTON 1941

VOLUME I
ALABAMA NARRATIVES

Prepared by
the Federal Writers' Project of
the Works Progress Administration
for the State of Alabama

CONTENTS

Charlie Aarons 1
Anthony Abercrombie 7
Molly Ammond(Ammonds) 11
Charity Anderson 15
Gus Askew 19
Tom Baker 23
Henry Barnes 27
Nathan Beauchamp 33
Oliver Bell 37
Nelson Birdsong 45
Ank Bishop 49
Siney Bonner 55
Jennie Bowen 61
Nannie Bradfield 65
Martha Bradley 69
Allen Brown 73
Gus Brown 77
Walter Calloway 83
Esther King Casey 89
Amy Chapman 93
Emma Chapman 99
Henry Cheatam 105
Laura Clark 113
Hattie Clayton 121
Wadley Clemons 125

William Colbert	129
Tildy Collins	133
Sara Colquitt	139
Mandy McCullough Cosby	143
Emma Crockett	147
Cheney Cross	151
Matilda Pugh Daniel	161
Carrie Davis	165
Clara Davis	171
George Dillard	173
Ella Dilliard	177
Rufus Dirt	183
Katherine Eppes	187
Reuben Fitzpatrick	191
Heywood Ford	193
Bert Frederick	197
Delia Garlic	201
Angie Garrett	207
Henry Garry	213
Georgia	223
Fannie Gibson	225
Frank Gill	227
Jim Gillard	233
Mary Ella Grandberry	237
Esther Green	247
Jake Green	251
Charity Grigsby	255

Charles Hayes 261
Lizzie Hill 265
Gabe Hines 269
Adeline Hodges 275
Caroline Holland 281
Jane Holloway 285
Joseph Holmes 289
Josh Horn 303
Emma L. Howard 315
Everett Ingram 321
Hannah Irwin 327
Martha Jackson 331
Jane 337
Hilliard Johnson 341
Randolph Johnson 347
Abraham Jones 349
Emma Jones 355
Hannah Jones 359
Josephine 363
Lucindy Lawrence Jurdon 365
Lucy Kimball 369
Ellen King 373
Mandy Leslie 377
Dellie Lewis 383
Lightnin' 387
Billy Abraham Longslaughter 389
Louis 393

Tom McAlpin	399
Anne Maddox	405
Mandy	411
Frank Menefee	415
Isaam Morgan	421
Tony Morgan	427
Mose	431
Sally Murphy	437
Hattie Anne Nettles	441
W.E. Northcross	445
Chapter 1—How Reared	445
Chapter 2—Entering The Ministry	447
Chapter 3—My Work	451
Wade Owens	455
Molly Parker	461
Lindy Patton	465
Simon Phillips	469
Roxy Pitts	475
Carrie Pollard	479
Irene Poole	483
Nicey Pugh	487
Sally Reynolds	493
Mary Rice	497
Cornelia Robinson	501
Gus Rogers	505
Janie Scott	509
Maugan Shepherd	513

Allen Sims	517
Frank Smith	521
John Smith	527
Annie Stanton	533
Theodore Fontaine Stewart	537
George Strickland	543
Cull Taylor	549
Daniel Taylor	553
George Taylor	557
Amanda Tellis	563
Ellen Thomas	567
Elizabeth Thomas	573
Mollie Tillman	575
Alonza Fantroy Toombs	579
William Henry Towns	583
Stepney Underwood	593
Charlie Van Dyke	597
Lilah Walker	603
Simon Walker	607
Lucindia Washington	611
Eliza White	617
Mingo White	621
Abe Whitess	633
Callie Williams	637
Silvia Witherspoon	643
George Young	647

CHARLIE AARONS

Personal contact with Uncle Charlie Aarons
Oak Grove, Alabama
—Written by Mary A. Poole

HE LOVED YOUNG MARSTER JOHN

Some friends driving to Oak Grove, Ala., gave the writer the opportunity on August 4th to interview an old ex-slave, Charlie Aarons, who is quite venerable in appearance, and who, when asked his age, replied:

"Madam I don't know but I sure been 'round here long time", and when asked how old he was at the time of the Surrender he answered:

"I was a man able to do a man's work so I 'spects I was eighteen or twenty years old."

Uncle Charlie, as he is known among his own color and the white people who know him, told the writer he was born at Petersburg Va., and his parents, Aaron and Louisa, were owned by a Mr. J.H. White, who had a store in the city, but no plantation. His parents had three children, two boys and one girl, and when Uncle Charlie was about ten years of age, he was sold by Mr. White to a speculator named Jones who brought him to Mobile. He recalled being placed on the block, at the slave mart on Royal and State streets, and the anxiety of hearing the different people bidding for him, and being finally sold to a Mr. Jason Harris, who lived near Newton Station in Jasper County, Miss.

Uncle Charlie never saw or heard of his parents or brother and sister again and never knew what became of them.

Uncle Charlie said Mr. Harris was a pretty rough master, and somewhat close. All rations were weighed out and limited. He had a white overseer and a negro driver, who was the meanest of all.

Mr. Jason Harris had about sixty slaves, and a large plantation of a hundred acres, the men and women worked in the fields from six to six, except on Saturday, when they had half day holiday to clean up generally.

The home of the Harris family was a large two story house and the quarters were the regular log cabins with clay chimneys. They cooked in their cabins, but during the busy season in the fields their dinners were sent out to them each slave having his own tin pail marked with his name. Water would be sent out in a barrel mounted on an ox cart.

The old men and women looked after the children of the slaves while their parents worked in the fields.

When the writer asked Uncle Charlie, if his master or mistress ever taught him to read or write, he smiled and said:

"No, Madam, only to work".

When asked if they had any special festivities at Christmas or any other holiday, he replied:

"No, we had no special jolifications".

Saturday nights they would sing and dance in the quarters and have prayer meetings, then on some Sundays, they would hitch up the mules to a big wagon and all go to the white folks church: and again there would be camp meetings held and the slaves from all the surrounding plantations would attend, going to same in these large wagons, sometimes having four mules to a wagon. They then would have a jolly time along the way, singing and calling to one another, and making friends.

Uncle Charlie, said, he drove many a load of cotton in the large mule wagons from Newton Station to Enterprise, Mississippi.

When asked if that wasn't a chance to run away, he replied:

"Git away, why Madam, those nigger dogs would track you and all you got was a beating."

Uncle Charlie seemed to look off in the distance and said: "You know, Madam, I never saw a slave rebuked until I came to Mississippi," and I just couldn't understand at first, but he grinned and said: "Lordy, Madam, some of those niggers were onery, too, and a nigger driver was a driver sure enough."

When the Master's son John Harris went to war, Charlie went with him as his body guard, and when asked what his duties were, he replied:

"I looked after Marster John, tended the horses and the tents. I recalls well, Madam, the siege of Vicksburg."

The writer then asked him if he wasn't afraid of the shot and shell all around him.

"No, Madam," he replied, "I kept way in the back where the camp was, for I didn't like to feel the earth trembling 'neath my feet, but you see, Madam, I loved young Marster John, and he loved me, and I just had to watch over that boy, and he came through all right."

Uncle Charlie said when they were told the Yankees were coming through from their headquarters in Meridian, Mississippi, and warned of their raids, they all made to the swamps and staid until they had passed on, but that the Yankees did not disturb the Jason Harris plantation.

After the Surrender Charlie came to Mobile and worked at the Yankee Camp, living in the quarters located in Holly's Garden. He drove their wagons and was paid $14.00 a month and his keep. After his discharge he worked on steamboats and followed different lines of work, being employed for several years at Mr. M.L. Davis' saw mill, and is at present living on the Davis place at Oak Grove, Ala., an old Southern home, with quarters originally built for the employees of the mill and still known as the "quarters", and like other ante-bellum homes they have their private burying ground on the place.

Uncle Charlie was married four times, but now a widower. He had four children, two boys who are dead, and two girls, one Carrie Johnson, a widow, living in

Kushla, Ala., and the other, Ella Aarons, a grass widow, living in Mobile, Ala.

Uncle Charlie says he saw Jeff. Davis as an old man, after the war at Mississippi City, Miss., and then his face lit up, and he said; "Wait a minute, Madam, I saw another president, let me think,—Yes, Madam I saw President Grant. He came through Mobile from New Orleans, and my! there was a big parade that day."

When asked about Abraham Lincoln, Uncle Charlie thought awhile, and answered:

"According to what was issued out in the Bible, there was a time for slavery, people had to be punished for their sin, and then there was a time for it not to be, and the Lord had opened a good view to Mr. Lincoln, and he promoted a good idea."

When he was asked about Booker T. Washington he replied:

"It was traversed out to him until the white folks took part with him and helped him carry on."

Uncle Charlie thinks the present day folks are bad and wicked, and dont realize anything like the old folks.

Charlie is a Baptist, became one when he sought the Lord and thinks all people should be religious.

United States. Work Projects Administration

ANTHONY ABERCROMBIE

Interview with Anthony Abercrombie
—Susie R. O'Brien, Uniontown, Alabama

OLD JOE CAN KEEP HIS TWO BITS

Uncle Ant'ny sat dozing in the early morning sunshine on his rickety front porch. He is a thin little old man with patches of white wool here and there on his bald head, and an expression of kindness and gentleness on his wrinkled old face.

As I went cautiously up the steps, which appeared none too safe, his cane which had been leaning against his chair, fell to the floor with a clatter. He awoke with a start and began fumbling around for it with his trembling and bony hands.

"Uncle Ant'ny, you don't see so well, do you?" I asked as I recovered the stick for him. "No ma'am, I sho' don't," he replied. "I ain't seed none outen one of my eyes in near 'bout sixty years, and de doctor say I got a catalac on de yuther one; but I knows you is white folks. I always is been puny, but I reckon I does purty well considerin' I is a hundred years old."

"How do you know you are that old?" I inquired of him. Without hesitation he answered, "I knows I's dat old 'cause my mistis put it down in de Bible. I was born on de fourth day and I was a full growed man when de war come on in '61.

"Yassum, my mind kinder comes and goes, but I can always 'member 'bout slave'y time. Hits de things what happen in dese days dat's so easy for me to disremember. I b'longed to Marster Jim Abercrombie. His plantation was 'bout sixteen miles north of Marion in Bibb county. When his son, young Jim, ma'ied, old Marse Jim give me to him and he fetched me to Perry county.

"No'm, old marster didn't go to war 'ca'se he was corrupted; he was deaf in bofe ears and couldn't see good nuther. But he didn't care much 'bout me 'caze I was puny like and warn't much 'count in de field.

"My mistis, Miss Lou, was raisin' me up to be a carriage driver, an' she was jes' as good to me as she could be. She useta dose me up wid castor oil, jimson root, and dogwood tea when I'd be feelin' po'ly, and she'd always take up for me when Marse Jim get in behind me 'bout somep'n. I reckon though I was a purty worrisome nigger in dem days; always gettin' in some kind of mischief.

"O yassum, I useta go to meetin'. Us niggers didn't have no meetin' house on de plantation, but Marse Jim 'lowed us to build a brush arbor. Den two years atter de surrender I took consideration and j'ined up wid de Lawd. Dat's how come I live so long. De Lawd done told me, 'Antn'y, you got a hundred and twenty miles to trabel. Dat mean you gwine to live a hundred and twenty years, if you stay on de straight an' narrow road. But if you don't, you gotter go jes' de same as all de yuthers.'"

"Tell me something about your master's slaves and his overseers," I asked of him.

"Well," he said, "Marse Jim had 'bout three hundred slaves, and he hed one mighty bad overseer. But he got killed down on de bank of de creek one night. Dey never did find out who killed him, but Marse Jim always b'lieved de field han's done it. 'Fore dat us niggers useta go down to de creek to wash ourselves, but atter de overseer got killed down dar, us jes' leave off dat washin', 'cause some of 'em seed de overseer's ha'nt down dar floatin' over de creek.

"Dar was another ha'nt on de plantation, too. Marse Jim had some trouble wid a big double-j'inted nigger named Joe. One day he turn on Marse Jim wid a fence rail, and Marse Jim had to pull his gun an' kill him. Well, dat happen in a skirt of woods what I get my lightwood what I use to start a fire. One day I went to dem same woods to get some 'simmons. Another nigger went wid me, and he clumb de tree to shake de 'simmons down whilst I be pickin' 'em up. 'Fore long I heared another tree shakin' every time us shake our tree, dat other tree shake too, and down came de 'simmons from it. I say to myself, 'Dat's Joe, 'cause he likes 'simmons too.' Den I grab up my basket and holler to de boy in de tree, 'nigger turn loose and drap down from dar, and ketch up wid me if you can. I's leavin' here right now, 'cause Old Joe is over dar gettin' 'simmons too.'

"Den another time I was in de woods choppin' lightwood. It was 'bout sundown, and every time my ax go 'whack' on de lightwood knot, I hear another whack 'sides mine. I stops and lis'ens and don't hear nothin'. Den I starts choppin' ag'in I hears de yuther whacks. By dat time my houn' dog was crouchin' at my feets, wid de hair standin' up on his back and I couldn't make him git up nor budge.

"Dis time I didn' stop for nothin'. I jes' drap my ax right dar, an' me and dat houn' dog tore out for home lickety split. When us got dar Marse Jim was settin' on de porch, an' he say: 'Nigger, you been up to somep'n you got no business. You is all outen breath. Who you runnin' from?' Den I say: 'Marse Jim, somebody 'sides me is choppin' in yo' woods, an' I can't see him. And Marse Jim, he say: 'Ah, dat ain't nobody but Ole Joe. Did he owe you anythin'?' An' I say: 'Yassah, he owe me two-bits for helpin' him shuck corn.' 'Well,' Marse Jim say, 'don't pay him no mind: it jes' Old Joe come back to pay you.'

"Anyhow, I didn' go back to dem woods no mo'. Old Joe can jes' have de two-bits what he owe me, 'cause I don't want him follerin' 'roun' atter me. When he do I can't keep my mind on my business."

MOLLY AMMOND (AMMONDS)

Interview with Molly Ammond (Ammonds)
—*Gertha Couric*

JESUS HAS MY CHILLUN COUNTED

I walked along a dusty road under the blazing sun. In the shade of a willow tree a Negro man was seated with his legs drawn up and his arms crossed upon his knees. His head rested face downward upon his arms, as he had the aspect of one in deep slumber. Beside him munching on a few straggly weeds, a cantankerous mule took little notice of his surroundings.

"Can you tell me where Aunt Molly Ammonds lives?" I asked in a loud voice. The Negro stirred slowly, finally raising his head, and displaying three rabbit teeth, he accompanied his answer with a slight gesture of his hand.

"Yassuh, dar her house raght across de road; de house wid de climbin' roses on hit."

"Thank you," I said.

"Yassuh," was the drawled response, and the Negro quickly resumed his former posture.

Aunt Molly Ammonds is as gentle as a little child. Her voice is soft and each phrase measured to the slow functionings of her aged mind.

Molly Ammond (Ammonds), Eufaula, Alabama

"Honey," she said, "you ain't gwineter believe dis, but I is de mammy of thirty chilluns. Jesus got 'em counted an' so is me. I was born in a log cabin dat had a loft, an' it was on Marse Lee Cato's plantation five miles wes' of Eufaula. My pappy's name was Tobe Cato an' my mammy's was Sophia. I had one sister, Marthy, an' two brothers, Bong and Toge. My pappy made all de furniture dat went in our house an' it were might' good furniture too. Us useta cook on de fiahplace. Us would cook ash cakes. Dey was made outen meal, water and a little pinch of lard; on Sundays dey was made outen flour, buttermilk an' lard. Mammy would rake all de ashes out de fiahplace, den kivver de cake wid de hot ashes an' let it cool till it was done.

"Yas Missy," she continued, "I recollects dat I was 'bout twelve or fo'teen when de s'render come, kaze a little atter dat I ma'ied Pastor Ammonds. We walked ober to Georgetown an' it was de fus' time I eber had shoes, and I got dem fum ole Massa. I remembers dat I ma'ied in a striped calico dress."

"Aunt Molly," I said, "you're getting a little ahead of your story, tell me something about your plantation life before the war."

"Well, honey, Massa Lee's place was 'bout three miles long an' two miles wide, and we raised cotton, cawn, 'taters and all sorts of vegetables. We had a mean oberseer dat always wanted to whup us, but massa wouldn't 'llow no whuppin'. Sometimes de massa whould ride over de place on a hoss, an' when he come up on de oberseer a-fussin' at a nigger, Massa say, 'Don't talk rough to dat nigger when he doin' de bes' he can.'

"My pappy had a little garden of his own back of his cabin, an' he raised some chickens for us to eat, an' we had aigs nearly ev'y mornin'.

"De only work I done on de plantation was to nuss some little niggers when dere mammy an' pappy was in de fiel's. Twarn't hard.

"Nawsuh! I ain't never seed no slave in chains.

Massa Lee was a good man. He had a church built called de brush house, dat had a flo' and some seats, an' a top made outen pine boughs, an' massa's pa, Mr. Cato, would preach eve'y Sunday. We sung songs lak 'I Heered De Voice of Jesus Say,' an' 'I'se Gwine to Die no Mo.' We was all babtized in de creek, but none of us was taught to read or write.

"No-suh, I ain't never seed no slave run away. Us was treated fine. Our folks was quality. We had plenty som'n t'eat, but dem slaves hadda work powerful hard though. Atter dey come home fum de fiel's dey was so tired dat dey go raght to sleep, except when de massa had barbecues. Christmas was de big time; dere was several days to res' an' make merryin' an' lots of dem no count niggers got drunk.

"When us slaves was sick, Massa Lee would send to Eufaula to fetch Dr. Thornton to give us some medicine. We had de bes' treatment ever.

"Yassuh, white folks, dem days is long ago. All my chilluns done died or wandered away an' my ole man been dead goin' on twenty years. I been here a long time by myself."

"Aunt Molly," I interrupted. "There's one thing I've always been wanting to ask one of you ex-slaves, and that is: what you thought of people like Abraham Lincoln, Jefferson Davis and Booker T. Washington."

A puzzled expression came of the face of the old Negro. "White folks," she said after a moments deliberation, "I don't believes I is had de pleasure of meetin' dem gent'mens."

CHARITY ANDERSON

Interview with Charity Anderson
—Ila B. Prine

Charity Anderson, who believes she is 101 years old, was born at Bell's Landing on the Alabama River, where her owner, Leslie Johnson, operated a wood-yard, which supplied fuel to the river steamers, and a tavern where travelers whiled away the delays of a dubious riverboat schedule.

Rheumatic and weak, she no longer ventures from her house in Toulminville, on the outskirts of Mobile, but sits, with her turbaned head and bespectacled eyes, rocking the long hours away in a creaky old chair and knitting or sewing, or just gazing into a past painted by the crackling flames in the fireplace.

Charity Anderson, Toulminville, Alabama

"I has so much trouble gittin' up and down de steps and ober de groun', I jist makes myself happy heah, cause—thank de Lawd—I'se on Zion's March," is her resigned comment.

"Missy, peoples don't live now; and niggers ain't got no manners, and doan' know nothin' 'bout waitin' on folks. I kin remember de days w'en I was one of de house servants. Dere was six of us in de ole Massa's house—me, Sarai, Lou, Hester, Jerry and Joe. Us did'n' know nothin' but good times den. My job was lookin' atter de corner table whar nothin' but de desserts set. Joe and Jerry, dey was de table boys. Dey neber tetched nothin' wid dere han's, but used de waiter to pass things wid.

"My ole Massa was a good man. He treated all his slaves kind, and took good kere of 'em. But, honey, all de white folks wan't good to dere slaves. I's seen po' niggers 'mos' tore up by dogs and whupped 'tell dey bled w'en dey did'n' do lak de white folks say. But, thank de Lawd, I had good white folks and dey sho' did trus' me, too. I had charge of all de keys to de house, and I waited on de Missis' and de chillun. I laid out all de clo'se on Sat'dy night, and den Sunday mawnin's I'd pick up all de dirty things. Dey did'n' have a thing to do. Us house servants had a hahd job keepin' de pickaninnies out'er de dinin' room whar ole Massa et, cause w'en dey would slip in and stan' by his cheer, w'en he finished eatin' he would fix a plate for 'em and let 'em set on the hearth.

"No mam, Missy, I ain't neber worked in de fields. Ole Massa he neber planted no cotton, and I ain't seen none planted 'tell after I was free. But, honey, I could sho 'nuff wash, iron and knit and weave. Sometimes I weaved six or seven yahds of cloth, and do my house work too. I lernt the chillun how to weave, and wash, and iron, and knit too, and I's waited on de fo'th generation of our fambly. I jes' wish I could tell dese young chillun how to do. Iffen dey would only suffer me to talk to dem, I'd tell dem to be more 'spectful to dere mammies and to dere white folks and say 'yes mam' and 'no mam', instid of 'yes' and 'no' lek dey do now.

"All dis generation thinks of is 'musement. I neber had seen a show in my whole life 'tell jes' dis pas' yeah when one of dem carnival things wid de swings, and lights, and all de doin's dey have stop right in front of our house heah.

"And I ain't neber been in no trouble in all my life— ain't been in no lawsuits, and ain't been no witness eben. I allus treat ebrybody as good as I kin, and I uses my manners as good as I knows how, and de Lawd sho' has took good keer of me. Why, w'en my house burnt up, de white folks helped me so dat in no time you couldn't tell I ebber los' a thing.

"But, honey, de good ole days is now gone foreber. De ole days was railly de good times. How I wish I could go back to de days w'en we lived at Johnson's landing on de riber, when de folks would come to ketch de steamboats and we neber knowed how many to put on breakfas', dinner or supper fo', cause de boats mought be behin' times. I ain't neber had to pay a fare to ride a steamboat needer. I was a good lookin' yaller gal in dem days and rid free wherever I wanted to go.

"But whut's de use dreamin' 'bout de ole times? Dey's gone, and de world is gettin' wicked'er and wicked'er, sin grows bolder and bolder, and 'ligion colder and colder."

GUS ASKEW

Interview with Gus Askew
—*Gertha Couric*

"Dat was one time when de ban' was playin' and flags was flyin' dat us lil' niggers didn't get no joy outen it." Gus Askew smiled at the thought of the occasion as he sat on the sunny steps of his comfortable house in Eufaula. Gus was telling about the investment of Eufaula during the War between the States.

"Gen'l Grierson and his men marched right through town," Gus went on with his story of his boyhood. "Mr. Lincoln done said we was free, but us lil' niggers was too skeered to lissen to any ban' music, even iffen the so'jers had come to set us free. 'Pears like us was allus gittin' in somebody's way in dem days and gittin' skeered of somepin'. But we went on away from the so'jers and had a good time 'mongst ourselves like we always done when there wasn't any cotton pickin'. Cotton pickin' time was when we didn't have any chance to do any playin'.

"After the surrender I didn't have to do any more cotton pickin' and I went blacksmithin' for Joe Sturgis. He was the first blacksmith in dis here town. I was the second. Now my son done took on de work. They ain't so much sence all dese here automobiles done got so plentiful and might 'nigh ruint de business. But for seventy years I riz wid de sun and went to dat blacksmith shop. I's enjoying a little misery now; so I's takin' my rest."

Gus Askew, Eufaula, Alabama

Gus Askew was born a slave of the Edwards family in Henry County in 1853. He was brought to Eufaula just before the close of the war and stayed on as a blacksmith after he was freed. In his seventy years of hard work he saved enough to buy his home and some property which maintains him and his wife since age and infirmity forced him to turn over the work to his son. He has been married 54 years, numbers his white friends by the hundreds and is held in great respect by his own race.

United States. Work Projects Administration

TOM BAKER

Interview with Tom Baker
—Susie R. O'Brien

"Sho, I recollects about de slabery days," said uncle Tom as he whittled shavings from a soft piece of white pine. "I lived on a plantation down in Perry County an' I remembers a story bout somp'n dat happen to me a way back dar.

"I was a water boy for fifty fiel' han's dat worked in de sun all day long, an' I hadda carry many a bucket from de spring dat was one fiel' ober from where most of dem was workin'. De spring run down between some willow trees an' it was powerful cool down dere in de shade. I use' to lie on de moss an' let my bare belly git cool an' put my face in de outlet of de spring an' let de water trickle over my haid. Jus' about de time I gits a little rest one of dem niggers would call: 'Water boy! Bring dat bucket!' Den I grab up de bucket an' run back out in de hot sun.

"One day, on my las' trip, I was mighty tired an' I flop down on dat moss wid de sweat a-drippin' from my body, an' 'fo' I knowed it I done fell slap to sleep. When I woke up, it was almos' dark, an' I couldn't hear de slaves a-singing' in de fiel's, so I knowed dat dey had gone home. I shake my haid, an' look about me, an' my eyes came to res' on a little black bear cub a-drinkin' outen de spring. He so was a cute little boogar an' I made up my mind right den to try an' kotch him. I was jus' a little nigger 'bout ten year old an' didn't have no sense, but I sho' wanted dat little bear. He ain't seed me a-settin' dere, so I snuck up real cautious like, an' afore he knowed it I had dat little debil a-squealin' in my han's. I was jus' about to start home wid him, when I hears a rustlin' in de bushes an' afore I went ten feets, here come a big, black bear a-lopin' along right outen dem willow trees. I drop dat little critter 'caze I knowed dat was his mammy an' she was ravin' mad. When I let de little feller fall it must have hurt him somp'n awful caze he howl mo' dan eber, an' went a limpin' up to his mammy. Well, suh, dat ole woman she got so mad she made fo' me lak two bolts of lightnin', but dese here feets of mine begin a-doin' dere stuff. I knowed she was a-gainin' on me so I lets out a whoop for help. She chased me 'cross dat empty field an' 'bout dat time I seen big Jim a-comin' through a row of cawn. 'Hurry Big Jim,' I calls, 'a bear is atter me!' Big Jim was de biggest nigger on our place. He must have weighed as much as half a bale of cotton. I was jus' 'bout gittin' to de aidge of de cawn when dat bear ketched me. He give me a slap wid his paw an' I goes down wid my mouf a-scoopin' up de dus'. My back felt like somebody done put a hot iron on it. Dat bear was a mean one. I was expectin' her to chaw me up an' I drawed my body up in a knot and kivered my haid wid my hands an' waited. But dat bear neber touch me agin'. I kinda snuck my eye aroun' an' I saw big Jim havin' it out wid her. Jim, he had a long knife an' dey was a-tumblin' an' a-rollin' in de dust, while I sot dere wid my eyes a-poppin' outen my haid an' my back feelin' like it was broke. Jim he wrap his legs roun' dat bear an' 'fore you knowed it he had done stuck dat ole critter a dozen times wid dat knife.

"About fifteen minutes later me an' Jim was a-walkin' back through de cawn fiel' an' I guess we looked a sight, 'caze I was all tore up an' Jim he looked like he done mess up wid a fambly of wildcats. He was bleedin' from haid to foot. When we walked into de big house to git some treatments an' medicine for our hurts, Mistis was a-standin' dere, and when she seed me an' Jim, she almost faint. She say: 'Whut done happen to my niggers?'

"Atter me an' Jim got fixed up I was jus' as happy, kaze I done seed de bes' fight dere eber was, an' I had me a little orphan bear cub."

United States. Work Projects Administration

HENRY BARNES

Interview with Henry Barnes
—Ila B. Prine, Mobile

HE MISSES DEM 'SET-DOWN HAWGS'

In Prichard, a suburb of Mobile, lives an old, blind Negro, "Uncle Henry" Barnes, who says he was born in 1858, near Suggsville, Clarke County, Alabama.

"Cose I was borned a slave, but I don't 'member much 'bout hit, 'caze I was li'l. Dere is one t'ing I does 'member, an' dat was when dey cut watermelons at de oberseer's house an' dey want us li'l niggers run races to git our piece. I jes wouldn't run an' my mammy she whup me 'caze I so stubborn an' when I git my piece o' melon, I fly down de lane whar our log cabins was. Dem cabins was daubed wid clay, an' de chimbleys was built outten clay an' stick. Our beds was homemade an' had t'ree legs wid de yuther side nail to de wall. I 'member atter I got a big boy, my mammy had a bed made outten lumber an' I slep' in dat bed 'twel I was growed an' ma'ed.

"I 'members us's Ole Mistis, Miss Dell. Miss Dell was a good Mistis an' she useter hab Sunday School ebber' Sund'y mornin' at de Big House an' all us li'l niggers went up dar for her to teach us 'bout de Bible an' Jesus.

"Marse John was good to all he slaves an' he wouldn't stan' no rush er meanness to his niggers. Iffen de o'seer got mean, Ole Marster would turn him off. Ole Marster allus tuk good keer of he slaves, 'caze when dey got sick, he hab de doctor, jes lak when de white folks got sick. One o' Marse John's boys, Marse Bennie, was a doctor, an' he was a good doctor, cep'n' he gin us bad med'cin', but he cyured you.

"Cose us hab our med'cin' sich lak elderbush tea. Hit was red 'mos' lak whiskey an' us used hit for feber. Den dere was red sassafrac tea fer spring feber, an' dey made Jerusalem oak candy full o' seeds an' gib to de chilluns to eat so dey could git rid of worms. Den us had mullen an' pine-top tea for colds an' feber. An' when us had a swellin' dey made a poultice of mullen leabes to take de swellin' out.

"Sometimes I wishes dat I could be back to de ol' place, 'caze us did hab plenty to eat, an' at hog-killin' time us had a mor'n a plenty. Ole Marster kill eight or ten set-down hawgs at one time, an' de meat, an' de lard an' de hawgjowl an' de chitt'lin's—m'm' I kin see 'em now.

"What a set-down hawg? Hit's a hawg what done et so much corn he got so fat dat he feets can't hol' him up an' he jes set on he hin' quarters an' grunts an' eats an' eats an' grunts, 'twell day knock him in de head.

"Dem was sho' good times, 'caze us had all us could eat den, an' plenty sugar cane to make 'lasses outten. An' dey made up biscuits in de big wood trays. Dem trays was made outten tupelo gum an' dey was light as a fedder. Us had plenty den, all de time, an' at Chris'mus an' when de white folks get ma'ed, dey kill hawgs, turkeys, an' chickens an' sometimes a yearlin'. En dey cook de hawgs whole, barbecue 'em an' fix 'em up wid a big apple in he mouf. When de big weddin' come off, de cook in big pots, so's to hab 'nough for eber'body. Cose us didn't hab eaten' lak dat all de time, 'caze de reg'lar rations was t'ree pound of meat an' a peck of meal fer eber' han' from Sat'day twell Sat'day.

"De niggers was 'lowed to hab a li'l patch of dey own, dat dey could wuk at night an' Sat'day ebenin'! What dey make on dis patch was dey'n, an' Ole Marster pay 'em money for hit. Nobody didn't make de niggers wuk dey patches—iffen dey want de grass to took 'em, dat's all right wid Ole Marster. Ole Martser hab a big gyarden, 'mos' big as a fiel', whar dey raise greens an' collards an' turnups fer de whole place.

"My granpappy was a carpenter an' Ole Marster contrac' him out to de yuther plantations to build dey houses. De grown niggers had to be up 'fo' day. De oberseer blow he horn fust to git up by an' de nex' time he blow dey hatter be ready to go to de fiel'.

"Dere was a ol' 'oman what kep' all de li'l niggers, whilst dey mammies was in de fiel'. Dis ol' 'oman cooked fer de li'l uns an' fed 'em all day, an' dey mammies tuk 'em at night.

"Us's clo's was made outten osnaburg cloth an' dyed wid cop'rus an' sometime dey mix terbaccy an' peach tree leabes wid de dye. Us had a big orchard wid apples an' peaches an' pears, more'n us an' de hawgs togedder could eat up.

"When a nigger died, dey was buried in de graveyard

lak dey do now, an' dey shouted an' hollered an' sometime a 'oman she faint an' hab to be tote home. De song dey sing mos' at de fun'ral was: Hark from de Toom'.

"Us sho' did hab plenty singin' o' hymns an' shoutin' at night in de cabins. Iffen de men want to break a night res' he go possum huntin' or rabbit huntin' jes' so he git pass from Ole Marster an' was at de fiel' nex' mornin' on time wid de yuther han's.

"I knowed Ole Marster went to de war, 'caze I heerd de folks talkin' bout hit an' wonder iffen Ole Marster gwine git kilt. Den I heerd 'em say de niggers was free, but us didn't leave Ole Marster for 'bout a year atter de s'render. Den us went to lib on de young mistis' place at Barlow Bend, atter she ma'ed Mr. Bob Flynn. Right dar I stayed twell I was grown and ma'ed. Den de fust move to town, us come up de Alabama Ribber to James' Landin'. I members all de big boats on de ribber. Dey sho' was fine 'uns.

"Den, I 'members atter I growed up dey tell 'bout how de Yankees comin' here an' how dey pester de white folks an' de niggers, too. Broke in dey smoke-houses, burn 'em up an' t'row t'ings away an' lef' nobody nottin' to eat. I don't 'member dat 'caze I was too li'l.

"Lady, you ax me iffen us knowed anyt'ng 'bout hoodoo? Yes, ma'am dere sho' was folkses what could put spells on you. I sho' was skeered o' dem kin' too. Atter I was nearly growed, dere was a gal name Penny what been down sick a long time an' dere was a cunjer doctor wukkin' on her tryin' cyure her, but her wan't 'greeable, so he let her die. Den a boy, name Ed, he had a mis'ry in he foot, an' hit went up he leg an' he cripple. Dere was a hoodoo doctor in de forks o' 'Bigbee Ribber come tend on him, an' he tol' ebber'body git outten de house 'cep'n' him an' Ed an' de Debil. He cyured Ed smack well.

"My mammy said I was borned wid a 'zernin' eye to see sperits, an' I seed sump'n lak a cow wid no haid. So mammy made me stir de fresh lard when dey was rendin' hit, 'caze dat cyures you of seein' de sperits. Atter I stirred de lard, I didn't see 'em no mo'.

"One time I was splittin' rails wid a nigger what could do anythin', but he was a bad man an' I was 'feered of him. I tol' him, iffen I had a pain or anything hurt me, I sho' would kill him wid my ax. I wudda split dat nigger wide open, jes' lak I split dem rails, iffen he try dat hoodoo on me.

"Talkin' 'bout fishin', I 'members when us would be plowin' down by de ribber, when hit come dinner-time an' whilst de mules eatin', us go down to de ribber an' fish. Den eb'ry Sat'day ebenin's us'd fish. Us kotch trout, gyar, jack an' carp. May was when de carp bite. Dey was so fat den dat you could cook em by deyse'f widout no grease. Den us ketch turkeys in pole pens baited wid corn.

"Lor' what's de use me talkin' 'bout dem times. Dey all pas' an' gone. Sometimes I gits to studyin' 'bout all de folks mos' is dead, an' I is here yit, libin' an' blin'; but I 'spec's hit won't be long twell I is ober de ribber wid de bles'."

NATHAN BEAUCHAMP

Interview with Nathan Beauchamp
—*Gertha Couric, Eufaula, Alabama*

HALF BREED

I walked up a little path bordered with small stones, an atmosphere of solitude surrounding me. In the sky, large, white cumulous clouds like great bolls of cotton, floated leisurely northward. Far down the road a ramshackle buckboard disappeared over a slight hill; directly in front the path ran at twenty yards into the dilapidated steps of a Negro cabin, while an old colored man in a vegetable garden to the left to the cabin broke the stillness with the intermittent metallic sounds of his spade digging into thirsty soil. I knew at a glance that this was Nathan Beauchamp.

"Hello, Uncle Nathan," I called.

Nathan Beauchamp, Eufaula, Alabama

"Mornin', white folks," he answered, as he discontinued his spading and raised his hand in a friendly gesture.

I walked over to where Uncle Nathan was standing and stopped in the little furrows of brown earth. Already a thick coat of dust had formed on my shoes.

"Uncle Nathan," I said, "I'd like to have a brief chat with you about slavery days, if you can spare a few minutes from your garden here?"

"Yassuh, boss," he said, punctuating his reply with a spat of tobacco that was soon nothing but a dark mark in the parched ground, "glad to be of any 'sistance."

We moved to the shade of a large oak where we sat down together on a sturdy, home-made bench.

"Well, white folks," he went on after taking a long turn at the dipper hanging on the tree which shades a well. "I'll tell you a story of my mammy an' pappy. Nathan Beauchamp, my pappy, belonged to Massa Green Beauchamp at White Oak Springs, near Eufaula.

Massa Green was a member of de legislature when de capital was at Tuscaloosy. He had many a acre of land an' hund'eds of slaves. Pappy use to dribe de wagon in to Eufaula to git supplies an' on de way he would meet up wid an Injun gal a-carryin' big baskets dat she was a goin' to sell dere. He would ask her iffen she wanted to ride, an' she always say yes. So one day pappy came to de massa and tell him dat dere was an Injun gal on de St. Francis Indian Village dat he wanted fo' a wife, an' de boss say all right so pappy married de Indian gal. Her name was Mimi. So I is half nigger an half Injun. My mammy died 'bout five year after freedom, but I can remembers dat she had long black hair, and I remembers de way de sun sparkle on her teeth when she smile. Atter she married pappy, she still carried her pretty baskets to Eufaula to sell. Sometime she walk all de way dere and back, twenty fo' miles. I been libin' here in Eufaula fifty year or mo', white fo'ks, an' I owns my little cabin an' de lan' around it. T'ain't much, but its enough to keep me a-goin', dis wid de little sto' I owns."

OLIVER BELL

Interview with Oliver Bell
—Ruby Pickens Tartt, Livingston

DE BES' FRIEND A NIGGER EVER HAD

Oliver Bell says the first thing he remembers was seeing his mother whipped. He was born in slavery, but most of his knowledge of the evils, as well as the joys of ante-bellum days, is by hearsay only.

"I was borned on de De Graffenreid Place," he said, "nine miles west of Livingston-Boyd Road. My mother was Luella De Graffenreid an' my pappy was Edmund De Graffenreid. Den dey changed my name to Bell. I had one brother, Nat, an' two sisters, Jestina an' Clara. I has 'bout sixteen chilluns, all born on de same place an' most of dem is livin' dere yit. My chillun by my firs' wife are Ed, Jack, Holly, Buck, Clarence, Sally, Liza, Mag an' Luella. Dey ma was Mandy Powell, frum York. Den my second wife, Bettie Brown, gived me de res' of my chilluns. Le's see, dey is Jimmy, J.W. Alfonso Wallace, Henry, Edna an' ——" He hesitated, explained, "Dat's as many as I kin 'member jest now.

Oliver Bell, Livingston, Alabama

"My gran'ma's name was Cely De Graffenreid an' my gran'pa's name was Peter. He was a shoemaker fur de place an' made plows, too. He was a worker an' he learnt me how to pull fodder an' chop corn an' cotton when I was jest a little scamp jes' a little black nigger.

"Us all b'longed to Mr. Tresvan De Graffenreid an' Mistus Rebecca; an' dey was all good to us. Ol' Mistus read de Bible to us an' got us baptized in de river at Horn's bridge, but dat was atter de surrender. In slavery times dey didn't like for us to sing an play loud in de quarters.

Honey, I 'members when us had de big prayer meetin's. Dey would shut de door so de voice won't git out, an' dey would turn de washpot down de door. Dat was to keep de voice inside, dey tol' me."

Oliver mused a moment, recalling the old times.

"Us chilluns useta have a good time singin' an' a-playin'," he said. "I 'members one of our little verses run somethin' lak dis:

> Shoo, shoo, shoo gander
> Th'ow yo' feathers 'way yander.

"Us had ol' corn hollers, too, but I fergits um now. I does remember though you could hear dem niggers holler a whole mile.

"No'm, it warn't so bad wid us. De white folks was good to us niggers. Us had 'nough to eat, lak greens, frum de big house. Us had our rations weighted out; peck o' meal, three pounds of meat, half gallon of 'lasses, made at home in wodden mills; an' dat was for a week. An' sometimes, on a Sunday us had a little sugar, coffee an' flour. No'm, us didn't know what rice was.

"What I seed of slavery was a bad idea, I reckon, but ev'ybody thought dey marster was de bes' in de lan'. Us didn't know no better. A man was growed plum' green 'fo he knew de whole worl' didn't belong to his ol' marster.

"Us didn't have no bought medicine in dem days; jes' whut us got outta de woods lak slippery ellum fer fever an' poke salad root; dey he'p a lot. An' May-apple root would he'p you same as castor oil.

"Didn't nobody he'p us learn nothin' much, but mos'

of my chilluns went to Booker T's school. Dey say he's a mighty smart man, an' my chilluns thinks so, too. It's all right; I wish I could read an' write; den I'd tell you things you'd lak to know."

His face clouded for the briefest moment.

"I tell you de fust thing I 'members, an' I don't know whut started it. One day my mammy done sumpin' an' ol' marster made her pull her dress down 'roun' her waist an' made her lay down 'crost de door. Den he taken a leather strop an' whooped her. I 'members dat I started cryin' an' Mistus Beckie said, 'Go git dat boy a biskit.'

"I reckerlecks my mammy was a plow han' an' she'd go to work soon an' put me under de shade of a big ol' post-oak tree. Dere I sat all day, an' dat tree was my nurse. It still standin' dere yit, an' I won't let nobody cut it down.

"Mammy say I never did learn to walk; jes' one day she sot me down under de oak, an' fust thing she knowed she look up an' dere I was walkin' down de middle of a cotton row.

"'Nother thing I 'members when I was a little boy; dat dey was 'vidin' de corn atter de s'render. Dr. DeGraffenreid measured de corn out to all of 'em whut was share han's. He'd take a bushel an' give 'em a bushel. When he mos' through he'd throw a ear of corn to dis one, an' give himse'f a ear; den he break a ear in two, an' he take part an' give dem part. Dat was close measurin', I tell you.

"Us lived in de third house frum de big house in de quarter, an' when I was a boy it was my job to set out shade trees. An' one day de Ku Klux come ridin' by an' dey leader was Mister Steve Renfroe. (Alabama bandit of Reconstruction days). He wore long hair an' he call my pappy out an' ax him a heap of questions. While he sittin' dere his horse pull up nigh 'bout all de trees I done sot out.

"Atter talkin' to my pappy, he rode on 'cross Horn's bridge, 'bout two miles souf of here, an' dere he met Ol' Man Enoch Sledge an' Frank Sledge. Dey was darkies whut b'longed to Marsa Simmy Sledge's father, Ol' Doctor Sledge. Slaves on dat plantation was 'lowed pretty good privilege atter de s'rrender an' was workin' on halvens. Uncle Enoch an' Frank was in town tradin' some, an' Mr. Renfroe didn't want 'em to have anything. When dey lef' town, dey pass de Ku Kluxes raght on de slough bridge. Mister Renfroe ax Enoch to give him a piece of string to fix his saddle wid; den shot him. Frank run to de river, but de Ku Kluxes cotched him an' shot him, too.

"De niggers went down to de river dat night an' got de bodies an' buried 'em in de ol' Travis graveyard. My mammy an' daddy is buried dere, too.

"Didn' nobody do nothin' 'bout Mister Renfroe 'till he went on an' got to messin' wid Marsa Simmy Sledge's things; stole a pair of mules an' de white folks rambled atter him 'till dey foun' him in Linden. Dey got so hot atter him dat he went to his camp in de flat woods down on Bear Creek. Dem was skeery times, 'case dat man never had no mercy for nobody.

"Dey's a cave down by de burial grounds whut de slaves dug when dey run away, an' Mister Renfroe stayed dere. It's on de river bank an' its dug up. You digs an' starts low an' pushes de dirt out an' digs up an' makes a big room up so de water won't git you. I knows whar dey's two of de caves on de place; my cow fell in one yestidy.

"When Ol' Marster Amos Travis come out here from Californy, he taken a lakin' to me an' wanted me to leave t'other side of de place an' move down dis side of de big house to take keer of dis swamp an' look atter de han's. But I wanted a big house wid four rooms an' two brick chimneys, an' I had to talk five years to git it. I's got some rosebushes now dat was at de big house raght atter de s'rrender, an' dey's growin' in my yard now.

"Speakin' 'bout graveyard, I was passin' dere one night, ridin' on 'bout midnight, an' sumpin' come draggin' a chain by me lak a dog. I got down off'n my horse, but couldn't see nothin' wid no chain, so I got back on de horse an' dere raght in front of me was a Jack-Me-Lantern wid de brightes' light you ever seed. It was tryin' to lead me off, an' ev'y time I'd git back in de road it would lead me off ag'in. You sho' will git los' if you follow a Jack-Me-Lantern.

"One of dem led a man down to de creek by dem double bridges; said he foun' he was travelin' in de wrong direction, gittin' frum home stidder clo'ster, so he jes' sit down under a tree an' waited 'til daylight. I ain't skeered of nothin' but dem Jack-Me-Lanterns, but dey stirs you up in yo' min' till you can't tell whar you's at; an' dey's so bright dey nigh 'bout puts yo' eyes out. Dey is plenty of 'em over by de graveyard raght over yonder whar all my white folks is buried, an' mammy an' pappy, too. Dey's all dere 'cept Marsa Jess Travis; he was de nex' whut come in line for de place, an' he was de bes' frein' dis here nigger ever had.

"Fac' was, dat's whut he call me; 't was 'nigger'. He an' Mistus Mag lived raght dere in de big house; den dey move into town an' dat's whar he died. Me an' Marsa Jess made a 'greement an' he said if he was de longes' liver, he'd see me buried, an' if I be de longes' liver, I see him buried. So dat day I went to his office in de co'thouse an' he say he want to talk wid me. He say, 'You 'members us 'greement?' An' I say, 'Whut 'greement, Marsa Jess?' An' he say, 'Bout buryin'.' Den I say, sho', 'I 'members dat.'

"Den he got up an' give me some papers 'bout some lan', an' I say, 'Whut do all dis here mean, Marse Jess?' He say, 'nothin', nigger, 'cept I's jes' goin' outta business.' Den I say, 'Goodbye, Marse Jess,' an' he say, 'Goodbye, nigger,' an' I walked on 'crost de street. Den Mr. Killian say, 'Oliver, whut's happened over at de co'thouse?' An I say, 'Ain't nothin' as I knows of.' Den he say, 'Yes, dey is; jes' look at de peoples gwine in a hurry.' Den I turn 'roun' an' run back an' dere lay Marse Jess. Mr. Smith was gettin' him up an' Marse Jess say to me, 'Well, nigger, I didn't do whut I tended to; I missed it.' An' I say, 'Boss, fer God's sake go to de hospital; I'll go wid you an' stay wid you.' Mistus Mag, she ast me to beg him, but he shuck his head an' say 'If I had a-wanted to live I wouldn't of shot myself.' He res' a minit, den say, 'Nigger, write Miss Calline an' tell her I says to always be good to you as long as you lives.'

"Yassum, I was raght dere, done jes' whut I tol' him I'd do; kep' my 'greement an' followed him to de grave. Co'se dat last 'bout Marse Jess ain't no slavery tale, but I thought you was atter hearin' all 'bout de family whut owned dis ol' place; an' Marse Jess was de bes' white frein' a nigger ever had; dis nigger, anyhow.''

United States. Work Projects Administration

NELSON BIRDSONG

Personal interview with Nelson and Virginia Birdsong Summerville, on Front Street
—Ila B. Prine, Mobile, Alabama

NELSON BIRDSONG REMEMBERS HIS MASTER

Nelson Birdsong, who lives on Front Street in the old suburb of Summerville, about three miles from Mobile, Alabama, was born a slave. A tall dark Negro man, with white hair and whiskers, he says he was born at Montgomery Hill, Alabama in Baldwin County, and that his people and he were owned by Mr. Tom Adkins.

Nelson said he was very small at the time of the Surrender, and could not tell very much about slavery days. In fact, he adds, "You know, missie, old folks in dem days did'nt 'low chillun to stan' 'roun' when dey was talking. We chillun was lack a shot out of a gun when anybody come in. We was glad when folks come in 'cause we c'ud run out an' play. Chillun now-a-days knows as much as we did when we was twenty-five years old."

Nelson does remember his "massa" saying he neber was going to 'let dat little nigger work.'

He did not remember much about coming to Mobile,

but "seemed lack" his "mammy worked for Mrs. Dunn on Monroe street, and later dey moved out in old Napoleonville" (which is now Crichton, Alabama, a suburb of Mobile). He said his "Pa and Mammy den worked fo' gris' mill out dere, and also owned a big gris' mill in de fork whar de big fire station is now" (which is located at the intersection of St. Francis street and Washington Avenue, the latter formerly Wilkinson street). This grist mill was burned in the 1870's.

Nelson says the first work he remembered doing was "nussing a baby boy of Mr. Bramwell Burden, a gran'son of old man Burden."

Nelson has owned his little farm and three-room house until the past two or three years. He said he scuffled and tried to pay de taxes, but had got so old and his "knees had give out on him, and I seed I was agoin' to lose mah place so I turned it over to a man to keep up mah taxes, so I'd have a place to lib. De relief gibes me a little he'p now, an' me an' my wife makes out de bes' we can."

The house is the familiar type of two-room Negro house, with a porch across the front, and a shed room on the back. The bedroom had been papered with scraps of wallpaper of varied designs and so old that most of it had fallen off. The mantel is covered with the colored comics section, cut in a fancy pattern of scallops. At the entrance of the house is a sack nailed to the floor and used for a foot mat, and at the two upper corners of the door are horse shoes for good luck. Nelson said he is a member of the African Methodist Episcopal Zion Church, and has been a Methodist all his life; that he and his wife Virginia "had only two chillun' and dey were bofe dead."

Nelson's wife, Virginia, came from a family of slaves, although she was not one herself. She said her folks were owned by Mr. Joe Pickett of Camden, Wilcox County, Alabama. She said she just can remember Mr. Joe taking her in his buggy, and she called him "Toe-Toe," as she couldn't say his name plainly. She also said as she grew older she always spoke of Mr. Joe, as "my Papa," instead of "my master," for "he sho' was good to me." She remembers her mother being chambermaid on the "Old Eleanora," a boat on the Alabama river, and as a small child going back and forth on the boat with her. When they finally settled in Mobile, her mother worked for the family of Dr. Heustis who lived in the corner house now occupied by the new Federal Court House and Custom House, at St. Louis and St. Joseph streets.

ANK BISHOP

Interview with Ank Bishop
—Ruby Pickens Tartt, Livingston, Alabama

GABR'EL BLOW SOF'! GABR'EL BLOW LOUD!

When "Gabr'el take his silver trump," he is going to blow soft for the saved and loud for the lost souls, according to Ank Bishop who was born into slavery eighty-nine years ago, and lives in Livingston, Alabama. The days before the war were as good as the present, Ank believes. He tells of them in the following story of his life:

"My name is Ank Bishop, en I was born in 1849, August 16th, at Ward, Alabama. My mother's name was Amy Larken, an' my father was Tom Bishop. I had three brothers, Alf, Volen an' Jim, an' two sisters, Cely an' Matildy. Us belonged to Lady Liza Larkin at Ward, right nigh Coke's Chapel.

"My mother was brought out from South Car'lina in a speculator drove, an' Lady Liza bought her at de auction at Coke's Chapel. She lef' her mammy an' daddy back dere in South Car'lina an' never did see 'em no more in dis life. She was bidded off an' Lady Liza got her, jes' her one from all her family. She was got fer Lady Liza's house gal. But sometimes she cooked or was de washer, den ag'in de milker. 'Twas my job for to min' de ca'ves. Sometimes I went to Mr. Ed Western's sto' at Gaston, three miles from us house, to see iffen was any mail for Lady Liza, but 'twa'n't none.

"Dey was good to us 'caze Lady Liza's son, Mr. Willie Larkin, was de overseer for his ma, but co'se sometime dey git among 'em an' thrashed 'em out. One time one de niggers runned away, old Caesar Townsy, an' dey sarnt for Dick Peters to come an' bring his "nigger dogs." Dem dogs was trained to ketch a nigger same as rabbit dogs is trained to ketch a rabbit. So Mr. Willie Larkin told Stuart for to say to old man Dick Peters when he come, 'I'm gone,' but for him to come on. 'I'm gwineter keep de road,' he say, 'an' cross 'Bigbee at Moscow landin'.' So ol' Dick Peters, he kept de road lack he tole him to, an' he cross 'Bigbee at Moscow landin' over in de cane-brake. But dem nigger dogs didn't never ketch ol' man Caesar. He stayed right wharever he was at 'twell after S'render, an' de War done ceased. Den he come out, but iffen he had a been caught, dey'd a used him up pretty rough, but he stayed hid twell de time done passed.

"All de women on Lady Liza's place had to go to de fiel' ev'y day an' dem what had suckerlin' babies would come in 'bout nine o'clock in de mawnin' an' when de bell ring at twelve an' suckerlin' 'em. One woman tended to all of 'em in one house. Her name was Ellie Larkin, an' dey call her 'Mammy Larkin.' She all time sarnt me down in de fiel' for to git 'em come suckle de chillen, 'caze dat made hit hard on her when dey gets hongry an' cry.

"Us didn't get to go to church none, an' us wa'n't larnt nothin'. I'm nigh 'bout ninety an' I can't read a line. I got some chillun kin read; one can't whut is sixty-five, but Henry he fifteen an' he kin. De ma, she go by de name of Pearlie Beasley, she can't read neither, but she's a good fiel' han' an' she patched dese breeches I'm wearin' an' dis ole shirt. Miss, I ain't got a coat to my name. Can't go to church, so I doan' know dat dis any better'n slav'y time. Hit's hard, anyway you got to travel, got yo' nose on de groun' rock all de time. When pay day come, ain't nothin' pay wid. Come git de rent, den you out do's ag'in. Bred an' bawn in Sumter County, wore out in Sumter County, 'specks to die in Sumter County, an' whut is I got? Ain't got nothin', ain't got nothin', ain't got nothin'.

Ank Bishop, Livingston, Alabama

"But I'm a believer, an' dis here voodoo an' hoodoo an' sper'ts ain't nothin' but a lot of folk's outten Christ. Ha'nts ain't nothin' but somebody died outten Christ an' his sper't ain't at res', jes' in a wand'rin' condition in de world.

"Dis is de evil sper't what de Bible tells about when hit say a person has got two sper'ts, a good one an' a evil one. De good sper't goes to a place of happiness an' rest, an' you doan' see hit no mo', but de evil sper't ain't got no place to go. Hit's dwellin' place done tore down when de body died, an' hit's jes' a wand'rin' an a waitin' for Gabr'el to blow his trump, den de worl' gwineter come to an en'. But when God say, 'Take down de silver mouf trump an' blow, Gabr'el,' an' Gabr'el say, 'Lord, how loud shell I blow?' Den de Lord say, 'Blow easy, Gabr'el, en ca'm, not to 'larm my lilies.' De secon' time Gabr'el say, 'How loud mus' I blow, Lord?' Den de Lord say, 'Blow hit as loud as seben claps of thunder all added into one echo, so as to wake up dem damnable sper'ts sleepin' in de grave-ya'ds what ain't never made no peace wid dey God, jes' alayin' dere in dey sins.'

"But de Christ'en Army, hit gits up wid de fus' trump, an' dem what is deef is de evil ones what anybody kin see anytime. I ain't skeered of 'em, though. I passes 'em an' goes right on plowin', but iffen you wants 'em to git outten your way, all you gotter do is jes' turn your head least bit an' look back. Dey gone jes' lack dat! When my fus' wife died 'bout thirty years ago, I was goin' up to Gaston to see Sara Drayden, ole Scot Drayden's wife, an' I tuck out through Kennedy bottom 'bout sundown right after a rain. I seed sompin acomin' down de road 'bout dat high, 'bout size a little black shaggy dog, an' I says,

'What's dat I sees commin' down de road? Ain't nobody 'roun' here got no black shaggy dog? Hit kep' a-comin' an' kep' a-gittin' bigger an' bigger an' closer an' closer, an' time hit got right to me 'twas as big as a ha'f growed yearlin', black as a crow. It had four feet an' drop years, jes' lack a dog, but 'twa'n't no dog, I knows dat. Den he shy out in de bushes, an' he come right back in de road, an' hit went on de way I was comin' from, so I went on de way hit was comin' from. I ain't never seed dat thing no mo'. But I'ze gotter pretty good notion 'bout who hit 'twas."

United States. Work Projects Administration

SINEY BONNER

Interview with Siney Bonner
—W.F. Jordan

"Hear dat whistle?" The speaker was Siney Bonner, an ex-slave, now living in the Norwood section of Birmingham. She had stopped for a "confab" where a group of other elderly Negroes of the neighborhood had gathered. "De whistles on dem Big Jacks what pull dese highsteppin' I.C. trains mind me of dem steamboats what used to pull up at de landin' at ole Pickensville on de Tombigbee River.

"'Cose dar wa'n't no railroads dem days an' de onlies' way folks had trabbelin' about was de steamboat which passed most every week, and de stage coach which passed twice a week.

"Lawsy, man, dem was de days, and many de time atter my daddy, whose name was Green Bonner, heard dat steamboat blow below Pickensville, he would hitch up de mules to de waggin and foller Massa John on hossback down to de landin' to fetch back de supply of sugar and coffee and plow-tools needed on de plantation. Dey would take me 'long to hold de mules and watch de waggin and it was a reglar picnic to me to see de big shiney boat and watch de goin's on.

"Massa John Bonner sho' did 'pend on my daddy. De massa paid a thousand green-back dollars for him down to Mobile. 'Nuf green-backs to wrap him up in, he said, so he named him Green Bonner.

"Yes suh, we was all Baptis'—de deep water kind, and every Sunday dey used to pile us into de waggins and pull out bright and early for Big Creek Church on the Carrollton road. Everybody fetched a big basket of grub and, sakes alive! sech another dinner you never see, all spread out on de grassy grove by de ole graveyard. Mos' all de quality white folks belonged at Big Creek and when dere slaves got sho' nuff 'ligion, dey have 'em jine at Big Creek and be baptized at de swimmin' hole. Some of de niggers want to have dere own meetin's, but Lawd chile, dem niggers get happy and get to shoutin' all over de meadow where dey built a brush arbor. Massa John quick put a stop to dat. He say, 'if you gwine to preach and sing you must turn de wash pot bottom up'; meanin', no shoutin'. Dem Baptis' at Big Creek was sho' tight wid dere rules too. Turn you out sho' if you drink too much cawn licker, or dance, or cuss.

"Massa John had a big fine bird dog. She was a mammy dog and one day she foun' six puppies out in de harness house. Dey was mos' all girl puppies so massa gwine drown 'em. I axed him to give 'em to me and purty soon de missus sent me to de pos'office, so I put de puppies in a basket and took 'em wid me. Dr. Lyles come by whar I was settin' and he say, 'Want to sell dem pups, Siney?' I tell him, uh-huh. Den he say, 'What 'nomination is dey?'. I tell him, dey's Methodis' dogs. He didn' say no mo'. Bout a week atter dat ole missus sent me to 'de pos'office again, so I took my basket of puppies. Sho' nuff, 'long come Dr. Lyles and he say, 'Siney, see you still ain't sold dem pups'. I say, 'Naw-suh'. Den he axed me ag'in what 'nomination dey b'long to. I tole him dey was Baptis' dogs. He say, 'How come? You tole me las' week dem was Methodis' pups'. Ha-ha! Bless God!, look like he had me. But I say, 'Yas-suh, but you see, Doctah, dey got dere eyes open since den!' He laff and go on down to his newspaper office.

Siney Bonner, Birmingham, Alabama

"How old is I? Law chile, I don't know. My mammy say I was fifteen year old time of de surrender. I 'members dat mighty well. Massa John call all de niggers on de plantation 'round him at de big house and he say to 'em 'Now, you all jes' as free as I is. I ain't your marster no mo'. I'se tried to be good to you and take keer of all of you. You is all welcome to stay and we'll all wuk togedder and make a livin' somehow. Ef you don' want to stay, dem dat go will jes' have to root, pig, or die.' Some stayed and some lef'. My daddy stayed wid Marse John till he was called home to glory. Now dey all gone but Siney, and I'se jes' here, waitin' for 'em to call me.

"Yas suh, I been 'round Carrollton a heap. Atter Marse John and my daddy bofe died, I wuk'd 'round from place to place. Used to wuk for Mrs. Roper at de old Phoenix Hotel. I recollect when de new brick court house was built. De ole court house had been burned and dey 'rested a nigger named Bill Burkhalter for settin' it on fire. Dey sent him to de pen' an' some officers started wid him to Montgomery. When dey got to Sipsey River a mob ketched up wid 'em an' took Bill and hung him dere in de swamp. 'Bout dat time a bad cloud come up. Dey axed Bill did he have anything to say. He say, 'I ain't burn no court house, an' ef you all kill me, my face gwine always ha'nt you'. Whilst he still hangin' dere in dat swamp de lightnin' flash and de thunder an' wind was somp'n awful. Nex' mornin' when de sun come up, bless my soul, right dere on de winder in de court house tower was a photygraf of de face of de nigger dey done hung for burnin' de old court house. Yas suh, I done seen dat wid my own eyes an' I speck dat picture still dere.

"But lawsy me, I got to get goin', kase I'se cookin' me a mess of poke sallet I picked down by de railroad tracks dis mornin'. Dat poke sallet and young ernions gwine to be mighty good, and dey sho 'mind me of dem good old days in Pickens county."

United States. Work Projects Administration

JENNIE BOWEN

Interview with Jennie Bowen
—Mary A. Poole, Mobile

NO BELL BRUNG HIM

Jennie Bowen was surrounded by numerous little colored children as I came upon her sitting on her front porch. She answered my questions through a mouth void of teeth and with a constant blinking of her brown eyes with their muddy whites. Her little grandchild had to act to some extent as an interpreter, as her speech was at times most indistinct.

"Yassum, I remembers lots of things dat happened back in de days of de Cibil War," she said. "I remembers de place whar I lived. It were de prettiest house you ever seed. It were on a high hill overlooking a small creek and de flowers 'roun' in de yard was somp'n to see, sho' 'nuff.

"I was bawn in 1847 on Massa Fisher's and Mistis Fisher's plantation near Camden, Alabama. Us slaves lived in a row of whitewashed cabins in de rear of de big house. We useta have a mean oberseer, white folks, an' all de time dere was slaves on our place a runnin' away.

"I acted as nuss for massa's three chilluns, an' dey learnt me to read an' write. My pappy was named Burl Fisher an' he come f'um Virginny when Cap'n Fisher brung him. My mammy was named Grace Fisher, an' she was 'roun' de big house mos' of de time a weavin' an' a cardin' wool for de slaves, who wo' calico spun in de summer an' wool in de winter.

"An ole nigger man rung a bell for us to get up by, an' to call de fiel' han's in de evenin's. Atter Surrender, dis ole nigger stayed right on de plantation an' was a workin' in de fiel's one day when de Fisher boy rung de bell for de niggers to come in. All of 'em came 'cep'n dis ole man an' later on dey ax him why he don't come when dey ring de bell. He answer: 'Tain't no mo' bell ringin' for dis nigger, 'caze I is free.'

Jennie Bowen, Mobile, Alabama

"De Fishers was Pres'terians an' dey had dere own church on de place. Eve'ybody had to go on Sunday; de white folks sittin' in de front, de colored folks in de back. De onl'es' holidays us niggers had was Chris'mas an' New Years. On dese days us all exchanged gif's.

"My pappy an' mammy atter de war farmed on shares wid Cap'n Fisher. I was ma'ied 'bout dis time, white folks, to Sam Bowen, who long been daid. Us had a big weddin' an' de two Mistis Fishers (Massa's daughters) baked us a cake an' I sont a piece to all my white frien's for dem to dream on. Atter I come to Mobile, I changed my 'ligion to bein' a Babtist.

"I had ten chilluns, but seven of dem is daid. I is even got fo' great gran' chilluns.

"Yassum, us had po' white trash back in dem days of de war. Dey lived near our place, an' some of 'em didn't have no niggers at all. Dey worked deyse'f in de fiel's. Us didn't fool 'long wid dem kinds of people dough, white folks. Us kep' mostly to ourselves.

"Yassum, us house niggers et in de kitchens, dat was separated f'um de main buildin' by a walkway, kivered at de top but not at de sides. All de slave chilluns had a grown nigger woman and a young gal 'bout sixteen to look atter dem. We-alls had a good time an' us was happy an' secure."

NANNIE BRADFIELD

Interview with Nannie Bradfield
—*Susie R. O'Brien, Uniontown, Alabama*

WHAT I KEER ABOUT BEIN' FREE?

Nannie Bradfield is a fat little old woman almost as broad as she is long, with a pleasant face and a broad smile which displays white teeth still good at the age of eighty-five. She lives alone in a dilapidated cabin which rests in a clump of trees by the side of the railroad. The sagging roof is patched with pieces of rusty tin of many shapes and sizes.

"Nannie," I said, "aren't you afraid to live here alone?"

"How come I be skeered? Ain't nobody gwine bother me lessen it be a spirit, and dey don't come 'roun' 'cep'n on rainy nights, den all you got to do is say 'Lawd have mercy! What you want here,' and dey go 'way and leave you 'lone.

"Any how I's gittin' pretty old and I won't be here so ve'y much longer so I jes' as well start gittin' 'quainted wid de spirits."

"Tell me something about yourself and your family,

Nannie," I said. "Dere ain't nothin' much to tell 'cep I was born in slav'y times and I was 'bout twelve year old in May when 'mancipation come. My Pa and Ma b'longed to Mars James and Miss Rebecca Chambers. Dey plantation was jes' on de aidge of town and dat's what I was born. Mars James' son William was in de war and old Miss would send me to town whar all de sojers tents was, to tote sompen good to eat to dem. I don't 'member much 'bout de war 'cep de tents and de bum shells shootin'. I was little and couldn't do much but I waited on Miss Liz'beth, my young Miss, and waited on table, toted battie cakes and sich like. No ma'am I don't know nothin' 'tall 'bout de patterollers or de Klu Kluxers but I know all 'bout de conjer doctors. Dey sho' kin fix you. Dey kin take yo' garter or yo stockin' top an drap it in runnin' water and make you run de res' of yo' life, you'll be in a hurry all de time, and if dey gits holt of a piece of de seat of yo' draw's dey sprinkles a little conjer powder on it and burns it den you can't never set down in no peace. You jes' like you settin' on a coal of fiah 'till you git somebody to take de spell offen you."

"Nannie, were you glad when the war was over and you were free?"

"What I keer 'bout bein' free? Didn't old Marster give us plenty good sompin to eat and clo's to wear? I stayed on de plantation 'til I mah'ied. My old Miss give me a brown dress and hat. Well dat dress put me in de country, if you mah'ie in brown you'll live in de country."

"'Marry in brown you'll live out of town?'" I quoted. "Dat's it—my remembrance ain't so good and I fergits.

"No ma'am, I ain't got no chillun, but Bradfield had

plenty un um, I was his fouf wife. He died 'bout three years ago and he done well to live dat long wid all dem wimmens to nag him. De Bible say it's better to climb on top of the house and set, den to live inside wid a naggin' 'oman."

United States. Work Projects Administration

MARTHA BRADLEY

Interview with Martha Bradley
—*Mabel Farrior, Montgomery, Alabama*

IN SLAVERY TIME

Aunt Martha—as she is known to all her "white folks"—claims to be 100 years old. She was a slave to Dr. Lucas of Mt. Meigs neighborhood long before the War between the States. Dr. Lucas is one of the well known Lucas family, with whom General LaFayette spent some time while touring the United States in 1824.

"Our Marster wuz sho good to all his 'niggers'," she said. "Us allus had plenty to eat and plenty to wear, but de days now is hard, if white folks gin you a nickel or dime to git you sumpin' t' eat you has to write everything down in a book before you can git it. I allus worked in the field, had to carry big logs, had strops on my arms and them logs was put in de strop and hauled to a pile where they all was. One morning hit was rainin' ad I didn' wanna go to the field, but de oversee' he come and got me and started whooping me. I jumped on him and bit and kicked him 'til he lemme go. I didn't know no better then. I didn't know he was de one to do dat.

"But Marster Lucas gin us big times on Christmas and July. Us 'ud have big dinners and all the lemonade us could drink. The dinner'd be spread out on de ground an' all the niggers would stand roun' and eat all dey wanted. What was lef' us'd take it to our cabins. Nancy Lucas was de cook fer eber' body. Well, she'd sho cook good cake and had plenty of 'em but she wouldn't lak to cut dem cakes often. She keep 'em in a safe. One day I go to dat safe and I seed some and I wanted it so bad till I jes' had to have some. Nancy say to me, 'Martha, did you cut dat cake?' I say, 'No sir! dat knife just flew 'roun by itself and cut dat cake.'

"One day I was workin' in de field and de overseer he come 'roun and say sumpin' to me he had no bizness say. I took my hoe and knocked him plum down. I knowed I'se done sumpin' bad so I run to de bushes. Marster Lucas come and got me and started whoopin' me. I say to Marster Lucas whut dat overseer sez to me and Marster Lucas didn' hit me no more. Marse Lucas was allus good to us and he wouldn' let nobody run over his niggers.

"There was plenty white folks dat was sho bad to de niggers, and specially dem overseers. A nigger whut lived on the plantation jinin' ours shot and killed an overseer; den he run 'way. He come to de river and seed a white man on udder side and say, 'Come and git me.' Well, when dey got him dey found out whut he'd done, and was gwine to burn him 'live. Jedge Clements, the man dat keep law and order, say he wouldn't burn a dog 'live, so he lef'. But dey sho burn dat nigger 'live for I seed him atter he was burned up.

Martha Bradley, Montgomery, Alabama

"Us'd go to meetin' to de Antioch Church some Sundays. Us'd go to de house and git a pass. When us'd pass by the patterole, us jes' hold up our pass and den us'd go on. Dar was a 'vidin' 'twixt de niggers and de white folks. De white preacher'd preach; den de colored man. Us'd stay at church most all day. When we didn' go to church, us'd git together in the quarters and have preachin' and singin' amongst ourselves.

"In cotton pickin' time us'd stay in de field till way atter dark and us'd pick by candle light and den carry hit and put hit on de scaffold. In de winter time us'd quilt; jes' go from one house to anudder in de quarter. Us'd weave all our ever' day clothes but Marster Lucas'd go to Mobile ever' July and Christmas and git our Sunday clothes, git us dresses and shoes and we'd sho be proud of 'em.

"In slavery time dey doctored de sick folks dif'funt frum what dey does now. I seed a man so sick dey had to put medicine down his tho'at lak he was a horse. Dat man got well and sho lived to turn a key in de jail. Ef it was in dese days dat man would be cay'd to de hospital and cut open lak a hawg.

"Dere was a slave whut lived in Macon county. He run 'way and when he was catched dey dug a hole in de ground and put him crost it and beat him nigh to death."

ALLEN BROWN

Interview with Allen Brown
—Gertha Couric

IS NIGH A HUNDERD

Uncle Allen is a thin little man with a short white beard that hides nothing of his ready, toothless smile always evident when conversing with "de white folks" and contributes to his dignified mien when solemnly lecturing to "de niggers" about their "no 'count ways." He is as deaf as the proverbial post, and, once launched into a discourse, rambles on to its end without regard to interruptions. Asked to tell something of his early life, he said:

Allen Brown, Eufala, Alabama

"I is nigh on to a hundred yeahs old, Suh, and I was brung to dis country from Virginny whar I was bawn. My mammy's mahster was movin' from Virginny to Texas, and when he go dis fur he sole me and my mammy to Mahster McRea. Den Mahster McRea he give me to Miss Julia; den Miss Julia she mah'ied Mahs Henry Young and I was dere ca'iage driver. Mahs Henry soon went off to de wawh and was kilt in de battle of Gettysbu'g and dat nearly bout kilt Miss Julia.

"A'ter de Surrender nothin' neber was de same. Jest hahd times mos'ly. Neber been any times lak de days when I was drivin' my ca'iage amongst de Eufaula high steppers, and I reckon dere neber will be ag'in.

"De ole man too ole and bruck down to wuhk now, and I gits along wid whut de Welfare gives me."

GUS BROWN

Interview with Gus Brown
—Alexander B. Johnson, Birmingham, Alabama

GUS SAW MASSA'S HAT SHOT OFF

"They is all gone, scattered, and old massa and missus have died." That was the sequence of the tragic tale of "Uncle" Gus Brown, the body servant of William Brown; who fought beside him in the War between the States and who knew Stonewall Jackson.

"Uncle Gus" recalled happenings on the old plantation where he was reared. His master was a "king" man, he said, on whose plantation in Richmond, Virginia, Uncle Gus waited on the tables at large feasts and functions of the spacious days before the War. He was entrusted to go with the master's boys down to the old swimming hole and go in "washin." They would take off their clothes, hide them in the bushes on the side of the bank, put a big plank by the side of the old water hole and go in diving, swimming and have all the fun that youngsters would want, he said.

Apparently his master's home was a plantation house with large columns and with all the glitter and glamour that the homes around Richmond have to offer. About it were large grain storage places for the master was a grain dealer and men on the plantation produced and ground large quantities into flour.

Gus worked around the house, and he remembers well the corn shuckings as he called them on which occasions the Negroes gave vent to emotion in the form of dancing and music. "On those occasions we all got together and had a regular good time," he said.

"Uncle," he was asked, "do you remember any of the old superstitions on the plantation? Did they have any black cat stories?"

"No sir, boss, we was educated Negroes on our plantation. The old bossman taught his Negroes not to believe in that sort of thing.

"I well remember when de war came. Old massa had told his folks befo' de war began dat it was comin', so we was ready for it.

"Beforehand the master called all the servants he could trust and told them to get together all of the silver and other things of value. They did that, he explained and afterward they took the big box of treasures and carried it out in the forest and hid it under the trunk of a tree which was marked. None of the Negroes ever told the Yankees where it was so when the war ended the master had his silver back. Of course the war left him without some of the things which he used to have but he never suffered.

"Then de war came and we all went to fight the Yankees. I was a body servant to the master, and once a bullet took off his hat. We all thought he was shot but he wasn't, and I was standin' by his side all the time.

"I remember Stonewall Jackson. He was a big man with long whiskers, and very brave. We all fought wid him until his death.

"We wan't beaten, we was starved out! Sometimes we had parched corn to eat and sometimes we didn't have a bite o' nothin', because the Union mens come and tuck all the food for their selves. I can still remember part of my ninety years. I remembers we fought all de way from Virginia and winded up in Manassas Gap.

"When time came for freedom most of us was glad. We liked the Yankees. They was good to us. 'You is all now free. You can stay on the plantation or you can go.' We all stayed there until old massa died. Den I worked on de Seaboard Airline when it come to Birmingham. I have been here ever since.

Gus Brown, Birmingham, Alabama

"In all de years since de war I cannot forget old massa. He was good and kind. He never believed in slavery but his money was tied up in slaves and he didn't want to lose all he had.

"I knows I will see him in heaven and even though I have to walk ten miles for a bite of bread I can still be happy to think about the good times we had then. I am a Confederate veteran but my house burned up wid de medals and I don't get a pension.

"Thank you, mister bossman, fer the quarter. It will buy me a little grub. I'se too old to work but I has to."

The reporter left him sitting with his little pack and a long fork in his hands; in his eyes, dimmed with age, a far-off look and a tear of longing for the Old Plantation.

United States. Work Projects Administration

WALTER CALLOWAY

Interview with Walter Calloway
—W.F. Jordan

OLE JOE HAD REAL 'LIGION

Walter Calloway lives alone half a block off Avenue F, the thoroughfare on the southside of Birmingham on which live many of the leaders in the Negro life of the city. For his eighty-nine years he was apparently vigorous except for temporary illness. A glance at the interior of his cabin disclosed the fact that it was scrupulously neat and quite orderly in arrangement, a characteristic of a great many ex-slaves. As he sat in the sunshine on his tiny front porch, his greeting was: "Come in, white folks. You ain't no doctor is you?"

To a negative reply, he explained as he continued, "Fo' de las' past twenty-five years I been keepin' right on, wukkin' for de city in de street department. 'Bout two mont's ago dis mis'ry attackted me an' don't 'pear lak nothin' dem doctors gimme do no good. De preacher he come to see me dis mornin' an' he say he know a white gemman doctor, what he gwine to sen' him to see me. I sho' wants to git well ag'in pow'ful bad, but mebby I done live long 'nuff an' my time 'bout come."

Quizzed about his age and antecedents, he began

his story: "Well, sir, Cap'n, I was born in Richmond, Virginny, in 1848. Befo' I was ole 'nuff to 'member much, my mammy wid me an' my older brudder was sold to Marse John Calloway at Snowdoun in Montgomery county, ten miles south of de town of Montgomery.

"Marse John hab a big plantation an' lots of slaves. Dey treated us purty good, but we hab to wuk hard. Time I was ten years ole I was makin' a reg'lar han' 'hin' de plow. Oh, yassuh, Marse John good 'nough to us an' we git plenty to eat, but he had a oberseer name Green Bush what sho' whup us iffen we don't do to suit him. Yassuh, he' mighty rough wid us but he didn't do de whuppin' hisse'f. He had a big black boy name Mose, mean as de debil an' strong as a ox, and de oberseer let him do all de whuppin'. An', man, he could sho' lay on dat rawhide lash. He whupped a nigger gal 'bout thirteen years ole so hard she nearly die, an' allus atterwa'ds she hab spells of fits or somp'n. Dat make Marse John pow'ful mad, so he run dat oberseer off de place an' Mose didn' do no mo' whuppin.

"Same time Marse John buy mammy an' us boys, he buy a black man name Joe. He a preacher an' de marster let de slaves buil' a brush arbor in de pecan grove ober in de big pastur', an' when de wedder warn't too cold all de slaves was 'lowed to meet dar on Sunday 'fo' preachin'.

"Yassuh, ole Joe do purty good. I spec he had mo' 'ligion dan some of de hifalutin' niggers 'tendin' to preach nowadays. De white folks chu'ch, hit at Hope Hill ober on de stage road, an' sometimes dey fetch 'dere preacher to de plantation to preach to de slaves. But dey 'druther heah Joe.

"Nawsuh, we didn' git no schoolin' 'cep'in' befo' we got big 'nough to wuk in de fiel' we go 'long to school wid de white chillun to take care of 'em. Dey show us pictures an' tell us all dey kin, but it didn't 'mount to much.

Walter Calloway, Birmingham, Alabama

"When de war started 'mos' all I know 'bout it was all de white mens go to Montgomery an' jine de army.

My brudder, he 'bout fifteen year ole, so he go 'long wid de ration wagon to Montgomery 'mos' ebry week. One day he come back from Montgomery an' he say, 'Hell done broke loose in Gawgy.' He couldn't tell us much 'bout what done happen, but de slaves dey get all 'cited 'caze dey didn' know what to 'spect. Purty soon we fin' out dat some of de big mens call a meetin' at de capitol on Goat Hill in Montgomery. Dey 'lected Mista Jeff Davis president an' done busted de Nunited States wide open.

"Atter dat dar warn't much happen on de plantation 'cep'in' gangs of so'jers passin' th'ough gwine off to de war. Den 'bout ebry so often a squad of Confederate so'jers would come to de neighborhood gatherin' up rations for Gin'ral Lee's army dey say. Dat make it purty hard on bofe whites an' blacks, takin' off some of de bes' stock an' runnin' us low on grub.

"But we wuk right on 'twell one day somebody sen' a runner sayin' de Yankees comin'. Ole mistis tell me to hurry ober to Mrs. Freeman's an' tell 'em Wilson's Yankee raiders was on de way an' comin' lak a harrikin. I hop on a mule an' go jes' as fas' as I can make him trabel, but befo' I git back dey done retch de plantation, smashin' things comin' an' gwine.

"Dey broke in de smoke house an' tuk all de hams an' yuther rations, dey fin' what dey want an' burn up de res'. Den dey ramshack de big house lookin' fo' money an' jewelry an' raise Cain wid de wimmin folks 'caze dey didn't fin' what dey wanted. Den dey leave dere ole hosses an' mules an' take de bes' we got. Atter dey done dat, dey burn de smoke house, de barns, de cribs an' some yuther prop'ty. Den dey skedaddle some place else.

"I warn't up dar but I heern tell dey burn up piles an' piles of cotton an' lots of steamboats at Montgomery an' lef' de ole town jes' 'bout ruint'. Twarn't long atter dat dey tell us we'se free. But lawdy, Cap'n, we ain't neber been what I calls free. 'Cose ole marster didn' own us no mo', an' all de folks soon scatter all ober, but iffen dey all lak me dey still hafter wuk jes' as hard, an some times hab less dan we useter hab when we stay on Marse John's plantation.

"Well, Cap'n, dat's 'bout all I know. I feel dat misery comin' on me now. Will you please, suh, gimme a lif' back in de house? I wisht dat white gemman doctor come on iffen he comin'."

United States. Work Projects Administration

ESTHER KING CASEY

Interview with Esther King Casey
—Edward F. Harper, Birmingham

Living with her grandchildren at 801 Washington Avenue, Birmingham, Alabama, Esther King Casey, former slave of Capt. Henry King of Americus, Georgia, recalls from fading memory a few vivid scenes of the days when men in gray moved hurridly about the town, suddenly disappeared for a while and then returned, one by one, with weary, halting tread and hollow faces, while gloom and despair hovered over the town like a pall of desolation.

Less vivid in her memory are the stories told her by her grandmother of a long voyage across the ocean, of the arrival in a new land called Mobile, and of slaves being sold at public auction. Less vivid, too, are the memories of her own journey to Georgia, where she, with her parents and brother, were brought to be the slaves of Captain King.

"I was only four or five years old when we came to Captain King's big house," said the old woman, brightening with pride in her ability to recollect. Her manners bore the marks of culture and refinement, and her speech was surprisingly void of the usual Negro dialect. She is an example of the former slave who was educated along with the white children in the family.

"There were eight or ten slaves in all," Esther continued. "We lived in a house in the backyard of Captain King's Big House. My mamma was the cook. Papa was a mechanic. He built houses and made tools and machinery. Captain King gave me to the 'white lady;' that was Miss Susan, the Captain's wife. Captain King was a fine man. He treated all of us just like his own family. The 'white lady' taught us to be respectable and truthful."

When asked if she had ever been punished for misbehavior the old woman smiled and said: "Once the 'white lady' whipped me for playing with the jailer's children. She had told me not to play with them because they were not good company for me. She said that she wanted to raise me to be good and truthful, and that the jailer's little white children told lies and talked bad."

Esther remembers well the mobilization of gray-uniformed troops at the courthouse which stood only a block from the King residence. "The town was filled with soldiers for several days," she said. "They assembled about the courthouse and had speakings. One day I passed there with my papa and saw Abraham Lincoln hanging from a noose in the courthouse square. Of course, it was only an effigy of Abraham Lincoln which was used to show what the soldiers thought of him. Papa told me that the soldiers shot the effigy full of bullet holes before they left town.

"Before Captain King left he brought a man with him from the courthouse to value his property. The slaves were valued, too. I remember Captain King lifting me high above his head and saying to the man: 'I wouldn't take a thousand dollars for this little gem.'"

She paused a moment. The light in her eyes showed that she was reliving the thrill of that childhood incident.

"Then Captain King left with the other soldiers. Papa stayed and took care of the 'white lady' and the house. After a while my brother ran away and joined the troops to fight for Captain King. He came back after the war, but Captain King did not. Several years later I saw a man down in south Georgia who told me that he belonged to Captain King's troops. He said that he was standing near him when he was killed.

Esther King Casey, Birmingham, Alabama

"After the proclamation the slaves were free. Most of them leased out to plantation owners. I stayed with mamma and the 'white lady.'"

Mrs. King had taught the little slave girl to read and write, and when schools were opened for the freed slaves she told the child's mother to send her to school. Fees of fifty cents a month were charged, which Mrs. King paid as long as the child remained with her. At eighteen years of age the girl had acquired sufficient education to qualify to teach in the public schools for Negroes. After three years of teaching she married Jim Casey, an ex-slave, who took her to his "three-plow" farm in south Georgia.

"No man ever lived who was finer than Jim," said the old woman. "My daughter used to say that I loved him more than God, and that God was jealous and took him away from me."

After her only daughter's death in 1919, Esther was brought to Birmingham by her grandson who has kept her comfortably ever since. Her hair is just turning gray, though she was born in 1856. The little briar pipe, which she endeavors to conceal from strangers, is the only outward evidence that she has anything in common with others of her generation.

AMY CHAPMAN

Interview with Amy Chapman
—Ruby F. Tartt, Livingston, Alabama

DE MASTERS GOOD, BUT OVERSEERS MEAN

Aunt Amy paused as she worked among the small plants in her garden, removing a weed here and there. She pushed back the sunbonnet that shaded her eyes and began:

"I was bawn on Governor Reuben Chapman's place five miles north of Livingston on May 14, 1843. My name is Amy Chapman. My mother was Clary Chapman an' my pappy was Bob Chapman. Dey both come from Virginny; my mammy from Petersburg an' my pappy f'um Richmond. Dey was driv' down to Alabamy lak cattle an' Marse Reuben bought 'em. He had a lot of slaves caze he had a heap of plantations, but him an' his wife stay most of de time in Huntsville an' dey had a heap of white oberseers. I had a plenty of chilluns but not as many as my mammy.

"Who was my husban'? Law chile, I ain't never had no special husban'. I even forgits who was de pappy of some of dese chilluns of mine.

"Us had a mean oberseer, an' since Marse Reuben

warn't never at home, dem oberseers useter treat us somp'n awful. One day Marse Reuben come home an' when he foun' out dat de oberseer was mean to de slaves he commence to give him a lecture, but when Miss Ferlicia tuk a han' in de business, she didn't stop at no lecture, she tol' dat oberseer dis: 'I hear you take my women an' turn dere clothes ober dere haids an' whup 'em. Any man dat's got a family an' would do sich a thing oughter be sham' of hisself, an' iffen Gov. Chapman can't make you leave, I kin, so you see dat road dere? Well, make tracks den.' An' Mistis, he lef' raght den. He didn't wait for no coaxin'. He was de meanes' oberseer us ever had. He tuk my ol'est brother an' had him stretched out jus' lak you see Christ on de cross; had him chained, an' I sot down on de groun' by him an' cried all night lack Mary an' dem done. Dat oberseer was de fus' one dat ever putt me in de fiel', an' he whupped me wid de cat er nine tails when I was stark naked.

"Den dere was anudder mean man named [...] who was always a-beatin' nigger women caze dey wouldn't mind him.

"Us warn't learned to read an' write, but Mr. Jerry Brown's slaves were. He owned a big plantation. Us didn't go to no nigger church, caze dere warn't none. I was babtized in Jones Creek, an' Dr. Edmon's a white preacher, j'ined me to de Jones Creek Babtist Church long fo' de war, an' de song I lacked bes' was a white folks song. Twarn't no nigger song. It was lack dey sing it now, 'cep' mo' lovely, Miss, mo' lovely.

> Dark was de night
> Col' was de groun'
> On which my Savior lay

> Blood in draps of sweat run down
> In agony he pray.
>
> Lawd, move did bitter cup
> If sich dy sacred will
> If not content I'll drink it up
> Whose pleasure I'll fullfil.

"An' anudder one us niggers useter sing was might pretty:

> In evil long I tuk de light
> An' led by shame an' fear
> When a new object stopped my flight
> An' stopped my wild career.
>
> I saw him hangin' on a tree
> In agony an' blood
> He fixed his languid eyes on me
> As near his cross I stood.
>
> Sho' never till my latter breath
> Kin I forgit dat look
> He seemed to change me wid his death
> Yit not a word he spoke.
>
> My conscience felt an' owned de quilt
> An' plunged me in despair
> I saw my sins his blood had spilt
> An' helped to nail him dere.

"Yassum, I kin tell you things about slavery times dat would make yo' blood bile, but dey's too turrible. I jus' tries to forgit.

Amy Chapman, Livingston, Alabama

"I could tell you 'bout bein' run myself wid dem nigger dogs, but I ain't gwineter do it. I will tell you dough 'bout a mean man who whupped a cullid woman near 'bout to death. She got so mad at him dat she tuk his baby chile what was playin' roun' de yard and grab him up an' th'owed it in a pot of lye dat she was usin' to wash wid. His wife come a-hollin' an' run her arms down in de boilin' lye to git de chile out, an' she near 'bout burnt her arms off, but it didn't do no good 'caze when she jerked de chile out he was daid.

"One day I seed ole Unker Tip Toe all bent over a-comin' down de road an' I ax him whut ail him an' he say: 'I's been in de stocks an' been beat till de blood come. Den ole Massa 'ninted my flesh wid red papper an' turpentine an' I's been most dead but I is somewhat better now.' Unker Tiptoe belonged to de meanes' ol' marster around here.

"But, honey, I ain't never tol' nobody all dis an' ain't gwine tell you no mo'. Ride me home now, caze I's cripple; a cow was de cause of it. She drug me roun' dat new orchard whut I planted las' fall. She done run away wid me. Mistis I wished you would do me a favor an' write my son in Texas an' tell him dat I say, iffen he 'specks me to make him anymo' of dem star quilts, he better come on here an' kiver my house. De roof sho' does leak bad."

EMMA CHAPMAN

Interview with Emma Chapman
—Mary A. Poole

Living in a small room in the rear of a house at 361 Augusta Street, Mobile, Alabama, the writer located an interesting ex-slave, Emma Chapman, who when first approached was somewhat reticent. I soon learned I had arrived just as she was ready to have her breakfast, which consisted of bread and coffee, and insisted she eat first and talk afterwards, as she had made just about enough fire in the open fireplace to boil the coffee.

While she followed my suggestion I glanced about the room and found it very neat and tidy and an unusually comfortable looking double bed, a mirrored door chifferobe and two trunks, one rocking chair and a couple of straight chairs, a table containing all cooking utensils and food containers. The walls were covered with sheets of manilla wrapping paper, tacked on, and part of the ceiling patched with odds and ends of corrugated paper. Emma is small in stature, of light complexion with greying hair arranged in neat braids around her head, very clean in appearance.

Emma said she was about 13 years of age at the time of the surrender, and that she was born on the plantation of Rev. Mr. Montgomery Curry of Charleston, S.C. When she was about 3 years of age Mr. Curry moved to Pickens County, Alabama, about 5 miles from Carrollton and 8 miles from Pickenville. When I asked why they moved to Alabama, Emma laughed, and said they expected to find money growing on trees in Alabama, and that she as a child came near being "snake bit" many a time, digging around the roots of old trees, trying to find money.

Rev. Montgomery Curry, said Emma, was married to Ann Haynie, whose parents were Aaron and Francis Hudson Haynie, and Emma's grandmother was Lucy Linier, who was born in Virginia and was sold to Mr. Haynie to pay a debt. Lucy Linier was nurse for his daughter Ann and when she married Mr. Curry, she brought Lucy with her to her new home. The Currys had three children, a boy and two girls, and it was Lucy Linier's daughter, Patsy, who acted as their nurse.

The home of Rev. and Mrs. Montgomery Curry was a two-story log house with wide open hall running the entire length of the house and with rooms opening off either side. The kitchen was out a short distance from the main house, with the dairy between the two, under a large hickory tree.

The slave quarters were also built of logs, with space between for a shed room and small garden plot and a few chickens. The slave women did not go to the fields on Saturday as that was their day to clean up around their homes. They usually washed their clothes at night and hung them on the bushes where they were left to dry in the sunshine, maybe a couple of days, as no one could or would disturb them.

Rev. Montgomery Curry was a Baptist preacher and had no overseer, except Lucy Linier and her husband, Emma's grandparents, who kept a supervision over the slaves about 40 in number. There was no whipping allowed on the Curry plantation, and after the death of Reverend Curry, Mrs. Ann Curry (his widow) ran the plantation under the same system. The patrollers had no jurisdiction over the Curry slaves, they were given permits by the Currys to go and come, and Emma said if one of those patrollers whipped one of "ole Miss's slaves, she would have sure sued them.

Emma laughingly said the slaves on other plantations always said the Curry slaves were "free niggers," as they could always get permits, and had plenty to eat and milk to drink. The slaves cooked their breakfasts in their own cabins, but dinner and supper was cooked in the kitchen and each came with their pan to be filled and had their own gourds which were grown on the place to drink their milk and of which they could have full and plenty.

During the war they cooked for the Confederate soldiers encamped nearby and great quantities were prepared. Emma was one of those delegated to carry the food to the camp. All she ever saw of the Yankees were two who stopped at the house and asked for something to eat. Mrs. Montgomery invited them in and served the best she had. One of the men wanted to take the last mule she had and the other said "No, Mrs. Montgomery is a widow and from the appearance of her slaves she has treated them well."

Mrs. Montgomery told them that someone had stolen her saddle horse and the soldier who had remonstrated with the other replied: "Madam, your saddle horse will be returned in three weeks," and sure enoug, one night about midnight they heard a horse whinny and Emma's grandfather said "there is old Spunk," and there was old Spunk waiting outside.

Emma said the first whipping she ever had, was after the Surrender, given her by her own father when they left Alabama and went to live near Columbus, Miss.

She had always lived in the house with the "old Miss" and her young Miss, and when she had to leave them, she cried and so did they.

Her grandmother Lucy Linier nursed "Miss Ann"; Lucy's daughter Patsy nursed "Miss Ann's" children, and was the special property of Fannie Montgomery Curry, who married a Mr. Sidney Lipscomb and whose children Emma helped to look after, so the three generations were interwoven.

Emma only wishes she could go back to plantation days. All her trials and suffering came after she left "Ole Miss," and went to live with her father and mother, George and Patsy Curry, who had fourteen children and of which Emma was the eldest. Her father who was a quadroon in cast was cruel to his family, and especially so to her. He made her work like a man, cutting timber, splitting rails, digging, planting and all work of the farm.

Now, Emma is the only member of her family left. She married three times, having only two children, a girl and a boy, these by her last husband, Frank Chapman, now dead, and Emma has no knowledge of her children's whereabouts. She gave them an education so they could write to her if they wanted to. The girl married and left

Mobile, the boy went to Chicago, was chauffeur for some rich folks. His last letter several years ago, in which he enclosed $25.00, stated he was going on a trip to Jerusalem with one of the young men of the family.

United States. Work Projects Administration

HENRY CHEATAM

Interview with Henry Cheatam
—Ila B. Prine

I HEARD LINCOLN SET US FREE

"White folks, I'se glad you drapped by to have a talk wid me. I was gittin' powerfully lonely," said Henry Cheatam, who lives in Marysville, a Mobile suburb. "Sho' I'll be glad to tell you some about de slave days. I sho' 'members plenty. Well, to begin wid, I was born in 1850 near West Point. Dat's in Clay County, Mississippi, you know. I b'longed to Mr. Tom Hollingshead who was killed in de Cibil War. I 'members all de slaves agoin' in to take a last look at him atter dey done brung his body home.

"My mammy's name was Emmeline Cheatam, an' my pappy's was Sam Cheatam. I don't remember my grandpappy an' grandmammy atall.

"Us slaves libed in log cabins what was daubed wid clay to keep de rain an' win' out, an' de chimneys was made of clay an' sticks. De beds was home-made an' nailed agin' de wall wid legs on de outer side. De Massa's house was build of logs too, but it was much bigger'n de nigger cabins an' sot way out in front of ourn. Atter de massa was kilt, old Miss had a nigger oberseer an' dat was de meanest debil dat eber libbed on de Lawd's green yearth. I promise myself when I growed up dat I was agoin' to kill dat nigger iffen it was de las' thing I eber done. Lots of times I'se seen him beat my mammy, an' one day I seen him beat my Auntie who was big wid a chile, an' dat man dug a roun' hole in de groun' an' put her stummick in it, an' beat an' beat her for a half hour straight till the baby come out raght dere in de hole.

"Why de Mistis 'low such treatment? A heap of times ole Miss didn't know nuthin' 'bout it, an' de slaves better not tell her, 'caze dat oberseer whup 'em iffen he finds out dat dey done gone an' tol'. Yassun, white folks, I'se seed some turrible things in my time. When de slaves would try to run away our oberseer would put chains on dere legs wid big long spikes tween dere feets, so dey couldn't git away. Den I's seen great bunches of slaves put up on de block an' sol' jus' lak dey was cows. Sometimes de chilluns would be seprated from dere maws an' paws.

"I come pretty near to bein' tuk away from my maw. When de slaves was bein' 'vided, one of ole Miss' datters was agoin' to Texas, an' I was goin' to have to go when somebody hollered 'Freedom', an' I sho' was glad 'caze I could stay wid my mammy now.

"In dose days us had plenty of good, plain food; such as pot likker, greens, cornbread, 'taters, peas, pears, an' at hog killin' us had chittlin's an' pig jowls an' back bone. Den us would cotch 'possums at night when dey come up in de corn fiel'. Us neber seed no flour dough.

"As for fishin', we neber did none, 'caze we hadda work too hard. We worked from 'can to can't.' Git up at sunrise, go to de fiel' an' stay till dark. In de middle of de day dey would sen' our somp'n t'eat to de fiel' wid a barrel of water. But for breakfas' an' supper, us hadda cook our own grub dey gib us.

"Our clo's warn't many. Us chilluns wo' a one-piece suit made outen osnaburg, an' us would hab to take dat off at night, wash it an' put it back on de nex' day. As for shoes, chillun neber had none. You see, white folks, I was jus' a chile, jus' big enough to tote water to de fiel's.

Henry Cheatam, Marysville, Alabama

"I 'members when de Yankees was acomin' th'ough I hoped to ca'y de hosses to de woods an' hoped to hide de meat an' bury de valu'bles, 'caze dem Yankees tuk whatever dey wanted, an' you better not say nothin' neither 'caze dey had dem long swyords ahangin' at dere sides.

"In dem days, de slaves done all de work an' carried all de news. De marsters sont notes from one plantation to anudder, an' when dey wanted de niggers to come to de Big House dey would blow an ole cow horn. Dey had certain number of blows for certain niggers. Dat is, de niggers dat was somp'n. Dey would also use dis horn for 'possum an' coon huntin' at night. De li'l niggers at night went to de big house to spin an' weave. I'se spun a many roll an' carded a many bat of cotton. I'se also made a many tallow candle by tyin' strings onto a long stick an' droppin dem down into moulds filled wid tallow. I'se hid many a night in de fence corners when I'd be agoin' som'ers to git my mammy some 'bacco. De pattyrollers would be out lookin' for slaves dat didn't hab no pass from dere oberseer, an' I'd hear dem acomin' an' I'd hide till dey pass on, 'caze iffen dey cotch me I sho' gwine have a sound beatin'.

"De owners always tuk care of us, and when us got sick dey would git a doctor, an' ole Miss was all right, but dat oberseer was a debil. He wouldn't 'low no meetin' on de place. Sometimes us would slip down de hill an' turn de wash pot bottom up'ards so de soun' of our voices would go under de pot, an' us'd have a singin' an' prayin' raght dere.

"Mos' of de slave could go sometimes to de white folks church when dey gits a pass from dere Massa, but dat mean oberseer always tried to keep us from goin' so's us couldn't learn nothin'. He didn't want us to learn to read or write neither.

"No'm us didn't have nothin' lak matches till I was growed. Us used flint rocks an' cotton to start de fires.

"Us didn't have nothin' but food an' clothes. We didn't have no garden of our own an' der wan't no celebratin', 'ceptin' at hog killin'. Dat was de bigges' day of de year.

"On Sat'day afternoon we was 'lowed to play, but I can't 'member none of de games. Us jus' played lak all li'l niggers did den. At night time us jus' went to our cabins an' went to bed, 'caze we warn't 'lowed to do no singing. Mos' of de singin' was done in de fiel's.

"Cornshuckin' time come when dey wanted to git de seed corn for plantin', an' us would commence de shuckin' when it commence rainin'.

"You axed me 'bout funerals an' weddin's. Us niggers nebber ma'ied an' don't 'member any big weddin's of de white folks. But dey buried folks den de same as dey does now, in a box. Dey would bury de slaves same as dey done de white folks, but us didn't eben have no babtizin' on 'count of dat oberseer. He didn't lak for us to git no religion. Cose all slaves didn't have hard treatment lak us did, 'caze dere oberseer an' Marster warn't as mean as ourn.

"No'm we didn't know nothin' 'bout no hoodoo stuff in dem days. Dey only had homemade medicines, dat is unless dey got sho' nuff powerful sick an' den dey would go to see a doctor. Us used bone-set tea made from a weed. Lawd, it was bitterer dan quinine, an' it were good for de chills an' fever, an' it would purge you too. Den us used life-everlastin' tea for fever, an' Jerusalem brush-reed to get rid of worms.

"But, Miss, I knows dere is gostes, 'caze when I was a little boy my mammy come in from de fiel' an' laid across de bed an' I was sittin' in front of de fireplace an' a big somp'n lak a cow widout no haid come in de do' an' I commence to beat on it wid my fists. Den my mammy say: 'What matter wid you, nigger?' Den dat critter he walk raght out de do'. I looked outen de window an' dere it was a-goin' in Aunt Marfa's cabin. I neber did see it no mo'. Den anudder time a white man died an' my mammy was a stayin' wid his sister an' dis spirit lak an angel come to my mammy an' tol' her to tell de white lady to read de Bible back'ards three times, 'caze dere was one talent 'tween her an' Jesus. Atter dat she were comforted. Anudder time, my pappy, Sam Cheatam, who was a wicked man, was a-sittin' in front of de fire an' a big brindle dog come to de do' an' started barkin'. My pappy say: 'What in de Hell am dat?' an' snapped his fingers at de dog. De dog he den dropped daid. Some folks say dat dere ain't no sich things as gostes, but I know dere is, 'caze dere is good spirits an' bad spirits.

"Dem was good ol' days, Mistis, even iffen us did have a hard time an' I don't know iffen it warn't better'n it is now. I has to almos' go hongry, an' I can't git no he'p from de government, 'caze I is over 65 years old. Fact is, I believe I 'druther be alivin' back dere dan today 'caze us at least had plenty somp'n t'eat an' nothin' to worry about. An' as for beatin'; dey beats folks now iffen dey don't do raght, so what's de difference? Yassum, Mistis, I worked as long as I was able an' didn't axe nobody for nothin', but now it's diff'rent, 'caze I ain't able to do no work. I'se tried to do raght and ain't never been in but one fight in my life. I now belongs to de Corinthian Babtist Church, an' I's tryin' to live so when de good Lawd calls I'll be ready to answer wid a clean soul.

"I'se had two wives, but I was only a young nigger when I had de fust un, an' had two chilluns by her, den I lef' her 'caze she warn't no 'count. Dat's been forty year ago, an' I ain't neber seen my chilluns in all dem years. My second wife I got when I lived thirty miles below Birmingham, Alabama, at de ol' Bank Mines. Dat's been thirty-five year ago an' us is still together. Us ain't neber had no chilluns. No'm, I don't know nothin' 'bout Abe Lincoln 'ceptin' dey say he sot us free, an' I don't know nothin' 'bout dat neither."

United States. Work Projects Administration

LAURA CLARK

Interview with Laura Clark
—Ruby Pickens Tartt, Livingston, Alabama

CHILLUN IN EV'Y GRABEYARD

Laura Clark, black and wrinkled with her eighty-six years, moved limpingly about the tiny porch of her cabin on the outskirts of Livingston. Battered cans and rickety boxes were filled with a profusion of flowers of the common variety. Laura offered me a split-bottomed chair and lowered herself slowly into a rocker that creaked even under her frail body. "Po'ly, Miss, po'ly," she responded to my query about her health. "Tain't lack de old days. I's crippled and mos' blin' now atter all de years what I got.

"I was born on Mr. Pleasant Powell's place in North Ca'lina, and when I was 'bout six or seven years ole I reckon hit 'twas, Mr. Garret from right up yonder in de bend, 'bout eight miles from Livingston gwine no'th on de Livingston and Epes road, bought ten of us chillun in North Ca'lina and sont two white men, and one was Mr. Skinner, to fotch us back in waggins. En he fotch ole Julie Powell and Henry to look atter us. Wa'n't none of dem ten chillun no kin to me, and he never bought my mammy, so I had to leave her behine.

"I recollect Mammy said to old Julie, 'Take keer my baby chile (dat was me) an iffen I never sees her no mo' raise her for God.' Den she fell off de waggin where us was all settin' and roll over on de groun' jes' acryin'. But us was eatin' candy what dey done give us for to keep us quiet, and I didn't have sense 'nuff for to know what ailed Mammy, but I knows now and I never seed her no mo' in dis life. When I heered from her atter S'render she done dead and buried. Her name was Rachel Powell. My pappy's name I don't know ca'se he done been sole to somewhars else when I was too little to recollect. But my mammy was de mother of twenty-two chillun and she had twins in her lap when us driv' off. My gran'mammy said when I lef', 'Pray, Laura, and be er good gal, and min' bofe white and black. Ev'body will lack you and iffen you never see me no mo' pray to meet me in heaven.' Den she cried. Her name was Rose Powell.

"Us all started den for Mr. Garrett's plantation down yonder in de bend, ten chillun and two ole uns, and two white men, and us was travellin' solid a month. Fuss thing Ole Marsa say was 'Now be good ter dese motherless chillun.' Den he went to war, and de overseers forgot all 'bout dey promise. When Ole Marsa come back he done got his arm shot off, but he let bofe dem overseers go, ca'se dey done whupped dat ole 'oman what come wid us to deaf. She brought her two little boys, Colvin and 'Lias, but Joe, dey pappy, didn't come—he was sole 'fo 'Lias was bawn. Joe never seed 'Lias.

Laura Clark, Livingston, Alabama

"I sets cross de road here from dat church over yonder and can't go 'ca'se I'm cripple' and blin', but I heers um singin':

> A motherless chile sees a hard time
> Oh, Lord, he'p her on de road.
> 'Er sister will do de bes' she kin
> Dis is a hard world, Lord, fer a motherless chile.

"And I jes' busts out cryin'. Dat was de song I had in view to sing for you, hit's so mournful. I knowed 'twa'n't no reel, 'twa'n't nothin' lack no reel, 'ca'se I been b'longin' to de church for fifty-five years, and I don't fancy no reel. I'm glad I got hit to my min' 'fo' you lef'. But my recollection is shaller. I ain't never read no verse in no Bible in my life, ca'se I can't read. Some my chillun kin, though. My husban' died and lef' me wid nine chillun, none of um couldn't pull de others outer de fire iffen dey fell in. I had mo'n dat, but some come here dead and some didn't. I got chillun dead in Birmingham and Bessemer. Dey ain't a graveyard in dis here settlement 'roun' Prospect where I ain't got chillun buried. Hettie Ann, right up dere ter Mr. Hawkins' graveyard, and my boy whut got killed settin' on de side de road eatin' his dinner, he' buried in Captain Jones' place in de bend yonder.

"Yassum, I been drug about and put through de shackles so bad I done forgot some of dey names, and I mos' blin' now and can't hear good neither. But my eyes is good nuff for to see ghosts, but I don't b'lieve in 'em, 'ca'se I'd see dem chillun sometime effen dey was ghosties. I know I'd see my boy, ca'se dey showed me his head whar dat Miller boy hit him in de head wid a spade and split his head wide open, slip up behin' him and all he said was 'Squeek,' jes' lack a hog, and he was dead. And de murderer live right here but dey move and now I'm here. When hit rain us jes' gets under de bed 'ca'se de house ain't got no top on hit.

Laura Clark's House, Livingston, Alabama

"I can't say Marse Garrett wa'n't good to us motherless chillun but de overseer, Mr. Woodson Tucker, was mean as anybody. He'd whup you nigh 'bout to deaf, and had a whuppin' log what he strip 'em buck naked and lay 'em on de log. He whup 'em wid a wide strop, wider'n my han', den he pop de blisters what he raise and 'nint 'em wid red pepper, salt, and vinegar. Den he put 'em in de house dey call de pest house and have a 'oman stay dere to keep de flys offen 'em 'twell dey get able to move. Den dey had reg'lar men in de fields wid spades, and iffen you didn't do what you git tole, de overseer would wrop dat strap 'roun' his han' and hit you in de haid wid de wooden handle 'til he kilt you. Den de mens would dig a hole wid de spades and throw 'em in hit right dere in de fiel' jes' lack dey was cows—didn't have no funeral nor nothin'.

"Us had a heap of houses in de quarters right on bofe sides de Big House. Us could step outer one house to 'tother. But, Miss, I didn't work so hard or have no trouble either. I was in de house atter Marsa come home and foun' me splittin' rails and plowin'. He 'lowed dey done put me in too hard a ship, and I was too little, so he tuck me to de house to draw water and wash dishes, 'ca'se I was a little motherless gal. Ole Marsa done a good part by me, and I was married to my fuss husban', Cary Crockett, right dere in de parlor. He tole de overseer dat us was human and had feelin's same as him, so he rejected de paterrollers and made 'em git off de place. I was treated good, 'ca'se I 'membered what my gran'ma say, and whatever dey tole me to put my han' to, I did, and I was obedient and wasn't hardheaded lack some de res.' I had no trouble, and wasn't 'buked none. But I's had mo' trouble las' ten years wid my own chillun den I ever did in slav'y time. Dey gives me sich bitter words till I can't swaller 'em and I jes' sets and cries. I can't read no songs to comfort me, jes' ketch 'em from de preacher on de stan' and hole 'em, dat's de way I ketch my larnin'.

"Las' sermon I hyard, he tuck his tex' en said, 'Don't nobody rob God.' Den he say, 'Effen you is goin' to 'tend to serve God, serve Him in de full, 'ca'se God don't never bat a eye, nor turn His haid and he kin see you. He frowns at ev'y sin, but He's a sinforgivin' man.' I use to know a heap 'bout de Lord, but I'm so cripple' an blin' since de ca'f jumped on my foot I can't go to church no mo', so I done forgot.

"You ax 'bout dem flowers on de po'ch—I sho' wish dey was mine, you could have 'em 'ca'se dey ain't room nuff wid dem for me ter sit whar I desire. Us ain't got no meal and here 'tis jes' Tuesday—no mo' till Saddy. Sho' is bad; us jes' 'pends on de neighbors and borrys."

United States. Work Projects Administration

HATTIE CLAYTON

Interview with Hattie Clayton
—Preston Klein

DE YANKS DRAPPED OUTEN DE SKY

"Aunt' Hattie Clayton said, "I'se gittin' erroun' de ninety notch, honey, an' I reckon de Kingdom ain't fur away."

She lives in a tiny cabin not far from Opelika. Her shoulders are bent; her hair gray, but she still does a large amount of housework. She likes to sit on the tumbledown front porch on summer afternoons, plying her knitting needles and stretching her aged legs in the warm sunlight.

"'Twas a long time ago, honey," she observed when talk of slavery days was brought up, "but I 'members as ef 'twas yestidy. My ol' mistus was de Widder Day. She owned a plantation clos't to Lafayette an' she was mighty good to us niggers.

"Ol' Mistus boughten me when I was jus' a little tyke, so I don't 'member 'bout my pappy an' mammy.

"Honey, I 'members dat us little chilluns didn't go to de fiel's twel us was big 'nuff to keep up a row. De oberseer, Marse Joe Harris, made us work, but he was good to us. Ol' Mistus, she wouldn't let us wuk whin it was rainin' an' cold."

Asked about pleasures of the old plantation life, she chuckled and recalled:

"I kin heah de banjers yit. Law me, us had a good time in dem days. Us danced most eb'ry Sattidy night an' us made de rafters shake wid us foots. Lots o' times Ole Missus would come to de dances an' look on. An' whin er brash nigger boy cut a cute bunch uv steps, de menfolks would give 'im a dime or so.

"Honey, us went t' de church on a Sundays. I allus did lak singin' and I loved de ol' songs lak, 'Ol' Ship of Zion,' an' 'Happy Land.' Ol' Mistus useter take all de little scamps dat was too little for church an' read de Book to dem under de big oak tree in de front yahd."

"Aunt Hattie," she was asked, "do you remember anything about the War between the States?"

"You mean de Yankees, honey?"

"Yes, the Yankees."

Her coal black face clouded.

"Dey skeered us nearly to death," she began. "Dey drap right outen de sky. Ol' Mistus keep hearin' dey was comin', but dey didn't nebber show up. Den, all ter once, dey was swarmin' all ober de place wid deir blue coats a-shinin' an' deir horses a'rarin'.

"Us chilluns run en hid in de fence corners en' behin' quilts dat was hangin' on de line. An' honey, dem

Yankees rid deir horses rat onto Ol' Mistus flower beds. Dey hunted de silver, too, but us done hid dat.

"I 'members dey was mad. Dey sot de house a-fire an' tuk all de vittals dey could fin'. I run away an' got los', an' whin I come back all de folks was gone."

'Aunt' Hattie said she "wint down de big road an' come to a lady's house where she remained until she married."

"Us moved to Lafayette an' den to Opelika," she concluded, "an' I bin' here eber since."

She lives with one of her numerous granddaughters now. She finds her great happiness in "de promise" and the moments when she can sit in the shade and dip her mind back into memory.

United States. Work Projects Administration

WADLEY CLEMONS

Interview with Wadley "Shorty" Clemons
—G.L. Clark

He was bent over the lawn, carefully trimming the border into a neat line. A small black figure in overalls, clean but worn blue chambray shirt, the misshapen remains of shoes and a nondescript hat, from under which protruded thin white sideburns.

"Good morning, Uncle," I said, "Mr. Lee was telling me about you. He said you lived back in slavery times. Is that right?"

"Yes suh, I sho' did. I'll be 92 years old de second of August, and I was a slave for 20 year. I had a good ole massa and mistis, de bes' dere was. Ole massa was a great big man, an' he wa'n't scared of nothin' dey was. He wouldn't go nowhere without me. He always took me wid him. My grandma was a cook and my ma was a house girl.

"We lived in Pine Hill, a summer resort in Jefferson County, Georgia, across the river from Louisville. From home we could look over and see de people walkin' about in Louisville.

Wadley (Shorty) Clemons, [TR: Village Springs?], Alabama

"I remembers de day de Yankees come to Louisville. We could see them goin' about from one house to anudder, settin' fire. Den dey come on to de river and sot fire to de bridge. Dey wouldn't use our bridge. Dey built dese here pontoon bridges and dey could build dem before you could look away and look back. Den dey come across de river to Pine Hill.

"Ole massa had his hosses an' mules hid down in de swamp but my uncle Tom went and got 'em an' brung 'em to de Yankees at de big gate. He didn't had to do it. He was jes' mean. He hadn't been much good to massa since de war commenced; lay off in de swamp mos' of de time. Arter he brung massa's hosses an' mules to de Yankees he went wid dem into massa's bedroom and dey jes' throwed massa and mistis close all outa' de closet and wardrobe and he give em' mistis gold yearings and bracelets and dey took de yearings and put dem on de hosses' years and put de bracelets on de hosses' ankles.

"Ole massa was sittin' on de long porch smokin' one of dese Meerschaum pipes wid a stem way so long and dat pipe was white as snow. He had a big can of tobacco on de table in front of him. In dem days people made dey own tobacco and I wisht I had some of it now.

"Massa had 'bout thutty fattening hogs and de Yankees jes' went in de pen and cut dem hogs in two. He had jes' lots of turkeys and guineas an' de Yankees shot dem down. He had thutty hives of bees in one long row an' one Yankee run up to de firs' hive an jump in it head first, and de bees stung him till he died. De udders pull him out and took him to de well and poured water over him but he stayed dead so dey just dug a hole down by the side of the road and bury him in it. Yessir, dat's de trufe!

"Dey stayed dere all night and camped out and cooked massa's good smoked meat and burnt down de barns and done all de devilment dey could. I couldn't see no use in dere doin' what dey did, but dat's what dey done.

"Massa had 71 slaves when dey was made free. De next county wasn't fit for much farming and atter we was freed my Uncle Andy went dere an' bought a place. De land sold for 50 cents de acre atter de timber was cut off. Uncle Andy had a brudder Sam and Sam had a steer. Dey plowed wid de steer.

"Uncle Andy worked at de sawmill in daytime an' at night he cut two cords of wood before he go to bed. He make two bales of cotton de first year and de next year he make four. Den he tuk up preachin'. He was a Methodist preacher.

"Den ole massa die and ole mistis lose all her land. Uncle Andy was right good fixed so he took keer of her a year or more 'fore she died. Den when she died, he went to pay all de expenses of de funeral but de white folks won't let him kase dey say he done his share already.

"My massa's name was William Clemons and dey name me Wadley for ole man Wadley, de president of de Center Road.

"Dem days is gone a long time an' I still heah, but dey was good times den. I had plenty to eat, plenty close to wear and when I gets sick, ole massa come to give me some medicine and I don't need no doctor.

"People worship God in dem days and not bother wid church houses so much. Ev'ry Sunday ole massa get out by de back do' and teach us Sunday school. Den we cut tree limbs and make brush arbors for preaching. In de summer atter crops been laid by, us all, black and white, go to camp meetin' and stay a week. De white preacher preach on one side and de nigger on de udder. We carry lots of vittles and feed everybody. Niggers sho' was better off in slavery times."

WILLIAM COLBERT

Interview with William Colbert
—John Morgan Smith

MY MASTER WAS A MEAN MAN

"Sho. I remember de slavery days. How could I forgits?"

Slowly Uncle Will spoke these words as he made his way up a few rickety steps with the aid of an old broomstick to his cabin door. "We can jes' set in de swing effen you wants to hear a little 'bout dem ole days, kaze I can sho tell it."

"Well, first, Uncle Will, what's your full name and where are you from?"

"My name am William Colbert and I'se fum Georgia. I was bawn in 1844 on my massa's plantation in Fort Valley. My massa's name was Jim Hodison. At one time he had 165 of us niggers."

Uncle Will, a gaunt, black figure with two weeks growth of gray hair upon his face, spoke in a soft, quaking voice scarcely audible ten feet away. His eyes had a far-off, sad expression of one who had known suffering. They were set deep back in bony caverns.

"Well, Uncle Will, tell me something about the slave days. Was your master good to you?"

William Colbert, [TR: Birmingham], Alabama

"Nawsuh, he warn't good to none of us niggers. All de niggers 'roun' hated to be bought by him kaze he was so mean. When he was too tired to whup us he had de oberseer do it; and de overseer was meaner dan de massa.

But, Mister, de peoples was de same as dey is now. Dere was good uns and bad uns. I jus' happened to belong to a bad un. One day I remembers my brother, January was cotched ober seein' a gal on de next plantation. He had a pass but de time on it done gib out. Well suh, when de massa found out dat he was a hour late, he got as mad as a hive of bees. So when brother January he come home, de massa took down his long mule skinner and tied him wid a rope to a pine tree. He strip' his shirt off and said:

"'Now, nigger, I'm goin' to teach you some sense.'

"Wid dat he started layin' on de lashes. January was a big, fine lookin' nigger; de finest I ever seed. He was jus' four years older dan me, an' when de massa begin a beatin' him, January neber said a word. De massa got madder and madder kaze he couldn't make January holla.

"'What's de matter wid you, nigger' he say. 'Don't it hurt?'

"January, he neber said nothin', and de massa keep a beatin' till little streams of blood started flowin' down January's chest, but he neber holler. His lips was a quiverin' and his body was a shakin', but his mouf it neber open; and all de while I sat on my mammy's and pappy's steps a cryin'. De niggers was all gathered about and some uv 'em couldn't stand it; dey hadda go inside dere cabins. Atter while, January, he couldn't stand it no longer hisself, and he say in a hoarse, loud whisper:

"'Massa! Massa! have mercy on dis poor nigger.'

Will's eyes narrowed down to fine creases as his thick lips came together in smacking noises, and the loose skin beneath his chin, and jaws seemed to shake with the impact of dread memories.

"Den," he continued, after a brief pause in which time there was no sound except the constant drop of a bead of water in a lard bucket, "de war came. De Yankees come in and dey pulled de fruit off de trees and et it. Dey et de hams and cawn, but dey neber burned de houses. Seem to me lak dey jes' stay aroun' long enough to git plenty somp'n t'eat, kaze dey lef' in two or three days, an' we neber seed 'em since. De massa had three boys to go to war, but dere wasn't one to come home. All the chillun he had was killed. Massa, he los' all his money and de house soon begin droppin' away to nothin'. Us niggers one by one lef' de ole place and de las' time I seed de home plantation I was a standin' on a hill. I looked back on it for de las' time through a patch of scrub pines and it look' so lonely. Dere warn't but one person in sight, de massa. He was a-settin' in a wicker chair in de yard lookin' out ober a small field of cotton and cawn. Dere was fo' crosses in de graveyard in de side lawn where he was a-settin'. De fo'th one was his wife. I lost my ole woman too 37 years ago, and all dis time, I's been a carrin' on like de massa—all alone."

TILDY COLLINS

Interview with Tildy Collins
—*Susie R. O'Brien, Uniontown, Alabama*

In the Negro section of Uniontown, locally known as "Rabbit Yard" (named by the Negroes themselves), lives "Aunt Tildy" Collins, a typical "black mammy" of orthodox type. She is a talkative old soul, running over with slavery tales and greatly beloved by a wide range of acquaintances among both races. Although eighty-four summers have passed over her snow-white head, Aunt Tildy's spirit is unconquered by time and her physical activity is truly remarkable for her age. She does her own housework and cares for her home without assistance. In front of her one-room cabin is a neat garden of vegetables and flowers combined, with morning glories trained carefully over the fence nearly all the way around. There is a saying in the South, that cotton will grow better for a Negro than for any other race, and this might well be extended to include morning glories in Aunt Tildy's case; since none in Uniontown are quite so fine in growth or brilliance of coloring.

Like nearly all old Negroes, Aunt Tildy goes to sleep very readily. She was dozing in a rocker on her small porch, while the scent of wood smoke and the odor of boiling vegetables issued from the cabin. An iron pot, hanging from a crane in the fireplace, sending forth clouds of steam and an appetizing aroma. She clings to old fashioned equipment and disdains a stove for cooking. Her "biled" vegetables or meats in the hanging pot, with baked potatoes and "pone" bread from the oven make up a meal that leaves little to be desired, as many visitors who have shared her repasts well know.

As the gate squeaked, Aunt Tildy awoke with a start and a smile.

"Come in, white folks, I was jes' a-settin' here waitin' for my greens to bile, an' I musta drapped off to sleep. Set down in dat cheer right dar, an' tek off your hat; you sho' is lookin' well, an' I'se proud to see you.

"Yas, ma'am, I sho' was borned in slavery times, an' I wish to Gawd I could git now what I useter hab den, 'caze dem was good times for de black folks. Dese free niggers don't know what 'tis to be tuk good keer of.

"Co'se I means dat! I was borned on a big plantation near 'bout to Linden, an' my Ole Marster was name Harris, yassum, Dick Harris, an' my Ole Mistis was Miss Mandy. Bofe dey boys fit in de wah, an' I 'members when dey went off wid de sojers, ole Mistis she cry an' hug dem boys an' kiss 'em goodbye, an' dey was gone a long time. I was a leetle gal whenst dey went to de wah, an' I was mos' a grown 'oman when dey come home, an' dey bofe had whiskers. Young Massa Richard he limpin' an' look mighty pale, an' dey say he been wounded an' stay in prison on Mister Johnson's island, summuz up de ribber; but Marse Willis, he look all right, 'cep'in' whiskers. Ole Marster had a big house, an' dat same house standin' dar right now. Us had plenty to eat an' plenty to wear, an' dat's mo'n what some folks got now.

"Ole Marster was good to all he niggers, an' my pappy and mammy bofe belonged to him. Dey was a slave-yard in Uniontown, an' ev'y time a spec'later cum wid a lot of new niggers, Ole Marster he buy four or five niggers, an' dat's how he come to buy my pappy, atter de spec'later brung him an' a whole passel of niggers from North C'lina. My mammy here already 'long to Ole Marster. Her was borned his'n.

"Sometime a no 'count nigger tek an' runned erway; but de oberseer, he put de houn's on he track, an' dey run him up a tree, an' de oberseer fetch him back nex' mawnin', all tuckerd out, an' he' glad to stay home for a spell an' 'have hese'f. Ole Marster had a good oberseer, too. 'Cose he wan't no quality, lak Ole Marster an' Ole Mistis, but he was a good, kin' man an' he didn't hab no trouble on de whole plantation.

"Us alluz had a Chris'mus tree in de quarter, jes' lak de white folks an' dey was presents for ev'ybody— nobody wan't lef' out, big or little. Dere was a meetin' house on de plantation an' Ole Marster had a rule dat all de chilluns had to go to Sunday school soon as dey was big 'nuff, an' dey had to go in clean white clo'se, too. Us chilluns hate to see Sunday come, 'caze Mammy an' Granmammy dey wash us an' near 'bout rub de skin off gittin' us clean for Sunday school, an' dey comb our heads wid a jimcrow. You ain't neber seed a jimcrow? Hit mos' lak a card what you card wool wid. What a card look lak? Humph! Missy, whar you been raise—ain't neber seed a card? Dat jimcrow sho' did hurt, but us hadder stan' hit, an' sometimes atter all dat, Mammy she wrap our kinky hair wid t'read an' twis' so tight us's eyes couldn't hardly shet.

"My Granmammy, her de head cook 'oman at de big house, an' us had to mine her lak us did Mammy. I ho'p Granmammy in de kitchen, atter I got big 'nuff an' she sho' did keep me humpin'. Chilluns had to mine dey olders in dem days. Dey wan't lak dey is now, don't mine nobody, not eben dey Pa.

"When de surrender come, Ole Marster he tole all de niggers dey was free now, an' some was glad an' some was sorry an' welst dey might be sorry, iffen dey knowed what a hard time dey goner had knockin' 'roun' de worl' by deyself; no Ole Marster an' no Ole Mistis ter look atter 'em an' feed 'em when dey sick an' when dey well. Look lak ter me, when de surrender parted de white folks an' de black folks, it hurt 'em bofe. Dey oughter be tergedder, jes' lak de Good Lord 'tended dey be."

Aunt Tildy sighed deeply and, gazing afar off, said: "Iffen Ole Marster was livin' now, I'd be all right an' not hafter worry 'bout nuffin."

In spite of her eighty-four years, Aunt Tildy makes her living as a mid-wife and serves as a "doctor man" in cases of minor ailments; but her practice is so closely interwoven with "conju'in'" that it is difficult to say which is the more important to her. For example: she prescribes wearing matches in the hair or a little salt on the mole of the head for headache. Her sovereign remedy for rheumatism is "'nint de j'ints wid a little kerosene oil an' put some mullen leaves on it." "A good dost of turpentine is good for mos' anything de matter wid you." A coin with a hole in it, usually a dime, tied around the ankle will keep you from getting "pizen." Furthermore, this same treatment warns against the ill effects of getting "conju'ed." "Iffen you gits conju'ed, de dime turn black, an' you kin go to de conju' doctor an' git de conju' took off."

"Is you got to go, Missy? Come back agin. I's allus proud to see you," Aunt Tildy called after me from the edge of the porch.

United States. Work Projects Administration

SARA COLQUITT

Interview with Sara Colquitt
—*Preston Klein, Opelika, Alabama*

SHE JUST CAN REMEMBER HER HUSBAND'S NAME

Sara Colquitt, who used to till the fields in slavery days, now has a handmaiden of her own. Sara does not know the date of her birth in Richmond, Virginia, but she says it was more than a century ago. (1937). The "girl," whom her daughter has employed to take care of the nearly blind and helpless centenarian, is well past eighty herself, yet she keeps her charge neat and clean and the cabin in which they live tidy. Sara's daughter works in the fields nearby at Opelika, Ala. to keep the family going.

"Mr. Bill Slaughter and Miss Mary Slaughter was our marster and mistess and dey had two chilluns, Marsa Robert and Marsa Brat," Sara said. "I had four brothers and sisters, Tate, Sam, Jennie, and Tenner. Us lived in log cabins wid dirt floors and dey was built in two long rows. Us beds was nailed to de wall at one end and us used corn shucks and pine straw for mattresses.

"Miss Mary was good to us, but us had to work hard and late. I worked in de fields every day from 'fore daylight to almost plumb dark. I usta take my littlest baby wid me. I had two chilluns, and I'd tie hit up to a tree limb to keep off de ants and bugs whilst I hoed and worked de furrow. All us niggers was fed from de big kitchen and wasn't hongry, but sometimes us would steal more food dan was give us anyhow.

Sara Colquitt, Opelika, Alabama

"I was one of de spinners, too, and had to do six cuts to de reel at de time and do hit at night plenty times. Us clothes was homespun osnaburg, what us would dye, sometimes solid and sometimes checked.

"'Sides working de fields and spinning, sometimes I'd ho'p wid de cooking up at de Big House when de real cook was sick or us had a passel of company. Us cooked on a great, big fireplace what had arms hanging out over de coals to hang pots on to bile. Den us had three-legged skillets what set right over de coals for frying and sech like. Us cooked sho' 'nuff bread in dem days, ash cakes, de best thing you ever et. Dey ain't nothing like dat dese days.

"I was sold oncet before I left Virginia. Den I was brung down to Alabama and sold from de block for $1,000 to Mr. Sam Rainey, at Camp Hill, Ala. I still worked in de fields, but I would cook for de white folks and hope around de Big House on special 'casions. Our overseer was Mr. Green Ross, and he was a bad one, too. Mean, my goodness! He'd whup you in a minute. He'd put you in de buck, tie your feet and den set out to whup you right.

"He would get us slaves up 'fore day, blowing on his big horn, and us would work 'twell plumb dark. All de little niggers'd get up, too, and go up to de Big House to be fed from wooden bowls. Den dey'd be called ag'in 'fore us come from de fields and put to bed by dark. I useta stop by de spring house to get de milk, it was good cold too, and tote it up to de Big House for dinner.

"I had two chilluns. Dey was named Lou and Eli, and dey was took care of like de rest. Us useta have some good times. Us could have all de fun us wanted on Sa'dday nights, and us sho' had it, cutting monkeyshines and dancing all night long sometimes. Some would pat and sing, 'Keys not arunning, Keys not arunning,' and us sho' did more'n dance, I'm telling you. Sometimes our Mistess would come down early to watch us dance.

"Next to our dances, de most fun was corn-shucking. Marsa would have de corn hauled up to de cribs and piled as a house. Den he would invite de hands 'round to come and ho'p shuck it. Us had two leaders or generals and choose up two sides. Den us see which side would win first and holler and sing. I disremembers the hollers jest now. My mind is sorter missing. Marsa would pass de jug 'round, too. Den dey sho' could work and dat pile'd just vanish.

"Us used de white folks' church in de morning. I j'ined de church den, 'cause I always tried to live right and wid de Lord.

"When de Yankees come through Dadeville, Ala., us heard 'bout hit and Marsa hid his money and lots of his fine things in de colored folks's houses. Dey never found 'em neither.

"Lemme see who I married? I mighty nigh forgot who it was I did marry. Now, I knows. Hit was Prince Hodnett.

"No'm, I don't want no more slavery. I hope dey don't have no more such, 'cause hit was terrible.

"Yes'm, I'd be proud to have my picture took."

So pridefully Sara's chair was dragged out on the porch by her maid, and the "picture was took."

MANDY MCCULLOUGH COSBY

Interview with Mandy McCullough Cosby
—*Margaret Fowler, Fruithurst, Alabama*

THEY CALLED US MCCULLOUGH'S FREE NIGGERS

Mandy McCullough Cosby puffed reflectively at her mellowed corncob pipe and began her story:

"My Massa, Bryant McCullough, was a Chambers county man. He had so many slaves I can't tell you de numbah. He didn't know hisself how many he had. I is now ninety-five years old an' what I remembers mos' is de way de chillun roll aroun' in de big nurses room." Mandy lives at 1508-Pine Street, Anniston, Alabama. She was cutting collards for dinner and left her dishpan and butcher knife to receive her caller.

"Mist' McCullough, he raised niggahs to sell—an' the little black chillen play aroun' until 'bout sundown, dey is give dey supper. A long trough out in a cool place in the bak yard is filled wif good, cold buttermilk an' cornbread crumbed in, an' dey each is give a spoon, an' dey eats dey fill. Den dey is ready fo' bed. Some of dem jes' fall ovah on de groun', asleep, and is picked up, and put on dey pallet in de big chillens room. Dey was old woman called de nurse, look after 'em. Dey git good care fo' de master expects dey will bring good money.

"Ol' Miss, she don't lak to see dem sold, an' she cry ever' time, she so tender-hearted. But Mist' McCullough is jes' lak mens is today. He jes' laugh an' go on.

"But he was good to his black folks. Folks called us 'McCullough's free niggers.' Wasn't much whippin' went on 'roun' our plantation, but on some places close to us, they whipped until blood run down. Some places they even mixed salt an' pepper in water an' bathed 'em with it. The salt water'd heal, but when the pepper got in there, it burned lak fire, an' they'd as well get on to work quick, cause they can't be still nohow.

"One woman, on a plantation not so far from us, was expectin', an' they tied her up under a hack-a-berry tree, an' whipped her until she died. Mos' any time at night ef you go 'roun' that tree, you could hear that baby cry. I 'spect you could hear it yet.

"Everybody said that was murder, an' that something ought to be done about it, but nothin' ever was.

"Mist' McCullough always give his folks plenty of sumpin' t'eat an' then he say, 'I's lookin' for plenty uv work.' 'Niggahs fat an' greasy can't do nothin' but work.

"My mother was a loomer. She didn't do nothin' but weave. We all had reg'lar stints of spinnin' to do, when we come from the fiel'. We set down an' eat a good supper, an' ever'night until ten o'clock we spin cuts of cotton, an' reel the tread, an' nex' day, the rolls is carded an' packed in a basket to be wove.

"Spinnin' wheels was in every cabin. Dere was so many of us to be tuk care of, it took lots of spinnin'."

United States. Work Projects Administration

EMMA CROCKETT

Interview with Emma Crockett
—*Ruby Pickens Tartt, Livingston, Alabama*

On the old east road from Livingston to Epes, about six miles north-east of Livingston, is the "double house" built of widely assorted materials, where Emma Crockett lives. The older part of the house is the "settin' room" where the stick-and-clay chimney of its earlier days has been replaced by a new brick chimney. A roof of corrugated sheet metal tops the warped, roughly hewn logs which form the walls. The "new room" is built in the later shanty style—pine boards, unplaned, and nailed upright to a frame of 2X4's, the cracks of the flat joints "stripped" with narrow siding. A roof of "bought" shingles covers this room. Connecting the two rooms is an open hall roofed with heavy boards "rived" from pine blocks. Despite its conglomerate architecture this is a better "colored folks'" house than many in the Black Belt. These "double houses" often have no roof for the hall and some also lack a floor, the hall being made entirely of earth, sky and imagination.

Emma settled herself on the top step at the front of the hall to talk to me, after first ironing a tiny wrinkle out of her "string apron" with her hand.

Emma Crockett, Livingston, Alabama

"Miss, I'm 'bout sebenty-nine or eighty year old," she told me, "and I belonged to Marse Bill Hawkins and Miss Betty. I lived on deir plantation right over yander. My mammy was called Cassie Hawkins and my pappy was Alfred Jolly. I was Emma Jolly 'fore I married Old

Henry Crockett. Us had five chillun and dey's two of 'em livin' in Bummin'ham, Fannie and Mary.

"Sometimes I kain't git my min' together so as I kin tell nothin'. I fell out t'other day and had a misery in my head ever since. I wish I could read, but I wa'n't never l'arnt nothin' 'ceptin' atter Surrender Miss Sallie Cotes she showed us how to read printin'; but I kain't read no writin. I kain't tell you so much 'bout de wah' ca'se my recollection ain't no 'count dese days. All I knowed, 'twas bad times and folks got whupped, but I kain't say who was to blame; some was good and some was bad. I seed the patterollers, and atter Surrender de Ku Kluxes dey come den, but didn't never bother me. See, I wan't so old and I minded ev'ybody, and didn't vex 'em none. Us didn't go to church none, but I goes now to de New Prophet Church and my favorite song is:

>Set down, set down, set down,
>Set down, set down,
>Set down, chile, set down.
>Soul so happy till I kain't set down.
>
>Move de member, move Dan-u-el,
>Move de member, move Dan-u-el.
>Dan-u-el, member, don' move so slow.
>Dan-u-el, member, don' move so slow.
>Got on my rockin' shoes, Dan-u-el.
>Got on my rockin' shoes, Dan-u-el.
>
>Shoes gwine to rock me home,
>Shoes gwine to rock me home, Dan-u-el,
>Shoes gwine to rock me home, Dan-u-el,
>Shoes gwine to rock me home, Dan-u-el,

Dan-u-el.

Shoes gwine to rock by faith,
Shoes gwine to rock by faith, Dan-u-el,
Shoes gwine to rock by faith, Dan-u-el.

Love de member, move Dan-u-el.
Love de member, move Dan-u-el.
Got on my starry crown, Dan-u-el.
Got on my starry crown, Dan-u-el.

"Dat's all I kin tell you today, honey. Come back when dis misery leave my head and I gwine to think up some tales and old songs.

Emma Crockett's House, Livingston, Alabama

"But I didn't never fool wid no hoodoo and no animal stories neither. I didn't have no time for no sich foolishness. And I ain't scared of nothin' neither.

"I lives here wid my grandchile now on Mr. Bob Davis' place. Us gits enough to eat, I reckon, but it's tight, I tell you dat!"

CHENEY CROSS

Interview with Cheney Crossss
—Annie D. Dean

GITTIN' MY PENSION

From all accounts, Aunt Cheney Cross must be quite ninety years old. "In jewin' de war," she says, "I had done long pass my thirteenth birthday." Today Aunt Cheney is a true reflection of slavery days and the Southern mammy.

Away from highways and automobiles, she lives several miles from Evergreen on a small farm in the piney woods with her "baby boy."

Talk with Aunt Cheney reveals that Evergreen's city marshall, Harry L. Riley, "put out to hope" this old family servant who had "tended" to his father, George Riley; his mother, "Miss Narciss," and "Miss Lizzible," his sister. She also helped bring his own "chillun" into the world.

Aunt Cheney had promised Mr. Riley that she would come in town on a certain Saturday morning in May, 1937, and would bring a letter from her young "mistis" for me to read.

It was past noon on that particular Saturday when she

came up the back steps, a little out of breath, but smiling. "Lawd, honey," she said, "here 'tis pas' dinner time an' I'se jes' makin' my arrivement here. No'm, I don't wants no dinner, thank you jes' de same. Whut makes me so late here now, I stopped by Miss Ella Northcutt's. She's my folks too, you know, an' she done made me eat all I kin hole! No'm, honey, I can't eat no cabbage. Me an' cabbage never is set horses together much, but I will thank you for the ice tea."

Settling herself down in a low chair, she sighed and began taking off her shoes. "Honey, you don't mind ef I resses my feets does you? My white folks is sp'ilin' me here today. I'll be lookin' for it tomorrrow, too, an' I won't be gittin' it." Her black eyes twinkled in her shiny, old, wrinkled face as she talked on.

"I tole Mr. Harry I'se comin'. An' here I is! How'd I come? I come on Mack and Charlie, dat's how! Yes, ma'am! Dese two boys here, dey brung me." Pushing her feet out for inspection, she leaned forward, smiling and pleased. "Dese here foots, dey's Mack an' Charlie. Dey's my whole pennunce for gittin' about. Don't you worry none. Mr. Harry he'll git be back home 'gainst dark come on.

"Lawd, honey, I don't want to know no better folks'n Mr. Harry an' Miss Emma. I follow dem good folks clean up to Muscle Show! Yessum, I sho' did. At fust, I tole'm I couldn't go nohow. But dey pull down on me so hard, look lack I couldn't he'p myself.

"I stayed on up dere at Muscle Show twell I got so homesick to see my baby boy I couldn't stan' it no mo'. Now, cose, my baby boy he was den de father of his own, a boy an' a girl, but to me dat boy is still jes' my baby, an' I had to come on home."

Aunt Cheney's little, old body shook with laughter as she leaned back and said: "Yes, ma'am! I ain't been home no time atall neither, 'twell here come Mr. Harry back to Evergreen wid his own self. Yes, Lawd! I kin see'm now, comin' up de big hardwood road, his haid raired back, asmokin' a sugarette lack he's a millinery! Lawd, Lawd! Me nor Mr. Harry neither one ain't never gona be contentious nowheres but right here. An' dat's de Gawd's trufe!

"Iffen Mr. Harry hadn't come on back here, I never woulda seed no pension. Dat's de Gawd's trufe, too. Nobody here didn't know my eggzack age, cause dis wasn't my originally home. All dem whut did know close onto my age done died out an' I knows it. So when Mr. Harry put out to hope me, I says in my heart 'Thank Gawd!'

"I tole Mr. Harry dat iffen anybody in de world knowed my age, it was my young mistis, an' I didn't know eggzackly where she at, but her papa was Captain Purifire (Purifoy). Back yonder he was de madistra of our town, an' he had all of dem lawin' books. I figgered dat my birthright would be down in one of dem books. I knowed in reason dat my mistis still got dem books wid her, 'cause dey ain't been no burnin's dat I done heard about. I knowed, too, dat Mr. Harry was gona fine out where she at.

"I 'members Captain Purifire jes' lack a book. I does dat! Now, cose, when he come on in home from de war he didn't 'zackly favor hisse'f den, 'cause when I seed him comin' roun' de house he look so ragged an' ornery I tuck him for de ole Bad Man hisse'f. I tuck out behind de smoke house, an' when I got a good look at him th'ew a crack it look lack I could recognize his favor, but I couldn't call his name to save my life. Lawd, honey! He's a sight! All growed over an' bushy! You couldn't tell iffen he's man or beas'. I kep' on alookin' whilst he's comin' roun' de corner, an' den I heard him say 'Cheney, dat you?' I'se so happy, I jes' melt down."

Aunt Cheney was really living over her past. "You see, it's lack dis," she said: "My fore parents, dey was bought. My Mistis an' my daddy's mistis, too, was Miss Mary Fields, an' my daddy was Henry Fields. Den de Carters bought my daddy from Miss Mary Fields. Well, dey mix up an' down lack dat, twell now my young mistis, what used to be little Frances Purifire, she's married to Mr. Cunningham.

"I was brung up right in de house wid my white folks. Yessum, I slep' on de little trundler bed what pushed up under de big bed, in durinst de day. I watched over dem chillun day an' night. I washed 'em an' fed 'em an' played wid 'em. One of de babies had to take goat's milk. When she cry, my mistis say, 'Cheney, go on an' git dat goat.' Yes Lawd! An' dat goat sho' did talk sweet to dat baby! Jes' lack it was her own. She look at it an' wag her tail so fas' an' say: "Ma-a-a-a-a!" Den she lay down on de flo' whilst us holes her feets an' let de baby suck de milk. All de time dat goat bees talkin', 'Ma-a-a-a-a,' twell dat baby got satchified.

"When us chillun got tuck wid any kind of sickness or zeezes, us tuck azzifizzity an' garlit. You know, garlit what smell lack onions. Den we wore some roun' us necks. Dat kep' off flu-anz.

"Dese days it look lack somepin t'eat don't tas'e lack dat we cooked back yonder. De coffee us used had to be fresh groun' ever' day. An' when it commence to bile, I put dese here knees down on de flo' befo' de fire an' stir dat coffee for de longes'. Den my gran'ma she hung dat pot up on dem pot hooks over de fire an' washed de meat an' drap it in. Time she done pick an' overlook de greens an' den wrenched 'em in spring water, de meat was bilin'. Den she take a great big mess of dem fresh turnip greens an' squash 'em down in dat pot. Dey jes' melt down an' go to seasonin'.

"Nex' thing I knowed, here come my mistis, an' she say: 'Now Cheney, I wants some pone bread for dinner.' Dem hick'ry coals in dat fire place was all time ready an' hot. They wouldn't be no finger prints lef' on dat pone when Cheney got th'ew pattin' it out neither. Better not! Look lack dem chillun jes' couldn't git 'nuff of dat hard corn bread.

"Plenty of fancy cookin' went on 'roun' dat fire place, but somehow de pot licker an' pone bread longside wid de fresh buttermilk stirs my mem'ry worse'n anything.

"All dis good eatin' I'se speakin' 'bout tuck place befo' de Yankees raided us. It was den, too, dat my mistis tuck me down to de spring back of de house. Down dere it was a holler tree stump, taller'n you is. She tell me to clam' up to de top of dat holler tree, den she han' me a big heavy bundle, all wropped up an' tied tight. Hit sho' was heavy! Den she say: 'Drap it in, Cheney.' I didn't know den whut she's up to, but dat was de silver an' jew'lry she was hidin'.

"Yes honey, I 'members dat Yankee raid lack it was

jes' yistiddy. I'se settin' dere in de loom room, an' Mr. Thad Watts' lil' gal, Louise, she's standin' at the winder. She say: 'O-o-oh! Nannie! Jes' look down yonder!' 'Baby, what is dat?' I says. 'Dem's de Yankees comin'!' 'Gawd hep us!' I says, an' befo' I kin ketch my bref, de place is kivvered. You couldn't stir 'em up wid a stick. Feets sounded lack mutterin' thunder. Dem bayonets stick up lack dey jes' setting on de mouf of dey guns. Dey swords hangin' on dey sides singin' a chune whilst dey walk. A chicken better not pass by. Iffen he do, off come his head!

"When dey pass on by me, dey put' nigh shuck me outa my skin. 'Where's de men's?' dey say an' shake me up. 'Where's de arms?' Dey shake me twell my eye balls loosen up. 'Where's de silver?' Lawd! Was my teefs drappin' out? Dey didn't give me time to ketch my bref. All de time, Miss Mary jes' look 'em in de eye an' say nothin'!

"Dey tuck dem enfield rifles, half as long as dat door, an' bus' in de smoke house winder. Dey jack me up off'n my feet an' drag me up de ladder an' say: 'Git dat meat out.' I kep' on th'owin' out Miss Mary's hams an' sawsidges, twell dey holler 'stop'. I come backin' down dat ladder lack a squirrel, an' I ain't stop backin' twell I retch Miss Mary.

"Yes, Lawd! Dem Yankees loaded up a waggin full of meat an' tuck de whole barrel of 'lasses! Takin' dat 'lasses kilt us chillun! Our mainest 'musement was makin' 'lasses candy. Den us cake walk 'roun' it. Now dat was all gone. Look lack dem sojers had to sharpen dey swords on ever'thing in sight. De big crepe mullen bush by de parlor winder was bloomin' so pink an' pretty, an' dey jes' stood dere an' whack off dem blooms lack folkses heads drappin' on de groun'.

"I seed de sargeant when he run his bayonet clean th'ew Miss Mary's bestest feather bed an' rip it slam open! Wid dat, a win' blowed up an' tuck dem feathers ever' which away for Sunday. You couldn't see where you's at. De sargeant, he jes' th'owed his head back an' laugh fit to kill hisse'f. Den fust thing next, he done suck a feather down his win'pipe! Lawd, honey, dat white man sho' struggled. Dem sojers th'owed water in his face. Dey shuck'm an' beat'm an' roll'm over, an' all de time he's gettin' limberer an' bluerer. Den dey jack him up by his feets an' stan'm on his haid. Den dey pump him up an' down. Den dey shuck'm twell he spit. Den he come to.

"Dey didn't cut no mo' mattrusses. An' dey didn't cut nothin' much up in de parlor, 'cause dat's where de lieutenant an' de sargeant slep'. But dey lef' de nex' day, de whole place was strewed wid mutilation.

"I 'members well back dere in jewin' de war how ever' oncet a month that come 'roun' a big box, longer'n I is an' wider too, was tuck to our sojer boys on de battle fiel'. You never seed de lack of sawsidges dat went in dat box! Wid cake an' chicken an' pies, an' Lawd! de butter all rolled up in corn shucks to keep it fresh. Ever'body from ever'where come to fix dat box an' he'p pile in de stuff. Den you hear 'em say: 'Poor sojers! Put it in here!' Den ever'thing look sorta misty, an' dey haids droop over, lack. Den you see a mother's bres' heave wid her silent prayer.

"Directly atter de surrender, de Ku Kluxes sho' was bad atter de Yankees. Dey do all sorts of things to aggivate 'em. Dey's continual' tyin' grape vines crost de road, to git 'em tangled up an' make 'em trip up an' break dey own necks. Dat was bad too, 'cause dem poor Yankees never s'picioned no better'n dat dem vines jes' blowed down or somepin.

"'Long about den, too, seem lack ha'nts an' spairits was ridin' ever'thing! Dey raided mostly 'roun' de grabeyard. Lawd, honey, I ain't hankerin' atter passin' by no grabeyards. 'Cose, I knows I got to go in dere some day, but dey do make me feel lonesome an' kinder jubus.

"I 'members one night, way back dere, when I'se walkin' down de big road wid Bud, an' he say: 'Look! Didn't you see me give dat road? Dat ha'nt done push me clean outa my place.' Now let me tell you somepin. Iffen you ain't never been dat clost to a ha'nt, you don't know nothin'! I 'lowed he gwine follow me home. When I got dere I shuck mustard seeds down on my flo'. When you sprinkles 'em lack dat he can't git outa dat room twell he done count ever' las' one of dem seed. Well sir, de nex' mawnin' all us could see was somepin lack a lump of jelly layin' dere on de flo' 'mongst dem seeds. Look lack he done counted hisse'f to a pulp.

"After dat night, I puts a big sifter down at my do'. You know ha'nts has to count ever' hole in dat sifter befo' dey can come th'ough. Some folks puts de Bible down dere, too. Den de poor spairit has to read ever' word of dat book befo' he crosses over.

"I reckon 'bout de terriblest thing ever happen to me was dat big lookin' glass. De lookin' glass was all laid out in de top of my trunk, waitin' for my weddin' day. One night I'se standin' by de trunk wid hit wide open. I seed somepin black befo' my eyes an' den a screech owl lit in my winder an' screech right in my face. I'se so scared I sot right down in de middle of dat lookin' glass. Hit bus' in a million pieces! Mamma th'owed up her han's an' holler, 'Git up from dere, gal. You gona have seven years of bad luck. Shoo dat hootin' owl away befo' you dies in your tracks!' Den I swoons off. I feels dem ha'nts gittin' ready to ride me clean down in my grabe. 'Bout den somepin kep' sayin' to me, over an' over: 'Th'ow dem pieces of lookin' glass in runnin' water.' Den hit say: 'Burn your mammy's ole shoe an' de screech owl leave.' Atter I does dat my min' was at res'.

"Soon as my daddy hear 'em firin' off for de Surrender, he put out for de plantation where he fust belong. He lef' me wid my mistis at Pine Flat, but 'twan't long twell he come back to git me an' carry me home wid him. I hates to leave my mistis, an' she didn't want to part from me. She say: 'Stay here wid me, an' I'll give you a school learnin'.' She say to Captain Purifire: 'You go buy my li'l nigger a book. Git one of dem Blue Back Websters,' she say, 'so I kin eddicate her to spell.' Den my daddy say: 'Her mamma tole me not to come home widout her an' she has to go wid me.'

"I never will fergit ridin' behin' my daddy on dat mule way in de night. Us lef' in sich a hurry I didn't git none of my cloze hardly, an' I ain't seed my mistis from dat day to dis!"

MATILDA PUGH DANIEL

Interview with Matilda Pugh Daniel
—*Gertha Couric*

MATILDA WAS WED IN DE WHITE FOLKS' PARLOR

Near Eufaula, Alabama, on a bluff stands a little three room cabin neatly furnished with plain, well worn, but nicely kept furniture. Surrounding the house are small beds of pretty flowers, and rows of fresh vegetables. Here resides in peace and tranquility Aunt Matilda Pugh Daniel, an old Negro slave, aged 96 years. Aunt Matilda was a full grown buxom gal when the War between the States was raging. She belonged to United States Senator, James L. Pugh, and was born on his plantation, near Eufaula. Even though time has dimmed her sight, and slightly diminished her hearing powers, she is still active of mind and accurate in her memories. We will let her speak for herself:

"Yassuh, white folks, I remembers lots of things dat happen in de slabery times. I works aroun' de house for mistis, who was de daughter of Gen'l John Linguard Hunter befo' she ma'ied de massa. When I was a little pig-tailed nigger, I usta play 'roun' wid Massa's chilluns. We play injuns in de woods, an' buil' dams down on de creek an' swing in de yard an' sometime we sho do devilish things. We hid red pepper in ole Black Bob's chewin' bacca, an' you ought to seed de faces he made. It makes me laugh still yit. Den we tuken a skunk dat us little white an' black debils kotched an' turn him loose in de slave quarters. You ought ter seed dem niggers come a flyin' outer dere. Dey come out like a swarm of wet antses.

"Atter I grew up I ma'ied Joe Daniel, a house nigger, an' Gen'l Hunter, de Mistis's pappy 'formed de ceremony. We was ma'ied in de parlor, an' I wo' a party dress of Miss Sara's. It sho' was purty; made outen white tarleton wid a pink bow in de front. I had a pink ribbon 'roun' my haid too, an' Joe, he look proud of me. Atter de weddin' all de niggers on de plantation gathered about an' we had a soiree in de back yard. Me an' Joe moved to de quarter den, but I still worked in de house. Mistis warn't goin' ter let nobody wash dem julep glasses but me, an' warn't nobody a goin' ter polish dat silber but dis here nigger. Nawsuh.

Matilda Pugh Daniel, Eufaula, Alabama

"Durin' de war us warn't bothered much, but atter de surrender, some po' white trash tried to make us take some lan'. Some of 'em come to de slave quarters, an' talk to us. Dey say 'Niggers, you is jus' as good as de white fo'ks. You is 'titled to vote in de 'lections an' to have money same as dey,' but most of us didn't pay no 'tention to 'em.

"Den Massa James an' Mistis moved to Washington, an' Miss Sara wanted me to go wid her to be her house maid. She said she'd pay me money fo' it, but I couldn't leave my ole man, Joe, kaze he had a case of consumption. Joe died a year later an' lef' me wid fo' little chilluns. Us stayed 'roun' on de plantation an' de new massa paid us good money fo' workin', but soon de house kotched fire an' burn to de groun', an' I have to move to Eufaula. I bought dis little house wid de money I saved. I has kinfolks in Detroit dat sen's me a little money, an' some good peoples in Eufaula helps me out some so I is in purty good financial shape. I ain't neber 'sociated wid no trashy niggers an' I ain't neber 'ten' to. I is goin' to be a proud an' good nigger to de las'."

CARRIE DAVIS

Interview with Carrie Davis
—Preston Klein, Lee County, Alabama

PLANTATION PUNISHMENT

Carrie Davis said "Honey, dere was a lot of cruel things done in slavery times."

She was washing when I arrived at her shanty near Smith's Station, Alabama. She asked, as so many of the old Negroes do, "Has you come to help me?" I said: "No, Carrie; I want you to tell me about slavery."

She shook her gray head, recalled: "Dem was good an' bad times, Mistus; good an' bad. I had a purty good marster; but de marster on de plantation dat j'ined our'n was mighty mean. He was a bad man, no matter if de slaves behaved or not.

"Honey, I 'members dat he had regular days to whup all de slaves wid strops. De strops had holes in 'em so dat dey raised big blisters. Den dey took a hand saw, cut de blisters and washed 'em in salt water. Our Ol' Mistus has put salve on aheap of backs so dey could git deir shirts off. De shirts'd stick, you see. De slaves would come to our house for water an' Mistus would see 'em."

Asked about her life as a slave, she said: "I was borned in Harris County, Georgia, an' was 'bout ten or twelve when freedom come. My mammy an' pappy was Martha an' Nathan Perry and had seben chillun. Besides me, dere was Amy, Ida, Knoxie, Jim, Abraham, an' Franklin.

"Us lived in de Perry quarters. De cabins was made of split logs, put up edgeways and daubed wid mud inside an' out. Dey was 'bout a hundred yards from de big house, whar Marster Billy an' Mistus Nancy Perry lived. Deir chillun was Clara Maria, Malinda, Sara, Alec, Jim, an' Bill. Dey was real good to us, too. Us et at de big house. 'Course de food was cooked on de fireplace, but us had meat and greens but not much biscuits. Us had collards an' cabbage, too.

"Sometimes us would have wild game, 'ca'se de men hunted lots an' kotched rabbits, 'possums and coons. Dey also kotched a lot of fish.

"No'm, our beds warn't so good. Dey was homemade and de sides was scantlings wid legs nailed on. Den slats was nailed on top of it to put our shuck-and-straw mattresses on.

"My grand-parents was from Virginny. When I was a slave I was used as a house-girl and to help keep de yards clean and bring in water. Us wore mostly slips, wove in homemade looms; an' dey was osnaburg an' homespun. We wore 'em Sunday and Monday de same. Us shoes was made at a tanyard and dey was brogans as hard as rocks.

"I 'members dat some of our white neighbors was poor and didn't have no slaves. Dey would help us work. De overseer couldn't whip dem, but he would make dem work hard and late. I 'members, too, dat de overseer waked us up wid a trumpet.

"Dey useta tell us dat if us didn't work dey was going to sell us to help feed de rest; and bless yo' soul, us niggers'd go to work, too. Marster wasn't mean. He would jest lock de slaves in de crib fer punishment. When slaves was sold, I seed many a nigger put on de block for five and six hundred dollars.

"Us couldn't leave de plantation widout a pass; and you better not let 'em kotch you wid a book. Us walked to de white church an' set in de back. Mr. Davey Snell preach and baptize, and dey had foot-washin's. Sometimes de niggers'd git so happy dey would shout. Den dey would keep shoutin' in de fields next day and git a whipping.

"If a nigger got out widout a pass, dey sot de hounds on you; and de patrollers'd tear you up too, if you stayed out too late.

Carrie Davis, Smith's Station, Alabama

"Us had sech good times on Sattidy nights; frolic, dance an' cornshuckin's. Most of 'em would be drinkin' and sing and holler:

> Sheep's in de cotton patch;
> Got 'im out Monday.
> Had it been a white man;

Got 'im out Sunday.

"Kid Kimbrough was our leader, and he could sing 'Dixie,' too.

"Christmas mornin' us'd have a better breakfast and dey would give us rations at de big house. When any of de slaves got married dey went up to de white folks' house an' jumped over de broom. Dat was de ceremony at de weddin'. And if marster wanted to mix his stock of slaves wid a strong stock on 'nother plantation, dey would do de mens an' women jest lak horses. I 'members dat when two niggers married, dey got a big supper.

"All us chilluns had a big time; played 'Pretty Pauline,' 'Turn, Charlie,' an' sech-lak.

"No'm I never did see nor b'lieve in ghosts.

"When us got sick Mistus'd give horse-mint, life-everlasting, goldenrod, an' holly teas, yessum. And us wore asafetida and pop-ball seed.

"When de Yankees come, dey handcuffed our folks and took 'em off. Marster had his meat, corn, fodder, and sech hauled in de swamp near de plantation. Dem Yankees went as straight to it as if dey had seed us put it dere. Dey burned it all up and took some niggers from de other farm.

"When freedom come, I 'members dat marster told us dat us was free, but dat we could stay on if we lacked. Most of us stayed on wid him for a spell. Now and den de Ku Klux Klan'd come around and beat on a nigger.

"I married Charlie Gibson and had two chillun, twelve grand-chilluns and nine great-grandchilluns.

"Honey, I's heard Abraham Lincoln's name, but don't know nothin' 'bout him. I got tired livin' 'mong wicked peoples; and I wanted to be saved. Dat's why I j'ined de church and still tries to de right."

CLARA DAVIS

Interview with Clara Davis
—*Francois Ludgere Diard*

AUNT CLARA DAVIS IS HOMESICK FOR OLD SCENES

"I was bawn in de year 1845, white folks," said Aunt Clara, "on de Mosley plantation in Bellvy jus' nawth of Monroeville. Us had a mighty pretty place back dar. Massa Mosely had near 'bout five hundred acres an' mos' near to one hundred slaves.

"Was Marse Mosely good to us? Lor', honey, how you talk. Co'se he was! He was de bes' white man in de lan'. Us had eve'y thing dat we could hope to eat: turkey, chicken, beef, lamb, poke, vegetables, fruits, aigs, butter, milk ... we jus' had eve'y thing, white folks, eve'ything. Dem was de good ole days. How I longs to be back dar wid my ole folks an' a playin' wid de chilluns down by de creek. 'Tain't nothin' lak it today, nawsuh. When I tell you 'bout it you gwine to wish you was dar too.

"White folks, you can have your automobiles an' paved streets an' electric lights. I don't want 'em. You can have de busses an' street cars an' hot pavements an' high buildin' 'caze I ain't got no use for 'em no way. But I'll tell you what I does want. I wants my ole cotton bed an' de moonlight nights a shinin' through de willow trees an' de cool grass under my feets as I runned aroun' ketchin' lightnin' bugs. I wants to hear de sound of de hounds in de woods atter de 'possum, an' de smell of fresh mowed hay. I wants to feel de sway of de ol' wagon a-goin' down de red, dusty road an' listen to de wheels groanin' as dey rolls along. I wants to sink my teeth into some of dat good ol' ash cake, an' smack de good ol' sorghum offen my mouth. White folks, I wants to see de boats a passin' up an' down de Alabamy ribber an' hear de slaves a singin' at dere work. I wants to see de dawn break over de black ridge an' de twilight settle over de place spreadin' a sort of orange hue over de place. I wants to walk de paths th'ew de woods an' see de rabbits an' watch de birds an' listen to frogs at night. But dey tuk me away f'om dat a long time ago. 'Twern't long befo' I ma'ied an' had chilluns, but don't none of 'em 'tribute to my suppote now. One of 'em was killed in de big war wid Germany and de res' is all scattered out ... eight of 'em. Now I jus' live f'om han' to mouth; here one day, somewhere else de nex'. I guess we's all a-goin' to die iffen dis 'pression don't let us 'lone. Maybe someday I'll git to go home. Dey tells me dat when a pusson crosses dat ribber, de Lawd gives him whut he wants. I done tol' de Lawd I don't want nothin' much ... only my home, white folks. I don't think dat's much to axe for. I supposed he'll sen' me back dar. I been a-waitin' for him to call."

GEORGE DILLARD

Interview with George Dillard
—Alice L. Barton

I LOVED TO PICK DAT BOX

George Dillard, born in Richmond, Va., in 1852, now idles about his little home at Eutaw and recalls days when he was a slave. The memories bring smiles to his wrinkled, black face.

"Honey, dar was a dance every Sattidy night," he chuckled, "an' all de niggers nigh 'bout broke dey legs adancin'."

"And didn't you dance just as hard as the others, Uncle George?"

"Well, Mistus, I was right spry; but I was at my best in de job of pickin' de banjer. I shorely did love to pick dat box while de other niggers danced away."

George said his family came from Virginia to Mississippi, and that he came to Greene County about 60 years ago. His two masters were a Mr. Dillard and Bob Steele.

George explained that he was a field hand and had to work hard most of the time.

"But us had plenty to eat," he said. "De food was cooked in Ol' Mistus' kitchen an' sont to de fiel' on a big cart. I 'member dat a bell would ring for us to git up, an' we would work as long as it was daylight."

George said that Mr. Steele owned about 200 slaves and that he always had plenty of everything. The plantation, he said, consisted of about 2,000 acres.

"Ol' Massa had a church right on de plantation for us niggers," he continued. "Many's de time I danced late in de night an' den had to git up an' go to church wid de rest. All of us had to go. A white man would preach, but I allus enjoyed de singin' most of all."

George believes earnestly that ghosts exist, but admits they have never bothered him.

George Dillard, Eutaw, Alabama

"Dey is all aroun'," he maintains, "but dey don't follow me. No'm, I's not 'fraid of 'em; but I knows plenty of niggers dat'll run if a ghost so much as brushes by 'em."

The old darkey said that "atter freedom come to de

worl'" he continued to live with his master and worked a share crop. He said that Mr. Steele was always fair and good to him; always giving him the best of everything.

George married Celia Shelton, and to them were born twenty-four children.

"It was a bunch of dem," he said, "but I loved ebry one. I had a nice weddin' an' de white folks helped me to git myself a 'oman an' then to git married to her."

ELLA DILLIARD

Personal interview with Ella Dilliard
756 Canal Street, Mobile, Alabama
—Ila B. Prine

ELLA'S WHITE HEN IS HEAPS OF COMPANY

Ella Dilliard, an old Negro woman who lives at 756 Canal Street, Mobile, says she was a small girl during slavery time, and does not know the hardships of it, because she was owned by good people. Her mother's name was Mary Norris, owned by Mrs. Calvin Norris, who lived in Selma, Ala., but had a homestead in Mobile. Her father belonged to people by the name of Childress, and his name was Green Childress. She doesn't remember much about him because his white people took him to Texas.

Ella said that her mother was her madame's hairdresser, and that Mrs. Norris had her mother taught in Mobile. So Ella's life was very easy, as she stayed around the big house with her mother, although her grandmother, Penny Anne Norris, cared for her more than her mother did. One of the things she remembers quite distinctly was her grandmother's cooking on the fireplace, and how she would not allow any one to spit in the fireplace. She said her grandmother made corn-pone and wrapped it in shucks and baked it in ashes.

Ella said she did not know many colored people, since the quarters were quite a ways from the big house, and that the plantation was managed by an overseer. She said the quarters were built in rows with streets between them.

She also remembers the first boat she ever saw that was when she was brought to Mobile after the surrender, and when she saw the boat she said to her mother: "Look at that house sitting on the water."

Ella said that there were three cooks at the big house, their names being Hannah, Judy, and Charlotte, and the gardener's name was Uncle John. Ella also said that one thing that she remembers so well about the kitchen in the big house was a large dishpan, that had a partition in the middle of it, one side you washed the dishes in, and the other side was used for scalding them.

The slaves always had Saturdays to wash their clothes and do things for themselves. Ella, not having lived among Negroes, does not know much about their habits and customs, but she does remember seeing the big white covered wagons that the slaves were carried in to be sold; and remembers hearing talk of the "Pattyrollers." She said when the slaves were sold, they were put on a block, and that the man who were buying would look in their mouths just like they did horses.

Ella said she was born in Greensboro, Alabama, but the plantation where she later lived was on the Alabama river near Selma, Ala. She doesn't know how many acres it comprised, or how many slaves that her master owned. She remembers her madame made her stop calling her mother "mammy," and her father "daddy." She said: "You know, Miss, that the white children now-a-days calls their parents 'mammy and daddy' like the colored people used to. The children now do not respect their parents as they should, and in fact everything is so different the truth done 'be under the table.' You know, miss, I am telling the truth, because the Bible says, 'Woe be unto the one that lies; Judgment is on the land.'

"In those days people had to work to live, and they raised most everything they used, such as cattle, hogs, cotton, and foodstuff. Then the women spun the thread out of the cotton, and wove the cloth."

Ella helped her grandmother at the weaving by picking up the shuttles for her. She said they generally used the cloth as it was woven. The shoes were made on the place and were called red brogans.

As for the churches, the white folks had the brush arbor camp meetings, where the people would go and camp in little cabins for weeks, so they could attend the church. They had newspapers then, Ella said, "but 'course they ain't like you have now, there warn't so many as there is now.

"You asked something, miss, about medicines. I don't remember much about any medicine, because Mr. Calvin Norris was a doctor, and he always treated us when we were sick. There was a Dr. Browder who 'tended the plantation."

Ella is a bright colored, small woman, whose eyes are

very keen. She says that a short time ago she had some trouble with her eyes, and she got something from the drug store to bathe them with, but it did not help them. So she caught some pure rain water and "anointed" her eyes with that, and now she can see to thread a needle. Her life has been very colorful in many respects. She recalled as a small child, that, during the war, a minie-ball came through a brick wall of the servant house where they were living, but it fell without harming any of the servants. She said when Wilson's raid was made on Selma, that the Yankee men went through the houses just like dogs, taking whatever they wanted.

"I 'members Mr. Parkman putting two sacks of money down in his big well, and him getting it out with hooks after the Yankees left."

Later when she was brought to Mobile she worked for Judge Oliver Semmes for twenty years. Judge Semmes was the son of Admiral Raphael Semmes, and she said he was a blessed, good man. For the past fourteen years she has been working for the Frank Lyons family of Mobile.

Ella lives in a double tenement house, having one room and a small kitchen. The room is full of old furniture and odd things. On the mantle is a lovely old china pitcher that once was owned by Judge Semmes and which Ella prizes very much. The thing that puzzles Ella most among the modern inventions, she said, are the aeroplanes, and the way ice is made. She said:

"Miss, we never had any ice way back yonder. We had nice, old, open brick wells, and the water was just like ice. We would draw the water and put around the milk and butter in the dairy. It's a mystery to me how they make that ice, but, my goodness! I guess I need not worry my head about things, because I am not here for long. All my family is dead and gone now, and the only companion I have is this here little white hen. Her name is Mary. You see, I bought her last year to kill for Christmas, but I couldn't do it. She is so human; and you ought to see the eggs she lays. I even have a few to sell sometimes. I just keeps Mary in the room at night with me, and she is heaps of company for me."

RUFUS DIRT

Interview with Rufus Dirt
—Woodrow Hand, Birmingham, Alabama

RUFUS WOULD TALK A LOT FOR A DIME

Foreword: This Negro, Rufus Dirt, was found on one of Birmingham's busiest streets begging for coins. Because of his inability to read, he was unable to give the number or location of his home. All he knew was "jes' som'ers on Southside, boss."

"I'll drop a dime in your hat uncle if you'll stand here and talk to me for a few minutes."

"Sho' boss, iffen you wants, I'll talk all day fo' dat much money. I'se been here fo' a long time an' I knows plenty to talk 'bout. What does yo' want to know?"

I explained my interest in slavery days and my search for ex-slaves, but he began telling me before I had time to finish. His ability to talk had somehow escaped what his age had done to his hair, which was sparse as well as snowy white. His eyes were a glazy red. One hand and arm seemed to be crippled, but the other waved around in the air as he talked and finally settled on my shoulder.

"Boss, I don' rightly know jes' how old I is. I was a

driver (Negro boss of other slaves) during slavery and I reckons I was about twenty sompin'. I don' remember nothin' in particular that caused me to get dat drivin' job, ceptin' hard work, but I knows dat I was proud of it 'cause I didn' have to work so hard no mo'. An' den it sorta' made de other niggers look up to me, an' you knows us niggers, boss. Nothin' makes us happier dan' to strut in front of other niggers. Dere ain't nothin' much to tell about. We jes' moved one crop atter de other till layin' by time come and den we'd start in on de winter work. We done jes' 'bout de same as all de other plantations.

"My massa's name was Digby and we live at Tuscaloosa befo' de war. An' 'bout dat war, white folks. Dem was some scary times. De nigger women was a-feared to breathe out loud come night an' in de day time, dey didn't work much 'cause dey was allus lookin' fo' de Yankees. Dey didn' come by so much 'cause atter de first few times. Dere wa'nt no reason to come by. Dey had done et up ever'thing and toted off what dey didn' eat. Dey tuk all Massa's stock, burned down de smokehouse atter dey tuk de meat out, an' dey burned de barn, an' we'all think ever' time dat dey goin' to burn de house down, but dey musta forgot to do dat.

"When de war was finally over an' I was free, my family went to Vicksburg, Mississippi where we made a livin' first one way an' den de other. I don't know how long we stayed dere, but I was livin' in Bummin'ham when dere wa'nt nothin' much here a'tall. I watched all de big buildin's 'round here go up and I see'd dem build all de big plants and I'se still watchin', but I still don' know how to tell folks where places is, 'cause I don' know how to read numbers. I goes anywhere I wants to go an'

I don't ever get lost, but jes' de same, I can't tell nobody where I am. I don' even know where we is standin' talking like dis right now. An' boss, I ain't beggin' 'cause I'se too lazy to work. I'se worked plenty in my time till I crippled dis arm in de mines and befo' my eyes got so bad," and with a grace and gentleness that may be called a characteristic of his generation, he added, "I hope I'se told you what you wants to know."

He had. I felt well repaid for the dime I had given him. As he walked off down the street, I noticed for the first time the large crowd that had gathered around us. Evidently slave tales carry more interest than this writer realized.

United States. Work Projects Administration

KATHERINE EPPES

Interview with Katherine Eppes
—Susie R. O'Brien, Uniontown, Alabama

CABINS AS FAR AS YOU COULD SEE

"Ma" Eppes sat on the steps of her weather-beaten, unpainted little cabin, duplicate of the dozens that make up Rat Row, Negro quarter of Uniontown, and looked down the vista of memory to her childhood when she lived in "where de log cabins stretched as far as you could see in de slave qua'ters."

Despite her eighty-seven years, Katherine Eppes, known to everyone as "Ma," came as spryly to her tiny porch as her rotund body would permit. She smiled broadly at her interviewer and seated herself slowly.

"Sho', honey, I can tell you mo'n anything you want to know 'bout the big fight, 'ca'se I been here a long time," she began her story. "Dey ain't many lef' to tell 'bout dem days. My mammy an' pappy was Peter an' Emma Lines an' us all belonged to Marsa Frank and Miss Sarah Lines. I was born on dey plantation five miles below Faunsdale 'bout 1850 so dey tells me.

"I is right ol' but thank Gawd I still got my teefies an'

my ha'r lef'." Proudly the old woman unwrapped her "head rag" to display a thick mop, woolly white but neatly parted into squares. Dozens of little plaits, wrapped with yards of twine, just as her hair had been dressed in the slave quarters before the War, adorned her head. She sat with uncovered head unblinking in the bright June sunshine, as she took up the tale of her health. "I sees pretty good, too, but I's so hebby I ain't able to toe myse'f 'roun' as pert as I useter.

"It was diff'rent back in dem days when I belonged to rich white folks. Dey had plenty of niggers an' dey was log cabins in de quarters jes' as far as your eyes could see. Marsa Frank an' Miss Sarah was good to de black folks, too. Dey son, young marsa Frank, fit in de big war. Atter de war was over I stayed on de Lines' place 'twell atter I ma'ied, an' Ol' Miss gin me my weddin' dress an' a long veil down to my foots.

"When us was chillun in de quarters we did a mighty lot of playin'. Us useta play 'Sail away Rauley' a whole lot. Us would hol' han's an' go 'roun' in a ring, gittin' faster an' faster an' dem what fell down was outa de game.

"My mammy wukked in de Big House, aspinnin' an' anussin' de white chillun. All of dem called her 'mammy.' Ah 'members one thing jes' lack it was yestiddy. Miss Sarah went to 'Mospolis (Demopolis) to visit wid her sister, an' whilst she were gone de oberseer, what go by de name of Allen, whupped my Mammy crost her back 'twell de blood runned out.

"When Miss Sarah comed back an' foun' it out, she was de maddes white lady I eber seed. She sont for de oberseer, an' she say: 'Allen, what you mean by whupping

Mammy? You know I don't allow you to tech my house servants.' She jerk her dress down an' stan' dere lookin' like a sojer wid her white shoulders shinin' lack a snow bank, an' she say: 'I 'druther see dem marks on my own shoulders dan to see 'em on Mammy's. Dey wouldn't hurt me no wuss.' Den she say: 'Allen, teck your fambly an' git offen my place. Don't you let sundown ketch you here. 'So he lef'. He wasn't nothin' but white trash nohow."

"Ma" Eppes sat silent for a time as she recalled the vision of Miss Sarah standing straight and regal in her dismissal of the overseer. Finally she turned with an abrupt change of subject.

"Honey, is you a Christian?" she asked earnestly. "I hopes you is, ca'se you is too fine lookin' for to go to Hell. I b'longs to de Baptis' Church, an' dey calls me Ma Eppes 'ca'se I's de mother of de church. I loves to sing de gospel Hymns."

She began to sing in a high, cracked voice, her body swaying with the rhythm. The song rose until her neighbors had gathered to form quite an audience. With much moaning between every line, she sang:

> "I am a sojer of de Cross,
> A follerer of de Lam'.
> I'm not afeard to own His name,
> Nor to 'fen' His cause."
>
> (Chorus)
>
> "I wan' you to come,
> I wan' you to come,
> I wan' you to come

An' be saved."

She was still singing as I left her, the neighbors joining in the choruses. Suppers would be late in the row of weatherbeaten cabins, because the spirit of song was on the gathering.

REUBEN FITZPATRICK

Interview with Reuben Fitzpatrick
—[HW: Mabel Farrior, Montgomery, Alabama]

A HORN FOR A HEADACHE

Reuben Fitzpatrick, of Eugene Street, Montgomery, was born Jan. 9, 1854, (83 years old). He says:

"My Marster was Mister Gholson frum Bullock county. He had lots uv slaves 'cause he was a rich man. I was jes' a boy ten years ole an' he was a squire dat tried cases, so he rode all over de country to dif'funt places. I rode wid him to hole his horse. He wore a high top black hat and had a buggy wid a top dat let back. When we went we was gone a long time an' when night come he would fix it fer me to sleep wid some uv de niggers in de quarters where we stopped. I sho' lacked to go 'bout wid him.

"My mother was de cook. She had rule over all the cookin'. She spinned thread an' reeled it off too.

"When de Yankees come through de country I seed 'em all runnin' so I thought it was jedgment day an' I runned an' hid under de chimney an' stayed dere 'tel night. Dey didn't tarry long, but dey drove de horses right up on de piazza, and throwed ever' thing out de houses, eben knocked down de smoke 'ouse doors. Dat's de trufe'.

"One time I was taken to the slave market and I was screwed on the block and Mr. Martin bought me and my Mamma. The man that was selling us would holler, "Who'll bid? Who'll bid?" We was supposed to be spry and fidgety so as to make the men want to buy us. My fust Marster was Wash Jones. He wan't good to us. He would hit us wid his cane jes' as if it had been a switch. Ben Jones didn't like the way Marse Wash treated us niggers. He bought us for his son.

"We didn't have no doctors much in dem days, but us had a horn us use when we got sick. If us had the headache that horn would go right over the spot and it wouldn't be no time 'fore the pain'd be gone. We'd use that horn anytime we was ailing an' it'd sho' do the work. I used to have the horn but I don't know jes' where it is now."

HEYWOOD FORD

Interview with Heywood Ford
—*Susie R. O'Brien, Uniontown, Alabama*

HEYWOOD FORD TELLS A STORY

"White folks," said Heywood Ford, "I'se gonna tell you a story 'bout a mean oberseer an' whut happened to him durin' de slabery days. It all commenced when a nigger named Jake Williams got a whuppin' for stayin' out atter de time on his pass done gib out. All de niggers on de place hated de oberseer wuss dan pizen, 'caze he was so mean an' useta try to think up things to whup us for.

"One mornin' de slaves was lined up ready to eat dere breakfas' an' Jake Williams was a pettin' his ole red-bone houn'. 'Bout dat time de oberseer come up an' seed Jake a pettin' his houn' an' he say: 'Nigger you ain't got time to be a-foolin' 'long dat dog. Now make him git.' Jake tried to make de dog go home, but de dog didn't want to leave Jake. Den de oberseer pick up a rock an' slam de dog in de back. De dog he den went a-howlin' off.

"Dat night Jake he come to my cabin an' he say to me: 'Heywood, I is gonna run away to a free State. I ain't a-gonna put up wid dis treatment no longer. I can't stand much mo'. I gibs him my han' an' I say: 'Jake, I hopes you gits dere. Maybe I'll see you ag'in sometime.'

"'Heywood,' he says, 'I wish you'd look atter my houn', Belle. Feed her an' keep her de bes' you kin. She a mighty good possum an' coon dog. I hates to part wid her, but I knows dat you is de bes' pusson I could leave her wid.' An' wid dat Jake slip out de do' an' I seed him a-walkin' toward de swamp down de long furrows of cawn.

"It didn't take dat oberseer long to fin' out dat Jake done run away, an', when he did, he got out de blood houn's an' started off atter him. It warn't long afore Jake heered dem houn's a-howlin' in de distance. Jake he was too tired to go any further. He circled 'roun' an' doubled on his tracks so as to confuse de houn's an' den he clumb a tree. T'warn't long afore he seed de light of de oberseer comin' th'ough de woods and de dogs was a-gittin' closer an' closer. Finally dey smelled de tree dat Jake was in an' dey started barkin' 'roun' it. De oberseer lif' his lighted pine knot in de air so's he could see Jake. He say: 'Nigger, come on down fum dere. You done wasted 'nuff of our time.' But Jake, he neber move nor make a sound an' all de time de dogs keppa howlin' an' de oberseer keppa swearin'. 'Come on down,' he say ag'in; 'iffen you don't I'se comin' up an' knock you outen de tree wid a stick.' Jake still he neber moved an' de oberseer den began to climb de tree. When he got where he could almos' reach Jake he swung dat stick an' it come down on Jake's leg an' hurt him tur'ble. Jake, he raised his foot an' kicked de oberseer raght in de mouf, an' dat white man went a tumblin' to de groun'. When he hit de earth dem houn's pounced on him. Jake he den lowered hisself to de bottom limbs so's he could see what had happened. He saw de dogs a-tearin' at de man an' he holla: 'Hol' 'im, Belle! Hol' 'im, gal!' De leader of dat pack of houn's, white folks, warn't no blood houn'. She was a plain old red-bone possum an' coon dog, an' de res' done jus' lak she done, tearin' at de oberseer's th'oat. All de while, Jake he a-hollerin' f'um de tree fer dem dogs to git 'im. 'Twarn't long afore dem dogs to' dat man all to pieces. He died raght under dat maple tree dat he run Jake up. Jake he an' dat coon houn' struck off through de woods. De res' of de pack come home.

"I seed Jake atter us niggers was freed. Dat's how come I knowed all 'bout it. It musta been six years atter dey killed de oberseer. It was in Kentucky dat I run across Jake. He was a-sittin' on some steps of a nigger cabin. A houn' dog was a-sittin' at his side. I tells him how glad I is to see him, an' den I look at de dog. 'Dat ain't Belle,' I says. 'Naw,' Jake answers, 'Dis her puppy.' Den he tol' me de whole story. I always did want to know what happen to 'em."

United States. Work Projects Administration

BERT FREDERICK

Interview with Bert Frederick
—Preston Klein

WANTS MY FRIENDS TO GO WID ME

"Wants my friends to go wid me,
New Jerusalem;
Wonder ef I'll ever git to heaven,
New Jerusalem!"

Nappy-headed, humble little Bert Frederick sang the old song in a voice that trembled and broke on the high notes. His black face beamed when he had finished, and "de old times" came flooding back into his mind.

"Honey, Ol' Master us'ta sing dat good song to us niggers; an' he allus could sing it so purty."

Uncle Frederick, like all the other gray-bearded Negroes of the Old South, is occupied mostly these days with getting ready to meet "de Sweet Jesus." As well as he can remember, he was around 12 years old when "de hawn of freedom sounded."

He shook his white head when the interviewer asked his age, a slow smile spreading over his face.

"Honey chile, you's axed me a riddle. I disremember 'bout dat. De bes' I kin till you is dat I is eighty-odd—but as to 'zackness, I can't tell."

Some years ago, Uncle Frederick suffered a broken back in an accident. Since then he has been unable to stand erect, but can straighten his back when seated. Therefore, he politely asked to sit down when he was asked to pose for a picture.

His first master, he says, was Dr. Rich Vernon, who lived in Chambers County. Afterward, he was sold to William Frederick.

He chuckled as he recalled the old days.

"I was a shirt-tail nigger," he laughed. "Dat is, I wore jes' a long shirt 'twel I was a big scamp more dan twelve year old. Honey, I was a sight to look at!

"Whut did I do about de plantation? Well, I driv de cows an' sheep to pasture an' seed dat no eagles kotched de lambs. Us had big eagles 'roun' den, an' us had to be keerful wid de small stock. Ef us warn't, ol' eagle ud swoop down an' tote off a whole lamb.

"Us had a time in dem days. I 'members dat us had a pen to ketch wild turkeys in. An' us kotched a few of dem, too."

Uncle Frederick's mother was Harriett Lumpkin, who lived below Opelika. He had three sisters, Mary Dowdell, Anne Carlisle and Emma Boyd; but all are dead.

Bert Frederick, Opelika, Alabama

"When de Yankees come to Alabama," he recalled, "Ol' Master tol' de niggers to hitch up all de wagons an' load all de food an' sech on 'em. Us had 'bout forty acres of swamp land, so us hid de stuff dere.

"'Fore long I seed a long string of black an' white horses, wid mules behin' dem. Dey had packs on dey back. In de packs was grub de Yankees had tuk off'en de white peoples."

"Did you enjoy the old slavery days, Uncle?"

"Yes, chile, dey was good days. Some of de white peoples was bad to de niggers, but my Ol' Master warn't dat kind. Dat de reason he would let all de niggers sit aroun' whilst he was a singin'; an' he could sing."

Uncle Frederick putters about his tiny home in Opelika, managing to grow a profusion of flowers and vegetables despite his bent back. He was hoeing in his garden when the interviewer came upon him, but he eagerly laid down the hoe when told what he sought.

"Uncle, I want to talk with you about the old times."

"Lordy me, chile," he beamed, his eyes twinkling, "you done foun' de raght nigger!"

DELIA GARLIC

Interview with Delia Garlic
—Margaret Fowler, Fruithurst, Alabama

DEM DAYS WAS HELL

Delia Garlic lives at 43 Stone Street, Montgomery, and insists she is 100 years old. Unlike many of the old Negroes of the South, she has no good words for slavery days or the old masters, declaring: "Dem days was hell."

She sat on her front porch and assailed the taking of young children from mothers and selling them in different parts of the country.

"I was growed up when de war come," she said, "an' I was a mother befo' it closed. Babies was snatched from dere mother's breas' an' sold to speculators. Chilluns was separated from sisters an' brothers an' never saw each other ag'in.

"Course dey cry; you think dey not cry when dey was sold lak cattle? I could tell you 'bout it all day, but even den you couldn't guess de awfulness of it.

"It's bad to belong to folks dat own you soul an' body; dat can tie you up a tree, wid yo' face to de tree an' yo' arms fastened tight aroun' it; who take a long curlin' whip an' cut de blood ever' lick.

"Folks a mile away could hear dem awful whippings. Dey was a turrible part of livin'."

Delia said she was born at Powhatan, Virginia, and was the youngest of thirteen children.

"I never seed none of my brothers an' sisters 'cept brother William," she said. "Him an' my mother an' me was brought in a speculator's drove to Richmon' an' put in a warehouse wid a drove of other niggers. Den we was all put on a block an' sol' to de highes' bidder.

"I never seed brother William ag'in. Mammy an' me was sold to a man by de name of Carter, who was de sheriff of de county.

"No'm, dey warn't no good times at his house. He was a widower an' his daughter kept house for him. I nursed for her, an' one day I was playin' wid de baby. It hurt its li'l han' an' commenced to cry, an' she whirl on me, pick up a hot iron an' run it all down my arm an' han'. It took off de flesh when she done it.

"Atter awhile, marster married ag'in; but things warn't no better. I seed his wife blackin' her eyebrows wid smut one day, so I thought I'd black mine jes' for fun. I rubbed some smut on my eyebrows an' forgot to rub it off, an' she kotched me. She was powerful mad an' yelled: 'You black devil, I'll show you how to mock your betters.'

"Den she pick up a stick of stovewood an' flails it ag'in' my head. I didn't know nothin' more 'till I come to, lyin' on de floor. I heard de mistus say to one of de girls: 'I thought her thick skull and cap of wool could take it better than that.'

"I kept on stayin' dere, an' one night de marster come in drunk an' set at de table wid his head lollin' aroun'. I was waitin' on de table, an' he look up an' see me. I was skeered, an' dat made him awful mad. He called an overseer an' tol' him: 'Take her out an' beat some sense in her.'

"I begin to cry an' run an' run in de night; but finally I run back by de quarters an' heard mammy callin' me. I went in, an' raght away dey come for me. A horse was standin' in front of de house, an' I was took dat very night to Richmon' an' sold to a speculator ag'in. I never seed my mammy any more.

"I has thought many times through all dese years how mammy looked dat night. She pressed my han' in bofe of hers an' said: 'Be good an' trus' in de Lawd.'

"Trustin' was de only hope of de pore black critters in dem days. Us jest prayed fer strength to endure it to de end. We didn't 'spect nothin' but to stay in bondage 'till we died.

Delia Garlic, Montgomery, Alabama

"I was sol' by de speculator to a man in McDonough, Ga. I don't ricollect his name, but he was openin' a big hotel at McDonough an' bought me to wait on tables. But when de time come aroun' to pay for me, his hotel done fail. Den de Atlanta man dat bought de hotel bought me, too. 'Fo' long, dough, I was sol' to a man by de name of

Garlic, down in Louisiana, an' I stayed wid him 'till I was freed. I was a regular fiel' han', plowin' an' hoein' an' choppin' cotton.

"Us heard talk 'bout de war, but us didn't pay no 'tention. Us never dreamed dat freedom would ever come."

Delia was asked if the slaves ever had any parties or dances on her plantation.

"No'm," she replied, "us didn't have no parties; nothin' lak dat. Us didn't have no clothes for goin' 'roun. I never had a undershirt until jest befo' my first chil' was borned. I never had nothin' but a shimmy an' a slip for a dress, an' it was made out'en de cheapes' cloth dat could be bought; unbleached cloth, coarse, but made to las'.

"Us didn't know nothin' 'cept to work. Us was up by three or four in de mornin' an' everybody got dey somethin' to eat in de kitchen. Dey didn't give us no way to cook, nor nothin' to cook in our cabins. Soon as us dressed us went by de kitchen an' got our piece of cornbread. Dey wasn't even no salt in dem las' years. Dat piece of cornbread was all us had for breakfus', an' for supper, us had de same.

"For dinner us had boiled vittles; greens, peas an' sometimes beans. Coffee? No'm, us never knowed nothin' 'bout coffee.

"One mornin' I 'members I had started to de fiel', an' on de way I los' my piece of bread. I didn't know what to do. I started back to try to fin' it, an' it was too dark to see. But I walk back raght slow, an' had a dog dat walked wid me. He went on ahead, an' atter awhile I come on him lyin' dere guardin' dat piece of bread. He never touched it, so I gived him some of it.

"Jus' befo' de war I married a man named Chatfield from another plantation; but he was took off to war an' I never seed him ag'in. Atter awhile I married a boy on de plantation named Miles Garlic.

"Yas'm, Massa Garlic had two boys in de war. When dey went off de Massa an' missis cried, but it made us glad to see dem cry. Dey made us cry so much.

"When we knowed we was free, everybody wanted to git out. De rule was dat if you stayed in yo' cabin you could keep it, but if you lef', you los' it. Miles was workin' at Wetumpka, an' he slipped in an' out so us could keep on livin' in de cabin.

"My secon' baby soon come, an' raght den I made up my min' to go to Wetumpka where Miles was workin' for de railroad. I went on down dere an' us settled down.

"Atter Miles died, I lived dere long as I could an' den come to Montgomery to live wid my son. I'se eatin' white bread now an' havin' de best time of my life. But when de Lawd say, 'Delia, well done; come up higher,' I'll be glad to go."

ANGIE GARRETT

Interview with Angie Garrett
—Ruby Pickens Tartt, Livingston, Alabama

MULES BE EATIN' AND NIGGERS BE EATIN'

She sat in the door of her small cabin, a short distance from Livingston, Alabama, in philosophical reflection. Time has not softened her memories. As she told these facts an occasional expression of bitterness passed over her face.

"I's Angie Garrett," she said. I was about sixteen years at beginning uv de Wa'. I was born in De Kalb, Mississippi. My mother was Betty Scott, an' I didn't know my father's name. I had four brothers, Ember, Johnny, Jimmie, and Henry; and three sisters, Delphie, Lizzie Sue, and Frankie, and my grandmother was Sukie Scott. She lived five miles from Gainesville across Noxubee Creek (in full, Oka Noxubee) an' I lived wid her. Never axed 'bout my grand-daddy, 'caze wa'n't no tellin'. My mammy lived right here in Gainesville an' belong to Mr. Sam Harwood.

"I b'longed to de Moorings and Cap'n Mooring run on a boat to Mobile from Aberdeen, Mississippi, 'twus on de 'Bigbee river, an' 'twus called de *Cremonia*. I was de house gal an' nuss an' I slep' on a pallet in old Miss's room. I had plenty to eat long as us was on dat boat, and dat sho' was good. But when us was in De Kalb, vittles was giv' out at de smoke house, a slice o' meat and piece of bread and peas, and 'twus sarnt out ter de fiel'. Mules be eatin' and niggers be eatin'.

"I nussed de Moorings little boy Johnny. De little gal had died. Mr. Scott in De Kalb had 'bout fifty slaves and a big plantation and a overseer name' Barnes. He was a haughty man, and niggers was skeered to death 'caze he would come in a-cussin'.

"Us would git up 'fo' daylight. 'Twus dark when go out, dark when come in. Us make a little fire in de fiel' some mawnin's, hit beeze so cold; dan us let it go out 'fo' de overseer come. Ef he seed you he'd make yer lay down flat on yo' belly, foots tied out and han's tied out and whoop yer wid slapper leather strap wid a handle. But I was laid 'cross a cheer. I been whooped 'tel I tell lies on myself to make 'em quit. Say dey whoop 'till I'd tell de troof, so I had ter lie 'bout myse'f keep 'em from killin' me. Dis here race is mo' lac de chillun uv Isreal, 'cept dey didn't have ter shoot no gun ter set um free.

"I was sole ter Mr. Johnny Mooring, 'caze de property was in debt. And den fuss I b'longed ter Mrs. Scott at De Kalb, and her sole me, an' I sho' was glad. I walked here to Gainesville frum De Kalb, Mississippi. Us wa'n't 'lowed to learn nothin'. Sometimes us sing and have a little prayer meetin', but 'twus mighty easy and quiet like. Gran'ma Sukey use' to sing, "Travel on, travel on, Soon be Over."

"Ef any us died in dem days, buried us quick as dey could and got out of dere and got to work. At night dey blow'd de horn for 'em to bring in de cotton w'ut de women spinned. Dey made all de clof. Us worked nights too, but us rested Sundays. Us didn't git no presents at Christmas. Sometimes us had a corn shuckin', and no celebration for no marriage. Dat was called "jumpin' de broom," jes' taken up wid 'em. Dey all want you to have plenty of chillun, though.

"Us wo' asafetida 'roun' us neck keep off de small pox and measles. Us didn't have much medicine and some of um was always full of bad complaints lac' Carrie, my neighbor, whut you axed about. I bees a-hurtin', but I can't never git in edgeways for her. Always got a lot excuses; doan' never 'spects to die 'thout folks knows whut ails her. But she brought me some black-eyed peas today, and I lac's um 'caze dey biles sof', and I say 'ef de devil brought hit, God sarnt hit.' Sometimes I bees hongry, an' I say, 'Whut is I'm gwinter eat?', and along come somebody wid sumpin'.

Angie Garrett, Livingston, Alabama

"Wish you could of heered dat calliope on de Cremonia. Dey dance some time 'mos' all night, but dey didn't act lac' dey do now. 'Twus nice behavior. Look lac' ev'ything goin' back ter heathenism, and hits on de way now. But de good Lord he'ps me. He hol's my han'. I ain't got nothin' 'gin nobody. I doan' see no need of fussin' and fightin' an' a-drinkin' whiskey. Us livin' in a new worl' and I go on makin' de bes' I kin of hit. Some I lac, some I doan'.

"I got one daughter, Fannie Watson, a good washer and ironer right here in Gainesville, and I got a son, too, say he ain't gonna marry 'tel he kin treat de 'oman good as she kin treat herse'f. I makes him wait on me, and he gits mighty raw sometimes, but I tells him I'm jes' much older den he is now as I was when he was bawn. Den he gives me a old dirty dime, but now wid dese here tokens, you gotter pay some of hit fer spendin'. Dey tells me hit's de Governor, and I say 'let him carry 'em; he kin tote 'em, I ain't able.' Well, once ain't always, and twice ain't forever.

"No'm, I doan' never go ter church no mo'. De preachers here is goin' bline about money. Dey ain't interested in dey soul. Some folks b'longs ter de church an' ain't been changed. De church ain't all of hit. I 'members day uv 'manicpation. Yankees tole us we was free, and dey call us up frum de fiel' to sign up an' see ef us wanted to stay on wid 'em. I stayed dat year wid de Moorings, den I bargain for lan', but couldn't never pay fer hit. Turned loose 'thout nothin'.

"But dey was a coal black free born nigger name George Wright, had a floatin' mill right here on de 'Bigbee River, stayed at de p'int of de woods jes' 'bove de spring branch, and hit did a good service. But he got in debt and he sole his five boys. Dey was his own chillun, and he could sell 'em under de law. De names was Eber, Eli, Ezekiel, Enoch, and Ezra, an' he sole 'em ter de highes' bidder right yonder 'front of de Pos' Office for cash. And Jack Tom was another free nigger here and he bought some of 'em, and dey others de white folks bought, and I never heerd no complaint and I seed 'em long as dey lived. Dey was a heap of things went on. Some I lac's to remember, some I doan'. But I'd rather be free now. I never seed Mr. Lincoln, but when dey tole me 'bout him, I thought he was partly God.

"But Mr. John Rogers right here, (he's dead an' gone now), he was whut he was and wasn't 'ceitful. Go to him ef you got into anything, and he more'n apt to tell you whut to do. He was wile when he was young, but he settle down and was de bes' white man to de niggers I ever know'd. He'd he'p me right now ef he was livin' and seen me wearin' dis here rag nasty, he sho' would."

HENRY GARRY

Interview with Henry Garry
—W.F. Jordan, Birmingham, Alabama

MR. RENFROE HANGS ON A CHINYBERRY TREE

"Howdy Cap'n! Kin you tell me how to fin' Jedge Ab's co't? I knowed 'zactly whar hit was in de ole co't house, but I gits all bumfuzzled tryin' to fin' anybody in dis new buildin'."

His name was Henry Garry. He wore a suit of faded and extensively patched Confederate gray and a cap of the regulation porter's style. His face bore the expression worn only by those of his race who had lived and toiled in a much earlier and in many instances, happier day. In the presence of "white folks" he was at ease, indicating an intimate association and relationship among them and in their service.

"What business have you in Judge Abernathy's court? You don't look like a criminal," was the response.

"Oh, nawsah, I ain't neber done nothin' to nobody no time. But I sho' don't know what dis new generation of nigguhs comin' to. Hit war bad 'nough when dey couldn' git nothin' but bootleg cawn licker; now dey kin buy all de gin dey wants right here in Bummin'ham, an' dem rapscallions git out on Sat'd'y night, fill up on gin an' git all lit up lak a meetin' house. Den de fust thing dey know dey gits tangled up wid somebody wid a razor or a meat axe or somp'n an' 'long come de law, locks 'em up an' de debil's to pay."

"But why should all that disturb you? They haven't run you in have they?" he was asked.

"Nawsuh, hits dat triflin' nevvew of mine. Dat boy kin sho' git into mo' kin's of trouble dan a pet monkey. He in jail now for some debilment or yuther an' I 'spect I'se gwine to hab to git him out ag'in. Dat's what I'se gwine to see Jedge Ab 'bout. Wisht I could git dat boy back down in Sumter County on Marse John Rogers' plantation. Dat's whar he b'long at. Betcha Marse John wouldn' take none of his foolishment."

"Are you familiar with the people and history of Sumter County?" he was quizzed further.

"Lawd man, I was bawn in de back yahd whar Marse John Rogers live right now. Dat was right atter de surrender an' my mammy b'long to de Vandegraaf family who useter live dar an' owned all dat plantation. My daddy's name was Daniel Grady. Dey come f'um Virginny long time 'fo' de wah. All dem ole peoples is dead now. Onlies' kinfolks I hab lef' down dah is a cousin. She mos' a hundert yeahs ole an' still libs on her little farm a few miles from Gainesville. An' Cap'n when I says libs, I means libs. Ain't nothin' dat grow outten de groun' nor in de groun' in Alabama dat's good for folks to eat but what she got it an' plenty. I goes down dar to visit her twicet a yeah, an', man alive, hit am a sin de 'mount of grub I puts away endurin' dem two weeks I stays dar.

Yassah, I'se 'bout due to go down dah now, 'caze dat gyarden sass en' spring chickens jes' 'bout ripe.

"My mammy was a seamstress for de Vandegraaf plantation an' made all de clothes for bofe black and white. She neber did leave de plantation atter de slaves was freed but stayed right dar till she died, she an' my daddy bofe. But dey was good hones', 'spectable, chu'ch-goin' people, my daddy an' mammy was. De little log chu'ch house is still dar an' de niggers still keeps up de services. De ole pastor nearly a hundert yeahs ole now, but it would s'prise you how spry he gits 'bout an' conduc's de meetin's.

"I don't know 'bout yuther parts, but from what my mammy tell me de slaves in Sumter County mus' hab had a mighty good time, had plenty of ebery t'ing an' nothin' to worry 'bout. Seems lak dar warn't no trouble 'mongst de whites an' blacks 'twell atter de wah. Some white mens come down from de Norf' an' mess up wid de niggers. I was a mighty little shaver, but I 'members one night atter supper, my daddy and mammy an' us chilluns was settin' under a big tree by our cabin in de quarters when all at wunst, lickety split, heah come gallopin' down de road what look lak a whole army of ghos'es. Mus' hab been 'bout a hundert an' dey was men ridin' hosses wid de men and hosses bofe robed in white.

"Cap'n, dem mens look lak dey ten feet high an' dey hosses big as elephan's. Dey didn't bodder nobody at de qua'ters, but de leader of de crowd ride right in de front gate an' up to de big dug well back of our cabin an' holler to my daddy. 'Come heah nigguh! Ho-oh!, 'cose we skeered. Yassuh, look lak our time done come.

"My daddy went ober to whar he settin' on his hoss at de well. Den he say, 'Nigguh git a bucket an' draw me some cool water.' Daddy got a bucket, fill it up an' han' it to him. Cap'n, would you b'lieve it? Dat man jes' lif' dat bucket to his mouf' an' neber stop twell it empty. Did he hab 'nough? He jes' smack his mouf an' call for mo'. Jes' lak dat, he didn' stop twell he drunk three buckets full. Den he jes' wipe his mouf an' say, 'Lawdy, dat sho' was good. Hit was de fust drink of water I'se had sence I was killed at de battle of Shiloh.'

"Was we good? Cap'n, from den on dar wasn't a nigger dare stick his head out de do' fo' a week. But nex' day we fin' out dey was Ku Kluxes an' dey foun' de body of a white man hangin' to a pos' oak tree ober by Gran' Prairie. His name was Billings an' he come from de Norf. He been ober 'roun' Livingston messin' up de niggers tellin' 'em dey had been promised forty acres and a mule, an' dey ought to go 'head an' take 'em from de white folks.

"But dat carpetbagger couldn' do nothin' wid ole Slick 'dough. Slick? Yassah, dat what ebe'ybody call him. He hang 'roun' de co'te house at Livingston an' listen to de lawyers argufy. He try to 'member all de big words dem lawyers use. When dat carpetbagger come to town dat nigger Slick was carryin' his bag to de hotel an' when dey pass de mineral well in de street, de man axed Slick, 'What dat water good for? Hab it been tested?' Slick say, 'Oh yassah, dat water been scanalyzed by de bes' fenologists in de country, an' dey say hit's three quarters carbolic acid gas, an' de yuther seben eights is hydrophobia.'

"Yassah, dat ole cannon in de co'te house yahd at Livingston was drug outten de Tombigbee ribber whar de Yankees done sunk it time of de wah. De Men's useter load 'er up an' shoot 'er off on big days at Livingston. Dey had to spike de ole gun, 'dough, to keep de deblish boys 'roun' town from shootin' it off jes' fo' fun.

"Git rid of de carpetbaggers? Oh yassah, dey vote 'em out. Well, sah, tell you how dey done dat. De 'publicans done paid all de niggers' poll tax, an' gib 'em a receipt so dey could vote same as de whites. Dey made up to 'lect de officers at de co't house all niggers an' den sen' yuther ones to Montgomery to make de laws. Same day de 'lection come off dar was a circus in Livingston an' de Demmycrats 'suaded de boss man of de circus to let all Sumter County niggers in de show by showin' dere poll tax receipts. Yessah, when de show was ober de 'lection was ober too, an' nobody was 'lected 'cepin' white Demmycrats.

"'Cose dat made Sumter County a mighty onhealthy place for carpetbaggers an' uppity niggers.

Henry Garry, Birmingham, Alabama

"Yo' ax me 'bout de old songs de slaves useter sing. Well, I don't 'members many of dem. Atter de S'render all de ole slaves what stayed on de plantations 'roun' Gainesville useter gather at de landin' dar waitin' to see de steamboats pull in from down de Tombigbee on dere way to Columbus, (Miss.), an' somebody'd start a song, an', Law' man, how dem niggers sing. Here one I heerd my mammy sing so much I learnt it:

> "Read in de bible, understan'
> Methuselah was de oldes' man.
> He lived nine hundred an' sixty nine
> Den died an' go to Heben in de Lawd's due time.
>
> Methuselah was a witness
> For my Lawd,
> For my Lawd.
>
> "Read in de Bible, Understan'
> Samson was de stronges' man.
> Went out to battle to fight one time
> Killed a thousan' of de Philistines.
>
> Samson was a witness
> For my Lawd,
> For my Lawd.
>
> "Daniel was a Hebrew chile,
> Went to de Lawd to pray a while.
> De Lawd tole de angels de lions to keep,
> So Daniel lay down an' went to sleep.
>
> An' dat's anoder witness
> For my Lawd,
> For my Lawd.

"Now 'bout de ghos' tales. I neber heerd many ghos' yarns 'cep' 'bout de chinyberry tree whar dey hung Mistah Steve Renfroe. He was 'lected High Sheriff dat time dey got all de niggers to go to de circus 'stead of goin' to de 'lection. He a fine lookin' man an' ride a big white hoss an' ebe'ybody lak him a lot 'cep' de carpetbaggers an' boddersome niggers. No matter whar, if he meet one of 'em, he look 'em squar' in de eye for a minute, den 'bout all he say would be, 'Get to hell outten heah!' An' man, iffen dey could fly dat would be too slow trabelin' for 'em, gettin' outten de county. But atter while he got in trouble 'bout money matters. Dey say he got color blind, couldn' tell his money from de county's. So dey 'rest him an' put him in jail, but he bust right out an' run off. Atter while he sneak back an' 'caze his Ku Klux frien's wouldn' help him outten de trouble when he got back in jail, he give 'em away an' tell what dere name was. One night a gang took him outten de Livingston jail an' go 'bout a mile outten town an' hang him to a chinyberry tree. I'se hyeard iffen you go to dat tree today an' kinda tap on hit an say, 'Renfroe, Renfroe; what did you do?' De tree say right back at you, 'Nothin'.'

"Nawsuh, folks down 'roun' Gainesville didn' pay much min' to signs an' conju' an' all dat stuff. My mammy wouldn' let us tote a axe on our shoulder th'ough de house, an' she wouldn' 'low a umbrella to be opened in de house, say hit bring bad luck. She neber fail to hab cown-fiel' peas an hawg-jowl for dinner on New Yeah's Day. She say hit a sign you hab plenty to eat balance ob de yeah. She put a ball of asafetida on a string an' make all us chillun wear it 'roun' our neck to keep off sickness. If a owl begin to hoot ober in Tombigbee bottom too close to de house, she put de shovel in de fire to make him stop.

"Wall, sir, I come to Bummin'ham mos' forty yeahs ago when Marse Josiah Morris finish de Morris Hotel. I fust run de elevators a while, den dey wukked me in de saloon what useter be jes' back of de office. I been heah eber sence. I 'speck 'bout de las' thing dat'll happen to dis ole nigguh will be to haul him away from de Morris Hotel in a black box.

"But Lawdy, Cap'n, I got to git up to Jedge Ab's co't. Lissen, Cap'n, iffen I gits dat no'count nevvew outten jail I sho' would lak to git him a job. You don't know nobody what don't want to hire nobody to do nothin' does you?"

GEORGIA

Interview with Georgia
—Gertha Couric

DEY PLANTED DE SILVER IN DE FIEL'

"No, honey, I neber seed my mammy. She died when I was bawn, an' my Mistis Mary Mitchell raised me in de Big House. I was named a'ter her sister, Miss Georgia. I slep' in her room an I was a house nigger all my days. I neber went to a nigger chu'ch 'tell I was grown an' ma'd, didn' sociate wid niggers 'cause I was a nu'smaid. I raised Miss Molly, her las' baby.

"I was bawn at 'Elmoreland', Massa Americus Mitchell's place, mor'n ninety yeahs ago, an' a'ter freedom I stayed dah 'tel ole Massa died an' my Mistis moved to Eufaula to live wid her son, Mahs Merry.

"'Bout all I know of de wawh is when dey said—'de Yankees is comin', de Yankees is comin'.'

"Us sho' was skeerd, an' dere'd be some fas' doin's about de place. All de cattle an' hawgs an hosses we driv' to de swamp on de nawth creek, an' de feather beds down dere too an' hid 'em in de brush an' leaves. My Mistis tied her trinkets in sacks an' put 'em in outlandish places lak de hen-house an de hay lof'. An' de silver, dey planted in de fiel."

FANNIE GIBSON

Interview with Fannie Gibson
—J.R. Jones, Columbus, Georgia

Fannie Gibson was born the slave property of Mr. Benajer Goff, a planter of near Roanoke, Alabama. She says that during her girlhood she "piddled in de fiels an hepped in de kitchen o' de big house."

She has very pleasant memories of slave days, and "wishes to God dat she was as comforbly (comfortably) fixed now as she was den."

Her ante-bellum owner she pictures as a very humane, Christian gentleman—a man that took great interest in the material and spiritual welfare of his slaves.

Two hymns, sung by 'Aunt' Fannie for her interviewer, are appended.

Going Home To Live With The Lord.

Goin' home soon in de mornin',
Goin' home soon in de mornin',
I's goin' home to live with de Lord.

In de mornin' so soon,
In de mornin' so soon,
I's goin' home to live with de Lord.

I's goin' home to live with de Lord,
I's goin' home to live with de Lord,
I's goin' home soon in de mornin'.

O, de Lord is a-waitin' for me,
O, de Lord is a-waitin' for me,
I's goin' home soon in de mornin'.

Where Were You When You Found The Lord?

My brother, where were you,
My brother, where were you,
My brother, where were you,
When you found the Lord?

I was low down in the valley,
I was low down in the valley,
I was low down in the valley,
When I first found the Lord.

My sister, where were you,
My sister, where were you,
My sister, where were you,
When you found the Lord?

I was low down in the valley,
I was low down in the valley,
I was low down in the valley,
When I first found the Lord.

This song can be extended indefinitely by addressing the question to various members of one's family, and to friends.

FRANK GILL

Personal interview with Frank Gill
708 South Hamilton Street, Mobile, Alabama
—Ila B. Prine, Mobile, Alabama

A SLAVE BOY ESCAPES WHIPPINsG BY PULLING TAIL OF FROCK COAT

A low, stout, sleek headed Negro man, sat in an old rocking chair in an end room of a long row of rooms of a tenement house at 708 South Hamilton Street, Mobile, Alabama. This old darkey said, when asked by the writer if he lived during slavery times: "I not only lived durin' slavery times, but I was here before a gun was fired, an' b'fore Lincoln was elected. I tells you, Miss, de fust time I 'members anything—a tale of any kind. I was livin' in Vicksburg, Lee County, Mississippi, an' mah maw an' paw's names was Amelia Williams an' Hiram Gill. I couldn't tells you whar dey war from, dough. But I does know dat Mista Arthur an' George Foster owned us, up 'til I war a big boy. De way it was, dere mother, Ol' Missy, was a widow, an' her had dese two boys, an' she had money, I tells you she had barrels ob money; so when de two boys got old enough she divide de slaves, an' property 'tween 'em. Me an' mah maw fell to Arthur Foster, and sum ob our kindred fell to George

Foster. Mister George was a Captain in de army an' was killed near Vicksburg.

"De Ol' Missy's place shore was big, I couldn't say how many acres dere was, but hit run four or five miles, an' she owned hundreds ob slaves. She had lots ob log cabin quarters, whut had de cracks daubed wid mud, an' den ceiled wid boards. I'se tellin' you dey was twice as warm as de houses we lib in now. Dey had chimbleys built ob mud an' sticks, an' had big wide, fireplaces, dat we cooked on, an' de beds was homemade, but Lor' dey was heaps stronger dan dey is now, in dese times. Dem beds was morticed together.

"As I said b'fore I was a boy between fourteen or fifteen years old b'fore de slaves was divided, an' when I was on de Ol' Missy's place, I stayed aroun' de house, an' wait on dem, an' 'tend de horses. Anudder thing I had to do, dey would send me for the mail. I had to go twelve miles atter hit an' I couldn't read or write, but I could bring everybody's mail to dem jes' right. I knowed I had better git hit right. You see I could kinder figure, so I could make out by de numbers.

"Ol' Missy an' Mister Arthur both was good to me an' all de slaves, dey 'low de slaves to make dere own patch ob cotton, an' raise chickens, an' he would sell hit for dem. Cotton was de main crop, in dem days, hit would sell as high as twenty-five cents a pound. 'Course dey raises corn, pears, an' other things on de plantation, too, but dey made de cotton. Master Jesus! dey sumtimes made from fifty to one hundred an' fifty bales.

"I 'members how all de women had looms, both black and white, weavin' cloth for de clothes; an' den dey raised sheep to git de wool to make dem gray uniforms. Lord, at sheep shearing time! hit was big times. Let me tell you, Miss, dem uniforms was made out ob all wool, too, but I cain't 'member whut dey used to dye 'em gray, but I 'members dey dyed wid red oak bark, walnut bark, an' also a brush whut growed down on the branch, also dey used de laurel leaves to dye yellow, as well as clay. Dey so't de dye wid salt, an' hit really stayed in.

"Let me tell you, dey really fed us slaves good, up 'til such a length o' time atter de war broke out, den food began to git scarce.

"You see de Government taxed 'em, an' dey had to gib so much to feed de soldiers. Even den us had a good time, I 'members how de li'l chillun played ball, and marbles, 'specially marbles, hit was our big game. Even atter night dey had a big light out in de backyard, an' us would play. Sometimes us would hunt at night, and well I 'members one Sat'day night I went huntin' wid mah uncle, an' didn't git in 'til daylight nex' mawning, an' I was sleepy an' didn't git de shoes all cleaned before church time. So ol' Marsar called me an' tuk me to de carriage house to gib me a whippin'. Ol' Marser's boy was about de same age as me an' he beg his paw not to whip me, an' I was beggin', too, but he carried me on, an' when we got in de carriage house, Ol' Marser had to climb up on de side wall to git de whip, an' he had on one ob dos long tailed coats, an' hit left dem tails hangin' down, so I jes' grabbed hold ob dem, an' made him fall, an' den I run to de Ol' Missy's room, 'ca'se I knowed when I got in dere, dat Ol' Marser would neber hit me.

"De Ol' Missy got up out ob de bed an' wouldn't let Ol' Marster whip me, an' she got so mad dat she tol' him dat she warn't going to church wid him dat morning, an' dat lack to kill de Ol' Marster, 'ca'se he shore loved an' was proud ob Ol' Missy. She was a beautiful woman. Dat ended de whippin', an' dat's de only time I 'members him tryin' to whip me.

"Ol' Missy didn't 'low dem to whip de women either, an' dey wouldn't 'low de women to roll logs either. But dey did work dem in de fiel's. 'Course dey kept de young women wid babies 'roun' de house, an' dey eat de same grub as de white folks eat.

"Talking 'bout log rollin', dem was great times, 'ca'se if some ob de neighborin' plantations wanted to get up a house, dey would invite all de slaves, men and women, to come wid dere masters. De women would help wid de cookin' an' you may be shore dey had something to cook. Dey would kill a cow, or three or four hogs, and den hab peas, cabbage, an' everything lack grows on de farm. An' if dere was any meat or food lef' dey would gib dat to de slaves to take home, an' jes' b'fore dark de o'seer or Ol' Marster would gib de slaves all de whiskey dey wanted to drink. Sometimes atter de days work, dey would hab a frolic, such as dancin', an' ol' time games.

"Dey would hab dese same kind ob gatherin's at cornshucking time, an' cotton pickin' time, but dere warn't so much foolishness at cotton pickin' time, 'ca'se dey didn't call one anudder den, 'ceptin' when de cotton got so far ahead ob dem, an' was 'bout to set in fer a wet spell, or rainy season.

"You axed me 'bout de patty-rollers? You see de City policemen walkin' his beat? Well, dat's de way de patty-rollin' was, only each county had dere patty-rollers, an' dey had to serve three months at a time, den dey was turned loose. And if dey cotch you out widout a pass, dey would gib you thirty-nine lashes, 'ca'se dat was de law. De patty-rollers knowed nearly all de slaves, an' it wurn't very often dey ever beat 'em.

"You know folks was jes' de same den as dey is now, both black, and white. Some folks you could neighbor wid den, jes' lack you can now, an' dere was good folks den, jes' de same as dey is now.

"Christmas time was de bes' ob all, 'ca'se us allus had a big dinner, an' de Ol' Marster gib de women calico dresses an' shoes, an' de men shoes an' hats, an' would gib us flour, an' sugar, molasses, an' would buy beer, whiskey an' wine.

"De Ol' Marster tuk good keer ob us too, when any ob us got sick he send for de doctor, den when dey order de medicine to be giben at night, he'd see dat us got hit. But nowadays if you git sick, you hab to git de Doctor, an' den pay him yo' se'f. Den de Ol' Marster had to find clothes an' shoes for us, but now us has to scuffle an' git dem de bes' way us can.

"You know, Miss, I'se been here a long time, I eben 'members Jefferson Davis. I'se seen him many a time. He had a home 'tween here (Mobile) an' New Orleans, an' you knows he fust tuk his seat in Montgomery, an' den moved to Richmond, Virginny.

"I 'members, too, how I useta to think dat de Baptist was de only religion. You see John de Baptist come here baptizing, an' ever'body had to offer up sacrifices, a goat or a sheep or sumpin', jes' lack de man who was going to offer up his son for a sacrifice. But you knows, Jesus come an' changed all dat. De folks in dem times didn't hab nobody to worship; an' den one come, who said, 'Father, hand me a body, and I'll die for dem,' Dat's Christ, an' he was baptized, an' God gib Jesus dis whole world. So I believed, dat was de only religion.

"I 'members how us would hab big baptizings an' shout. Us allus went to church in de white folks church, dey had church in de mornings, us had ours in de afternoons. Us would hab to hab a pass, dough, 'ca'se de church was eight miles away from de plantation.

"Dere was plenty old songs us useta to sing, but I can't 'member 'em. Dere is dis one dat goes—

> Wonderful Peter,
> Wonderful Paul,
> Wonderful Silas,
> Who for to make a
> Mah heart rejoice.
>
> On Good Shepherds, feed a' mah sheep.
> Don't you hear de young lambs a bleatin'?
> Don't you hear de young lambs a bleatin'?
> Don't you hear de young lambs a bleatin'?
> Oh! Good shepherds feed a' mah sheep."

JIM GILLARD

Interview with Jim Gillard
—*Preston Klein, Opelika, Alabama*

SOLD AT THREE MONTHS FOR $350

Jim Gillard was eleven years old when the War between the States began. Thus, the memories of the conflict are fresh; with the retreat from Rome, Ga., to Salem, Ala., as a refugee, transcending the others.

Jim was born on a plantation at Pendleton, S.C., and was sold for $350 when he was only three months old. He was one of eight children belonging to James and Hannah Gillard.

"Atter bein' sold, I fust lived 'bout three miles from Rome, Ga.," Jim recalled. "Den, when de Yankees come into Georgy us refugeed fust to Atlanta, den to Columbus an' later to Salem. Us was at Salem when de war ended."

Jim remembers catching partridges as a boy, taking them to the train and selling them to Charlie Crowder for ten cents each.

"Game was plentiful in dem days," he said, "an' I never had any trouble catchin' dem birds.

"No'm, our houses wasn't nothin' to brag about. Dey

was built of hewn logs an' had slab floors, havin' two rooms an' a shed cook room. Us beds was lak tables, wid four legs nailed on to de sides an' den corded over de top wid ropes dat was tightened wid a big key. Us had shuck mattresses to sleep on.

"Us cooked on a great big fireplace. I 'members dat dere was plenty of meat in de winter, 'ca'se Ol' Marster used to kill as many as thirty hogs at a time. Us had meat an' bread an' home-made light bread an' de white folks was mighty kind. I 'members us was carried to Sunday School every Sunday at 3 o'clock in de evenin'. Ol' Mistus'd teach us de lesson. De white chilluns had dere Sunday School at 9 o'clock in de mornin.'

"I allus went to Sunday School, but on de week days us little niggers would slip off an' go huntin' when we could."

Jim recalls that "de little niggers" ate from tin plates on the plantation; but declared he didn't mind that because the food was always good.

"Yes'm, us had purty good clothes. Dey was dyed brown wid walnut leaves an' hazelnut bush, an' on Sunday us had striped gingham pants an' shoes. My father was de shoemaker an' had a gov'mint tan yard whar he would make ol' hard brogans fer $8 a pair.

"My marster an' Mistus was Steven an' 'Lizbeth Wilson. Dey fust lived in a big log house, but den moved into a planked house. Dey had nine chillun; Ann, Steven, William, Liza, Humie, Eddie, Laura, Mary an' Lizzie.

"I 'members lots 'bout Mistus 'Lizabeth, 'ca'se she

useter read de Bible to us niggers. She would talk to us 'bout de Good Book an' have prayer meetin' wid us.

"My dad useter look atter de fiel' hands. No'm, he war'nt no overseer, but Ol' Marster allus had confidence in him.

"I 'members dat when dey would be a funeral, us'd sing; marchin' befo' de body 'fore us'd get to de grave an' singin', 'Hark come de tune a doleful sound, my years a tender cry; a livin' man come view de ground whar you may shortly lie.'

"Us frolics on Sattidy night was fine an' us'd dance 'twel mos' day. Marster's brother would fiddle for us, an' at Christmas time us would have six days to frolic. Us also had a big time at de cornshuckin's, an' us'd whoop an' holler an' sing mos' all night. De big niggers had plenty of liquor de boss give 'um. High tables was filled up wid corn an' de niggers would shuck 'twel it was all done.

"My aunt married up at de big house an' dey give her a big dance. Dey had de fiddle and had a great big time. Dey jes' jumped over de broom to marry, so atter slavery dey had to git married agin.

"I acted as houseboy in slavery times. An' all de little niggers did have lots of fun.

"When de slaves got ailin', I 'members dat Marster had Dr. Word an' Dr. Dunwoody to come to see us.

"I 'members, too, how de Yankees come to Spring Villa, 'bout eight miles from Opelika, an' said to some mens, 'Halt'. De mens wouldn't stop so de Yankees throwed dey guns on dem. Two white ladies threw a white flag an' dey wouldn't shoot, but dey carried Mr. John Edwards to Spring Villa an' made a cross on his wrist; den turned him loose 'ca'se his wife was rale sick.

"When de Yankees come, us niggers buried a cigar box wid de jewelry in it under a certain pine tree 'twel dey went on.

"Atter de big war, I married Jane Davis fust time; den Carrie Cooper. Us had two chillun an' one gran' chile, Emanuel Trotter, ten year' old.

"Yassu'm, Mr. Abraham Lincoln died a warrior for dis country. I b'longs to de church, 'ca'se if a man dies outter de Ark he is not saved, an' I wants to be saved."

MARY ELLA GRANDBERRY

Interview with Mary Ella Grandberry
—*Levi D. Shelby, Jr., Tuscumbia, Alabama*

TODAY'S FOLKS DON'T KNOW NOTHIN'

Life as a child is not clear in the ninety-year old memory of Mary Ella Grandberry, who lives in Sheffield, but she remembers that she did not have time to play as do children of today.

"I don't know jes' how old I is," Mary Ella said, "but I knows dat I'm some'ers nigh ninety yars ol'. I was borned in Barton, Alabama. My father an' mother come from Richmond, Virginny. My mammy was name Margaret Keller an' my pappy was Adam Keller. My five sisters was Martha, Sarah, Harriet, Emma an' Rosanna, an' my three brothers was Peter, Adam, Jr., an' William.

"Us all live in a li'l two-room log cabin jes' off the Big House. Life wan't ver' much for us, 'caze we had to work an' slave all de time. Massa Jim's house was a little ol' frame buildin' lack a ord'nary house is now. He was a single man an' didn't hab so terr'ble much, it seem. He had a whole lot, too, but jes' to look at him you'd thank he was a po' white man. Dere was a lot o' cabins for de slaves, but dey wasn't fitten for nobody to lib in. We jes' had to put up wid 'em.

"I don' 'member much about when I was a chil'. I disremembers ever playin' lack chilluns do today. Ever since I kin 'member I had a water bucket on my arm totin' water to de han's. Iffen I wan't doin' dat, I was choppin' cotton. Chilluns nowadays sees a good time to w'at we did den. Ever' mornin' jes' 'bout hip of day de oberseer was 'roun' to see dat we was ready to git to de fiel's. Plenty times us had to go widouten breakfas', 'caze we didn' git up in time to git it 'fo' de man done come to git us on de way to de fiel'. Us wukked 'twell dinner time jes' de same before we got anythang to eat.

"De food we et was fix jes' lack hit is now. My mammy fixed our grub at home. De on'y diffe'nce 'tween den an' now was us didn' git nothin' but common things den. Us didn' know what hit was to git biscuits for breakfas' ever' mornin'. It was cornbread 'twell on Sundays den us'd git fo' biscuits apiece. Us got fatback mos' ever' mornin'. Sometimes us mought git a chicken for dinner on a Sunday or some day lack Chris'mas. It was mighty seldom us gits anythin' lack dat, dough. We lacked possums an' rabbits but dey didn' come twell Winter time when some of de men folks'd run 'crost one in de fiel'. Dey never had no chanst to git out an' hunt none.

"Dere was no sech thang as havin' diffe'nt clo's for winter an' Summer. Us wore de same thang in summertime as in de wintertime. De same was true 'bout shoes. Us wore brogans from one yeah to de yuther.

"My Ol' Massa was a putty good man but nothin' exter. One thang 'bout him, he wouldn' 'low none of de oberseers to whup none of us, lessen he was dar to see hit done. Good thang he was lack dat, too, 'caze he sabed de blacks a many a lick what dey'd got iffen he hadn' been dar. Massa Jim was a bach'lor, an' he ain't never had much truck wid women folks. Iffen he had any chilluns, I never knowed nothin' 'bout 'em.

"De oberseers was terrible hard on us. Dey'd ride up an' down de fiel' an' haste you so twell you near 'bout fell out. Sometimes an' most inginer'ly ever' time you 'hin' de crowd you got a good lickin' wid de bull whup dat de driver had in de saddle wid him. I hearn mammy say dat one day dey whupped po' Leah twell she fall out like she was daid. Den dey rubbed salt an' pepper on de blisters to make 'em burn real good. She was so so' 'twell she couldn' lay on her back nights, an' she jes' couldn' stan' for no clo's to tech back whatsomever.

"Massa Jim had 'bout one of de bigges' plantations in dat section. I guess he had nigh onto a hun'erd blacks on de place. I never knowed 'zackly how many thar was nor how big de place was.

"De folks now'days is allus complainin' 'bout how dey is havin' sech hard times, but dey jes' don' know nothin'. Dey should hab come up when I did an' dey'd see now dey is libin' jes' lack kings an' queens. Dey don' have to git up 'fo' day when hit's so dark you kin jes' see your han's 'fo' your eyes. Dey don' know what it's lack to have to keep up wid de leader. You know dey was allus somebody what could wuk faster dan de res' of de folks an' dis fellow was allus de leader, an' ever'body else was s'pose to keep up wid him or her whatsomever hit was. Iffen you didn' keep up wid de leader you got a good thrashin' when you gits home at night. Hit was allus good dark when de han's got in from de fiel'. Co'se iffen dar was a lady what had a baby at home, she could leave jes' a little 'fo' de sun sot.

"Younguns now'days don' know what it is to be punish'; dey thank iffen dey gits a li'l whuppin' from dey mammy now dat dey is punish' terrible. Dey should of had to follow de leader for one day an' see how dey'd be punish' iffen dey gits too far behin'. De bigges' thang dat us was punish' for was not keepin' up. Dey'd whup us iffen we was caught talkin' 'bout de free states, too. Iffen you wan't whupped, you was put in de 'nigger box' an' fed cornbread what was made widouten salt an' wid plain water. De box was jes' big 'nough for you to stan' up in, but hit had air holes in hit to keep you from suffocatin'. Dere was plenty turnin' 'roun' room in hit to 'low you to change your position ever' oncet in a while. Iffen you had done a bigger 'nough thang you was kep' in de 'nigger box' for months at de time, an' when you got out you was nothin' but skin an' bones an' scurcely able to walk.

"Half de time a slave didn' know dat he was sol' 'twell de massa'd call him to de Big House an' tell him he had a new massa from den on. Ever' time dat one was sol' de res' of 'em'd say, 'I hopes nex' time'll be me.' Dey thought you'd git a chanst to run away to de free states. I hearn my mammy say dat when she come from Virginny dat she come on a boat built outten logs. She say she never was so sick in all her life. I seed a 'hole wagon load of slaves come through our farm one day what was on dere way to Arkansas. Dey was de mos' I ever seed travel at de same time.

"De white folks didn't 'low us to even look at a book. Dey would scol' an' sometimes whup us iffen dey caught us wid our head in a book. Dat is one thang I sho'ly did want to do an' dat was to learn to read an' write. Massa

Jim promised to teach us to read an' write, but he neber had de time.

"Dere wan't but one chu'ch on de place what I lived on, an' de colored and de white both went to hit. You know we was neber 'lowed to go to chu'ch widoutten some of de white folks wid us. We wan't even 'lowed to talk wid nobody from anudder farm. Iffen you did, you got one of de wus' whuppin's of your life. Atter freedom Massa Jim tol' us dat dey was 'fraid we'd git together an' try to run away to de No'th, an' dat was w'y dey didn' wan' us gittin' together talkin'.

"A few years 'fo' de war my pappy learnt to read de Bible. (Mary Ella apparently forgot her previous comment on penalties for learning to read). Whenever we would go to chu'ch he would read to us an' we'd sing. 'Bout de mos' two pop'lar songs dey sung was 'Steal Away' an' 'I Wonder Whar Good Ol' Dan'el Was.' 'Steal Away' is sech a pop'lar song what ever'body knows hit. De yuther one is done mought' nigh played out, so I'll sing hit for you. It goes lack dis:

> I wonder whar was good ol' Dan'el,
> I wonder whar was good ol' Dan'el,
> I wonder whar was thankin' (thinking) Peter,
> I wonder whar was thankin' Peter.
>
> (Chorus)
>
> I'm goin' away, goin' away.
> I'm goin' away, goin' away.
>
> I wonder whar was weepin' Mary,
> I wonder whar was weepin' Mary,

> I'm goin' away, I'm goin' away,
> I'm goin' away to live forever,
> I'll never turn back no mo'.

"De slaves would git tired of de way dey was treated an' try to run away to de No'th. I had a cousin to run away one time. Him an' anudder fellow had got 'way up in Virginny 'fo' Massa Jim foun' out whar dey was. Soon as Massa Jim foun' de whar'bouts of George he went atter him. When Massa Jim gits to George an' 'em, George pertended lack he didn' know Massa Jim. Massa Jim as' him, "George don't you know me?" George he say, 'I neber seed you 'fo' in my life.' Den dey as' George an' 'em whar did dey come from. George an' dis yuther fellow look up in de sky an' say, 'I come from above, whar all is love.' Iffen dey had owned dey knowed Massa Jim he could have brung 'em back home. My pappy tried to git away de same time as George an' dem did, but he couldn' see how to take all us chillun wid him, so he had to stay wid us. De blacks an' de whites would have de terr'bles' battles sometimes. Dat would be when de blacks would slip off to de No'th an' was caught an' brung back. De paterollers'd ketch de colored folks an' lock 'em up twell de owner came atter 'em.

"Iffen a slave was cotched out after nine o'clock he was whupped. Dey didn' 'low nobody out atter it was dark 'lessen he had a pass from de Massa. One night, 'fo' George an' dis fellow (I disremembers his name, but I thinks it was Ezra) runned away, George tried to git over to de bunk whar he lived an' one of de oberseers seen him an' dey put him in de 'nigger box' for three weeks. Jes' as soon as he got out again, George an' dis Ezra slipped off. Dey had a sign dat dey would give each yuther eve'y night atter sundown. George would hang de lantern in de window, an' den he would take it outen de window an' hang it raght back in dar ag'in. I couldn't never make no sense outen it. I axed him one day whut he was adoin' dat for. He say dat 'fo' long I'd know 'zackly what is all about. Dis was de sign of how long dey have to wait 'fo' dey try to git away.

"Atter de day's work was over, de slaves didn't have nothin' to do but go to bed. In fac', dey didn't feel lack doin' nothin' else. On Satiday dey sot up an' washed so's dey could have some clean clothes to wear de comin' week. We wukked all day, ever' day 'cep'n some Sat'days, we had a half day off den. Us didn' git many an' on'y when us as' for 'em. On Sundays us jes' laid 'roun' 'mos' all day. Us didn't git no pleasure outten goin' to church, 'caze we warn't 'lowed to say nothin'. Sometimes even on Chris'mas us didn't git no res'. I 'members on one Chris'mas us had to build a lime kiln. When us git a holiday us rested. Iffen dere was a weddin' or a funeral on our plantation us went. Odderways we don't go nowhar.

"De war come when I was a big gal. I 'member dat my uncle an' cousin jined in wid de Yankees to hope fight for de freedom. De Yankees come to our place an' runned Massa Jim away an' tuk de house for a horsepittil. Dey tuk all of Massa Jim's clothes an' gived dem to some of dere frien's. Dey burned up all de cotton, hay, peas an' ever'thing dat was in de barns. Dey made de white folks cook for de colored an' den serve 'em while dey et. De Yankees made 'em do for us lak we done for dem. Dey showed de white folks what it was to work for somebody else. Dey stayed on our place for de longes'. When dey did leave, dere warn't a mouthful to eat in de house. When de war was over, Massa Jim told us dat we had to find som'ers else to live. Co'se some of my folks had already gone when he come home. Us lef' Massa Jim's an' moved to anudder farm. We got pay for de wuk what we did on dis yuther place. Raght atter de war de Ku Klux got atter de colored folks. Dey would come to our houses an' scare us mos' to death. Dey would take some of de niggers out an' whup 'em an' dose dat dey didn't whup dey tied up by dere fingers an' toes. Dese Ku Klux would come to our windows at night an' say: 'Your time ain't long acomin'.' De Ku Klux got so bad dat dey would even git us in de daytime. Dey tuk some of de niggers an' throwed 'em in de river to drown. Dey kep' dis up 'twell some folks from de North come down an' put a stop to it.

"I ma'ied Nelson Granberry. De weddin' was private. I don't have no chilluns, but my husban' got fo'. I haven't heered from any of 'em in a long time now. I guess dey all daid.

"Abe Lincoln was de bes' president dat dis country eber had. Iffen it hadn't been for him we'd still be slaves raght now. I don't think so much of Jeff Davis 'caze he tried to keep us slaves. Booker T. Washington was one of de greates' niggers dat ever lived, he always tried to raise de standard of de race.

"I joined the church 'caze de Bible says dat all people should join de church an' be Christians. Jesus Christ set up de church an' said dat ever'body what wanted to be saved to come unto him. Sin is de cause of de world bein' in de fix dat it's in today. De only way to fight sin is to git together. Iffen we can do away wid sin raght now, de world would be a paradise. In de church we learn de will of God an' what he would have us do.

"Dere was no po' white trash in our 'munity; dey was kep' back in de mountains."

United States. Work Projects Administration

ESTHER GREEN

Interview with Esther Green
—Ila B. Prine

US CHILLUN WORE SHOES LIKE GROWNUPS

'A'unt' Esther Green, of 554 Texas Street, Mobile, Alabama, was all too ready to talk about her slavery days in spite of her assertion that she didn't remember much about the war.

"I was jus' a chile," she says. "You can figure for yourself. Somebody tole me I was born in 1855, so I couldn't of been very old. I was born in State Line, Mississippi, and was owned by Edward Davis. He owned my mother, Rachel Davis and her mother, Melinda Davis. I never did know who my pappy was 'cause I never did see him.

"To de bes' of my recollections, my whitefolks was allus good to us niggers. He neber allowed no overseers and he never whipped none of dem, 'ceptin' maybe a switching once in a while for us littl'luns when we didn't behave. I never saw a growed up nigger whipped in all my life. Ole Massa jus' didn't b'lieve in dat. Massa was shorely a good man. Lots of times he would get us little niggers up on de porch at de big house and have us dance for him. We sho used to have a big time out on dem big white porches.

"I never had no work to do myself, 'cause I always stayed in de big house wid Miss Mary Davis, ole Massa's wife. I was in de house one day and ole Massa asked me if I wanted to eat at de table wid dem, so I pulled up a chair and spite of de fact dere was all kinds of good stuff to eat in front of me, I called for lye hominy. I sho did love dat stuff better'n anything else I ever et. Ole Massa and de res' of dem jus' laugh fit to kill. I reckon dey thought I was crazy sho' nuff', but I et hominy jes' de same.

"As to de number of slaves ole Massa had, I never knew. Us had log cabins to stay in. De cracks was chinked up wid yellow mud to keep de cold out and de chim'ney was made of straw and de same kind of mud, but dem cabins was warmer dan de house is nowadays. We didn't have no furniture 'ceptin' a home-made bed which was nailed to de wall on one side and two legs out in de middle of de floor. De mattresses was made of straw and hay. All de cookin' was done on de big open fireplaces what had big potracks to hang de pots on.

"Massa rationed out de food every week and we usually got a peck of meal. We had plenty of 'taters and peas and other vegetables dat we growed on de place. At Chris'mas time, we was give meat and molasses to make cakes. Us always had plenty of plain food. And too, de men would go huntin' at night and come back wid lots of big fat 'possums and rabbits by de dozen, and mos' of de time, dey would even catch a coon. And old Ben, a nigger who had turkey traps, was always bringin' in lots of dem big fat birds.

"De men and women worked in de field all day, but I never picked a bit of cotton all my life. At night de women would spin and weave cloth, but I never did learn to do dat. Den dey would dye de cloth different colors, mostly red and blue though, and make dem into clothes. Us chilluns had a one-piece dress or slip. Our shoes was all homemade too. Massa had one man who tanned de leather. He would take it an put it into a long trough for a long time and den whatever was done dat was supposed to be done to it, he would take it out and cut it and make shoes. Us chilluns' had shoes same as de grown folks.

"On Sundays, we would got to de white folks' church. Dere was a shed built onto de church and we would sit on benches out under de shed and listen to de preacher. De white folks would have lots of big baptizings, but I never did see no niggers baptized den.

"Ole Massa had a big fambly, three boys and six girls. My own ma had eight chilluns. Us was always healthy and never had to have much medicine. 'Bout de only thing I remembers ever takin' was tea made from de root of de china berry tree. It made good tea for worms, but was to be used only at certain times of de moon. My man also used Jerusalem Oak seed for worms. I never fools wid tryin' to doctor nobody's chilluns now-a-days, things is all so different.

"My Grandma, Melinda, and ole Ben and his wife was three ole people Massa freed long time before de war. When all de niggers was freed, Massa called em up to de house and tole dem dat dey was loose to go wherever suited dem, but mos' of dem stayed on de place two or three weeks, and den one mornin' I woke up and all of dem had left durin' de night. I was de only nigger left on de place and I jus' cried and cried, mostly because I was jus' lonesome for some of my own kind to laugh and talk wid.

"I don't remember exactly what I did after de Surrender, but it was about four years afterwards dat I come to Mobile and I been here every since.

I's a member of de Mobile Delaware Baptist Church, but I can't attend very regular 'count of bein' all crippled up wid de rheumatisms. I reckon dat ailing is natural though, cause I been here a long time and I's got forty grand-chilluns and more dan dat many great-grandchilluns."

JAKE GREEN

Interview with Jake Green
—Ruby Pickens Tartt, Livingston, Alabama

A CONJU' WHAT DIDN' WUK

"Yessum, dem niggers sho' was scared when ole Buck showed up in de fiel'," Jake Green, former slave, laughed with a vigor that denied his eighty-five years as he described "a conju' what didn' wuk." Jake has a vivid memory of those days before the Civil War, though he was only a small boy when it started.

"Me an' my mother an' father b'longed to old man Lam Whitehead jes' a few miles from Coatopa, 'bout ten miles east of Livingston, Alabama," he began. "My mother was Molly Whitehead, my father was Dan Whitehead. I don't know nothin' 'bout my gran'mammy an' gran'pappy, but I had a heap of unkies.

"Mr. Whitehead owned Dirtin Ferry down to Belmont, an' dey had a darkey dere named Dick what claim sick all de time. So de Massa man said, 'Dick, dam it, go to de house. I can't get no work outten you.' So Dick went on. He was a fiddler so dey jes' tuck his vittuls to him for seven years. Den one day, Old Massa say to de overseer man, 'Let's slip up dere an' see what Dick doin'. So dey did, an' dere sot Dick, fat as he could be a-playin' de fiddle an' a-singin',

>'Fool my Massa seben years.
>Gwiner fool him seben mo'.
>Hey diddle, de diddle, de diddle, de do'.'

"'Bout dat time Ole Massa poked his head in de do' said 'Dam iffen you will. Come outten dere, you black rascal, an' go to work, 'An' I ain't never hyard of Dick complainin' no mo'.

"But dey wan't so mean. Sometimes us got whupped but Massa had fo' men he didn't 'low nobody to hit, white er black. Dey was Unker Arch, he was de main carriage driver; my father, he was de house servant; Unker Julius, de fo'man of de plow han's an' Unker Ed'erds, de fo'man of de hoe han's. Whenever anybody wanted to hire anybody to work for 'em, de Massa send dem fo' out an' hire 'em by de day to chop cotton or pick. An' dem fo' niggers could chop much cotton in a day as de mule could plow. Whenever dey'd stop de plow at twelve o'clock, dem niggers was right dere to lay de hoe handles on de plow, an' dat's choppin'. All four could pick a bale of cotton a day. Whenever anybody say, 'Mr. Whitehead, I want a bale of cotton picked today,' he'd send dem fo' men an' dey could pick five hundred pounds apiece an' leave de sun still runnin'. Dey was pickers in dem days!

"Cose dey had to begin, an' all us got up 'fo' day. Twan't nothin' strange to be standin' in de fiel' by your plow waitin' for de sun to come up. Ev'body was early risers in dem days. Dey was pretty good to us, but ole Mr. Buck Brasefiel', what had a plantation 'jinin' us'n, was so mean to his'n dat twan't nothin' for 'em to run away. One nigger, Rich Parker, runned off one time an' whilst he gone he seed a hoodoo man, so when he got back Mr. Brasefiel' tuck sick an' stayed sick two or three weeks. Some of de darkies tole him, 'Rich been to de hoodoo doctor.' So Mr. Brasefiel' got up outten dat bed an' come a-yellin' in de fiel', 'You thought you had ole Buck, but by God he rose agin'. Dem niggers was so skeered, dey squatted in de fiel' jes' lack partridges, an' some of 'em whispered, 'I wish to God he had a-died.'

Jake Green, Livingston, Alabama

"'Twan't long atter dat come S'render, but dat nigger done lef' dere, an' didn't nobody know whar Parker was at. Some of de niggers done bought an' paid for dey mule an' me an' Pappy was rentin' an' wukkin' on sneers, when here come Parker, jes' hyared 'bout S'render. He say 'Why didn't somebody come tell me 'twas S'render?' Den he start a-singin'

> Slav'y chain, slav'y chain,
> Thank God a'mighty I'm free at las',
> Free at las', free at las',
> Thank God a'mighty I'm free at las'.

"But dat wan't none of Old Massa's niggers. He had one, do' call him John, an' hit come a traveler an' stayed all night. Ole Massa p'inted out John, an' said, 'He ain't never tole me a lie in his life.' De traveler bet Massa a hund'ed dollars 'ginst fo' bits he'd ketch John in a lie 'fo' he lef'. Next mawnin' at de table de mice was pretty bad, so de traveler caught one by de tail an' put him inside a kiver-lid dish what was settin' dere on de table, an' he tole Ole Massa tell John he could eat sumpin' out of ev'y dish atter dey got th'oo but dat kiver-lid one, an' not to take kiver offen hit. An' John said, 'Nossuh, I won't.' But John jes' nachully had to see what was in dat dish, so he raise de lid, an' out hopped de mouse. Den hyar come Old Massa an' axed John iffen he done what he tole him not to do, an' John 'nied hit. Den de traveler look in de dish an' de mouse wan't dere, an' he said, 'See dere, John been lyin' to you all de time, you jes' ain't knowed hit,' an' I reckon he right 'caze us had to lie."

CHARITY GRIGSBY

Interview with Charity Grigsby
—R.P. Tartt, [HW: Livingston?]

I KNOWS I'S EIGHTY FIVE BUT 'SPECTS I'S MORE DEN DAT

Charity Grigsby lives in a tumbledown shanty about nine miles from Livingston on the old Epes road. She was sewing on a quilt when I arrived; humming an old plantation song that ran:

> Angels in de water, walkin' by de light;
> Po' sinners stand in darkness an' cannot see de light!

A broad smile flowed across her black face as I entered the cabin. She placed her needle aside, exclaimed: "Law me, honey, I's always proud when de white folks drap aroun'; an' dat's directly so."

"Charity," I said, "I want you to tell me about slavery times."

She lowered her head in thought a moment, said:

"Honey, what would I tell?"

"Just all you remember, Charity."

And this is what she told:

"Honey, I was borned Charity Grigsby, but I married Nelson Grigory; ain't much 'stinguish in de names; but 'twas a little. My pappy was Dan'l Grigsby an' my mammy was Mary Moore. See, us belonged to Ol' Mister Jim Moore right up yonder 'bove Sumterville near Ramsey Station.

Charity Grigsby, Livingston, Alabama

"You goes up de Gainesville an' Livingston Road an' turns off at de cross road 'bout nine miles from Livingston. Den you goes due west. It ain't far from dere; bout six miles, I reckons. 'Twan't no big plantation; 'bout a dozen of us dere; an' Marse Jim didn't have no overseer lak de rest. He had dem boys of his'n what seed to us. Dey was John an' William an' Jim. Dey was all tol'able good to us; but dey would whoop us if we wasn't 'bedient; jes' like a mother raisin' a chile.

"I can't say how old I is; it's done got away from me; but I was a stroppin' gal durin' de war. I knows I's eighty-five an' I 'spects I's more dan dat. I's de mammy of 'leven chilluns; I knows dat; but ain't but five of dem a-livin'. As you knows, I lives wid two of dem; Mattie an' Evie. Dey treats me good. Hattie an' Ellen an' my boy lives in Bessemer. Dat is all my individual chilluns, but I's got a few others. I can't recollect much to tell; been a good while since de war; but when you calls it to my 'memberance I can think it up.

"Honey, dem nigger dogs; dey sho' did run. Sometimes dey kotched a nigger, but dey didn't never run me. I was in de house weavin' an' spinnin' lak mistus showed me; an' I didn't never get in no trouble wid nobody.

"An' den again, Marse Jim was purty tol'able good to us, but Mr. Ervin Lavendar was sho' mean to his niggers, an' his plantation warn't far from our'n. He had a pack of dogs what run de niggers; an' dem was skeery times, I tell you. Us didn't l'arn no schoolin' nor go nowhere nor have no corn shuckin' nor nothin'; jes' 'quired to stay in de cabins. I hyared 'bout Bre'r Rabbit an' hoodoo; but I never takes up no time wid dat foolishness; never seed no sense in it. Us got on all right 'thout dat.

"Some of de other niggers 'sides me was all de time in trouble, dough. Mr. Fulton, who lived clost to Mr. Lavendar, had a nigger-driver an' overseer name Sanders, an' I bet he was de meanest one of dem all. You know, honey, dey planted wheat fields in de fall in dem days an' cut it in de spring. It would come off in time 'nuff to make corn.

"Dere was a flock of birds lak blackbirds; only dey was wheat birds; an' dey went in droves an' fly way up yonder. Us had planks to slap together to keep de birds out er de wheat, because dey et it up.

"Well'm, one day Mr. Sanders tol' one of de women what was one of de sucklers on de place, dat if she wouldn't do what he axed her to dey was a black coffin over her haid. She 'fused him; so when he was loadin' his gun dere in de wheat fiel', he was holdin' de gun barrel propped under his chin, jes' so, an de other end settin' on de ground. Well sir, it went off an' he killed hisse'f stid of dat sucklin' woman; an' dat was a awful time, 'ca'se de niggers got skeered an' run, an' dey sot Mr. Lavendar's pack of nigger dogs on 'em. De dogs kotched some an' chewed 'em nigh 'bout to death. It warn' none of us, but it were close.

"Us laid low, didn't go out nowhere. Us wasn't 'lowed to; couldn't go to prayer meetin' or nothin'.

Charity Grigsby's House, Livingston, Alabama

"You ax what dat song I singin' when you come? Dat was all of it, an' dat's 'nuff fer me, 'ca'se it's true. What dey gwine to be no mo' fer? Jes':

> Angels in de water, walkin' by de light;
> Po' sinners stan' in darkness an' cannot se de light.

"I don' want no mo' myse'f; jes' dat; dat's all. How come you wants some mo'? Don't dat much satisfy you? But honey, de sun gettin' low an' my chilluns will soon be comin' from de swamps. Ain't no bread cooked fer 'em. I'll tell you some mo' when I gets my mind on it, 'ca'se it's been a good while since de war.

"Yas'm, us has 'nuff to eat; but if us could get anymore, us would lak it. You know how 'tis; can make out wid mighty little. Us eats greens; lookin' forward to roas' in years comin' in."

United States. Work Projects Administration

CHARLES HAYES

Interview with Charles Hayes
—*Mary A. Poole, Mobile*

SHO' I BELIEVES IN SPIRITS, SAYS CHARLES

"Mistis," said Charles Hayes from his porch in Maysville, near Mobile, Alabama, "I was a little bitty nigger when de war broke out, an' I belonged to Massa Ben Duncan who lived at Day's Landin' on de Alabamy Ribber.

"Marse Ben's house was de regulation plantation wid slave quarters. Most of de things us used was made raght dere on de plantation, sich as: beds, buckets, tools, soap, brogans, breeches, an' chairs. Our mattresses was either made outen cornshucks or cotton bolls. Us cooked on an open fireplace, an' eve'y Sadday night us would go to de big house for supplies. Marse Ben was good to his slaves an' he 'lowed dem to have a little plot of groun' nex' to de cabins whar dey could raise dere own little crop.

"My mammy was a fiel' han' an' my pappy was a mechanic an' he use to be de handy man aroun' de big house, makin' eve'thing f'um churns an' buckets to wagon wheels. My pappy also useta play de fiddle for de white folks dances in de big house, an' he played it for de colored frolics too. He sho could make dat thing sing.

"Us useta have all sorts of cures for de sick people, f'rinstance, us used de Jerusalem weed cooked wid molasses into a candy for to give to de chilluns to git rid of worms. Den us'd bile de root an' make a kinda tea for de stomach worms. You know de kinds dat little puppies an' little chilluns has dat eats all de food dat goes in to de stomach, an' makes de chile or dog eat plenty but don't git no benefits f'um all dey're eatin'. Horehound, dat growed wild in Clarke County, was used for colds. Mullen tea was used for colds an' swollen j'ints. Den dere was de life everlastin' tea dat was also good for colds and horse mint tea dat was good for de chills an' fevers. Co'se, Mistis, us niggers had a regular fambly doctah dat 'tended to us when we was sho 'nough down raght sick, but dese remedies I's tellin' you 'bout us used when warn't nothin' much ailin' us. It was always to de owner's interest, Mistis, to have de niggers in a good, healthy condition.

"Does I believe in spirits, you says? Sho I does. When Christ walked on de water, de Apostles was skeered he was a spirit, but Jesus told dem dat he warn't no spirit, dat he was as 'live as dey was. He tol' 'em dat spirits couldn't be teched, dat dey jus' melted when you tried to. So, Mistis, Jesus musta meant dat dere was sich a thing as spirits.

"Atter de war my pappy an' mammy stayed on de Duncan plantation en' worked on share crops. Dere was a school on de groun's for us slave chilluns, an' my gran'mammy, Salina Duncan, taught de bible, 'ca'se she was f'um Virginny an' had been learnt to read an' write by her Mistis up dere.

"My fus' wife was named Alice Bush, an' us had ten

chilluns; my second one was named Caroline Turner an' us didn't have but eight. Both my ole womens is daid now, white folks, an' I stays here wid one of my daughters. You see, my eyesight is almos' gone due to one day when I was a workin' in de forge, a hot piece of iron flew up an' landed in my eye. 'Twarn't long befo' it started to hurtin' in my udder eye. Now both is 'bout to give out."

United States. Work Projects Administration

LIZZIE HILL

Interview with Lizzie Hill
—*Gertha Couric*

THE STORY OF AUNT LIZZIE HILL

Aunt Lizzie Hill, 94 years of age, moved from the Spurlock plantation, four miles out, to the city of Eufaula about 20 years ago. She was of such vigorous constitution, that until recently, she carried on her regular occupation of laundress or "wash-'oman," as she calls herself. Too feeble to work regularly, she now is cared for by a niece with whom she lives.

Sitting before the fire in a rocking-chair, smoking a clay pipe—her neat clothing, snow-white hair and wrinkled, kindly face make a pleasing picture of contentment. Her mind is, apparently, unimpaired, and she readily responds to her recollections of slavery:

Lizzie Hill, Eufaula, Alabama

"Sho, Missey, I 'members 'bout it! I was most grown when freedom come. My Marster (Richard Dozier) and my Mistis was good to all dey niggers and dey raised me right. I had two little mistises 'bout as old as me, and I played wid dem all de time and slep' on a pallet in dey room ev'y night. Dey slep' on de big bed. My clothes was jes' as good and clean as deyrn, an I et what dey et."

The little girls, she explained, were about six and eight years old when this association began, and it continued until close of the war, when all were nearly grown.

"Atter freedom come," continued Aunt Lizzie, "Mammy moved to Cuthbert and tuk me erway fum Old Mistis; but I runned away and went back to Mistis, and walked all de fourteen miles down de big road at night—I runned most ob de way. Three times I done dat, but Mammy come and tuk me back to work in de field ev'y time. I wanted to stay wid Old Mistis. Dey called her 'Miss Everline' and ev'ybody liked her. Bofe my little mistises got mai'ed and den Old Marster and Old Mistis moved off to Texas, and I ain't eber seed none ob 'em no more. I's had a hard time workin' in de field since de war. Fo' freedom come, I nebber worked cep'n in de house—I was a 'house-girl' and didn't do no field work."

GABE HINES

Interview with Gabe Hines
—*Gertha Couric*

GABE WAS KIDNAPPED BY CARPETBAGGERS

Old Gabe had been long in this world—close to one hundred years. He had experienced much but one incident had out-lasted all the others—even the stroke that made him older and more feeble. That experience had caused Gabe and his "ole woman" to stray far from the fold and to walk all the way back to its shelter.

That was back in Reconstruction days, when he was not "bandy in his knees" and long before Anna left him alone in his cabin with just memories of earlier and happier days.

Gabe was "birthed in Cusseta, Georgia," the son of two faithful old slaves, Hetty and Gabe Hines, and they "all 'longed to Marsa William Shipp an' Miss Ma'y. He told his story thus:

"Endurin' of de Wah, I was big enough to be water toter on de plantation. No, Li'l Missy, I doan' 'zactly know how old I is 'ceptin' by de squeakin' an' achin' of my bones. I 'members lots 'bout doze days. Dem was happy times, Li'l Missy. Arter we all was freed, I went to Silver Run to live and dar I mahied Anna. She lef' me nine yeahs ago an' that broke the happiness. I miss her ev'whar, jes' keep a-missin' her though nine yeahs hev gone since dey tuk her from de cabin an' lef' her up thar on de hill. Dere's nights when de mis'ry in dese ol' bones jist gits past standin' an' on sich nights she come ter me and holp me wid de linnymint jes' as she useter do. But she caint stay long when she come.

"I was a-tellin' 'bout Silver Run. Arter we was mahied and was gittin' use to bein' free niggahs, an' happy in our cabin, one night a gen'ulman from de no'th was to see us an' he tol' us if we'd go wid him he'd pay us big wages an' gin us a fine house to boot.

"Fer two nights we sot dere by dat chimbly a-thinkin' a sight to do or to don't and ponderin' this way and t'other one. Den we 'cided to go. We lef ev'y thing dar 'ceptin' whut we tied up in a bandana han'chief, and we tied that onto a stick for de gen'ulman from de no'th wouldn't let us take no baggage. We was goin' to Columbus, Georgia, but we didn't know dat.

"Li'l Missy, when we got dar, whar he was a-takin' us, we foun' the big wages to be fifty cents a month, and dat fine house tu'ned out to be mo' like a stable. Instid of our cabin and gyarden and chickens and our trees, we had a turrible place, right out under the hot sun wid watah miles away down a hill. And he wan't no gent'man from de no'th!

"Missy, I nebber will be able to tell myself whut made us do hit no mo' den I'll ebber be able to tell how skeered I was one night when de wind howled an' de lightnin' was sprayin' ober de place an' de rain was so turrible hit was a-sobbin' in de fire. We knowed de debbil was ridin' de win' dat night.

"We was a-sittin' dar befo' de fire, me an' my ol' woman, when we heard a stompin' like a million horses had stopped outside de do'. We tipped to de do' an' peeked out an', li'l Missy, whut we seed was so turrible our eyes jes' mos' popped out our haid. Dere was a million hosses all kivered in white, wid dey eyes pokin' out and a-settin' on de hosses was men kivered in white too, tall as giants, an' dey eyes was a-pokin' out too. Dere was a leader an' he heldt a bu'nin' cross in his hand.

"When we seed dat, we fell on our po' knees, skeered mos' to def an' we axed de Great Marster to holp two po' ol' niggers an' holp 'em quick.

"De fust thing we knowed dem Ku Kluxes had de gen'man from de no'th out of his hidin' place 'hind our house an' a-settin' on one of dem hosses. Dey nebber spoke wid him. Dey jes' tuk him off somewhar, we nebber knowed whar, but he di'n't come back no mo'.

"Li'l Missy, we heard arterwards dat dis gen'lman from de no'th was no qual'ty a-tall. Dat he was de wu'st leadah of all de debilment bein' done; one of dem carpet-baggin' men.

"Nex' day arter de Ku Kluxes cotched dis man, his wife lef' Columbus in a hurry, sayin' she couldn't sociate wid de Columbus ladies 'caze dey was so po'. Dey wa po'! Dey is no denyin' that. We was all po' caze the Yankees done ruint Columbus. But, li'l Missy, dey's a big dif'ence in bein' po' an' qual'ty and' bein' jes po' white trash.

Gabe Hines, Eufaula, Alabama

"What did I do then? Well, li'l Missy, we lef' Columbus arter whut happen'd an' we walked to Eufaula, whar twas safe to be. For forty yeahs I w'uked for de city and Anna, she tuk in washin'. Endurin' dat time we was gettin' along pretty likely, when one day Gabriel blew his horn for Anna, and Gabe was lef' alone.

"My ol' woman's gone. Li'l Missy, mos' ev'y one I knowed is daid. Dis heah cabin ain' home to me no mo'. Hits lonely ev'y whar. Maybe I'd orter be thinkin' 'bout Canaan, but hits ol' times crowds dis ol' darkey's heart.

Li'l Missy, may be whin I gits to whar Anna is hit will be ol' times all ovah ag'in."

United States. Work Projects Administration

ADELINE HODGES

Personal interview with 'Aunt' Adeline Hodges
3 Frye Street, Mobile, Alabama
—*Ila B. Prine, [HW: Mobile?]*

HONGRY FOR PUN'KIN PIE

'Aunt' Adeline, a tall, gaunt, bright-skinned Negro woman, lives on Frye St., Mobile, Ala. The day I called she was nodding in a cane bottom rocking chair on a wide porch that extended across the front of a cottage almost hidden in a grove of giant oaks. She opened her eyes, which were covered by a pair of steel-rimmed glasses with one lens badly cracked. The news that a search was being made for old people who had lived during slavery days acted like an electric shock on the old woman, who immediately sat up straight and said:

"Lor, yes'm, I libed in dose days, and I tells you I 'members all 'bout dem. Do come in and set down. De fust white people I b'longed to was a man named Jones, who was a colonel in de war, but I can't tell you much 'bout dem, 'caze I was jes' a li'l gal den. I was jes' big 'nuff to tote water to de fiel' to de folks wukking and to min' de gaps in de fence to keep de cattle out when dey was gatherin' de crops. I don't 'spec' you knows anything 'bout dose kind of fences. Dey was built of rails and when dey was gatherin' de crops dey jes' tuk down one section of de fence, so de wagons could git through.

"A'ter de war broke out ole Mister Jones went off to hit, and I 'members de day he lef'. He come to de fiel' to tell all de han's goodbye, wid a big white plume on his hat. Dat was in Bolivar County, Mississippi. A'ter ol' Mister Jones lef' for de war, den de nigger drivers an' oberseer begun to drive us 'round lack droves of cattle. Every time dey would hyar de Yankees was coming dey would take us out in de woods and hide us. Finally dey sold us a'ter carrying us away from Bolivar County. Some of us was sold to people in Demopolis, Alabama, an' Atlanta, Georgia, an' some to folks in Meridian and Shubuta, Mississippi. I don't any more know whar my own folks went to dan you does.

"I 'members afore leaving ole Mister Jones' place how dey grabbed up all de chillun dat was too li'l to walk and puttin' us in wagons. Den de older folks had to walk, and dey marched all day long. Den at night dey would strike camp. I has seen de young niggers what was liable to run away wid dere legs chained to a tree or de wagon wheels. Dey would rake up straw and throw a quilt ober hit and lie dat way all night, while us chillun slep' in de wagons.

"When us come to de big river at Demopolis, Alabama, I 'members seein' de big steamboats dere, and dey said dat de sojers was goin' away on dem. Hit was in Demopolis us was sold, and a man name Ned Collins of Shubuta, Mississippi, bought me."

'Aunt' Adeline said that the houses the slaves lived in on the Jones plantation were board houses, and that Mr.

Jones owned a big plantation and lots of slaves. She said that they had home-made beds, nailed to the walls, with mattresses made out of shucks.

After having been sold to Mr. Collins, of Shubuta, Mississippi, 'Aunt' Adeline said that life was very hard, not so much for herself, but she saw how hard the other slaves worked. She was the house girl and helped clean house, wash dishes, and take care of the children. After finishing that work, she had to spin thread. Each day she would have to spin so many cuts, and if she did not finish the required number, she was punished.

She said that her mistress kept the finished work on top of a large wardrobe, and 'Aunt' Adeline said that many times she would steal a cut of thread off that wardrobe to complete the day's task to keep from being punished.

As she grew older she did have to go to the field and pick cotton. 'Aunt' Adeline does not remember it pleasantly. She said:

"I jes' hates to hab to weigh anything today, 'caze I 'members so well dat each day dat de slaves was given a certain number of pounds of cotton to pick. When weighing up time come and you didn't hab de number of pounds set aside, you may be sho' dat you was goin' to be whupped. But hit wasn't all bad times 'caze us did hab plenty to eat, 'specially at hog killin' time. Dey would hab days ob hog killin' and de slaves would bake dere bread and come wid pots, pepper, and salt. A'ter cleanin' de hogs, dey would gib us de livers and lights, and us would cook dem ober a fire out in de open and hit sho' was good eatin'. De usual 'lowance a week of pickled pork was six or seven pounds, and iffen you had a big family of chillun dey gib you more. Den dey gib you a peck of meal, sweet 'taters, sorghum syrup, and plenty of buttermilk. At Christmas times, dey gib you extra syrup to make cakes wid and sweet 'taters to make 'tater pone. And, Lor', dey would hab big cribs of pun'kins. Hit makes me hongry to think 'bout dem good ol' pun'kin pies.

"And did dey raise chickens? You knows in Mississippi dat de minks was bad 'bout killin' dem. I 'members one time de minks got in de chicken house and killed nearly every chicken on de place. Ole Mister Jones had de cook to clean and cook dem, and he come out in de fiel' an' eat wid dem to let de slaves know dat hit was all right. Den us had dem good ol' cushaws and lye hominy, too.

"De clothes was made out ob homespun in one piece. I 'members I allus had mine split up de side so I could git 'bout in a hurry. De women had pantalettes made and tied to dere knees to wear in de fields to keep de dew off dere legs. De shoes was made of cow hide and was called red russets. De way dey got dem darker was to take a hog 'gristle' and hang up in de chimbley. When hit git full of soot, we rub de shoes wid dat. Den dey used de darker shoes for dere Sunday best.

"You asked me about huntin'? Lor', yes dey hunted in dem times. Up in dem swamps in Mississippi dere was bears as big as cows, and deers aplenty. Dey bofe was bad about comin' in de corn fiel's and tearin' down de corn. You could hyar dem at nights out in de fiel's. Dey also caught plenty of possums and coons.

"Of course, us got sick, but dey had de doctor. In dose days de doctor would cup you and bleed you. I seen a many a person cupped. De doctor had a li'l square lookin' block of wood wid tiny li'l knifes attached to hit. On top was a trigger lack is on a gun, and de doctor would put de block of wood at de nape of dere neck an' pull dat trigger. Den he hab a piece of cotton wid somepin' on hit to stop de blood when he had cupped you long 'nough. Dey would allus gib us calamus (calomel) to clean us out, and den de nex' mawnin' dey gib us a big bowl of gruel made out ob meal and milk. Den us'd be all right.

"De slaves warn't 'lowed to go to church, but dey would whisper 'roun' and all meet in de woods and pray. De only time I 'members my pa was one time when I was a li'l chile, he set me on a log by him an' prayed, an' I knows dat was whar de seeds ob religion was planted in my min'. Today I's happy to tell folks 'bout Jesus and thank Him for His goodness to me. Hit won't be long twell I meet Him face to face and thank Him."

CAROLINE HOLLAND

Interview with Caroline Holland
—*Mabel Farrior*

CAROLINE HOLLAND HAD MANY MASTERS

"Yassuh, I was a slave," spoke Aunt Carry from her vine-shaded porch at No. 3 Sharpe Street, Montgomery, Alabama. "I was borned in 1849 on Mr. Will Wright's plantation on the Mt. Meigs road. Massa Will had a big slave house an' us niggers sho' use to have a good time playin' 'roun' down at de slave quarters. We had a row of houses two stories high, an' dey was filled wid all sorts of niggers. When I was twelve year old, I was made nu'ss fer my mistis's little girl an' at de fus' I couldn't do nothin' but rock de cradle. I didn't know how to hol' de baby. Us niggers had gardeens (guardians) dat look 'atter us lak dey did atter de hosses and cows and pigs.

"One night atter we had all gone to bed I heered a noise at de window, an' when I look up dere was a man a climbin' in. He was a nigger. I could tell eben do I could scarce see him, I knowed he was a nigger. I could hear my mistis a breathin', an' de baby was soun' asleep too. I started to yell out but I thought dat de nigger would kill us so I jes' kep' quiet. He come in de window, an' he see us a sleepin' dere, an' all of a sudden I knowed who it was. 'Jade,' I whispers, 'What you a doin' here?' He come to my bed and put his rough han' ober my mouf.

"Listen you black pickaninny, you tell em dat you saw me here an' I'll kill you,' he say, 'I th'ow yo' hide to de snakes in de swamp. Now shet up.'

"Wid dat he went to de dresser an' taken mistis' money bag. Atter dat he went to de window an' climb down de ladder an' I didn't do nothin' but shake myself nearly to death fum fright. De nex' day de oberseer an' de pattyrollers went a searchin' th'ough de slave quarters an' dey foun' de money bag under Jade's cot. Dey tuk him an' whupped him for near fifteen minutes. We could hear him holla way up at de big house. Jade, he neber got ober dat whuppin'. He died three days later. He was a good nigger, 'peer to me lak, an' de bes' blacksmith in de whole county. I ke'pa-wonderin' whut made him want ter steal dat purse. Den I foun' out later dat he was a goin' to pay a white man ter carry him ober de line to de No'thern States. Jade jus' had too big ideas fo' a nigger. I us'ta see Jade's ghos' a walkin' out in de garden in de moonlight; sometime he sit on de fence an' look at his ole cabin, den sometimes he stroll off down de cotton fiel'. When de Lawd git th'ough a punishin' him fo' a stealin' dat money, I guess he won't make us no mo' visits. He jus' go right on in heaben. Dat's what ghos'tes is, you know; peoples dat can't quite git in heaben, an' dey hadda stroll 'roun' little longer on de outside repentin'.

"Soon atter dat my gardeen tuk me to Tallasse when de massa died. My gardeen was a good man. He was always a-makin' speeches fo' de slaves to stay under bondage till dey was twenty-one. One dey he was in front of a sto' talkin' 'bout de slaves an' a man come up to him an' said he don't like de way Capt. Clanton talk (dat was my gardeen's name). Capt. Clanton ask him whut he goin' ter do 'bout it an' de man tuk out a pistol an' kil't de Cap'n raght dere on de spot.

"Den I was sold to another man, a Mr. Williamson, 'bout de time de war broke loose, an' Massa Williamson tuk me ober ter lib wid some mo' peoples. He said he had mo' slaves dan he could take keer of. Dis was de Abernathy plantation. While de massa was a standin' in de slave quarters a takin' to Mr Abernathy, I noticed a boy wid a bad eye. I didn't lak him at all an' I tol' de massa I don't wanna stay, kaze I didn't lak de way dat boy Lum wid de bad eye looked at me. Den Mr. Abernathy brung a boy 'bout sebenteen year old; a big strong lookin' boy named Jeff. He say 'Jeff, look out after Carry here. Don't let her git into no trouble.' Fum dat time on till 'bout five year ago, Jeff he always look after me, kaze atter de war I ma'ied him. Now I ain't got nobody but myself."

JANE HOLLOWAY

Interview with Jane Holloway
—*Preston Klein, Opelika, Alabama*

DEY BRUNG WHUPPIN'S ON DEYSELVES

Jane Holloway was ill. For weeks she had been in bed, and the untidy condition of her cabin brought profuse apologies when I entered.

"Jane, do you remember me?" I asked.

"I don't know, honey. I been sick so long wid de fluse I can't 'member much of anything," she answered peering up at me from her pillow. Suddenly she smiled, "Shucks. Co'se I 'members you, honey. Your daddy sho' was good to my boys. Watt worked for him so long. Res' yourself in dat cheer and I'll tell you all about myself and slavery times what I can recollect.

"I'se all alone now 'ceppen for my grandson. He ain't but twelve and he can't ho'p much. But I guess I got no right to complain I guess I done got me plenty outa life.

"I was borned up in North Alabama. My mammy was Carrie Holloway and my pappy was Traylor Holloway. I had a brother Maryland. Dere nebber was but de two of us. Us lived in a mud and log house, jes' one room but it sho' had a big fireplace. Us had a good old time den, effen us jes' had knowed it, 'caze us was always fed good. Dey had long wooden troughs what dey poured our bread and milk in and us eat it wid a wooden spoon. When dey yell, 'Chillun, chillun! Bread!' you bet we jes' burnt de wind getting dere, 'caze us was always hongry.

"We had high tester beds in all de houses, what was 'bout a mile from de Big House. It had four rooms and was all planked up. Mr. Billy Taylor was mighty good to his niggers. He didn't have so many slaves, he jes' had a little plantation. Our oberseer was good, too. He had to whip some of dem sometimes, but dey wouldn't work. Dey brung it all on deyselves.

Jane Holloway, Opelika, Alabama

"When de Yankees come enduring de war, de men come arunning and a screaming dat de Yankees coming. And dey did come on horseback and took all our provisions what was in de smokehouse. Dey took everything we had in de way of victuals and stock, too.

"I j'ined de church when I was ten years old, 'caze

I was trying to live right and do what de Bible said. De white folks had deir services in de morning, and in de evening would let us niggers have ourn."

Jane forgot her misery long enough to come out to the porch of her comparatively comfortable cabin and she was "plumb proud" to have her "picture took."

JOSEPH HOLMES

I

Personal interview with Joseph Holmes
Grand Avenue, Prichard, Alabama
—Ila B. Prine, Mobile, Alabama

DEY KEP' NIGGERS IN GOOD CONDITION TO SELL

S tanding in the middle of the road at Prichard, suburb of Mobile, and gesticulating while talking to a small group of interested listeners an old Negro man ended his talk to the small gathering and punctuated his last sentence with a spat of tobacco.

"No'm," he continued after I had put in my appearance and asked him a question, "I doesn't know whether I was a slave, but jus' de same I seed Gen'l Grant's army when it went th'ough Virginny. Jus' as sho' as you is standin' dar, lady, I seed dem mens all dressed in blue suits, a-marching' side by side, gwine down de road pas' our place. It tuk 'em three days to go by our house.

"An' I remembers when dem Yankees came to our ole Mistis' house an' take a ladder an' clumb up to de roof an' tear de boards outter de ceilin' to git dem big hams an' shoulders my white folks done had hid up dar. When de Yankees find dat stuff dey give it all to de niggers. Den atter de solgers lef' ole Miss called us to her an' tol' us we was free, but for us to give back some of de meat an' things dat de Yankees done give us, 'ca'se she didn't have nothin' to eat 'roun' de place. 'Course we was glad to do it, 'ca'se Mistis sho' was good to us.

"I remembers ebery Sunday mawnin' dat she'd make de older slaves bring all de little niggers up to de big house, so she could read de Bible to 'em, and den she give us plenty of dem good biscuits and taters dat Susanne cook for us. She'd say: 'Git 'roun' dere, Susanne, and he'p dem little niggers' plates.' I really thought Mistis was a angel.

"Talkin' 'bout niggers bein' free. Ole Miss tol' us was free, but it was ten or twelve years atter de surrender befo' I knowed whut she meant. I was a big boy goin' to school befo' I had an understandin' as to what she meant.

"Ole Miss taught de niggers how to read an' write an' some of 'em got to be too good at it, 'ca'se dey learned how to write too many passes so's de pattyrollers wouldn't cotch 'em, an' on dem occasions was de onlyes' times dat I ever seed one of our niggers punished.

"Mistis never 'lowed no mistreatin' of de slaves, 'case dey was raisin' slaves for de market, an' it wouldn't be good bizness to mistreat 'em. Lor' Miss, my white folks was rich; dey had as many as five or six hundred niggers; men, women an' chilluns. De plantation was big, but I doesn't remember how many acres it was, but I does remember dat de cabins was all built in rows, an' dere was streets laid out among de cabins. De chimneys was built outten dirt an' sticks, an' you know up in Virginny it got powerful cold, so when dey built de cabins dey th'owed dirt up under 'em to keep de wind an' snow out.

"I was bawn in Henry County, Virginny, near Danville, an' I's been to Vicksburg an' Petersburg a many a time wid my pappy to de wheat an' 'bacca market. Lor', honey, Virginny is de bes' place on earth for good eaten' an' good white folks. If anybody tells you dat de white folks was mean to dere niggers, dey neber come from Virginny, 'case us was too near de free states, an' I done already tol' you dat dey raised niggers to sell an' dey kep' 'em in good condition. In dose days white folks an' black folks was black folks. Jus' lak Booker T. Washington was a riber between de niggers of dis generation an' learnin'. He had all dat was fine an' good, an' he give de bes' to his people iffen dey would take it. Dat was de way wid de white folks den; dey didn't do no whuppin'.

"I's de onlyes' rat lef' in de pond, an' 'case I ain't hung in de smoke house, folks thinks I's not as old as I say I is, but chile, I's been here a long time. I 'members how black Sam useta preach to us, an' when I growed up I useta think warnt nobody Christians cep'n us Babtists, but I know better now, an' de longer I lives de mo' I realizes dat de churches go 'way 'case dey leaves off de ordinances of God, although us has a Bible an' mo' Christian readin' dan ever befo'.

"My mammy's name was Eliza Rowlets an' my pappy's was Joseph Holmes. My pappy had de same name as de peoples dat owned him an' my gran'mammy name was Lucy Holmes. Gran'mammy Holmes lived to be over a hundred years old, an' she was de fust pusson I ever seed daid. In dem days it tuk three days to bury a pusson, 'case dey dug de graves as deep as de corpse was tall.

"Land sakes a-livin', us had great times, an' I forgot to tell you dat us had home-made beds wid two sides nailed to de wall an' de mattresses was made outen wheat straw.

"As for huntin' I done plenty of it an' one thing I got to git forgiveness for was when I lef' Virginny, I lef' 'bout fifty or sixty snares set to cotch rabbits an' birds.

"My mammy had eight chilluns an' we was raised in pairs. I had a sister who come along wid me, an' iffen I jumped in de river she done it too. An' iffen I go th'ough a briar patch, here she come along too.

"'Bout de fruit; it makes my mouth water to think about dem cheese apples, dat was yaller lak gold, an' dose Abraham apples, an' de cherry tree as big as dese oaks here. I's eaten many a big sugar and sweetheart cherry. But dere was another kind called de Gorilla dat growed as big as de yaller plums down dis way. Now let me tell you somp'n 'bout Virginny; 'dey had dere laws 'bout drink. Dey had de bes' peach an' cherry brandy an' mos' any kin' you eber heared of, but dey didn't 'low you to make drink outten anything you could make bread wid; sich as corn or rye. Us had our brandy same as you would coffee, 'case it was cold, an' some mawnin's my pappy would git de brandy out an' my mammy would putt a little water an' sugar wid it an' gib it to us chilluns. Us neber thought nothin' 'bout drinkin'. I kinda believes lak dat ole infidel Ingersoll who said dat anything dat was a custom was dere religion.

"Now you axed about hog-killin' time? Dat was de time of times. For weeks de mens would haul wood an' big rocks, an' pile 'em together as high as dis house, an' den have several piles lak dat 'roun' a big hole in de groun' what had been filled wid water. Den jus' a little atter midnight, de boss would blow de ole hawn, an' all de mens would git up an' git in dem pig pens. Den dey would sot dat pile of wood on fire an' den start knockin' dem hogs in de haid. Us neber shot a hog lak us does now; us always used an axe to kill 'em wid. Atter knockin' de hog in de haid, dey would tie a rope on his leg an' atter de water got to de right heat, fum dose red-hot rocks de hog would be throwed in an' drug aroun' a while, den taken out an' cleaned. Atter he was cleaned he was cut up into sections an' hung up in de smoke house. Lawsie, lady, dey don't cure meat dese days; dey jus' uses some kind of liquid to brush over it. We useta have sho' 'nuff meat.

"Den come cawnshuckin' time. My goodness, I would jus' love to be dar now. De cawn would be piled up high an' one man would git on dat pile. It was usually a kinda nigger foreman who could sing an' git de work outten de niggers. Dis fo'man would sing a verse somp'n lak dis:

> Polk and Clay went to war,
> Polk come back wid a broken jaw.

Den all de niggers would sing back at him wid a kinda shoutin' sound. Near 'bout all de times de fo'man made up his own songs, by pickin' dem outen dat shuckin'! It war de jug dat dey brung aroun' eve'y hour. Dat's de onlyes' time de slaves really got drunk.

"In dem ole days I went to plenty of dances an' candy pullin's durin' de Yule season, but I doesn't do dat no mo'. I's a preacher an' when I fus' lef' Virginny, I come to Georgy an' stayed dar twenty years whar I kicked up plenty of dus'. I even taught school dar. Den I come to Alabamy an' lived in Evergreen for 'bout twenty mo' years. Since I been in Mobile I's worked for sich men as ole Simon, Damrich, an' Van Antwerp, an' all dere chilluns has been in dese here arms of mine. I's been a square citizen an' dere hasn't been a time dat I is had to call on nobody but Uncle Sam when ole man 'pression cotched me. But thank de Lawd I is still able to git about an' have all my senses 'cep' my eye-sight, an' it's jus' a little po'ly. I is got all my teeths 'cep' one, an' my mammy was always proud of my hair. See how silky an' fine it is? Not quite white, dough. I hope I lives long enough for it to turn white as snow. I think St. Peter will lak it better dat way."

II
Personal interview with Joseph Holmes
Grand Avenue, Prichard, Alabama
—Ila B. Prine, Mobile, Alabama

TWELVE YEARS 'TWELL I UNDERSTOOD SURRENDER

In the middle of the road near Prichard, an incorporated suburb of Mobile, stood an aged Negro man, gesticulating as he told a tale of other days to a small audience. Tall, straight, with gray hair and mustache, he was a picturesque figure. He does not know whether he was born in slavery, he said, but he knows his age to be about eighty-one.

"I doesn't know whether I was a slave, but jes' de same I seed Gineral Grant's army when hit went th'ough Virginny," he said "Jes' as sho' as yo' is standin' dar, lady, I seed him, and I seed dem men all dressed in dem blue suits a-marchin' side by side, gwine down de road pas' our place. Hit tuk dem three days tuh git pas' our house.

"An' does I 'member when dem Yankees come tuh Ol' Mistiss house an' tuk a ladder an' clim' up tuh de roof an' tear de boards outta de ceilin' tuh git dem big hams an' shoulders dey had hid up dar? I sho' does. De women folks makes de slaves hide wid de meat; an' when dem Yankees fin' dat stuff dey jes' gib hit all tuh de niggers, an' I 'members too, how Ol' Miss calls us all to her atter dey lef' an' tole us dat us was free, but she tole us dat us hab tuh gib back ob de meat an' 'serves 'case she didn't hab a bit tuh eat. 'Cose we was glad tuh do hit 'case Ol' Miss sho' was good tuh her slaves.

"I 'members ebery Sunday mawnin' dat she made de older slaves bring all de little niggers up to her big white, two-story house, so she could read de Bible to us, an' den she gib us plenty dem good biscuits an' 'taters dat she had de cook, Susanne, cook for us. She'd say 'Git 'roun' dere, Susanne, an' he'p dem li'l niggers plates,' I, railly thought Ol' Miss was an angel.

"Talkin 'bout niggers bein' freed, Ol' Miss tole us us was free, but hit was ten or twelve years atter de Surrender, befo' I knowed whut she was talkin' 'bout. I was a big boy goin' to school befo' I had any understanin' as tuh whut she meant.

"Ol' Miss taught de niggers how to read an' write, an' some ob dem got to be too 'ficient wid de writin', 'case dey larn how tuh write too many passes so de pattyrollers wudn't git dem. Dat was de onliest time I ebber knowed Ol' Miss tuh hab de slaves punished.

"Ol' Miss nebber 'lowed no mistreatin' de slaves, case dey was raisin' slaves for de market, an' hit wouldn't be good business to mistreat 'em. Lor' mah white folks was rich; dey had as many as five or six hundred niggers, men, women and chillun. De plantation was big but I don't 'member how many acres I does 'member de cabins was all built in rows, an' streets was laid out 'tween de cabins. De chimbeys was built outta dirt an' sticks, an' sticks, an' yo' know up in Virginny hit got turrible cold an' de snow would pile up, so when de cabins was built, de men th'owed dirt up under de house to keep de snow an' cold out. Yo' might think dat dirt would wash out from under de house, but hit didn't. Hit jes' made dem so warm an' com'fo'ble we did'nt suffer.

"Dat was de way wid de white folks den; dey didn't do no whippin' an' mistreatin' ob de slaves. Oh, once in a while Ol' Miss might slap de cook's face an' tell her tuh bear down 'roun' dere, an' if she wanted de servin' boys to hurry, she would say 'Cutch hit,' meanin' fer dem to cut some steps an' git 'bout in a hurry.

"I's de ol'est rat in de pon', an' 'case I ain't hung in de smokehouse, folks think I's not as ol' as I says I is, but chile, I's been heah. I 'members how Sam useta to preach to us, when we was at Ol' Miss's place, an' when I growed up, I 'members how I useta think nobody was a Christian 'ceptin' us Baptists, but I knows better now. An' de longer I lib de mo' I realize dat de chu'ches go away 'case dey leabes off de ordinances ob God, 'tho us has got de Bible an' mo' Christian litterchoor dan eber befo'.

"My ma's name was 'Liza Rowlets, an' mah daddy's name was Joseph Holmes. My daddy had de same name as de people whut owned him, an' my gran'ma's name was Lucy Holmes. Gran'ma Lucy libed to be a hundred yeahs old, an' she was de fust pusson I ebber seed daid. Hit tuk three days tuh bu'y a pusson den, 'case dey dug de graves as deep as yo' is tall, which means mo' than five feet deep. Lor' sakes a-livin' us had great times. I forgot tuh tell yo' dat us had home-made beds wid two sides nailed tuh de wall, an' de mattresses was made outta wheat straw. Dat's 'minds me dat dere wa'n't no pore cattle in dem times, 'case yo' could go whar dey thresh de wheat an' git all de straw yo' wanted an' feed de dry cattle on hit. An' you wouldn't believe de fruit us did hab! Yo don't nebber see de like down dis way. Sich as apples, cherries, quinces, peaches an' pears.

"As fer huntin', I done plenty of it, an' one thing I got

to git forgiveness fer was when I lef' Virginny, I lef' 'bout sixty or seventy snares set to ketch rabbits an' birds.

"My ma had eight chillun an' we was raised in pairs. I had a sister who come along wid me, an' if I jumped in de ribber tuh swim, she did hit too; if I clum' a tree, or went th'ough a briar patch, she done hit right behin' me. Ma wanted to know why her clo's was so tore up, an' when dey was pretty, we'd make hit right wid Ma by havin' a rabbit or coon wid us, an' sometimes a mud turtle. An' as fer 'possums an' coons, us ketch dem in plenty.

"'Bout de fruit, hit makes mah mouf watah tuh think 'bout dem cheese apples dat was yaller lac' gold, an' dose Abraham apples de lack of which ain't now to be had. An' dose cherry trees as big as dese oaks, wid long limbs an' big sugar an' sweetheart, an' black heart cherries. Den dere was annudder kin' of cherry called de gorilla, dat was roun' an' growed as big as de yaller plums down dis way.

"Now, let me tell yo' sumpin' 'bout Virginny. Hit had hits own law 'bout drink. Dey made de bes' peach an' cherry brandy an' mos' any kin' yo' ebber heerd ob, 'ceptin' dey didn't 'low yo' to make drink out ob anythin' you could make into bread. Now yo' understan's, sich as corn and rye.

"Us had our brandy same as yo' would coffee, 'case hit was cold an' some mawnin's us would git up an' de snow would be halfway up de do', an' de men would hab to ditch hit out, so us could git out of de house. On dem rail cold mawnin's my daddy would git de brandy out an' my ma wud put a li'l water an' sugar wid hit an gib to us chillun. An' den she'd take some in her mouf' an' put hit in de baby's mouf an' hit wud open hits eyes an' stamp hits foot rail peart lack.

"Us nebber thought nothin' of drinkin'. I kinda believes lack dat ol' infidel, Ingersoll, who said dat anythin' dat was de custom, was de religion.

"Folks was a heap kinder-hearted den dey is now, 'case dey kep' big dogs to hunt up people los' in de snow. Dey all seemed mo' happy 'case dey was all busy. At night instid of wastin' dey time, dey wud go tuh de big house an' spin an' weave an' make clo's.

"I kin hyar dat ol' loom hummin' now, an' see great cards ob cloth comin' out, an' dem was clo's den dat was made from hit. Hit tuck fire tuh git dem offen' yo' dey was so strong. I doesn't 'member whut dey used fer dye, but I knows dey used copperas as sizin' to hol' de colors. Some of de cloth was dyed red, blue an' black. I jes' can't 'member 'bout de dye, but dey used copperas. 'Dat was the qualification of de intelligence ob de primitive age', in usin' dat copperas. Dey not only made our clo's, but also made out hats. Of co'se dey wa'n't very hatty, but was mo' cappy. Dey made 'em wid tabs ober de ears, an' to tie under de chin, an' was dey warm, I'll say!

"Now, when yo' axes 'bout hawg killin' time, dat was de time! Fer weeks de men would haul wood and big rocks, an' pile hit all together as high as dat house; den hab sev'ral piles like dese 'roun' a big hole in de groun' whut had been filled wid watah. Den jes' a li'l atter mid-night de boss would blow de ol' horn, an' all de men would git up an' git in dem hog pens. Den dey would set dat pile of wood on fire, an' den start knockin' dem hawgs in de haid. Us nebber shot a hawg like dey does now. Us allus used an ax to kill 'em wid.

"Atter knockin' de hawg in de haid, dey would tie a rope on hits leg, an atter de water got to de right heat from dose red hot rocks whut had been pushed out ob dat pile ob nu'in wood into de watah, dey wud th'ow de hog in an' drag hit aroun' awhile, an' take him out an' hab him clean in 'bout three pair o' minutes. Atter he was clean dey hung him up, an' den later cut him up an' hung him in de smoke house, an' smoke him wid great oak logs. Huh, dey don't cu'ah meat now, dey jes' use sum kinda brush an' liquid, but dey don't hab meat lack us did.

"Den come co'shuckin' time. Mah goodness, I jes' would love to be dere now. De co'n would be piled up high an' one man would git on dat pile. Hit usually was one who was kinda niggah fo'man dat could sing an' get de wuck out of de odder niggers. Dis fo'man would sing a verse somethin' lack dis:

> Polk an' Clay went to War,
> An' Polk come back wid a broken jar.

"Den all de niggers would sing back to him, an' hallo, a kinder shoutin' soun'. Ginerally dis fo'man made up his songs by pickin' dem up from whut he had heard white folks tell of wars. But Miss yo' know whut was de motor powah of dat co'n shuckin'? Hit was de ol' jug dat was brung 'roun' ebery hour. Dat's de onliest time any ob de slaves railly got drunk.

"I wish I could 'member dose ol' songs, but all dat hallo done lef' me, 'case de onliest singin' I hears now is de good ol' sisters singin' an' sayin' 'Amen.'

"In days gone by I went to plenty of dances an' candy pullin's but I doesn't do dat any mo'. I's a preacher, an' when I fu'st lef' Virginny I come to Georgia an' stayed dere twenty yeahs, an' I kicked up a plenty of dust in Georgia. I eben taught school an' built a plenty of chu'ches dere. Den I come on to Alabammy, an' libed in Evergreen fo' about twenty mo' yeahs, an' I built a two-story brick chu'ch dere. Since I's been in Mobile I's wu'ked by dat Bienville Squah for twenty-eight years, for sich men as ol' man Simon, Damrich, an' Van Antwerp, an' all dere chillun has been in dese arms. I's been a squah citizen an' dere hasn't been but one time in mah life I's had to call on anybody, an' dat was when I had tuh call on Uncle Sam when ol' man Depression got me. But thank God I's still able to be 'bout an' have all my faculties, 'ceptin' my eyesight is a li'l porely. I still has all mah teeth, 'ceptin' one, an' my ma allus tuck pride in mah haih, yo' see how fine an' silky hit is, an' hit ain't snow white yit. Dere is one thing to be thankful fer. Dat is 'case I's so near home."

JOSH HORN

Interview with Josh Horn
—*Ruby Pickens Tartt, Livingston, Alabama*

CHASING GUINEA JIM, THE RUNAWAY SLAVE

Seven miles East from Livingston on State Road No. 80, thence Left two miles via a dim road through the woods to a cultivated section, the beginning of a large plantation area, stands the old-timey cabin of Josh Horn, a well known and influential figure in the colored community. Vigorous and active despite his more than 80 years, Josh exemplifies the gentleness with which time deals with those dwelling in a healthful spot and living the simple lives of a rural people. I found him nodding on his front steps.

"Josh," I said, "I've come to get you to tell me some old war-time stories, and I want to ask you some questions about you and Alice and how you-all are getting along. I just want to know all about you and your family as far back as you can remember."

"All right, Miss Ruby, I's glad to tell you what I knows," said Josh, "and it ain't gonna be a lot of fibbin', but jes' lak everything was. I's telling you lak you axed me.

"Now, 'bout how us is getting along. I's telling you de troof, ef I was took 'fore God, I'd say jes' lak I's saying now, ef my chillun ever et a mouful dat wasn't honest, dey et it somewhar else, 'ca'se I ain't ever stole a mouful somepin' t'eat for 'em in all my life. It's honest vittles dey et, and varmints I's killed in de woods, 'ca'se us raised chillun fast, and us had a heap of 'em, sixteen, if I 'members right, and soon's I found out dat I could help feed 'em dat way, I done a heap of hunting. And everybody knows I's a good hunter. Alice used to make me go every Friday night; den us always had a 'possum or two for Sunday."

"Why," I asked, "didn't you go Saturday night?"

"Well, I'll tell you," Josh said, "Alice is a good Christian woman, and she knowed I'd hunt mighty nigh all night, and she didn't want nobody see me coming in Sunday morning wid no gun and no dogs; so I went every Friday night and went in de week too, and dat holp a lot to feed de chillun. I don't owe nobody, not a nickel.

"I lak to got in debt, when de Government come in and tried to help us wid dat cotton doings. Dey cut it down so on me, tell I couldn't make nothing; but I's getting on all right now, and so is my chillun. Us is got fourteen living, and dey's all been to school, but ain't but one been to Booker Washington's school, but dey kin all read and write, and some of 'em teaching school out here in de country. De doctor, he come clear out here to see us, 'ca'se I always pays him. He jes' here wid Alice last night. It's nine mile and two of dem's back here in de woods through Marse Johnnie's place, but he come when us went atter him 'bout midnight, and dat's a comfort to know he come."

I asked, what was the matter with Alice.

"Well, I'll tell you, Miss Ruby. She was back dere wid me in de kitchen, and I got through eating and I come out and set down in de swinger to git some air. De moon was shining, and Alice come out, saying loud as she could: 'Who is you? Who is you?' De chillun run to her wid a lamp and I run, and 'twan't nobody dere. Well, Alice said 'twas a big man standing right 'side her dressed in black, and she called it Death. Us couldn't do nothing wid her, and she didn't know nobody, me nor de chillun, so I went to Livingston atter Dr. McCain, and he come and set wid her 'bout a hour. He said 'twas de 'cute 'digestion or somepin' lak dat. I knowed 'twan't no sperrit; I don't b'lieve in nothing lak dat."

"Well," I said, "I don't know, Josh, I've been hearing some ghost tales that freeze the blood in my veins."

"Yassum," said Josh, "if you wants to hear ghost tales, I kin sho tell 'em, ca'se I seed dis here wid my own eyes. 'Tain't no made-up nothing, needer; jes' somepin' I seed jes' lak I tells you.

"Green Hale and Isham Mathews b'longed to New Hope church, and de Reverend Bird Hall pastored dere. Dey axed me down to hear him preach one night, and us three, me and Green and Isham, was riding along side and side. I's riding a mule, but it was a fast mule, and Green couldn't keep up, en Isham said: 'Somebody been hunting.' I looked up and 'twas a sapling right 'cross de road. He said, 'Fellow oughten leave nothing lak dat. When de moon git low, it hit him in de face.' De moon was straight up and down den, and I said: 'Dat's right', and I's telling you de troof, dat sapling jes' riz up, turned aroun' in de air, en de brush part tickled my mule and Isham's hoss in de face. If you ever seed 'em buck and rare and jump up, dey sho did. Den dey took off down de road, and we didn't hold 'em back, and here come Green. We lef' him behind, 'cause his mule couldn't keep up. If you ever heard a man pray more earnester dan old Green, I ain't! He come down de road a-yelling: 'Lord, us live togedder, let us die togedder.' He meant for us to wait on him, but I couldn't hold dat mule, and I wan't trying to hold him! I was gitting away from dar!

"When us come togedder, us was a mile from whar us done been, den us had to decide what to do. Isham said for us to go wid him, and Green said no, us nearer to his house; but us wan't near to nobody and I was so scared, hadn't been for Alice, I'd a jes' stayed right whar us was 'tell sun-up. I said, 'No, every man better take keer his own self,' en us did. When I got home, I didn't take nothing off dat mule but myself. I jes' left him standing at de do' wid de saddle on. What skeered Green so, was a man, he said, what was ridin' right 'side him en didn't have no head! 'Twas a good thing he didn't tell me dat den, I'd jes' nacherly drap dead!

"No'm, I don't 'zackly believes in ghosties, but I heared Mr. Marshall Lee say he was riding on home one night and a woman stepped out in de road and say: 'Marshall, let me ride.' He say: 'My hoss won't tote double.' She say: 'Yes it will,' and she jump up behind him, and dat hoss bucked and jumped nigh 'bout from under him, but when he got home, she wan't dere. He say, his sister had jes' died and it mout been her.

"'Nother time, one Friday night, Alice say us better git a 'possum for Sunday. She say she didn't want none caught atter midnight on Sadday. I went down whar I knowed dey was 'simmons, and dem dogs never treed nothing; dey jes' run 'round dat 'simmon tree lak dey gone crazy. I'm telling you de troof, somepin' jump outer dat tree, had a head back'erds and for'erds and look lak a flame shooting out it eyes! 'Twan't lak no possum I ever seed, 'twan't lak nothing. Dem dogs, Liz and Roger en Cuba, made a bluge at me. Cotton was waist high, and I run down de cotton row and cross de road and dey trail me. I say: 'What ail you, dogs?' And dey jes' come on a-barkin', and dey run me to de bridge over Konkabyer. So I clumb on de banisters. I seed dey had my trail an dey gonna ketch me, so I turn 'round and tore out for de slough. Dey lost my trail dere and when I got home, 'bout daylight, de thorns and de briars and all done tore my clothes plum off me. 'Twas t'ree days 'fore I ever seed dem dogs ag'in.

"And I kin tell you somepin' else. It's jes' lak I say, I's always been a hunter, en one night I went down in de post oak woods hunting by myself. Dis is a fact; 'tain't no lie. It's what I done. I had a mighty good dog, and I jes' kept walking and walking, and I got mighty nigh to Mr. Redhead Jim Lee's place, and I walked on and atter while I seed I'd lost my dog. I couldn't see him nowhar and I couldn't hear him nowhar, and den somepin' say to me, jes' lak dis: 'Josh, blow your horn!' Jes' lak dat, lak somebody talking to me. Well I give three loud, long blows and set dere awhile longer but dat dog didn't come. Co'se I knowed he'd come sometime, and so I jes' set dere on dat log and I jes' turned a fool, I reckon, but 'twas jes' lak somebody talking to me, lak it 'peared to me was whispering: 'Josh, you out here in dese woods by yo'self. You blowed dat horn and your enemy heard you.

You's a fool, you is.' And I whispered back: 'Dat's a fact.' I couldn't hear what it was a-whispering to me, but us jes' talk back to one 'nuther, and 'bout dat time I look up and here come three men ridin' on new saddles wid shiny buckles gwine, 'squeechy, squeechy', jes' lak dat. I hears de hosses feed jes' as nachel as could be. I thought sho I seed 'em, and it 'pears to look clean outer reason, but dem men come riding right on up to me, and I jump over dat log and lay down flat on de other side, and it look lak I could see right through dat log and heard 'em say: 'Dar he is, dar he is', and I seed 'em p'inting dey finger right whar I was. I knowed dem hosses gwineter step over de log on top me, and I's telling you de troof, I jump up from 'hind dat log and run 'bout two miles, and if it hadn't been for dat slough, I don't know whar I'd a went. I come to myself in de middle of dat water, up to hyar, waist high, and dar was my dog, old Cuba, done treed a 'possum.

"De fust thing I 'members 'bout slave'y time, I wan't nothing but a boy, 'bout fifteen I reckon, dat's what Marse Johnnie Horn say. Us belong to Marse Ike Horn, Marse Johnnie's pa, right here on dis place whar us is now, but dis here didn't belong to me den, dis here was all Marse Ike's place. Marse Ike's gin got outer fix and we couldn't get it fixed. Colonel Lee had two gins and one of 'em was jes' below old Turner house. Recolleck a big old hickory tree? Well dar's whar it was.

"I was plenty big 'nough to drive de mules to de gin. Set on de lever and drive 'em, jes lak a 'lasses mill, so dat night Marse Ike told us he want everybody go wid him to Colonel Lee's gin nex' morning, and didn't want nobody to git out and go ahead of him. Dat held up de ginning; made us not go to de ginhouse tell sunup.

"Us got de mules and jes' waited. 'Twixt daylight and sunup, us all standing dar at de gate and we heared a little fine horn up de road. Us didn't know what it meant coming to de house. And bimeby Mr. Beesley, what live not fur from Marse Ike, he rode up and had five dogs, five nigger dogs, what dey call 'em, and soon as he come, Marse Ike's hoss was saddled up and Marse Ike and him rode off down de road and de dogs wid em, 'head of us. Us followed 'long behind 'em, stay close as dey 'low us, to see what dey was up to. When dey got close to de ginhouse, ginhouse right 'side de road, dey stop us and Mr. Beesley told old Brown to go ahead. Old Brown was de lead dog and had a bell on him and dey was fasten togedder wid a rod, jes' lak steers. He turn 'em loose, and den he popped de whip and hollered at old Brown and told him 'nigger'. Old Brown hollered lak he hit. He want to go. And dey was a fence on bofe sides made it a lane, so he put old Brown over de fence on de ginhouse side, and told Brown to 'go ahead'. He went ahead and run all aroun' de ginhouse and dey let him in de gin-room and he grabbled in de cottonseed in a hole.

"Den somebody holler 'Guinea Jim', I looks and I didn't see him. Didn't nobody see him, but dey know dat's whar he been hiding. Mr. Beesley told old Brown he jes' fooling him, and Old Brown holler ag'in, lak he killing him, and Mr. Beesley say: 'Go git dat nigger' and old Brown started 'way from dar lak he hadn't been hunting nothing, but he went aroun' and aroun' dat gin and Mr. Beesley told him he hatter do better dan dat or he'd kill him, 'cause he hadn't come dar for nothing.

"Brown made a circle aroun' dat gin 'way down to de fence dat time, and he was so fat he couldn't git through de fence. You know what sort of fence, a rail fence it was. Den he stop and bark for help. Now I seed dis wid my own eyes. Dey put Brown on top de fence and he jump way out in de road, didn't stay on de fence. He jump and run up and down in de road, and couldn't find no scent of Jim. You knows how dey used to make dem rail fences?

"Well, Brown come back dar, and dis is de trufe, so help me Gawd. He bark, look lak, for dem to lift him back up on de fence, and bless God, if dat dog didn't walk dat rail fence lak he walking a log, as fur as from here to dat gate yonder, and track Jim jes' lak he was on de groun'. He fell off once, and dey had to put him back, and he run his track right on to whar Jim jumped off de fence way out in de road. Old Brown run right cross de road to de other fence and treed ag'in on t'other side de road toward Konkabia. Old Brown walk de fence on dat side de road a good piece, jes' lak he done on de other side, and dem other dogs, he hadn't never turned dem loose.

"When Brown he jump off dat fence, he jump jes' as fur as he kin on de fiel' side, lak he gwine ketch Jim lak a gnat or somepin' and he never stop barking no more, jes' lak he jumping a rabbit. Den, Mr. Beesley turn dem other dogs loose dat he hadn't never turned loose, 'ca'se he say old Brown done got de thing straight. And he had it straight. Dem dogs run dat track right on down to Konkabia and crossed it to de Blacksher side. Dey was a big old straw field dar den and dey cross it and come on through dat field, all dem dogs barkin' jes' lak dey looking at Jim. 'Reckley, dey come up on Jim running wid a pine brush tied behind him to drag his scent away, but it didn't bother old Brown.

"When dem dogs 'gin to push him, Jim drap de brush and runned back toward Konkabia. Now on Konkabia dere used to be beavers worse den on Sucarnatchee now. Dey was a big beaver dam 'twixt de bridge and de Hale place, and Jim run to dat beaver dam. You know when beavers build dey dam, dey cut down trees and let 'em fall in de creek, and pull in trash en brush same as folks, to dam de water up dar tell its knee-deep. De dogs seen him, old Brown looking at him, jes' 'fore he jump in 'bove de dam right 'mongst de trash and things dey'd drug in dar. Brown seed him and he jump in right behind him. Jim jes' dive down under de raff, en let he nose stick outer de water. Every once in a while Jim he put he head down under, he holding to a pole down dar, and once Mr. Beesley seed him, he jes' let him stay dar.

"Brown would swim 'bout 'mongst de brush, backerds and for'erds, and terreckly Mr. Beesley tole old Brown, 'Go git him.' Den all de men got poles and dug 'bout in de raff hunting him. Dey knowed he was dar, en Marse Ike had a pole giggen aroun' trying to find him too. Den he told Mr. Beesley to give him de hatchet and let him fix he pole. He sharpen de pole right sharp, den Marse Ike start to jug aroun' wid de pole, and he kinder laugh to hisse'f, 'ca'se he knowed he done found Jim. 'Bout dat time Jim poke he head up and say: 'Dis here me', and everybody holler. Den he ax 'em please, for God's sake, don't let dem dogs git him. Dey told him come on out.

"You see, Jim belonged to Miss Mary Lee, Mr. John Lee's Ma, and his Pa was kilt in de war, so Mr. Beesley was looking out for her. Well, dey took Jim outer dar, and

Mr. Beesley whipped him a little and told him: 'Jim, you put up a pretty good fight and I's gwine to give you a start for a run wid de dogs.'

"Jim took out towards Miss Mary's, and Mr. Beesley helt old Brown as long as he could. Dey caught Jim and bit him right smart. You see dey had to let em bite him a little to satisfy de dogs. Jim could have made it, 'cept he was all hot and wore out.

"Dat's 'bout all I knows, 'cept us belonged to Marse Ike Horn, and fust us belonged to Mr. Price Williams, what run de hotel in Livingston. He took my gran'ma to Mobile, den he died. Us Ma belonged to dey two chillun, Miss Nancy Gulley, Mr. Jake's wife, en Miss Burt Blakeney. Marse Ike Horn was dey uncle, and us all come 'round to him, and us been here ever since. My mammy was Ann Campbell, and my pappy was John Horn, and us ain't never had no trouble wid nobody 'bout nothing.

"We's having a barbecue on de fo'th of July and us wants you to come down to it, if Alice gits along well, and I's gwine tell you 'bout Rod and Big John, and John Graverson when dey runned away and about how old man Jim Devers, Alice's step-pa, hid em in de cave under he house whar dey had as nice hams as I ever et, co'se a little tainted, but sho was good. Dem niggers was fat as beavers, jes' settin' dar eatin' dat meat.

"And 'bout de time Marse Ike slip up on a heap of niggers at a frolic 'twixt Sumterville and Livingston and put a end to de frolic. De niggers having a big dance, and Marse Ike and de patterrollers having a big run, said dey wanted to have some fun, and dey did. Said he eased up on 'em wid a white sheet 'round him and a big brush in he hand, and somehow or 'nother, dey didn't see him tell he spoke. Den he holler 'By God, I'm bird-blinding,' and he say dem niggers tore down dem dirt chimleys and run t'rough dat house. He say he ain't never heerd sich a fuss in a corn field in his born days. What he mean 'bout bird-blindin'? When you goes in de canebrake it so thick, you takes a light to shine de bird's eyes and blind 'em, den you kin ketch 'em. Dat what he call bird-blindin'. Yassum, Marse Ike in dat too. He couldn't stand for 'em to have no fun 'thout he in it.

"Come back on de fo'th of July, and I's gwine tell you some sho-nuff tales. You sort of caught me when my min' wa'n't zackly on it. I ain't had no sleep, jes' settin' 'side de bed by Alice, ketching a nod now and den. I's too sleepy to sing you no song, but one I laks is dis: It suits me now in my age:

> My lates' sun is sinking fas'
> My race in nearly run,
> My strongs' trial now is pas',
> My triump' jes' begun.

"You come back and I'll sing de res', I's got to see 'bout things now."

EMMA L. HOWARD

Interview with Emma L. Howard
—Margaret Fowler, Fruithurst, Alabama

IS MASSA GWIN'ER SELL US?

"Mammy, is Ol' Massa gwin'er sell us tomorrow?
Yes, my chile.
Whar he gwin'er sell us?
'Way down South in Georgia."

'Aunt' Emma L. Howard sat in a huge, old-fashioned rocking chair at her home, 170 Elmwood St., Montgomery, and sang the old slave song. When she had finished, her memory recalled the time, years ago, when she was a slave on the plantation of William and Georgiana Shepherd in Lowndes County, between Mac's Switch and Morgansville.

"Dat was one of de saddest songs we sung endurin' slavery days," she mused. "It always did make me cry."

She thought a moment, smiled.

"I 'members I was de only light nigger in de fambly," she said proudly. "I was brung up in de house wid de white chillun. Twice a week I went to my mammy's cabin an' took a bath. I had my own sof' shoes an' my own nightgown an' jacket an' played games wid my massa's chilluns."

She explained her duties about the Big House as sweeping the rambling porches and yards. Sometimes she churned. Afterward she would join the white children and played most of the day.

"We played hot-scotch, ring-'roun'-the-rosy an' lots of yuther things I can't 'member," she explained. "I musta been 'bout seven years old den."

Emma says she is 84 or 85, but she looks older. She remembers very little about her brothers and sisters. She can only recall "Sist' Cellie, Sist' Harriett an' Sist' Liza." Liza helped Aunt Evalina in the kitchen.

Emma lifted her eyes toward the ceiling, endeavoring to recall the exact number of servants her master owned.

"Edie was de laundress," she recalled, "an' Arrie, she was de weaver. Den dere was Becky, Melia, Aunt Mary, Ed, John, and Uncle George the house man, who married Aunt Evalina. Jake was de over-looker (overseer). He was a great, big cullud man. Dar was more, but I can't 'member. I was jes' a little shaver den."

She remembers that the Big House was huge and white with a beautiful parlor and guest room, where the visitors were entertained. Gigantic white columns rose in front of the house, and clusters of magnolias surrounded it. The slave houses were located about two hundred yards back of the house.

"Massa Shepherd an' Mistis Georgiana was both good an' treated de servants kin'," Emma said. "I 'members dat I used to keep de flies offen Mistis Georgiana wid a big fan, an' once I went to sleep. She jest laugh when she foun' me sleepin' dar beside her.

"Massa would only whup a slave fer two things," she recalled. "One thing was if things warn't done up jes' right at hog killin' time, and de other was iffen a nigger warn't clean when he 'ported for work on Monday mornin's. Ol' Massa didn't do de whuppin's hisse'f. Jake did it, but Massa sat dar on his horse to see dat only a certain number of licks was give.

"How did we feel 'bout a white man who would be over-looker? We called him 'po white trash.' He wasn't thought much of by anybody."

Emma said that everyone went to church on Sundays and that she liked to sing the old religious hymns. When freedom came all the Shepherd servants had been taught to read and write, she said, and each family had enough money to buy a little home. "De Marster" would make each family keep pigs, hens and such; then he would market the products and place the money aside for them, Emma explained.

Talking further about work about the plantation, she said:

"Louisa cleaned de parlor an' kept Mistis' room nice." She took up a recital of work on the plantation. "Atter dat she didn't do anything but sew, an' Sist' Liza hoped her wid dat. After de weavin', we done sewin', and it took a lot of sewin' for dat family. Eve'body had two Sunday dresses, summer and winter, as well as clothes for eve'day.

"For de men's suits de wool had to be took off an' carded an' got ready to make. But we had plenty of wool from our own sheep.

"When dey kilt de hogs for winter meat, dey took some of de hands out of de field an' let dem ho'p. We had a smokehouse full of hams and middlin's, an' when rainy spells came, us chillun would rake up chips an' leaves an' make a smudge of smoke to keep de meat sweet.

"Massa Shepherd and Miss Georgiana was both mighty kin' hearted an' treated their servants good. Once when Marse Shepherd sent us chilluns down to de station wid a note, he say, 'Now, go fas'.' But we played 'long the way an' picked flowers. When we come steppin' back, he say, 'I told you to hurry.' I held out de flowers an' say, 'See, us brung you some flowers;' but he take up a little switch an' nettle my legs good.

"Massa always give us plenty of eve'thing. On Friday us worked an' washed, an' on Sattidy us cleaned for Sunday. Den on Sunday Massa would go 'roun' an' have a mouthful at every house to see dat eve'thing was done up jes' right, an' if they wasn't, somebody got a whuppin' next day.

"When us went to church on Sunday, Massa Shepherd, Miss Georgiana an' us three chilluns rode in de rock-a-way. Dat was a carriage shaped mos' like a bowl. De carriage was pulled by two big horses, an' de coachman what sat up on de high seat had on a long double-breasted coat, shiny black boots an' a tall silk hat. Massa had on a silk hat, too, but he wore a tight-waisted coat. An' Miss Georgiana, she look lak a bokay.

Emma L. Howard, Montgomery, Alabama

"She didn't lak to wear hoops, because she had sprained her ankle once an' walked wid a limp. She liked to wear thin, cool, flowery dresses wid lots of ruffles an' lace. She also wore a scoop of white straw, mighty sof' over de years' an' flarin' high an' spreadin' over de face.

It was filled wid flowers an' tied wid long streamers of ribbon."

Emma said that Mr. Shepherd died during the second year of the war, and that it was whispered he was poisoned because he was so good to his niggers. "Just before the war closed," she said, "Mrs. Shepherd married again and later moved to Texas.

"I was took on as a cook by a rich family named Marchiel, in Montgomery," she said. "Dey treated me lak I was deir own daughter. I was 'lowed to go out three nights a week, but no more, an' I had to be home by 'leven o'clock.

"I got engaged to be married an' de boy had to ax for me. I 'member dat Massa Marchiel say: 'If you don't take good care of her I'll take her back.' When de younges' daughter married she lef' me her veil an' wreath, an' dey give me a weddin' dress an' shoes.

"My husban' was a carpenter, an' we lived in dis house. When he died, I went to work for a family dat once was de richest family in de State. Dey comes to see me every few days, an' nex' week dey are comin' for me to spen' de day wid dem. De reason I has stayed so well is dat folks has always been so good to me."

EVERETT INGRAM

Interview with Everett Ingram
—*Preston Klein, Opelika, Alabama*

MY GRANDMA RAISED PLENTY CHILLUNS

Uncle Everett Ingram mused: "Honey chile, my gran'mammy was de beatenest woman to have chilluns dat you ever seen. I has hyared dat she raised so many of dem dat she brung a mighty heap on de block; somewhere near a thousan' dollars."

Uncle Everett is a familiar figure in East Opelika, where he has lived for years. He was "a right good-sized scamp at freedom time" and remembers much of what he has seen and heard. He was born in Russell County, the son of Prince and Fanny Ingram. They had seven other children; Jerry, Clara, Rubin, Jep, Lula, Eugene and Lucy.

Everett says of his life:

"Our house in de slave settlement was made of logs an' had one room. It had a mud an' stick chimney, a plank floor an' a boxed-up bed wid one leg at de foot. De mattress was stuffed wid shucks an' straw.

"My gran'pappy, Prince Walden, an' Lucy, his wife, come from Russell County, too, an' belonged to de

Covingtons. Later dey was sold to Dr. Walden, at Uchie. When dey come to Uchie de county was full of Indians. My gran'pappy useta drink likker wid 'em; but gran'ma, she was skeered an' runned away to Columbus, Georgy. On her way dere, my mammy was borned in de woods.

"I 'members dat when I was a strip of a boy, dey cooked ash-cake on leaves an' de chilluns et pot-licker an' bread an' greens outen wooden trays wid wooden spoons. Dey would sit under de trees an' eat. Each family had dey own bowl, an' us et a-plenty, too. In cold weather mammy kept all de chilluns in de house by de fire.

"Master had us a two-room house, 'ca'se my mammy was de cook an' weaver. Dey made dey own silk den, too, an' raised de silk worms. Us useta get mulberry leaves to feed de silk worms wid. Us used indigo, which us cooked an' used for dye. Us would wear any kind of clothes on everyday an' Sunday; an' didn't have no shoes 'til us was big chilluns.

"Ol' Marster an' Ol' Mistus, Mr. Bill an' Miss Lucy Ingram, lived in a big weather-boarded house wid a wide hall an' a chimney at each end. De kitchen was off from de rest of de house.

"I 'members dat de overseer useta whip mammy an' pappy, 'ca'se dey fight so much. He useta take my mammy to de carriage to whip her. Marster was in de war den. When he come home, de overseer tuk mammy by de han' to de house an' tell Marster 'bout havin' to whip her. He'd jest shake his head, sad-lak. He was mighty good to all of us.

"My gran'pappy was put in de speculator drove, put on de block an' sold.

"I 'members dat Mistus read de Bible to us an' my mammy was converted by de white preacher. He baptized her. De colored folks used de white church an' set in de back.

"An' honey, dey shorely did have good times dancin' on Sattidy nights; an' sometimes dey would dance 'till Sunday mornin'. When de corn needed shuckln', it was hauled up near de crib, an' on a purty moonlighted night Marster would pass 'roun' de likker. It wouldn't be long 'til dey was all happy an' had what dey called a general. De general led all de hollers an' songs. Dey shorely did get dat corn shucked fast, too.

"Gran'mammy was a great doctor; useta give us turpentine an' castor oil an' Jerusalem oak fer worms. She'd give us all kinds of teas, too. I 'members dat gran'mammy was also a midwife.

Everett Ingram, Opelika, Alabama

"De Yankees comed through de yard in May an' tol' us: 'You's free.' De Yankees wasn't so good. Dey hung my mammy up in de smokehouse by her thumbs; tips of her toes jest touchin' de floor, 'ca'se she wouldn't 'gree to give up her older chilluns. She never did, neither.

"Daddy stole both de older chilluns, dough, an' went off. De Yankees stole provisions an' stock an' hauled 'em off. De news got to Uchie an' everybody hid out; Marster wid 'em. Dey hunted de money whut was hid in de colored folks beds; nearly $2,000. De jewelry was dere, too. Dey foun' some money at de big house an' said: 'Dis money ain't worth a damn;' but dey tuk it jest de same.

"I married Hattie Graves. Den I j'ined de church an' was saved."

United States. Work Projects Administration

HANNAH IRWIN

Interview with Hannah Irwin
—*Gertha Couric, [HW: Eufaula?]*

KU KLUX RIDES WHEN DE NIGGERS STARTS TROUBLE

On a high knoll overlooking the winding Chewalla Creek is a little one room shack. Its rusty hinges and weather-beaten boards have seen many a glowing sunset; have stood against many high winds and rains; they have for many years sheltered Aunt Hannah Irwin, ex-slave. Now the old Negro woman is too old and feeble to venture very often from her small home. She lives almost in solitude with her memories of the past, and an occasional visit from one of her old friends who perhaps brings her some fruit or a little money.

"Yas'm, I'll be pleased to tell you 'bout whut I remembers aroun' de time of de War." Aunt Hannah sat stolidly in a chair that virtually groaned under her weight; and gave utterance to this sentiment through a large thick mouth, while her gold ear rings shook with every turn of her head, and her dim eyes glowed with memory's fires. "Dere ain't much I can tell you, dough," she went on, "kaze I was only twelve years old when de war ended.

"I was bawn on Marse Bennett's plantation near

Louisville, Alabama. Ma Mammy's name was Hester an' my pappy was named Sam.

"I remembers one night raght atter de war when de re'struction was a-goin' on. Dere was some niggers not far fum our place dat said dey was agoin' to take some lan' dat warn't deres. Dere massa had been kilt in de war an' warn't nobody 'ceptin' de mistis an' some chilluns. Well, Honey, dem niggers, mo' dan one hundred of 'em, commenced a riot an' was a-takin' things dat don't belong to 'em. Dat night de white lady she come ober to our place wid a wild look on her face. She tell Massa Bennett, whut dem niggers is up to, an' widout sayin' a word, Massa Bennett putt his hat on an lef' out de do'. Twarn't long atter dat when some hosses was heered down de road, an' I look out my cabin window which was raght by de road, an' I saw acomin' up through de trees a whole pack of ghosties; I thought dey was, anyways. Dey was all dressed in white, an' dere hosses was white an' dey galloped faster dan de win' raght past my cabin. Den I heered a nigger say: 'De Ku Klux is atter somebody.'

"Dem Ku Klux went ober to dat lady's plantation an' told dem niggers dat iffen dey ever heered of 'em startin' anything mo' dat dey was a-goin' to tie 'em all to trees in de fores' till dey all died f'um being hongry. Atter dat dese niggers all 'roun' Louisville, dey kept mighty quiet.

"No m'am, I don't believe in no conjurin'. Dese conjure women say dat dey will make my hip well iffen I gives 'em half my rations I gits fum de gover'ment, but I knows dey ain't nothin' but low-down, no-count niggers."

"Speaking of the Ku Klux, Aunt Hannah. Were you afraid of them?"

"Naw'm, I warn't afeered of no Ku Klux. At fu'st I though dat dey was ghosties and den I was afeered of 'em, but atter I found out dat Massa Bennett was one of dem things, I was always proud of 'em."

Hannah Irwin, [TR: Eufaula?], Alabama

"Well, what about the Yankees?" she was asked. "Did you ever see any Yankees; and what did you think of the ones that came through your place? Were you glad that they set you free?"

"I suppose dem Yankees was all right in dere place," she continued, "but dey neber belong in de South. Why, Miss, one of 'em axe me what was dem white flowers in de fiel'? You'd think dat a gent'men wid all dem decorations on hisself woulda knowed a fiel' of cotton. An' as for dey a-settin' me free! Miss, us niggers on de Bennett place was free as soon as we was bawn. I always been free."

MARTHA JACKSON

Interview with Martha Jackson
—*Ruby Pickens Tartt, Livingston, Alabama*

HEAPS OF DEM YALLER GALS GOT SONT NORF

"When de War fus' started," said Martha Jackson, who was born in 1850, "dey wouldn't let none of de cullud people go to chu'ch 'thout dey had a pass, and mighty few white folkses would give 'em a pass. Dere was a heap of men (hit mou't have been six or twelve, my recollection is short, but anyhow 'twas jus' a big crowd) whut went back'erds en ferwerds jes' lack sher'fs and de calls de'se'fs de 'Patterrollers.' Ef de white folks give de niggers a pass, den dey could go, and ef dey was to go'thout one, dem Patterrollers would have 'em a-runnin' thoo de woods jes' lack dey was a lot of deer, an ef dey ever cotch 'em, dey'd take 'em to dey Marster and he'd jes' natchelly wear 'em out!

"Den dey didn't 'low 'em for to go nowhurs much, eben when de plantation j'ined one ernudder did, dey'd ketch 'em over dere and fetch 'em back and dey'd git whooped ag'in, and dat's 'zackly how come a heap uv 'em run'd away. I knowed a nigger onc't whut was gone nigh 'bout a year, and he wa'n't gone nowhur but right up de big road a piece, livin' in a cave whut he dug outer de side uv a clay bank. And Miss Betty say, 'Marthy, whur you reckon Dan at?' And I never said nothin'. De Patterrollers couldn't fine him or nobody, and he ain't never showed hisse'f in daylight 'tel he peered up atter de S'render.

"And I knowed a woman name Tishie, Miss Mollie's house sarvant. She run away 'case dey so mean to her, I reckon, and de cullud folks harbored her and hid her up in de grain house wid de peas and sech lac', stedder down in de corn crib. And who ever 'twas 'trayed her I ain't sayin' but a crowd uv dem Patterrollers come and got 'er one night, and tuck her away, and I ain't nebber seed Tishie no mo'.

"And one uv Ole Marsa's niggers—'little boy' he go by—he tuck on might'ly, 'case dey say he wanted to marry Tishie. I know he fotch her up in de quarter fer ter git her sumpin' to eat atter de white folks done sleep. But couldn't nobody marry, 'twa'n't 'lowed, 'outer one or t'other uv de Ole Marsa 'greed to buy bofe uv 'em and ef dey didn't 'gree you sho' better keep 'way fum dey place. And Ole Marsa and Miss Mollie didn't nebber 'gree.

"I hear some uv 'em say one dem Patterrollers had 'bout three sets er cullud chillun over dere, and some uv 'em favor'd Tishie, and ev'y time hit come time fer 'em yaller gals ter work in de fiel', dey got sarnt Norf. I reckon 'case he never wanted see his own blood git beat up, and dat Jim Barton was er cru'l overseer, sho's yer bawn.

"'Twas a heap of dem yaller gals got sarnt Norf frum 'roun' here sho' was."

Martha says most of the meaness of pre-war days on the plantations may be charged up to cruel overseers.

"Ole Marsa's wife's sister had a husband whut kep' de meanest overseer durin' de war dat I ever is seed," she declares. "Dat man would make 'em niggers on de plantation plow up a gre't big fiel' big as all over yonder and den check hit fer corn. And checkin' corn in runnin' a straight row clean 'cross de fiel' bofe ways, and hit make a check 'bout two feet square. Den he'd make de niggers drap a grain uv corn right in de middle uv ev'y check, and ef hit didn't come up straight as deese here fingers on my han', he'd snatch hit up and make 'em eat hit right den and dere, stalk and all 'thout ever bilin' hit a anything. And that'll mighty ne'r th'ow you in de middle uv a spell uv sickness sho's yo' bawn.

"But dat didn't make no diffe'ns to dat man. And stidder dat, he'd nigh 'bout beat 'em ter deaf ef dey 'sputed his word 'bout hit, but den dey didn't 'spute, 'case dey was so skeered when dey drappin' hit dat hit ain't gwinter come up straight lack he say, dat dey couldn't drap hit good as dey could uv drapped hit. 'Case dey so skeered dey couldn't.

"Dem niggers jes' natchelly shuck lack dey havin' de black ague chill soon as dey heered him a-comin'. And when de Patterroles tole him de niggers was a-risin', 'case dey foun' papers 'bout in de cabins, he nigh 'bout kilt 'em. Some of dem niggers run 'way down in de woods lack deers and clam' up in de trees, 'case he sot dogs on 'em and some uv 'em stayed in a cave in de clay bank and tuck to comin' up to us house nights after vittles. And dat overseer man would send 'em Patterrollers jes' lack dey was de sher'f down to fotch 'em back, and he'd say,

'Dead or alive, doan' make no diffe'nce.' And sometimes dem dogs be done nigh 'bout chewed dem niggers up. Den he'd whoop 'em sho' 'nuff.

"'Twas a long and a wide stiff leather strop w'at he had whut hung back uv his do', and hit had big roun' holes in hit, and he'd git him a pot of warm salty water and set hit down by his side. Den he had 'em cotch de nigger and put his feet in de long block, and somebody helt dey han's, and he strip 'em stark naked, and he stretch 'em 'cross a log, and he dip de long stiff leather strop wid de roun' holes in hit in de briny salt water, and den look out 'case he comin' down on dat po' nigger's nekkid bottom. De holes in de strop dey sucks flesh up in th'oo 'em, and de nigger's a hollerin' and ev'ybody so skeered dey right ashy, and dey can't nobody say a mumblin' word 'case dey so skeered.

Martha Jackson, [TR: Livingston?], Alabama

"Lawdy, Lawdy, dem was tribbolashuns! Wunner dese here 'omans was my Antie and she say dat she skacely call to min' he e'r whoopin' her, 'case she was a breeder woman, and brought in chillun ev'y twelve mont's jes' lack a cow bringin' in a calf. And she say, dat whut make her mo' val'ble to her Ole Marster. He orders she can't be put to no strain 'casen uv dat. And she say she give him praise on his gretty grave fer dat. But dem others he worked 'em day en night, Sad'dy en Sunday too you'se sho' ter hear dem women uv er night battin' de clo'es on er log in creek wid de stick.

"But fo' long dat man tuck rale sick, en he b'lieved in conjurashun but spite everything he done he got worser en worser and fo' long he died.

"So dey sarnt down in de woods and all over de plantation er lookin' fer de niggers to come to de Big House 'case dey overseer was dead. And here dey comes a-shoutin' and a-clappin' dey han's and a-holl'rin' sumpin' awful.

>Ole John Bell is de'd en gone
>I hopes he's gone to hell!

"En dat was de onles' time I's ever seen dem niggers happy on dat plantation 'tel atter s'render."

JANE

Interview with Jane
—*Mildred Scott Taylor, Georgiana, Alabama*

DID THEY OWN US OR WE OWN THEM?

"Yas, chillun, I 'members de wah; 'caze I was here when de Yankees come t'rough an' I was about fourteen year ole. Ole Marster he went off to de wah wid a whole passel of sojers, en' he been gone a long time, en' nobody to home to look atter de plantation, 'cep Ole Mistis en' Unker Jude, what was Ole Marster's fust slave he ebber owned. Ole Marster en' Unker Jude was borned de same day, en' Ole Marster's pappy gin Unker Jude to him, whenst dey was leetle bitsy babies. When Ole Marster mai'ed Ole Mistis, dey was young folks, en' dey move to his own plantation. He tuk Unker Jude wid him, en' Unker Jude was de ca'i'ge driver. When Ole Marster went off ter de wah, he tole Unker Jude ter look atter Ole Mistis en' evy'ting on de place 'twell he come back. Whilst Ole Marster gone to de wah, Unker Jude was oberseer for Ole Mistis, en' he made de niggers wuk harder dan Ole Marster did, to make co'n, en' oats, en' fodder, en' meat fer de sojers.

"Ole Mistis made de womens card bats, en' spin en' weabe on de loom. What er loom look lak? It look lak er loom, dat what it look lak; what you spec' it look lak? All de womens, white en' black, wuk hard makin' jeans fer de sojers clo's en' makin' linsey fer de women's clo's. Us didn't hab no udder clo's 'cep dem linsey, but dey sho was good uns en' las' er long time, iffen yer didn't stan' too close ter de fire en' scorch 'em.

"Us kep' hearin' of de Yankees comin', en' one mawnin' Ole Mistis she say: 'Jane, you go down ter de front gate en' stay dar en' watch en' see iffen de Yankees comin' down de big road, en' when you sees 'em, you run tell me quick.'

"Bimeby, I seed de Yankees comin' about a mile down de road, en' I run tell Ole Mistis, en' she call de womens en' dey run down t'rough de orchard to de big woods, en' I run tell Unker Jude en' he onhitch de mules en' lead 'em down ter de big gully behin' de fiel'.

"Ole Mistis tole me to run back to de house, quick, fo' de Yankees get dar, en' git her gole watch en' chain outen de bureau drawer; but de Yankees come in whilst I was gitten de watch en' chain, en' one ob 'em grabbed it outen by han' en' put it in his pocket en' tole anudder Yankee: 'I'se gwine tek dis home ter my gal.'

"De house en' de yard was plum full of Yankees en' dey rid dey hosses en' tore up ev'yting, lookin' for money en' jewelry. Dey ax me whar it was hid, en' I tole em' I didn't know en' dey said I was lyin', en' iffen I didn't tell 'em, dey would kill me 'lak er dam Rebel', en' I sho was skairt.

"Dey et up all de sump'n' to eat in de kitchen en' tuk all de meat en' meal outen de smokehouse en' didn't lef' us nuddin', en' dey went to de crib en' tuk ev'y year co'n en' all de fodder en' put it in wagins en' tuk 'em off.

"De Yankees ax me don't I wanner be free en' I say: 'No, suh', en' dey say ev'body gwine be free an' I won't hab ter wuk fer Ole Marster no mo'. Den dey ax me whar Ole Marster at, en' I say: 'He gone to wah', en' dey ax me whar Ole Mistis, en' I say: 'I dunno whar she at; she done gone off summuz.' Dey ax me whar de guns, en' I tole 'em us didn't hab no guns.

"Dem Yankees mighter been dar till yit, iffen one ob 'em hadn't rid his hoss ober a bee gum en' Man! dem bees en' dem Yankees sho did mess up! In about a minute dere wan't no Yankees nowhar 'cep down de big road whar de dus' jes' foggin' up! 'Bout a week some mo' Yankees come, but dey muster heared 'bout de bees, 'caze dey lef' dey hosses outside de big gate en' walked up to de house, but dey didn't stay long 'caze dey wan't nuffin' lef' atter de fu'st Yankees done to' up ev'ything. En' when dey ready to go dey tuk dey guns en' stood way off en' shoot de bee gums all to pieces, en' dey flewed aroun' en' us had to stay 'way 'twel night. Unker Jude, he wuk all night long, makin' bee gums outen a hollow log, en' nex' day he hive ebery one ob dem bees en' put 'em in de new gums, en' de bees dey tote all dey honey en' put it in de new gums fas' as dey could make comb fer it. Dem bees sho' was smart.

"When de wah done gone, Ole Marster he come, wid one he arms shot plum off, en' Ole Mistis she cry, she so glad to see him en' Unker Jude he cry en' hug Ole Marster, en' us all cry en' tek on, we so glad Ole Marster come back en' so sorry he arm shot off. Ole Marster tell all de niggers dey free now en' don't hatter wuk fer him no mo', en' some er de young niggers went off atter de Yankees, en' neber did come back, but de res' ob us jes' stayed right whar we is. Us had a mighty hard time for a long time, but de white folks had de same hard time en' us didn't mek no diffunce. I mai'ed Rufus en' us raise a big fambly right dar on Ole Marster's plantation, en' outen us's twelve chilluns, ain't nary one eber seen de inside ob de jailhouse. I raise my chilluns jes' lak Ole Mistis raise her'n en' dat's de way to raise 'em, to wuk en' keep outen debilment. Ole Marster dead en' gone en' Ole Mistis too, but I 'members 'em jes' lak dey was, when dey looked atter us whenst we belonged to 'em or dey belonged ter us, I dunno which it was. De times was better fo' de wah. Us had good things to eat en' plenty of it, en' we had good clo's en' clean clo's fer Sunday. Dat's mo'n some triflin' niggers got now.

"I goes to church en' sings en' prays, en' when de good Lord teks me, I'se ready to go, en' I specs to see Jesus en' Ole Mistis en' Ole Marster when I gits to de He'benly Lan'."

HILLIARD JOHNSON

Interview with Hilliard Johnson
—*Ruby Pickens Tartt, Livingston, Alabama*

HOODOOIN' DE DOGS

Uncle Hilliard Johnson and his wife Callie live on the Johnson place about three and a half miles from Livingston, Ala., the same place Hilliard was brought as an infant of two in slavery days. He and Callie tend their own little patch of ground and they own a mule. White friends patch up the gaps in their financial structure and everybody knows them. Uncle Hilliard pulled up his mule in front of my house and climbed down from the high seat, leaving Callie sitting placidly in the sun.

He came around to the kitchen door and announced that he was here, "'ca'se he got de word I wanted to ax him somepin."

"Uncle Hilliard," I said, "I want to hear all about you and your family and whom you belonged to in slavery time."

"Well, Miss Ruby, iffen you is knowed me all dese years and still don' know who I'm is, and my family is, and who us belonged to, dey ain't no use of me stoppin' now to tell you. 'Sides, I's sick, I's been to de horspital in York, Dr. Hills', and he wants to operate. I's skeered of de knife and ain't got no money neither.

"I can't eat nothin' but tomato soup. Dem sho' is nice ones you got dere on de she'f, and oyster soup and rice soup and all lac dat. Can't eat no rough vittles lac collards. I ain't gittin' on well atall, but I'll 'blige you a while. I was thinkin' other day 'bout you and dem ole sperichel hymns I leads out to Mount Pilgrim. You's got 'Oh Lord, I'm a Waitin' on You', ain't you? I knowed you had dat 'bout 'And I Can't Do Nothin' Until You Comes. Sho Can't.' Well, here's one you ain't got, 'ca'se hit's a really old sperichel my gran'maw use to sing. I's sorter hoarse today, but hit go:

> Jes' carry me and bury me
> I'll rise at de comin' day.
> Jes' carry me and bury me,
> I'll rise at de comin' day.

"Now dat's jes' de chorus and de verse say:

> When I was in my worldly ways
> Nobody had nothin' to say.
> Now I'm ridin' de pale white hoss
> Ev'ybody got something to say."

"Den de chorus ag'in, and hit's a pretty one sho's you bawn."

I mentioned the figure of speech "pale white hoss", but he "didn't know nothin' 'bout no figures!"

"And another one, dey is so many, let me see. Here one but I jes' can't call to mine a heap of verses:

> Trouble here and dey's trouble dere,

> I really do believe dere's trouble ev'ywhere.
> Swing low, chariot, I'm gwine home.
> Swing low, chariot, I'm gwine home."

"Den hit goes on and tell 'bout de moaner, says:

> Oh, dey's a moaner here, dey's a moaner dere,
> I really do b'lieve dey's a moaner ev'ywhere.
> Swing low, chariot, I'm gwine home.
> Swing low, chariot, I'm gwine home.
>
> Oh dey's a sinner here, dey's a sinner dere,
> I really do b'lieve dey's a sinner ev'ywhere.
> Swing low, chariot, I'm gwine home.
> Swing low, chariot, I'm gwine home.
>
> Oh, dey's a Christun here, dey's a Christun dere
> I really do b'lieve dey's a Christun ev'ywhere
> Swing low, chariot, I'm gwine home.
> Swing low, chariot, I'm gwine home.

"Den dey's a heap of 'em to dat song lac a "deacon" and a "member" and a "prayer" and a "singer", jes' a whole passel dem verses, but I reckon dem will do today.

"Now what else you want, 'ca'se dem mules is tired and I is too. 'Sides I got to see a man and Callie in de waggin and she's hot too. You knows Callie, she my wife, my second wife, and us got twelve chillun in all, growed and married. Us still live on de Johnson place three and a half miles from Livingston right han' side de ole Boyd road west from town. Us belonged to Miss Ella Johnson, she was us young Mistis, and Mr. Nep Johnson, dat's de onliest ones I ever knowed. My mammy, Frances Johnson, and my pappy, Alf Johnson, come from down 'bout Cubie Station. Young Mist'iss bought 'em I reckon and my gran'maw, Rachel Johnson. Fus' thing I knowed, us was livin' on Johnson place. Dey was good to us, 'bout seventy-five of us all together, I reckon. All I 'members, dey looped de bridle rein over my feet an' let de mule drag me all over de orchard. It hurt my head. And dey beat some of 'em up scan'lous, but dey was pretty good to me, I reckon. See, I wa'n't so ole, jes' a young boy in slavery time, but I recall young Massa told Tom, a young nigger dere, one time not to go to de frolic.

"'Clean up dem dishes and go ter bed,' he say. And Tom said 'Yassuh' but Marse Nep watch Tom th'oo de do' and atter while Tom slip out and away he went, wid young Massa right 'hin' him. He got dere and foun' Tom cuttin' groun' shuffle big as anybody. Young Massa called him, 'Tom,' he say, 'Tom, didn't I tell you you couldn't come to dis frolic?' 'Yassuh,' says Tom, 'You sho' did, and I jes' come to tell 'em I couldn't come!'

"Young Massa didn't hurt Tom none, but I is seed 'em strip 'em plum nekked and nigh 'bout kill 'em. I did see 'em kill old Collin, but dey done dat wid a shot gun jes' 'ca'se dey couldn't control him. Did they have nigger dogs, you say? Yassum, dey sho' did, but I'm tellin' you de troof now some of de black folks knowed how to git away from dem nigger dogs jes' lac dey wa'n't dere. Mr. Joe Patton, you know Mr. Joe Patton don' you? Young Mr. Joe, I'm talkin' 'bout what's over here in town and use to be de sher'ff. Well, in his day, he done seed a nigger hoodoo dem dogs 'ca'se dey had nigger dogs after S'render too. I kin tell you what I seed, but what dey done now, I doan' know, I couldn't tell you dat. But hit was a fair day, fair as 'tis now, and dey sot de dogs on dat nigger and 'fo' yer knowed hit dat nigger done lef' dere and had dem dogs treein' a nekked tree. 'Twa'n't nobody dere. Dey calls hit hoodooin' de dogs. And I'se seen hit more times than one. Time I tell you 'bout, Mr. Patton was ag'in. 'Twas a feller right here in town. I forgits his name but he was a tall nigger, married Dennis Coleman's daughter. You 'members Dennis Coleman, had dat gal call Hettie? Well, he married Hettie, and he whooped her up mightily. She 'ported on him to de sheriff, and he went to git him. I can't think what dat nigger go by now, but anyhow Mr. Patton couldn't ketch him and he sot de dogs on him and dey couldn't ketch him. Dey knowed whichaway he went, down 'bout Bear Creek on Miss Mamie Smith's place in de flatwoods. 'Twa'n't no trouble to ketch nobody down dere, but dem dogs couldn't do hit, and fus' thing you know he run back to Hattie's.

"Now jes' give me a few tomatoes, Miss Ruby, and I mus' cut dis short. Dey's a cloud comin' up over yonder by Peter's washpot and dat's when us gits a rain. I got a fur piece to go for a old man. Yassum, I'se nigh 'bout seventy-nine years old and porely."

United States. Work Projects Administration

RANDOLPH JOHNSON

Interview with Randolph Johnson
—*Morgan Smith, [HW: Birmingham?]*

RANDOLPH AND THE LITTLE CRIPPLE

Randolph Johnson, age 84, although he admits he was "jes' a little picaninny" when the War between the States began, still recalls with vivid clarity the days of his childhood on the old plantation. Unlike most of the former slaves, he never worked hard. His hours were too filled with the joy of playing, for he belonged to a little crippled boy about his own age and guarded over him all the time. At night the little white master and his small black playmate slept in the same room; the latter having a pallet that he spread on the floor. During the day both little white and black played in the shade of the cedars on the grassy lawn. The kindly white owner of the plantation was always good to Randolph. Never a cross word was spoken to him, he says.

"But one day," Randolph said, "de little massa took very sick. Dey wouldn't even let me see him. I had a feelin' trouble was a comin', kaze little massa neber did have no real life like other boys. He was always a lookin' lak a sick puppy. I gues de Lawd jus' wanted him fo' hisself, and he took him.

"Adder dat I was put to work on a mule dat turned de wheel of de cotton gin. He jus' walk aroun' in circles lak de mule dat's pullin' a syrup press. Den de War came, and all de good clothes dat we had made on de loom turned to tatters. De food got low; some of de slaves run away and some of our houses was burned by de Yankees. Atter de war, de massa came back and told us niggers dat we waunt slaves no mo'. Said we could go, but if we wanted to stay we could do dat too. He gib' each fambly dat stayed a mule, a cow, some tools and money enough to run 'em till dey could git de crop harvested. He was de best massa dat any nigger ever had.

"Den I come to Bummin'ham. I worked on de railroad dey was puttin' through. I was a big nigger and I could make de others step. I was about six feet three inches and weighed near 200 pounds. I knowed my ole massa would have been proud of me if he coulda seed me a-workin' on de railroad and a liftn' dem ties and a sweatin' wid dem rails; I wished I coulda been in his cotton field and a-heard him talkin' fair like instid ob listenin' to dat foreman gibin' us de debil 'bout bein' lazy when we was a workin' our selfs nearly to death. Den one day I saw de foreman slap a nigger fo' drinkin' at de dipper too long. De nigger picked up a shovel and slam him in de haid, and run. Back in de slabery days dey didn't do somethin' and run. Dey run befo' dey did it, kaze dey knew dat if dey struck a white man dere want goin' to be no nigger. In dem days dey run to keep from doin' somethin'! Nowadays dey do it and den dey runs."

ABRAHAM JONES

Interview with Abraham Jones
—G.L. Clark

THE PATRIARCH ABRAHAM SAW THE STARS FALL

A lot of water passes under the bridge in 112 years. I thought of that as I talked to Abraham Jones, 112-year-old ex-slave of Village Springs, Alabama. "Uncle Abe" says he was born August 1, 1825, in Russell County, Alabama. Perhaps the day, the month and the year may not be exactly accurate. But they are near enough. He recalls the falling of the stars, the removal of the Indians from Russell County and the settlement of Auburn and other towns in that section. His great age is not apparent in his looks, actions or natural faculties. His hair is thin and white, but no more so than that of many men half his age, and his hearing is good. The mellow voice so characteristic of his race, is strong. He stands as straight as a soldier. And he works regularly to earn a living for his family. When we found him he was laying a flagstone walk in hard clay soil, and there was power in the swing of his pick and his tamping ax. His regular daily chores include milking a cow and chopping wood.

Abraham Jones, Village Springs, Alabama

He describes the phenomenon of falling stars as an event that occurred when he was "a little shaver 'bout eight year' old." November 13, 1833 was the date.

"Yes, sir, I saw de stars fall. Some folks say dey didn't never fall but I seen 'em. Dey fell jest like pitch from a torch, 'Z-z-z-z-zip, z-z-z-z-zip!' and big cracks come in de ground. I was settin' on de end of de porch, and I watched 'em. Dere was so many grown people crowdin' into de house, 'twa'n't no use fer me to try to git in so I jest sot still. We had a big sill under our house, more dan a foot thick, and so many people crowded in de house till dere weight broke de sill. Dey was cryin' and hollerin' but de stars didn't hurt nobody; dey jest fell and went out, and I don't know where dey went den; maybe into dem cracks in de ground. De cracks stayed a long time and it was dangerous for de people to go about at night; dey might fall into de cracks. One of dem I remember was two feet across and so deep dey couldn't find no bottom wid a long pole. I reckon dem stars kept fallin' for about a hour. Folks thought de end of time was comin' and ever'body got right after dat.

"Back at dat time de country was not settled much and dere was lots of Indians. My grandpappy was a full-blooded Indian but I don't know what kind. De Indians was good people but if dey thought you had done 'em wrong dey'd kill you right now. I saw some of dem when dey left dat country. Dey women carried de babies in some sort of sacks, hung down in front of 'em, and de men carried some of de bigger chillun on dey shoulders. Dey didn't have no property—jest lived wild in de woods.

Abraham Jones' Back Yard, Village Springs, Alabama

"A few years after de stars fell, a passel of people from de other side of Columbus, Georgia, moved over and started de town of Auburn so dey could have a place for a school.

"Before de war my people took me up to Blount County, and when de war come dey left me to run de grist-mill. I was de fust man in Alabama to try to grind a bushel of oats. I ground 'em too. A lady brung de oats and ast me could I grind 'em, and I told her I would try. She say dey didn't had nothin' for de chillun to eat. I ground de oats, and told her, 'Ole Mistis, I knows jest how 'tis and I'll be glad to give you a peck of meal if you will use it.' She say, 'of course I will; jest put it in with the oat meal, and I sure will appreciate it.' Her husband was off to de war and she didn't had no way to feed de chillun.

"I was workin' on de road a long time after de war and was tellin' de men about dat when her son hear me. She had told him about it and so he went home and told her he had found me. She sent word back for me to go to her house and let her see if I shore 'nuff was de same man. So I went and when she seen me she say, 'Yes, he is the same man,' and she called her husband and de other chillun and told 'em about it. Her husband say, 'Well, dey is jest one thing we kin do. If he ever need a place to stay or vittles to eat, we must see dat he gits dem.'

"In slavery time I belong to Massa Frank Jones, and Timothy Jones was de overseer on de place. Frank Jones had two plantations, de one whar I was born and another one close to Columbus. People ax me sometimes what kind of house I was born in and I tell 'em I wa'n't born in no house; and I warn't, I was born in de middle of de big road.

Abraham Jones' House, Village Springs, Alabama

"It's gittin' to where it's mighty hard for me to go now and do de work to make sompen for us to eat. I can't git about so fast and my head bother me a lot. I been workin' a long time now, and you does git tired after a hundred years of workin'!"

On his wrists were circlets of heavy cord. I asked him why they were there and he explained:

"To keep de pain out. Dey keeps it out purty good but if you can git a little leather band wid a buckle on it, dat is better yet. I wears dese all de time."

EMMA JONES

Interview with Emma Jones
—*Mrs.Preston Klein, Opelika*

EMMA TELLS HOW TO MAKE THEM "TEETHE EASY"

Emma Jones, eighty-three years old, was born in the Chattahoochee Valley between West Point and Columbus Georgia. She is very alert though quite deaf.

"White folks," she began, "I belonged to Marse Wiley Jones and his wife, Mistis Melba.

"I lived in a little two-room log cabin with high tester beds and mattreses filled with cawn shucks. Our food den was away better dan de stuff we eats today. It was cooked on a fireplace made outen rocks wid big hooks fastened into de side to swing de pots aroun' on. Us cooked hoe-cakes on a three-legged skillet dat sot ober hot coals an' us had a big oven for to bake meat an' cawn bread in. Dere ain't nothin' lak it nowdays, no'm.

"Ole Massa had a big garden an' we useta git de vega'bles we et f'um his garden. De folks was plenty good to us. Sometimes de mens would hunt 'possums an' rabbits an' wild turkeys. We sho' loved dem 'possums smothered in 'taters.

"An' talkin' 'bout medicines. Let me tell you a sho' 'nough cure for a baby dat's havin' a hard time teethin'. Jus' putt a string of coppers roun' he neck an' he won't have no trouble at all. Us useta do dat to de little white chilluns an' de black uns too; 'specially in hot weather when dey jus' seem to have de misery.

"Atter us got to be big gals, us wo' cotton dresses an' drawses in hot weather, an' when it git col' we had to wear long drawes an' homespun wool dresses an' home-knitted socks and shoes dat de cobbler made in his shop. You know, white folks, we useta make near 'bout eve'ything dat wes needed to run a body raght on our plantation. Us had eve'ything. On Sunday us wo' gingham an' calico dresses an' I ma'ied in a Swiss dress.

"I worked as a house gal an' when Miss Sarah ma'ied I went with her to nuss her chilluns. Besides Miss Sarah dere was Mista Billy, Mista Crick, Miss Lucy and Miss Emma. Dey had two uncles an' a Aunt of deres lived dere too.

"We had a happy fambly. At night some of de house niggers would gather 'roun' de fire, an' mistis would read us de scriptures, an' de white chilluns git tired an' slip out de do' but us little niggers couldn't 'ford to do dat; us hadda stay dere whether us liked it or not. Sometimes de massa let de niggers dance an' frolic on Saturday nights, but we warn't 'lowed to go offen de plantation, none ceptin' de ones dat had a wife or husban' on anudder plantation; den dey could only stay for a short time. Sometimes us could go off to church, an' I remembers a babtizin' in de creek. Some of dem niggers 'most got demselves drowned. Dey warn't used to so much water an' dey would come up outen de creek a spittin' an' a-coughin' lak de debil had a holt of 'em. Dere was so much shoutin' I 'spose ever'body fo' ten miles aroun' could hear dem niggers a-carrin' on in de creek.

"Durin' de war, my mammy helped spin cotton for de soldiers' clothes, an' when de Yankees come through, us hid all de valuables in de woods. Us had to feed dem an' dere hosses too. Dey et up near 'bout everything we had on de place.

"Dere warn't no schools in dem days for us colored folks. Us learned f'um de scriptures, an' by listenin' to de white folks talk."

HANNAH JONES

Interview with Hannah Jones
—*Pigie T. Hix, Greensboro*

AUNT HANNAH HAS A HUNDRED DESCENDANTS

Aunt Hannah Jones lives with her daughter in a small four room house on Tuscaloosa Street, Greensboro. "Lawdy," she said, "It's been so long dat I's 'mos' forgot 'bout dem slavery days, but I was bawn, in Bunker Hill, Amelia County, Virginny. My pappy was named Simon Johnson an' my mammy was Rhoda Johnson. My Marster was Alfred Wood an' my mistis was Miss Tabby Wood. When Massa died, de 'state was 'vided an' I fell to de son dat was too sick to take care of de place an' de slaves. Soon I was tuk to Richmond an' sold to Jedge Moore of Alabammy for twelve hundred dollars. Dat was de fust time I ever seed a slave sold. I was sixteen years old. When Jedge Moore's plantation was sold de niggers went wid de place an' it was bought by Marse Isaiah an' Marse Bill Smarr. It was called de Gillum Place and dat is east of Prairieville. I was a house girl an' ho'p wid de sewin' an' de spinnin'.

"Us had good houses built outten cedar logs an' de quarters looked jus' lak dis street dat I lives on now. We had good beds an' plenty vittels to eat: greens, cawn bread, meat an' all kinds of sweets. Some time de men folks would ketch a 'possum or rabbit. Marster had a big vegetable garden an' we was 'lowed to help ourselves f'um dis here garden. Us had two eve'y day dresses, an' we done our washin' at night. When I was ma'ied, de ceremony tuk place at my Mammy's house an' I wo' a pretty white dress.

"Our oberseer was Harvey Williamson an' he went 'roun' at nine o'clock to see iffen us niggers was in baid. Sometimes atter he done been 'roun', us'd git up an' have some fun. At de break of day all de slaves would git up an' go to work. Dose goin' way down in de fiel's would have to git up even befo' it was light so's to be dar when de dawn broke to commence de day's work. Den dey would come back at twelve o'clock for dinner an' res' awhile, den go back an' work till sun down.

"We useta have a man on de place dat played a banjo, an' we would dance an' play while he sang.

"Dis was one of his songs:

> White folks says a nigger won't steal
> But I cotched six in my cawnfiel'
> If you want to see a nigger run
> Shoot at dat nigger wid a gattlin' gun.

"My last Marsters was two brothers an' dey had one sister, Miss Sarah Smarr.

"We didn't have no jail on de place, an' most of us never went offen de plantation, jus' stayed 'roun' an' had a good time playin' amongst ourselves. Us niggers had a church dar on de place an' a white man preached to us, but in Virginny we went to de same church as de Marster did. I didn't jine no church dough till I come to Alabamy.

"None of us slaves ever tried to run away to de nawth 'ca'se dey was good to us.

"We useta have a doctor dat'd come roun' eve'y two weeks to see how de slaves was doin' an' iffen we was sick he would give us some medicine. Some of de women would tie asafetida 'roun' de chilluns necks to keep de sickness away.

"Some Saddays we had to work after dinner, but most of the time Marster would let us have a good time. On Christmas day us had a big celebration an' didn't do no work at all.

"Didn't nobody have no time to learn us how to read an' write.

"I don't know nothin' 'bout Mr. Lincoln 'cep'n he freed all us slaves, an' when we heard dat us was free all de niggers marched to Prairieville an' had a celebration.

"Honey, I's had nine chilluns, twenty five gran' chilluns, twenty seven great gran' chilluns an' thirteen great great gran'chilluns, an' I is expectin' mo' to come along pretty soon. I guess maybee I'll have 100 descendents fo' I shuffle off."

JOSEPHINE

Interview with Josephine
—*Gertha Couric, Eufaula, Alabama*

WHEN SHERMAN PASSED THROUGH

Aunt Josephine claims to be the oldest Negro in Eufaula. She says she was born ninety-four years ago in North Georgia on a plantation above Atlanta. She lives now in Eufaula, Alabama with a great-granddaughter.

"I used to belong to Marse Rogers," she said. "After surrender, Marse Rogers moved to dis country, and bought a plantation 'twixt Marse Josiah Flourney's and General Toney's. He said his plantation j'ined theirs." She was a nurse-maid all of her life, even in Slave days, and never was a "field nigger." Asked if she saw any soldiers during the war she said she saw "thousands."

"I and my Mistis and her baby hid in de swamps three days while Sherman and his army was passin' through," she explained. "Marse Rogers was in Virginny and when he got back home, there wasn't nothin' left but a well. Everything had been burned up. His house was gone and so was de smoke house; everything." She added that the well was a "dry well" where melons and butter and milk and meats were placed, in Summer, to keep them cool.

"Those three days my little brother hid in this well, while the soldiers were passin'," she said.

"'Fore God, Missy," she exclaimed, "when we got dat little nigger out ob dat well, he had almost turned white!"

Aunt Josephine is still a "nurse maid." She rocks her great-great-great-grandchildren.

LUCINDY LAWRENCE JURDON

Interview with Lucindy Lawrence Jurdon
—Preston Klein, Lee County, Alabama

IT AIN'T DE SAME

Lucindy Lawrence Jurdon bustled feverishly about her tiny Lee County cabin when she learned her picture was "goin' to be tuk." She got out her old spinning wheel; sat down before it and beamed. Her daughter coming in from the field, exclaimed: "Ma, I done tol' you dis lady was comin' to see you; an' you wouldn't believe me."

After she had posed, she seated herself to tell about slavery days. Her oldest grandson was sick in the next room with pneumonia; the cabin was stuffy and bare.

Lucindy said:

"Honey, I was borned in Macon, Georgy, on de twenty-eighth day of some month or other; I can't 'member which. But de year was 1858.

"My pappy an' mammy, Emanuel and Patsy Lawrence, come from Jasper County, Georgy. I had a sister named Jennie an' a brother named Phillip, but I was de oldest.

"Ol' Marster had 'bout three or four hundred acres on his plantation. His name was Marster LeRoy Lawrence, and he shorely was good to all us niggers. His daddy was Mr. Billy Lawrence; an' de marster had four chilluns.

"Us lived in a two-room log house wid a lean-to next it. Us was well off in dem times, but us didn't have sense enough to know it. I 'members dat us always had plenty of good victuals.

"Honey, us had meat broiled on hot rocks, roasted 'taters, ash-cake and sech. On Sunday us had ash-cake cooked in collard leaves; an' beef was served us when de killin' time come. Marster always gived de niggers plenty to eat.

"I can sit here an' picture dat house of marster's; a big, six-room house wid wide plank weather-boarding. Beside de house was a big garden, and it had palings 'round it.

"My mammy was a fine weaver and did de work for both white an' colored. Dis is her spinning wheel, an' it can still be used. I use it sometimes now. Us made our own cloth an' our stockings, too.

Lucindy Lawrence Jurdon, Lee County, Alabama

"No'm, us never did learn nothing. If us tried to read or write dey would whack our forefingers off. Us lived forty miles from de town an' it would take more dan two days to git to town. De women folks had to fix lunches every time dey went.

"My grandmammy had sixteen chilluns. I 'members

dat when us courted us went to walk an' hunted chestnuts. Us would string dem an' put 'em 'round our necks an' smile at our fellers.

"On Sattidy nights dey would have dances an' dance all night long. Somebody would clap hands, beat pans, blow quills or pick de banjer strings. When us had corns-huckin's, dey would pile de corn up, ring 'round it an' shuck, drink likker an' holler: 'Boss man, boss man, please gimme my time; Boss man, boss man, fer I'm most broke down.'

"I 'members dat one ol' sick man was freed 'fore freedom come. Dey let him go whar he wanted to, so he dug a hole in de ground an' used it fer a room. He put rafters inside to help hold it up an' it slanted down at de back."

Lucindy mused a moment, concluded: "Dem was good days, honey; mighty good. But us shorely is in a bad fix now an' needs help mighty bad. It jest ain't de same no more."

LUCY KIMBALL

Interview with Lucy Kimball
—Francois Ludgere Diard, Mobile, Alabama

THE FULFILLED WISH OF MAMMY LUCY KIMBALL

I made two visits to the home of Mammy Lucy Kimball. The first was during the month of April, 1937; the next was nearly a month later. On the first trip I had a very successful talk with the old Negro woman, but on the last, she wasn't at home, and so the information I sought had to wait. I was very disappointed that I couldn't see her on my second venture, but it was impossible.

Mammy Lucy had not grown very feeble when I last saw her, and her methodical mode of living can be attributed to her consciousness of the venerable age of eighty-five years which she had reached. She was born into slavery in 1851 at Swift's Landing near the town of Blakeley, in Baldwin County. She was a slave in the Charles Hall family of that county before and during the War between the States. In 1907, she came to work for the T.S. Fry and Santos Rubira families of Mobile.

Following the War between the States, Mammy Lucy Kimball worked in various families at the summer resorts of Baldwin County.

When a young girl, Mammy Lucy performed the duties of a children's nurse, and worked as a dining room servant. She had some education, and as she had worked in families of refinement and culture all her life, her manner was that of a well educated person. However, like the average educated Negro, she still displayed the characteristics of the Negro of the ante-bellum days. She said that she strictly adhered to old fashioned methods, such as: going to church twice a week, not believing in doctors, and always taking home-concocted remedies.

I asked her if she believed in carrying a rabbit's foot for luck, to which she responded:

"Honey, you don' think I'm like these other Negroes, who still believe in that old nonsense? I might tell the children that a rabbit foot brings good luck because it is an old custom for superstitions persons to carry one, but, honey, you'd have just as good luck if you carried brick-bats in your coat. My white people in Baldwin County never brought me up to believe in such things."

"Well, Mammy Lucy," I asked, "do you remember any strange or weird things that happened during the Civil War?"

"Yes," she answered slowly, "I remember during the Civil War some of the mischievous Sibley boys who were kin to the Hall family over in Baldwin County, tied a strange long black thread to the ankle of a black boy named Slow Poke.

"Some Negroes were going to town that night to fetch supplies and among them was Slow Poke. The boys jokingly asked him if he had his rabbit foot with him as he might need it to keep the rattling noises away at night. Slow Poke showed them his rabbit foot and, displaying his glistening teeth in a broad grin he said that there 'warn't goin' to be no ghosties atter him.' The boys deftly tied a string to Slow Poke's ankle while some of their friends held his attention. On this string were attached three cow bladders. Slow Poke hadn't gone far when he heard the bladders rattling at his heels. He immediately decided that there was a whole troop of ghosts after him, and so began to hit his fastest gait down the middle of the dark road. He ran till he reached Montgomery Hill some miles distant, where the string finally wore out. His people didn't find him till three days later. Then they took him home and gave him a sound whipping for running away."

Mammy Lucy talked of the Hall and Sibley families and of the wealth that they once had, and what happiness she found in being slave to such good people. She remembered all the summer resorts on the eastern shore of Mobile Bay when they were in their glory before the Civil War, and how the Mobile ferries landed bringing over all the fashionable Mobile families to their summer homes on the bay. She remembered hearing father Ryan, the poet-priest of the south, preaching at the dedication of the Catholic Church at Montrose and the storm in the '70's which almost demolished Alabama City (now Fairhope). She recalls the landing of the Confederate troops at Hollywood for wood when they left Mobile at the outbreak of the war on their way to Fort Pickens, Florida, to enter active service.

I found Mammy Lucy to be neat and prim as she must have been thirty years ago, when she first went to work for the Fry and Rubira families. She still walks with the agility of a young person, and her mind is fertile with fresh thoughts and with the deeds of the past. "I have found happiness," she said. "People have been good to me and I, in return, have tried to be kind to those around me. I have lived a plain life and have been rewarded with a ripe age that still finds me feeling young. I shall never grow old in my thoughts and actions, but always keep a place in my mind to welcome something new. I will have had a complete life if I can live only two weeks longer. There is something I'd like to see."

After a few more minutes I left her and returned home. There was something I wanted to ask Mammy Lucy; something that preyed on my mind for days. I wanted to ask her what the thing was that she wanted to see. She was so gentle and courteous; my interest seemed officious prying into her affairs. Someday I shall go to see her again, I decided, and bring up the subject casually. Then she'll never know of my unworthy curiosity.

Three weeks later I walked to the door of Mammy Lucy's cabin and on the porch stood a Negro girl watering a few pots of flowers.

"Is Mammy Lucy at home?" I asked.

The girl was silent for a moment, then she spoke in a high-pitched whining voice: "Mammy Lucy, she died."

"Oh, I'm sorry," I said. "When did she die?"

"Fo' days ago," was the reply.

I walked down the path of pebbles toward the bay. The question would never be answered, but I knew that Mammy Lucy died content.

ELLEN KING

Personal conversation with Aunt Ellen King
Mauvilla, Alabama
—Mary A. Poole, Mobile, Alabama

SATAN DONE GOT DIS JUKING GENERATION

Ellen King lives in a two room cabin nestling back in the woods near Mauvilla, Ala., about twelve miles above Mobile. A little Negro boy led me along a circuitous path to the ex-slave, showing the weight of her 86 years. After talking awhile she became interested and told that she was born at Enterprise, Miss. on the plantation of Mr. and Mrs. Harvey, but could not recall their given names, or the names of their children, of which there were three, two girls and one boy.

They lived in a big white house and the cabins in the slave quarters were built of planks, with streets between and little gardens in front of them. Some planted vegetables and others flowers.

The Harveys were good masters, they had plenty to eat, and good homespun clothes to wear and home-tanned leather shoes. The women gathered leaves, bark, and indigo to dye the cloth to make their dresses of different colors.

The plantation was large and had several slaves. Aunt Ellen, however, could not recall the number of acres or the number of slaves, but knew there was a crowd of them. The Harvey's raised wheat, cotton and corn, and lots of live stock.

Aunt Ellen sat quiet for a few moments and said:

"Lady, when I sits and thinks of all the good things us had to eat and all the fun we had 'course we had to work, but you knows lady, when a crowd all works together and sings and laughs, first thing you knows work's done."

Aunt Ellen recalled the Yankees coming through and telling all the slaves they were free, and that a lot of the slaves went with them, but Aunt Ellen laughed and said:

"My Pa and some of the others got scared and hid in a big cave and just stayed there until the soldiers left, and, lady, he still stayed on atter the war with the Harveys, and I was married there in the white folks church. They gave me a big wedding, lots to eat, plenty of music, singing and dancing. Jest like they used to say, we 'danced all night to broad daylight.'"

Aunt Ellen was asked how many times she was married and she replied:

"Twice, first one dead and don't know where t'other is, and had no children by either."

When asked about religion Aunt Ellen said:

"Lady, I prayed and prayed and religion came to me, and I jined the Big Zion Methodist Church, in Mobile, Ala., but moved here to Mauvilla where there was no Methodist Church, so I jined the Baptist Church."

Aunt Ellen says the people of today are going back not forward. "All they study is idleness and to do devilment these days. Young generation done gone, Satan got 'am, too much 'juking' these days, have no time to study 'bout the Lord and their dying day. All they do, is juke, juke, juke! When they closed the schools up here in Mauvilla, they had children all juking.

The writer was somewhat at a loss to know just what Aunt Ellen meant by "juking," but thought best to let her talk on and not make a direct inquiry, and after a little Aunt Ellen continued:

"No, lady, we used to call figgers for our dancing, had a big fiddle and two small fiddles, and a set in one room and one in t'other. None of this twisting and turning. I just can't stand all that juking, just won't look at it."

By "juking" Aunt Ellen meant rough dancing of the generation of today.

Aunt Ellen firmly believes the old-time religion was best for all, and tried to sing in a wavering voice the following:

> "Down by the river side,
> Jesus will talk and walk,
> Ain't going to study the world no more,
> Ain't going to study the world no more,
> For down by the river side,
> Jesus will talk and walk."

MANDY LESLIE

Interview with Mandy Leslie
—*Daphne L.E. Curtis, Fairhope, Alabama*

THE ORPHAN SLAVE-GIRL

In the suburbs of Fairhope, in a rough but neatly-kept cottage of two rooms, lives Mandy Leslie, a hard-working Negro woman whose energy belies the seventy-seven years to which she credibly lays claim. Twice widowed and her children scattered to the winds, Mandy is a pillar of strength and comfort to several white households, where she makes weekly calls to care for the laundry work, "wash and iron," as she calls it. The washing is done in the back yards, where a hot fire under an iron pot boils the garments to a state that permits Mandy's rubbing over a fluted wash-board to make them spotless. Strung on lines in the sun, the clothes are ready for ironing next day.

Using old-fashioned sadirons, heated at an open fire, Mandy turns out a "done-up" product that any modern laundry might envy. During the ironing process, which takes place in the hall or a spare room, the mistress of the house is entertained with a steady stream of biography, comment, and information from the lonely old woman who relishes this opportunity to talk to somebody, especially if there happens to be a visitor who is not familiar with her story. A typical episode runs like this:

"Yassum, I 'members de war, but I don't lak no wars. Dey give folks trouble and dey's full of evil doings. When de Yankees come t'rough here, dey took my mammy off in a wagon, and lef' me right side de road, and when she try to git out de wagon to fetch me, dey hit her on de head and she fell back in de wagon and didn't holler no more. Dey jes' driv' off up de big road wid Mammy lying down in de wagon—she mount a been dead, 'cause I ain't never seed her no mo'.

"Unker John Leslie and Aunt Josie and all dey chillun come along in a wagon, gwine up North, dey said, and dey said dey found me standing dar side de road crying for my mammy. Aunt Josie, she say: 'Pore little lamb, you gwine wid us. Us ain't got much, but us can't let you die.' And Unker John, he say: 'Poor chile, us mustn't leave her disaway.' He lift me up in de wagon and drive twell de mule gin plum' out, and den us stop and took up on a place not fur from Mon'gomery, on Mr. Willis Biles' place. Us live dar twell I was grown woman, and Mr. Biles sho' was a good man to live wid and he treat us right every year.

"Den I married Taylor and us kep' on living wid Mr. Biles and all t'ree of us's chillun was borned dere. Den Taylor died wid de fever, and he had insho'ance whet us pay a dollar a mont' for de longest and he say it take care me and de chillun when he gone. Bless God, dat money didn't take care nobody 'cept de doctor and de burying-man. Dey bofe got dey part and lef' me jes' two dollar and seventy cents, dat's all. Mr. Biles say dey ought to be whupped for chargin' me lak dey did. Den he went to see 'em, and cussed 'em out, and dey sont back twenty dollar. I ain't waste no more money on insho'ance, no ma'am!

"I had a hard time keeping my chillun and working de crop too; but Mr. Biles, he 'low me a mule, jes' lak he do Taylor 'fore he died, and us made four bags of cotton de fust year and five bags de nex' year. I pick every lock of it myself—jes' me and dem little chilluns.

"Den Rufus he come along and he thought us had all de insho'ance money, and he court me so hard and so reg'lar dat I act a fool and married him, and he turn out to be de no-countest nigger dat ever lived. 'Stead of him supporting me, us had to support him for nigh 'bout ten year, me and de chillun. He had misery in he back, and couldn't do no hard work lak plowing and hoeing. It hurt he back to pick cotton and pull fodder, and he jes' set 'roun' and make a few baskets and eat lak a hoss.

"Mr. Willis Biles he died, and he boy, Mr. Joe, he took de place and run it for he ma. Mr. Joe told Rufus 'twan't nothing de matter wid him but damn lazy, and if he don't git out and he'p me work, he gonna set de Ku Klux on him. Den us got scared and moved nigh 'bout to Uniontown, and us live wid Mr. Bob Simmons for seben years hand-running, and he treat us right every fall 'bout de settlement. Mr. Bob he say 'tain't nothing de matter wid Rufus jes' lak Mr. Joe say, and Rufus say he gwine move to town whar he kin git work to suit him.

"Us move to town, and Rufus he gone all day looking for a job and don't find nothing to suit him. I has to take in washing from de white folks to feed us and dey charge two dollars rent for de little shack us live in. 'Twan't right to do dat; 'cause I ain't never paid no house-rent in all my bo'n days, twell den. And de fust t'ing I know, dat trifling Rufus he done sell de mule and wagon and got drunk and lost de res' of de money. Us was sho' in a bad fix. Why didn't I quit Rufus? Yassum, I 'spects I ought to done dat; but he' so humble when he sober up and pray so strong. He say de Lord done call him outen he meanness and he gwine preach Jesus. He make lak he need dem preacher clothes, and us skimped along and saved 'nough to buy Rufus de suit of clothes wid a long-tail coat. He got a high-up hat and a Bible, and he sho did look gran'. Us was proud to see him all fix up and going out to labor in de vineyard of de Lord.

"Us give Rufus de las' t'ree dollars us could scrape up and he got on de train and went to Mon'gomery, but us ain't seen hair nor hide of dat nigger sence. In 'bout a year us got a letter from him in Juliet, wayup in Illinois, wharever dat is, and he say he in de pen'tenshry for ten year, 'cause dey 'scuse him stealing a woman's jew'lry, and would I get Mr. Biles and Mr. Simmons to do what dey can to get him out. He repent and been washed in de blood of de Lamb sence he been in jail. And he say if anybody write me dat he runned off from Mon'gomery wid 'nother woman and dat he got a wife in Chicago, it's a lie.

"Dat fix me wid dat triflin' nigger, and Mr. Sam Broady, what's a lawyer, he got me a 'vorcement and gin me back my fust name, Leslie. Now I's t'rough wid marrying. My chillun done all gone and got married, and I come back here whar I come from. 'Twix' here and Brantley, is de place.

"How old I is? I was five year old, come de Surrender—how old dat make me? Sebenty-seben? Dat's right and

I be sebenty-eight dis time nex' year. How I know I be living dis time nex' year? 'Cose, I will be living! I always notice dat when I lives t'rough March, I lives de res' of de year, and ain't March jes' now gone, huh?

"How de way wais' ironed suit you, Missy?"

DELLIE LEWIS

Interview with Dellie Lewis
—Mary A. Poole, Mobile, Alabama

DELLIE LEWIS KNOWS CURES AND 'CUNJER'

"To begin at de beginnin', white folks," said Dellie Lewis, "I was bawn on de plantation of Winston Hunter at Sunflower in Washington County, Alabama. It's on de Southern Railroad. De fus' thing dat I remembers was when de Gran' Trunk Railroad cut dere right of way through near Sunflower. Dey had a chain gang of prisoners dat warn't slaves aworkin' on de road, an' me an' anudder little nigger gal was sont wid big cans of buttermilk to sell 'em. One day a handsome white gent'man rode to our house an' axe me fo' a drink of cool water. He was de fo'man on de road. Jus' as soon as I handed it to him he done fell offen his hoss on de groun'. I run to de Mistis an' she got some of de niggers 'roun' de place to ca'ay de gent'man to de big house, an' do you know it, white folks, dat man, he neber open his eyes again! He keppa callin' de Mistis his mammy, but he neber open his eyes to see dat she warn't his mammy. He died a little later wid a conjested chill.

"Den I remembers one of de Alabama River floods, dat swep' ober de lan' an' washed away lots of de food. De gover'ment sont some supplies of meat, meal an' 'lasses. De barrels was marked U.S. an' one nigger, bein' tired of waitin' an' bein' powerful hongry tol' us dat de U.S. on de barrel meant Us, so us commence' to eat. When de oberseer come to gib us de meat an' 'lasses, us be done et it all up.

"Us slaves useta git up at dawn; de oberseer blowed a cow hawn to call us to work. De Hunter slaves was 'lowed to go avisitin' udder slaves atter work hours an' on Sundays, an' iffen we was to meet a pattyroller, an' he axe us whar we f'um an' who we b'long to all us had to say was we's Hunter niggers; an' dat pattyroller didn't do nothin', caze de Hunter niggers warn't neber whupped by no pattyroller. Some niggers when dey was kotched eben dough dey warn't Hunter niggers, dey'd say it jus' de same, caze dem pattyrollers was always 'fraid to fool 'long wid a Hunter nigger. Massa Hunter, he was somp'n'.

"Durin' de Christmas celebration, us all had gif's. Us had quilting bee's wid de white folks, an' iffen a white gent'man th'owed a quilt ober a white lady he was 'titled to a kiss an' a hug f'um her. Atter de celebratin' we all had a big supper.

"An' speakin' of cures, white folks, us niggers had 'em. My grandmammy was a midwife an' she useta gib women cloves an' whiskey to ease de pain. She also gib 'em dried watermelon seeds to git rid of de grabel in de kidneys. For night sweats Grandmammy would put an axe under de bed of de sick pusson wid de blade asittin' straight up. An' iffen yo' is sick an' wants to keep de visitors away, jus' putt a fresh laid aig in front of de do' an' dey won't come in. If you is anxious fo' yo' sweetheart to come back f'um a trip put a pin in de groun' wid de point up an' den put a aig on de point. When all de insides runs outen de aig yo' sweetheart will return.

"Yassuh, white folks, us useta hab games. Us useta play, 'Puss in de cawner,' 'Next do' neighbor' an' 'Fox an' geese.' I kin gib you some of de songs we useta sing:

>Old sweet beans and barley grows,
>Old sweet beans an' barley grows,
>You nor I nor nobody knows,
>Where old sweet beans an' barley grows.

>Go choose yo' east,
>Go choose yo' wes',
>Go choose de one dat you love best,
>If she's not here to take her part,
>Choose de nex' one to yo' heart.

"I is always been a 'piscopalian in belief, white folks. I ma'ied Bill Lewis when I was fifteen year old in Montgomery an' us had three chilluns. I is strong in my faith.

>In mercy, not in wrath,
>Rebuke me, gracious Lawd
>Les' when Dy whole displeasure rise,
>I sink beneath Dy rod.

"Yassuh, I remembers de war. I seed de Yankees a-marchin' through our place an' down de road dat led to Portland in Dallas County. Dey was mighty fine looking wid all dere brass buttons and nice lookin' uniforms. Dey didn't gib us much trouble. Dey had a Cap'n dat was good an' kin'. I heered him say dat dere warn't agoin' to be no stealin' an' atrampin' through folks' houses. Dey slep' outen de yard for one night; den dey went on in to Portland.

"Mr. Munger was our oberseer, but he had money of his own. He was better dan mos' oberseers, an' dere warn't no po' white trash, dem onery buckers libed further back in de woods.

"When us was sick Dr Lewis Williams, who was de doctor of de massa, 'tended to us slaves. I remembers sittin' in de doctor's lap while he tried to soothe my ailments.

"Us house servants was taught to read by de white folks, but my gran'-mammy, Alvain Hunter, dat didn't have no learnin' but dat knowed de Bible back'ards an' farwards, made us study. When me an' my brother was learnin' outen de Blue Back Speller she say:

"'How's dat? Go ober it.'

"Den we would laugh an' answer, 'How you know? You can't read.'

"'Jus' don't soun' raght. De Lawd tell me when its raght. You-all can't fool me so don't try.'

"When de marriages was performed, de massa read de ceremony an' de couples would step off over a broomstick for luck. Den we all had a big supper, an' dere was music an' dancin' by de plenty."

LIGHTNIN'

Interview with Lightnin'
—John Proctor Mills

Ignorant of the date of his birth, which occurred at Cahaba, the old State capital, Lightnin' was an overgrown, gangling youth of fourteen or thereabouts when the Civil War began. Born into slavery, he was the property of one Joel Matthews, cotton planter, whose fields lay near the then new capital city.

Lightnin' is happiest when spinning some yarn of the old days in Alabama for an interested audience, and when one such inquired as to how he came to be called "Lightnin'," the old man broke into a toothless grin and launched at once into another of the stories dear to his heart.

"Dat's Massa Joel's doin's, boss. I jist natcherly wa'nt neber any too peart an fas' on my foots, an de fus' thing Massa Joel eber sot me to fetch him was a cool drink o' water. De water done got wa'm 'fo' I brung it to him, an stid'er scoldin, he jist bus' out laffin' an' say: "Boy, you is so slow I gwineter call you after the fas'est thing on earth. Frum now on yo' name is Lightnin'." An I been Lightnin' eber since. Co'se I knowed Massa Joel was throwin' off on me, lil' as I was, but it looks lak I wa'nt bawn in no big hurry an I jist been movin' long slow-like eber since.

"Massa Joel musta been bawn on a sunshiny day 'cause he sho' was bright an' good natured. Eber' nigger on de place love him lak he was sont from Heaben. Mos' eber' day he come to de quarters wid de fambly doctor to look atter de niggers, fer he say a well-fed, healthy nigger, next to a mule, is de bes' propersition a man kin 'ves' his money in." An' us slaves fared as good as anybody.

"Naw suh! Massa Joel ain't neber hit me a lick in his life. He say a well nigger whut doan' wuhk, sho' ain't got no eats an care comin' his way, an ought'er be sont down de Ribber.

"Is I been mah'id? Yas suh. I done had fo' wives, an raise 'leben chillun. But 'taint lak in de ole days. Chillun all gone, an de ole nigger got no white folks, makes it mighty hahd to git along. 'Bout all de ole man kin do is fish an I does dat an gits a li'l somp'in to eat. 'Fo young Massa Tom passed on—he was Massa Joel's boy—I ain't neber wanted fer nothin'. I was Massa Tom's body guard. Us hunted an fished together, played wid de white chillun an sometimes I rid behin' him on de hoss, or on de fore seat wid de ca'iage driver when de fambly went to chu'ch.

"But dat's all in de pas', an de good Lawd say no man kin bring back de pas'. So I reckon, ef you all 'll 'scuse me, I better go fish my trotline an git somp'in to make the de skillit smell."

BILLY ABRAHAM LONGSLAUGHTER

Interview with Billy Abraham Longslaughter
—F.L. Diard, [HW: Mobile?]

HE CANED A CHAIR FOR PRESIDENT BUCHANNAN

On a bright April afternoon, while strolling along the Louisville and Nashville banana wharf and watching the crisp breezes from the gulf make small waves lick at the pilings, I met an old Negro man who was fishing for croakers off the pier. He had, sitting beside him, a basket containing wicker canes for making and repairing chairs. In the course of our conversation, I asked him his age.

"I'se eighty year old, white folks," he replied.

"Well," I said, "you must have been a slave back in the days before the war."

"Yassuh, boss. I were eight year old when Gen'l Grant freed de niggers." He spoke the words in a clear, strong voice and with a slight rolling motion of his gray bristly head.

"But General Grant didn't free the slaves, Uncle," I protested.

"Oh, yassuh he did too, white folks," he said respectfully; fo' I was right dere when de gen'l come into Richmond and sot us free."

"What about Abraham Lincoln?" I asked.

"Well, I guess he done a part of it, but he didn't do no fightin', kaze he hadda 'tend to de business in de White House. He lef' de freein' part to Gen'l Grant. I don' guess Mr. Abe lived long enough ter help us niggers much. He went to de Ford's Circus and got hisse'f shot."

"What's your name?" I asked.

"Billy Abraham Longslaughter. De niggers all calls me Billy, but ole Massa Longslaughter afore he died called me William."

"Where were you born, Uncle Billy?"

"On ole Massa Longslaughter's plantation near Richmond Virginny."

"Can you read and write?"

"Dey neber teach me no readin' and writin' kaze I had to work in de fields." His rusty hand rubbed across his woolly head, as my questions continued with the regularity of a metronome; nevertheless, Uncle Billy seemed always glad to answer them. I couldn't help but notice with what ease he moved about. He had the agility of a man twenty years his Junior, though his face, being caverned with wrinkles, gave him the appearance of great age.

"Where is your home now, Uncle Billy?" I continued.

"Most any place I goes, white folks. Ma wife, she died 'bout forty year ago in Virginny, and I been a trabelin' eber since."

"What do you do for a living besides fish?" I asked.

"Oh," he said, "I canes a few chairs," pointing to his basket of chair-canes beside him on the stringer of the wharf. "You see, white folks, when all dis repression came on an' dere war'n't no work fo' de people tuh do, jes lak all de young scallawags I hops me a train and goes on a trip."

"Where do you go next, Uncle Billy?"

"Well, I guess I mought run ober to New Orleans if I can catch me a freight train a goin' dat away."

"About your fixing chairs," I said. "Have you ever repaired any for well known people?"

"Lor', white folks, I caned a chair oncet fo' President Buchanan and he used it ter sit on in de White House. I'se made many a chair fo' famous people as I trabeled about. I guess I jus' keep on a goin' as long as I'se able, and when I goes on dat last trip across de quiet riber, I'se goin' ter make one for ole Gabriel, so's he can res' hisself in between times he blows on dat hawn."

United States. Work Projects Administration

LOUIS

Interview with "Uncle" Louis
—*David Holt, Mobile*

PSYCHOLOGY OF A RUNAWAY SLAVE

Of course you know that we always called the older colored men "Uncle" and the older colored women "Aunt." It was proper manners.

Old "Uncle" Louis was the oldest slave on the plantation, "Uncle" Toby having died. Louis was a "Guinea nigger." His ancestors had been brought from the Guinea coast of Africa. He had the characteristic marks of his tribe, being short, strong and very black, with heavy neck, thick lips, flat nose and eyes like those of a hog. He had great knowledge of wild plants, claimed to understand the language of birds and beasts. He prided himself on his powers as a hunter and also claimed intimate friendship with ghosts and spooks. Being what was known as a "yard servant," he had picked up much of the talk of his white masters and spoke his own version of their language.

Old Louis was what was called a "runaway nigger." He would run away in the latter part of the summer once in every two or three years and come back in time to help dig sweet potatoes. I was out in the sweet potato patch one morning when he returned. The doctor was there, also. When Louis walked up he simply said, "Hello, Louis; are you well?"

"Yes sir, Marster."

"Well, take that basket and go to picking up potatoes." Not a word was said about his running away. After the hands had knocked off work and Louis was sitting in front of his cabin, I went to him for an interview.

"Uncle Louis, what makes you run away? You don't get whipped or abused in any way."

The old slave scratched his grizzled head, puffed at his clay pipe and pondered the subject for some time before he replied:

"Marse Davie, I does cause de woods seems to call me. When de fall insec's is singin' in de grass an' the 'simmons is gettin' soft an' de leaves is beginnin' to turn, I jes natcherly has ter go. De wild sloes, de red haws an' de crab apples is ripe. De walnuts an de hickory nuts an de beach mast drappin' an de blue smoke comes over de woods, an de woods birds an de yard birds goes souf wid de cranes an ducks an wil' geese an de blackbirds an de crows goes in droves—it seem lack all dat is jes callin' me."

"Where do you go?" I asked.

"Lorsy, Marse Davie, I never goes off de plantation. I always go to de woods back o' de past'er. Ole Master knows whar I is an so does Henry. Don't you know dat holler dat come down on de lef' han' side of de branch—de fus holler you comes to, not more dan two hundred yards in de woods?" I knew it well.

"Don't you 'member a big green oak tree growin' on de right han' side of de holler bout a hunder yard up de path?"

"Well, sir, dat tree is my home. I done toted some poles an some sedge gress up dar an made me a bed—but you can't see it from de groun'. When I gets up dar I can see all 'roun'. I seen you an Marse Joe de las' time you go fishin'. I lays dar all day and listen to de birds and critters talkin'. A chicadee tole me you was comin' long befo' I seen you. Den a jay bird caught a sight of you an he tole me. Can't nobody come along widout de birds tellin' me. Dey pays no min' to a horse or a dog but when dey spies a man dey speaks. I done tame' a squi'l so he comes see me ever'day.

"De birds and critters sho is good comp'ny. I done made frens wid up all but de owl and de hawk. Dey is jes natchally bad an de other critters hates 'em. A ole red-breast' hawk come an lit in a daid pine tree. I seen him so plain til I knowed what he was thinkin' about. He was jes mad clean down in his craw and was cussin' ever'thin'. A little pewee bird seen him an begin to fuss. A crow fly over and hear de pewee, den fly down close an take a good look at mister hawk den he fly up and start callin' de other crows. In a little while a whole drove of crows is flyin' 'roun dat pine tree. Den de jay birds come an dey is callin' for a fight, but de ole hawk never move. Den de mocking birds come an dey sair right in and starts pecking at de hawk until he dove into de woods and gets away, an all de birds begin to talkin' 'bout bugs an things."

The old man was wound up for an interminable talk on his favorite theme, the talk of critters, and to change the subject I asked: "Uncle Louis, ain't you afraid of ghosts?"

"Lor', chile, I ain't feared of no ghos' or spook, as I's seed lots of both. All a ghos' do is jes show hise'f. You never hear of one doin' nothin' to nobody. Dey is sociable an wants to be near livin' people. When folks gets scared it hurts de ha'nt's feelin's an dey goes somewhere else. Dey has all de feelin's dey had when dey was livin'. You wouldn't stay by wid folks dat's fear'd of you an want to run away from where you is.

"Las' night, when I was up in my nes', an my fire had died out, all 'sept one little chunk, an de moon was shinin' like day, I lay down, I did, an I take a li'l nap o' sleep. Den I wakes up sudden an looks 'roun ag'in. Well, sir, de norf side of de hill was covered wid ghoses an spooks; dey was layin' down, standin' up and leanin' agin trees, but mos'ly dey was jes sittin' on de groun', all lookin' at me hard as dey could, widout battin' an eye.

"De neares' one to me was a little white ooman. She war sittin' flat on de groun', holdin' a baby in her lap. She look mighty pitiful an I say 'please Missis, can I ho'p you an yo' baby? I'd be 'bleeged if you tell me.' Her lips move but I couldn't hear no sound. Den I lay me down an drap off to sleep agin. When I wakes up de ghosses is all dere an de little white ooman look lak she want to say somethin', but can't, an I say, 'I ain' nothin' but a poor runaway nigger, but my Marster is a mighty kin' man, he'll sholy he'p you; but she didn't say nothin' an I goes back to sleep. De next time I wakes up de sun was risin' an I jes lays dere an watches de ghosses an spooks get thin, an fade away like a fog."

The old Negro was sitting in the twilight, talking in a low, impressive monotone, in a language we both understood but which I find difficulty in transcribing after all these years that intervene. A screech owl was "misery-flying" in the family grave yard back of the quarters, a fitting abligato to the narrative. Though creepy sensations crawled up my spine, I still had my doubts.

"Uncle Louis, do you really believe you saw all that, and didn't dream it while you were curled up in your nest?" I asked.

The old man seemed aggrieved at my doubts as he replied:

"It ain't no beleevin' about it. I knows what I knows an I sees what I sees. De ghos' is what lives when de body is done wore out, but it don't die."

"It's all imagination," I said, in defense of reason and nature, as I understood these things.

"I wants to ax you what does de imaginin'. It's your ghos' that does the imagin' so you can see other ghosses an spooks."

In recognition of Louis' knowledge and powers of reasoning my brother William wrote a diploma in Latin and presented it to him. After that he was called "Doctor" Louis.

I recall that it was about that time that I read a book on psychology but later discovered that there were those on the plantation who had a better working knowledge of the subject than was taught in the book.

Bibliography: Old Plantation Days, an unpublished

work by the Venerable David Elred Holt, late Archdeacon of the Sacramento Diocese (Protestant Episcopal) of California, and a native of Buffalo Plantation, near Natchez, Mississippi.

TOM MCALPIN

Interview with Tom McAlpin
—John Morgan Smith

A WHUPPIN' WID DE TRIMMIN'S

"Mornin' Boss," said uncle Tom McAlpin, "how is you dis mornin'?" The old former slave spoke cordially with a definite twinkle in his muddy eyes though his age had passed the four score and ten mark. His mind was alert; his memory vivid, and his faculties of speech quite unusual. Tom McAlpin was indeed a remarkable man. There was really a sincere note of welcome in his voice as he came forward, placed a large piece of cast-iron pipe against the steps of his house, 1928 Ave. D. So., Birmingham, and looked up at me showing a mouth of straggly teeth in a warm smile.

"Yassuh," he continued in his high-pitched voice after our salutations, "I'll be glad to serve you as bes' I kin wid my knowledge of de pas' years. Jus' you set down in dat chair," he pointed to what was left of an ante-bellum wicker seat; "I'll set on dese steps an' us'll go over de whole thing from de beginnin's.

"Fus' thing I guess you wants to know is whar an' when I was born. Yassuh, an' who I b'long to. Well, Boss, I was born in Martersville, Alabamy. Dat's five miles southwest of Talladega. I come into dis ole worl' on a sunny day in June, eighteen fawty fo'. I belonged to Dr. Augustus McAlpin, an' from dat day to dis, I is seed many things come an' go, an' I is aimin' to see a lot mo' befo' I cross to de udder side.

"De docta jus' had a small plantation, 'bout 100 acres, I s'pose, an' he didn't have but 12 slaves, 'caze dere warn't no need fo no mo'. He was busy in town adoctorin' folks. He didn't have no time to do any real farmin'.

"My job aroun' de place was to nuss de chilluns, white an' nigger. We all played 'roun' together. Sometimes we play coon an' rabbit, fox an' houn' and snatch, but what was de mostes' fun was a-ridin' ole Sut. Sut was a donkey an' us useta hitch him to a wagon, an' six of de chilluns would ride in de wagon an' I'd ride on his back. Sometimes us'd ride all de way into Talladega wid Sut.

"Nawsuh, I ain't neber got no whuppin' but one, an' it was a sho' 'nough complete one, boss, wid all de trimmin's. It all happened when de Massa told me he better not cotch dem hogs in de corn, an' iffen he did, I was agoin' to git a whuppin'. Well, boss, dere was one ole hog dat I jus' couldn't keep outten dere so I tuk a needle an' sewed up his eyes. 'Course I was jus' a little black 'un an' didn't know whut I was adoin', but I sho' sewed up dat hog's eyelids so's he couldn't see nothin'. Dat kep' him outten de corn all raght, but when de Massa found it out he gave me a lickin' dat I ain't forgot yit. Boss, dat was de onlies' lesson I ever needed in my life. It done de wuk.

"Yassuh, dere was pattyrollers 'roun' our place, but dey never cotched me, 'caze I was too swif' for 'em. Boss,

I could take holt of a hosses tail an' run 'roun' de pasture an' keep up wid him. I was sho' fas' on my feets.

"Nawsuh, us wan't never given no money for nothin', but I learnt how to make baskets an' I would take 'em in to Talladega on Sat'day evenings an' sell 'em to de white folks for fifteen cents. Den when I needed somp'n lak 'bacca or a little piece of chocolate, I could go to de sto' an' buy it. Lots of slaves on yuther plantations warn't 'lowed to make any money dough.

"Nawsuh, I ain't never had no schoolin', 'ceptin' what I could git outen de little white folks' books myself. Us niggers useta tote dere books to school for 'em an' on de way I would look in de book an' git a little learnin'.

"When us niggers on de McAlpin place et, us et raght at de same table dat de white folks et at. Atter dey finished dere meal, us slaves would sit down raght atter dem an' eat de same kinda food. Yassuh.

Tom McAlpin, Birmingham, Alabama

"Sho' I 'members de war. I 'members when de war commence', Jeff Davis called for volunteers; den a little later when de south needed mo' mens to fight, Jeff Davis' officers would go th'ough de streets, an' grab up de white mens an' put ropes 'roun' dere wrists lak dey was takin' 'em off to jail. An' all de while dey was jus' takin' 'em off to de war. Dey made all de white mens go. It was called de 'scription. Some niggers went too. Dem niggers fought raght side of dere masters. Some went as body guards an' some went as soldiers.

"Yassuh, Boss, I recalls de time dat de 'federate soldiers, bless dere souls, hid dere few hosses in de basement of de old Masonic Institute in Talladega an' hid dere amunition in de hollow stone pillars. Gen'l Wilson an' his raiders come th'ough dar, but dey never did fin' dem 'federate supplies. Dem Yankees jus' lak to scare eve'ybody roun' de place to death. Dey shot up de town an' dem blue coats tuk eve'ything we had: cotton, sugar, flour, hams, preserves, clothes, corn; eve'ything, Boss, eve'ything. Dey even burned up some houses.

"But Boss, dere ain't never been nobody afightin' lak our 'federates done, but dey ain't never had a chance. Dere was jes' too many of dem blue coats for us to lick. I seen our 'federates go off laughin' an' gay; full of life an' health. Dey was big an' strong, asingin' Dixie an' dey jus knowed dey was agoin' to win. An' boss, I seen 'em come back skin an' bone, dere eyes all sad an' hollow, an dere clothes all ragged. Boss, dey was all lookin' sick. De sperrit dey lef' wid jus' been done whupped outten dem, but it tuk dem Yankees a long time to do it. Our 'federates was de bes' fightin' men dat ever were. Dere warn't nobody lak our 'federates.

"I was in Richmond dat cold day dat Gen'l Lee handed his sword over to de yuther side, an' I seen Jeff Davis when he made a speech 'bout startin' over. I seen de niggers leavin' dere homes an' awandering' off into de worl' to God knows whar, asayin' good-bye to dere white folks, an' atryin' to make dere way de bes' dey kin. But, white boss, it jes' seem lak you let a nigger go widout a boss an' he jes' no good. Dere ain't much he kin do, 'caze dere ain't nobody to tell him. Yassuh, I was sont to Richmond to bring home some of our wounded 'federates. Dey sont me 'caze dey knowed I was agoin' to do my bes', an' caze dey knowed I warn't afeered of nothin'. Dat's de way I've always tried to be, white boss, lak my white people what raised me. God bless 'em."

ANNE MADDOX

Interview with Anne Maddox
—*Preston Klein, Opelika*

I SHOUTED THREE DAYS

Bible records place Anne Maddox's age at 113. She lives in a tiny cabin with her youngest child, Zora, about eight miles from Opelika. She is very feeble now and had to be wheeled out on the front porch to have her picture made.

Anne lives exclusively in the past. To her, the present world is "full of de devil an' gettin' worser every day." She likes to talk about the old days, but her voice is feeble and barely above a whisper.

"I'se heerd a heap o' talk 'bout Mr. Abraham Lincoln," she said, "an' I had a picture of him onc't; but I don't know nothin' 'bout him."

Anne takes her religion seriously and is devoutly confident that she will "inherit de promise."

"I jined de church in Gold Hill, Alabama," she recalled, "an' honey, I felt so good I don't know jest how I did feel. I shouted three days an' wouldn't eat a bite. I couldn't even drink water."

The old former slave was born in Virginia in 1824 and belonged to John Umford. She was later sold to Bill Maddox, of Alabama.

"When I come from Virginny," she said, "us travelled in wagons and slept in tents. Eve'y mornin' us was made to clean ourselves an' dress up; den us was put on de block an' bid on. White peoples was dere from everywhere; de face of de earth was covered by dem. I was thirteen den, an' I kin remember four wars.

"My mother and father was Charlie an' Rhody Heath, an' I had two brothers an' two sisters. Our houses was lak horse stables; made of logs wid mud an' sticks dobbed in de cracks. Dey had no floors. Dere warn't no furniture 'cept a box fer de dresser wid a piece of looking glass to look in. Us had to sleep on shuck mattresses an' us cooked on big fireplaces wid long hooks out over de fire to hang pots on to bile.

Anne Maddox, Opelika, Alabama

"Us fried on three-legged skillets over de fire an' cooked ash-cakes on de hearth wid hickory leaves on de bottom nex' to de hearth. 'Tain't no sech good cookin' now as den.

"'Bout four o'clock in de evenin' all de little niggers

was called up in de big yard where de cook had put milk in a long wooden trough an' crumbled ash-cake in it. Us had pot licker in de trough, too. Us et de bread an' milk wid shells an' would use our hands, but it was good.

"Ol' Marster hunted a heap, but us never did git none of what he brought in. Us had plenty of clothes, sich as was, but dey was spun an' wove at home. Us had home-made shoes, hard brogans, called 'Jackson ties.' Dey had brass caps on de toe an' would rub blisters on de feet.

"De plantation had several hundred acres. I was up wid de fust light to draw water and help as house girl. When dat task was done I had to go to de fiel'. Dey blew a big hawn to 'rouse de slaves in de morning's, sometimes 'fore day.

"Marster was good to us niggers, dough. He never 'lowed us to be whupped; jist scolded us. If us went anywheres, us had to be back by sundown. I once seed some slaves workin' roads in chains wid a iron ball hangin' on behin'. It was punishment fur meanness."

Anne said the slaves on the Maddox plantation were never allowed to learn to read and write, declaring: "It was too bad if dey kotched a nigger wid a pencil an' paper in his han!"

"I was made to carry Marster's chilluns to school, den go back fur 'em," she said. "Ol' Mistus read us de Bible, an' us went to de white folks church an' sat in de back, wid de white peoples sittin' up front.

"Oh, dem patterollers was bad. I sho' would run from dem things, too."

Anne's mind leaps in fast succession from one subject to another, and at times it is difficult to keep up with her intermingled thoughts.

"Ol' Marster give us plenty of licker," she said, "an' us laked dat. One of de funniest things us had aroun' de plantation was a little goat dat could walk a fence jist lak us little niggers."

"When de Yankees come, gran'daddy was at prayer meetin' an' Ol' Marster come runnin' an' told de niggers to hitch up de mules an' waggins. Dey was tol' to hide all de food an' jewelry, but 'bout dat time us seed de Yankees comin'. Dey didn't do us no harm; sho' did some places, dough.

"T'want long 'fore Marster call all us niggers up to de house an' tol' us dat us was free. He said us could go away or stay wid him. I stayed 'twel I was grown an' married Doc Maddox. Us had five chillun, Walter, Failer, Siney, Zora an' Johnny. I don't know how many gran'chilluns I'se got."

MANDY

Interview with Mandy
—*Daphne L.E. Curtis, Fairhope, Alabama*

"Howdy Miss. We is sure got a purty day fer de scrubbin' job. Hit will dry as fas' as we turns hit loose.

"Now jes' look a yonder, ef she ain't got gold-fishes an' ever'thing heart could wish!—Is they got ary increases?—Yassum,—dat's good; mebby so you can sell some.

"Me got chillun?—well I is borned three head uv em, but dey all died right now; didn't live a minute.

"Then I 'dopted me a baby boy. A little bitty girl borned him, an' she didn't want him,—he was in her way. She said she'd kill him, an' I didn't want her to git in no trouble, so I tooken him.

"But sho's you bawn I is sorry I done dat t'ing,—dat nigger so triflin', he is goin' on fourteen now, an' he ain't no help to me at all. He only come home when he hongry, an' that's plenty often.

"An' dis yere husbin' whut I is got now, he 'spicions me 'bout other men's all de time, and de boy an' him togedder, keeps ever't'ing riled up mos'ly, twell I'll be glad effen you was to say, you need me to sleep on your place.

"Go to school? Yassum I sho did. I had three months a year for three years, and a extra month onc't, that my mammy paid for. Dat made ten months for me. I was de forwardest chile my mammy had. When dey was any readin' to do my mammy sont fer me.

"Sis Kate kin turn off more work then I kin, but I can mek more cotton. Oncet I won a contest wid a man an' made 480 pounds. Dey gimme a hundred pounds for doin' it.

"Me and Taylor, he's my other husband, the one that died, we used to fo' mek bales near 'bout every year, but dis yer husband whut I got now, he don't do nothin' but jalous me, look lak he'd know I didn' want no man, but jes' fer company; an' dat boy I brung up, he jus' runs nights 'twell I am jes' plumb skeered. So one night I sont for my sister's boy, she is my dead brother's wife, an' Miss, dat rascal, he would steal my las' dime look like. Miss he would steal de har offen your haid could he jus' git a holt, so I jes' sont him back. I talk to him nice befo' I sont him, but hit didn' do no good so I up an' sont him.

"Then Miss Nellie (she that keeps the fillin' station) tooken him an' he stole a whole ginger ale an' a coky coly, an' she cotch him wid em. No'am he didn't git 'em open, effen he had uv, he would uv drunk 'em both, he would fo' sure.

"An' him tellin' folks he married a rich widow. Huh, Mr. Corte he say, 'Mandy you is getting yo'se'f messed for sho'.' He did so Miss, an' he done tole de truf' fo' God, he sho did. I is sho messed up wid 'em bofe.

"But Miss, hit was de bigges' cullud weddin', you ever see, an' me as black as I is. Dey was three tables for de white folks, an' I don' know how many cakes, an' Miss Bessie give me my marryin' dress, an' Mister Harry he give me a dollar, an' him? O yessum, he been married befo', he is got eight head uv chillun. His fust wife's bringin' em up, up in Dallas County, an' him carryin' on like he is down here.

"I allus wanted chillun, a house plum full of 'em, en I done los' all I could mek, so now effen I could of had me some widout 'em I never would of had ary husban' a tall. No'am.

"Me dance? No'am I is j'ined to de Church. Miss Emily she showed me some white folks dancin' oncet, but I thought they was gettin' too closet togedder. In my day they used to swing corners.

"House parties, yassum I is served a many of em. That's what breaks you down, though; day an' night an' day an' night.

"Well, good bye Miss, I sure do thank you for my dollar, an' my cup, an' ever'thing. I is shore enjoyed my day wid you. Me an' you is real good frien's now, ain't we? Hits been jes' like a partyin'.

"Now I'll be gettin' to Sis Katie's, she will mo'n likely want me to carry her Lodge dues up. An Miss, please you ast the bus man, wid yo' telephone, please sir wait for me jes' a minute."

FRANK MENEFEE

Interview with Frank Menefee
—*Preston Klein, Opelika, Alabama*

BROOM-STICK WEDDIN'S

Frank Menefee of Opelika is eighty-four years old and still healthy. He says, "Kids was brought up right in dem days but don't have no sich now, 'caze de switch was one of de best medicines ever made."

He was born in Loachapoka, Alabama. His mother and father were Susan and Monroe Menefee. They had six other children, Patsy, Sally, Lula, Mary, Melvina, and Philmore. Susan Menefee came from Jefferson County and Monroe from Gold Hill, Alabama, and belonged to Willis Menefee, near Roberson's Mill.

"My mother's father an' mother was Milton and Patsy Footman whut come frum Meridian, Miss., and dey paid $3500 for dem," Frank boasts.

"I'se never seed inside a jail, never paid a nickel in council, ain't never gwine to steal nothin' whut don't belong to me an' ain't never used a cuss word in my life. I always tried to do whut was right an' I plowed ever' day us could. Us cooked on dem great big fireplaces, 'bout six feet wide an' two an' three feet deep, with pots an' kittles hangin' out over hickory an' oak fires. Nobody better not spit in dat fireplace neither. Sho' never was better eatin' collards dan dem. All the chillun had a tin plate an' a tin cup with buttermilk in hit.

"I was whut dey called a shirt-tail fellow, had long shirt dresses of osnaburg dyed with red mud an' cinnamon bark. In winter dey doubled de osnaburg to be warmer. My daddy was a shoemaker. He made dem outer cowhides an' even lef' de hair on dem sometimes. Yuther times he clean 'em in de wash-pot to git de hair offen 'em.

"Us had good Marsa and Mistiss, iffen you wukked an' 'haved yourse'f. Dey was marsa Willis an' Miss Hanna Menefee. Dey jes' had two chillun Willis an' Willie. Willie weighed two hundred pounds when he was very young too. De 'Big House' stood in a oak grove wid one big oak tree raght by it.

"Mr. Sadler, de overseer, was good, too, but you sho' had to wuk. He's got a great-great-grandson, Sam Sadler, living now in Waverly, Alabama. De poor white peoples 'roun' dere used to ho'p us wuk. I disremembers our carriage driver's name but us had one dat drove Mistiss about, an' de carriage house was close to de Big House.

"Marsa had seven or eight hundred acres in de plantation an' I jes' don't know de number of slaves he did have. Dey got us up by daylight an' 'fo'. Blowed a cockle shell to get us niggers up. Iffen you didn't wuk, dey 'tended to you. Dey slashed one nigger an' he died nex' week. Us plowed 'twell dark an' lots an' lots of times all night long wid a lantern tied to front an' back of de plows. We was picking cotton all night long too, be ready to take dat wagon to de gin by three or four o'clock in de morning. Sometimes dey would put de slaves in chains. When dey wuk clearing up new groun' dey had chains put 'roun' dey ankles.

Frank Menefee, Opelika, Alabama

"On Sunday mornin' Mistiss would try to teach us niggers de Bible. Den us would go to church at white

church an' sit in de back wid white folks in front. De preacher was Rev'ren Frank Hugely. Dat Sunday mornin' breakfast sho' was good to us niggers. Us had meat, sugar, lard an' butter. I used to love to hear dem sing. When My Soul Be Resting in de Presence of My Lord, I'll Be Satisfied. I was baptized at eleven o'clock by Dave Hill an' I sho' got happy. I shouted an' sung: 'I'se never drunk no whiskey in my life.' When any of de niggers would pass on, old Mistiss would stand over de casket and weep. Us would pull off our hats an' marsa was nice as he could be, too. Hit was a home-made box dyed black. Mistiss she would see to de fixin' of de shroud.

"De patrollers sho' would get you an' dat's one thing made you stick to your wuk.

"On Sadday nights us would frolic an' dance all night long iffen you wanted to, buck-dance, sixteen-hand reel and cake walk. Dey would blow reed quills an' have all the licker dey wanted. Mistiss, dey ain't jes' now drinkin' licker. Oh, dem cornshuckings! Shuk corn, drink an' holler all night long. Sometimes dey'd sing:

> Dark cloud arising like gwine to rain,
> Nothing but a black gal coming down the lane,
> Nigger stole a pumkin an' started outer town;
> Nigger heered it thunder, Lord, an' throwed dat pumkin down.

"Mistiss, I don't wanter tell you no mo' of dat.

"When us niggers ma'ied, dey didn't have no preacher. We jes' jumped over de broom, an' went on an' lived together. Iffen a gal went wrong, dey beat her nearly to death. Iffen you moved de place when you ma'ied, de other marsa had to buy you.

"De li'l niggers had big times. Us used to play, 'Green grow the willow tree, you swing my gal an' I swing yourn. Green grow de willow tree.' Dey used to sceer up us niggers 'bout "Raw Head an' Bloody Bones," gwine to ketch us dat was so sceer bad iffen us didn't mind 'em, but I ain't never seed nor believed in ghostes. Us didn't get sick much 'caze us didn't have no trash to eat an' Mistiss giv' us ebony of yarbs an' us wore sacks of yarbs 'roun' our necks too.

"The Yankees did plenty of harm. Marsa shot at some of dem; an' dey took off our cabin wagons. When us was freed dey singed, 'I'se gwine back to Dixie, no more my heart to wander, never see my master no mo'.'

"Marsa called us all up an' told us we was jes' free as him. He give us all a suit of clo'es, some money, a mule, a cow, wagon, hog and a li'l corn to start off on. Us moved to Dr. Lawrence Smiths near La-Fayette, Alabama.

"Later years I ma'ied Jane Drake at the cafe in Opelika, Alabama, and by de jedge at twelve o'clock. She died, den I ma'ied Phoebe Ethen Drake. Some says de church can't save you, but I sho' feels safer in hit, an' I jined 'caze I wants to be better dan I was an' try to be saved."

ISAAM MORGAN

Interview with Isaam Morgan
—Mary A. Poole, Mobile, Alabama

"Mistis, I was bawn in 1853, 'cordin' to ole Miss's Bible, near Lotts Landing on the Alabama River." It was Isaam Morgan who spoke from his porch at 1657 Sligo Street, Mobile, Alabama. "I made a special trip back dar a few months back to de ole place, an' Mistis' daughter looked it up for me 'caze I done had forgot.

"Mr. James Morgan was my Massa, an' his wife, Miss Delia, was my Mistis. My mammy's name was Ann Morgan, an' as for my pappy, I done forgot his'n. I was raised raght dar in de white folks house, an' I had my own special place to sleep. I was de house boy, an' when I growed older I driv' Mistis aroun' in de Ca'iage.

"Us niggers lived in sho-'nuff style. Us had our regular quarters whar us lived in white log cabins chinked wid mud, an' de slaves had built-in beds an' a big open fireplace whar dey cooked. Us had plenty somp'n t'eat. All us had to do was to ask for it an' de Massa done de res'. Our rations was gib out to us eve'y Sadday. Some of de bes' food us ever had was 'possum an' taters. Us'd go out at night wid a big sack, an' a pack of houn's an' twarn't long befo' we done treed a 'possum. Atter we done treed him, de dogs would stan' aroun' de tree an' bark. Iffen de tree was small, us could shake him out. Iffen it was big, one of de niggers hadda climb up it an' git ole Mr. 'Possum hisself.

"Funny things about 'possums, Miss; de bigger dey is seem lak de littler de tree dey picks to go up. It is sho-'nuff fun, dough, to go a trailin' th'ough de woods atter a 'possum or coon. De coon'll give you de bes' chase, but he ain't no good eatin' lak de 'possum. I seen a coon one time when he was cornered bite de tip of a houn's nose off.

"Massa Morgan sol' wood to de steam boats, an' us slaves hadda cut de wood, an' split it up into smaller pieces. Any time a slave worked over time or cut mo' wood dan he s'pose' to, Massa pay him money for it, caze whenever one of us slaves seen somp'n we lak, we did jus' lak de white folks does now. Us bought it.

"Massa never whupped none of his slaves; he jus' tole us whut to do an' iffen we didn't do it, he'd call us to him an' he would say in his sorta way: 'Nigger! How many mo' times is I gotta tell you to do lak you tole?' Dat's all he would say, an' believe me Mistis, he hada a way of lookin' at you dat made you jump. When he bought a new slave dat wasn't use to doin' what he was tol', 'twarn't long befo' massa had him in line.

"No'm none of our slaves ever tried to run away. Dey all knowed dey was well off. We didn't have no oberseer but once. He was a mean un too. He tried to fight an' whup us slaves, an' one night six big nigger men jumped on him an' scairt him mos' to death. Atter dat de massa wouldn't never have no mo' oberseers. He tended to dat business hisself.

"Whut we do atter we finished work? Go to bed! Dat was de onl'es' place we was fittin' for. Us was so tired us wouldn't lie down two minutes 'fo us was 'sleep. On some moonlight nights us was 'lowed to pick de cotton. Den us'd git a little res' de nex' day.

"Massa an' his fambly used brass lamps an' candles for light, an' a few of us slaves had brass lamps too, but most of de niggers used torch lights.

"Some of de plantations had a calaboose whar dey putt de slaves dat wouldn't behave. Dis calaboose was built of logs fastened together wid stout ropes an' sunk into de groun', but Massa didn't need no calaboose to make his niggers behave.

Isaam Morgan, Mobile, Alabama

"Yassum, us had remedies for ailments. We used wild hoarhound tea for de chills an' fever, an' sweet gum turpentine, an' mutton suet. Dey wan all good uns too. But shucks! Warn't nothin' much ever de matter wid us niggers.

"Yassum, we used rock an' cotton to start de fires on de plantation, an' Massa had a flint lock rifle, too.

"De slaves had dere own special graveyard an' us'd make de coffins raght on de place dar. When someone die, he was taken in a ox cart to de grave, wid all de slaves a-walkin' 'long behine de cart singin' de spirituals.

"Our clothes was made mostly outen osnaburg wove on de plantation. We had wool clothes for de winter time dat was carded on de place. We had shoes made by our own cobbler an' tanned on de plantation. We called dese brogans.

"Atter de surrender, de Yankees camped near our place, an' bought aigs f'um us. Dey offered me a hoss iffen I would go nawth wid dem, but I jus' couldn't leave de Massa even dough I did wanted dat hoss mighty bad. I was twenty-one years old when Massa came to me one day an' say: 'Isaam, you is a grown man now. You is got to boss your own business. It's up to you to fin' work. I can't keep you no longer. Good luck Isaam. You has been a good nigger, an' you is gonna make somebody a good worker.'

"Atter I lef' Massa I worked at diff'ent jobs, sich as: loader, roustabout on different steamboats an' cotton picker. I worked on de *May Boyd*, *Lula D.* an' de *Gardner*. One of de ole songs sang on de boats went somp'n lak dis:

> De John T. Moore
> De Lula D.
> An' all dem boats is mine
> If you can't ship on de Lula D.
> You ain't no man o' mine.

"I been ma'ied three times, Mistis, an' Lawd chile I done forgot de name of my fust wife. I guess she still livin' somewhere caze she was too mean to die. My secon' wife was named Dora, an' she is daid. I got a wife now name Lily. She purty good.

"Yes maam you can take my picture, but lemme git my hat, caze I ain't got no hair on my haid, an' I looks better wid a hat. I'se got to be fixed up stylish."

TONY MORGAN

From record of a conversation in 1884
—*Francois L. Diard, Mobile, Alabama*

A SLAVE INTERVIEWS A SLAVE

George Washington extolling the virtues of a plain, homespun suit—granite-jawed Andrew Jackson defying the British at Pensacola—horror and massacre at Alabama's old Fort Mims—savages skulking near the fort, their bronzed bodies glistening in the hot August sunlight.

These were among memories of parchment-skinned Uncle Tony Morgan, who was interviewed on Oct. 1, 1884 by Jim Thomas, another slave, and a record of the conversation held in the files of a family in Old Mobile, Alabama. Uncle Tony was 105 years old then.

The story is told by Thomas, former slave of the Diard family. Uncle Tony was the slave of Mobile Judge H. Toulmin, grandfather of the later Judge H.T. Toulmin, who was appointed a judge by President Jefferson.

According to Jim Thomas, Uncle Tony told him:

"Did I knowed Gen'l Andrew Jackson? Lord bless you

honey, why, I knowed him and remember Gen'l George Washington afore him."

Uncle Tony explained that he accompanied General Jackson when the war-loving Tennessean marched from Mobile against Pensacola in 1814. He said he was serving as a wagoner, and remembered distinctly that the British surrendered on November 6. He recalled that, during the battle, Jackson was standing talking with a group of officers when an enemy shell exploded near him.

"Move away, general," the old Negro quoted one of the officers as saying, "they'll kill you!"

And Jackson replied in a characteristic manner:

"Damn 'em—I'll have 'em all in hell tomorrow!"

Concerning George Washington, Uncle Tony told Jim Thomas that the great American leader visited the town of Frankfort, Ky., and while there made an address. He wore a home-spun suit, which he pointed out as an example of what people might do in utilizing their products.

Frankfort was highly excited when Washington arrived in the city, and Uncle Tony told of a tiny urchin exclaiming with bitter disappointment in his voice:

"Why, Pa, he ain't nothing but a man!"

Uncle Tony's memory of what occurred at Fort Mims was vivid, according to Jim Thomas. The older slave related that he was one of many Negroes in the fort at the time. He said the defenders had been sleeping off a night of dissipation the morning William Weatherford's warriors attacked.

Men, women and children were butchered in the ensuing slaughter and the buildings were fired. The massacre continued until noon, Uncle Tony said, when the Indians retreated with scalps and several Negro prisoners to their camping site, called the Holy Ground. Here, the half-starved Negroes lived in constant dread that they would be butchered by war-inflamed Creeks.

Uncle Tony also recalled carrying the mail from Fort Stoddert, in Alabama, through the State and Mississippi. On several occasions he barely escaped being scalped by Indians, he said.

The old Negro related further that his father was a wagoner under Cornwallis when that general surrendered to Washington at Yorktown.

Concerning his age and birthplace, Uncle Tony told Thomas he was born in Danville, Ky., about 1779. He went to Mobile in 1805 with Judge Toulmin.

At the time of the interview the old slave was extremely feeble and lame, and walked with the aid of a cane. His skin was dried and wrinkled, and cataracts on his eyes had totally deprived him of his sight. Despite these handicaps, however, Thomas said the old man's mind was exceptionally clear, and his recollection of events occurring almost a century before were remarkable.

United States. Work Projects Administration

MOSE

Told by Edith Tatum, Greenville, Alabama
—*Mildred Scott Taylor, Georgiana, Alabama*

UNCLE MOSE—A TRUE STORY

The early spring sunshine sifted through the honey-suckle vines clustering around the cabin door, and made a network of dancing light upon the floor. A little Negro boy sat on the steps gazing silently up the dusty road and idly listening to the insistent buzzing of insects hovering about the honey-suckle blooms.

"Don't yer see nothin' of her yet, Jerry?" came in a querulous voice from a bed in a corner of the cabin.

"Naw, Unc' Mose. She ain't in sight yit, but it's mos' time fer 'er."

"Hit 'pear lak dis mis'ry is er gittin' wus all de time," the voice went on.

"Miss Sally say dat limerumunt gwine he'p it," essayed Jerry consolingly.

"It don' do no good 'cep'in jess whilst Aun' Judy is er rubbin'. De rubbin' does mo' good dan de limerumunt."

"Dar she is, rat now!" exclaimed Jerry presently.

"Praise de Lawd! fer de ole man sho is hongry en' got de mis'ry from his haid to his heels."

"Dar's ernudder lady wid Miss Sally. Sarter looks lak er gal."

"Mus' be some er ole master's gran'dahters come on er visit. Whyn't yer come an' sit some cheers out an' dus' em' an' straighten dis quilt 'stead er settin' dar lak er black patch on de sunshine? Don' yer know how ter ack when de quality is comin'?" By the time the chairs had been arranged to his notion the visitors were at the door.

"Good morning, Uncle Mose," said the older woman brightly, as she put a covered basket down on a table by the bed.

She had a strong, sweet face and smooth white hair, and the gracious dignity of a queen. "I hope you rested well last night and are feeling very much better. I have brought some one to see you. Now guess who she is," and she placed the girl where the sunshine fell across her face.

Uncle Mose turned his head on the pillow, and gazed eagerly at his visitor. Then his old black face wrinkled into a smile. "Lawd, honey, you sho' mus' be one er Mars' Eddard's dahters, frum de favor!"

"You are right, Uncle Mose. It's Miss Caroline."

"I'm so sorry to find you in bed, Uncle Mose," said the girl, coming closer, while Miss Sally began taking an appetizing breakfast from the basket and putting it on the table.

"Father told me not to come home without seeing Uncle Mose. He talks of you so often."

The old man beamed with pleasure. "Den Mr. Eddard's done fergive me for not choosing him dat time," he said with a chuckle. "Did you ebber h'yar 'bout dat time I choosed mah master?"

"Now, Uncle Mose, none of your reminiscence until Jerry has given you your breakfast. Then I know that Caroline will be delighted to hear all about it," and Miss Sally smiled indulgently. "Here, Caroline, put these flowers in water where Uncle Mose can see them, while I measure some medicine for him."

"Dat sho was er good breakfus', Miss Sally," said the old negro with a sigh of content, as Jerry gave him the last bit of waffle. "Ole Aun' Jincy allers was er good cook, en her ma befo' 'er. Couldn't nobody beat Aun' Lucy cookin' in dem days. Ginger cakes? She made de bes' ginger cakes! Miss Sally, you 'member dat time Ole Marster give me an Mars' Wat er whole silver dollar en we walked two miles to Mars' Walter's sto' en spent ev'ry bit er it fer ginger cakes? Er whole dollar's wuth er ginger cakes, an' Aunt Lucy rat dar at home er cookin' de bes' ones in de country! Mars' Wat sho was er sight!" and Mose lay looking with dim eyes into a happy, long-vanished past.

"Now tell me about when you chose your master," said Caroline, drawing a chair closer to the bed.

"O, dat time; I 'members dat mornin' jess lak it was yistiddy. Hit was in the spring-time lak dis, en ole Mose was er lil' black rascal lak Jerry dar. I was playin' roun' de cabin do' en h'yer come Jim de ke'ge driver, en say ole

Marster wanted me rat erway. I sho was skeered! But I couldn't think o' no meanness I had done so I jess helt up mah haid en marched up de road ter de Big House. En dar I foun' Ole Marster standin' on de steps, en in er row on de po'ch was Mars' Eddard, en Mars' Ted, an Mars' Wat, en Mars' Tom. 'Come h'yer Mose,' say Ole Marster in dat big way er his'n. 'Come h'yer en choose yer marster. I'm gwine to give yer ter de one you picks out.' I 'gan at Mars' Eddard. He was older 'en me an' sorter se'rus lak so I passed him by. I looked at Mars' Ted er long time sorter hes'tatin', but den I jess chanced ter look at Mars' Wat, en dem blue eyes er his'n was fa'rly dancin' wid sump'n sorter lak ole Nick, en I say ter mahself, 'dat's de marster fer Mose,' so I say out loud, 'I chooses Mars' Wat,' en bress yer heart, honey, I ain' nebber been sorry er minute sence. But de res' er Ole Marsters' boys nebber did fergive Mose fer dat," and he chuckled at the remembrance.

Caroline laughed. "Thank you, Uncle Mose, I've enjoyed hearing about it. I must go and see Mammy now. Next time I come I hope you will be better."

"De ole man ain' had his foots ter de flo' in five weeks dis comin' Sadd'y Miss Ca'line. Good bye, Miss Ca'line honey, come ergin."

"And now, Jerry, you run tell Aunt Judy to come up at once and rub Uncle Mose's ankles," said 'Miss' Sally as Caroline left the cabin. "I'll warm this liniment and have it all ready." She stopped before the open fireplace and raked up the embers into a little blazing fire, and putting the saucer of turpentine on the floor at some distance, she stood up and turned toward the bed. Just then a spark from the fire fell into the saucer, and the turpentine blazed up. 'Miss' Sally, startled, sprang back, but in so doing, her light cotton morning gown came in contact with the blazing turpentine and was quickly ignited. She caught up her skirts and tried to put it out with her hands, but could not. For several seconds 'Miss' Sally stood face to face with an awful death.

"My God-er-Mighty!" cried Uncle Mose, and with the agility of youth and health he sprang from the bed dragging a blanket with him, and throwing it around her, wrapped it close, extinguishing the flames just as Aunt Judy and Jerry appeared in the door.

"De Lawd in Hebben!" cried fat Judy, her swift glance taking in Miss Sally's white face, burned garments and helpless hands, and 'Uncle' Mose tottering back to his bed.

"Po' lamb! now jess look at dem han's! Lemme tie 'em up in wet sody this minute! You sho 'mos' got burned up, honey."

"I would have, but for Uncle Mose," said 'Miss' Sally faintly, as she sank into a chair.

Aunt Judy turned stormy eyes upon the poor groaning old man. "I'd lak ter know how cum Unc' Mose jess foun' out he kin walk?" she inquired belligerently. "I 'lowed some time ergo dat Mose was possumin'. I sho ain' gwine to waste mo' elbo' grease on dat old hyp'crite."

"Hush, Judy," said her mistress sternly, "Uncle Mose is no hypocrite. He has inflammatory rheumatism. It was a miracle," she added reverently.

"Dat's hit!" exclaimed Mose, eagerly. "Er miracle! Hit was de Lawd-er-Mighty let Mose git up den. Fer how you reckon I'd eber face Mars' Wat ergin' ef I had to tell him I jess lay in de baid en let my lil' mistress burn up? Mose done promus Mars' Wat ter tek keer er Miss Sally, an' ole man done de bes' he could."

SALLY MURPHY

Interview with Sally Murphy
—*Preston Klein, Lee County, Alabama*

SLAVERY WAS ALL RIGHT IN ITS PLACE

When I was looking for Sally Murphy, I went into a clean, four room cabin and found a small, neat Negro woman.

"Are you Sally Murphy?" I asked.

"I'm sho' is, honey, and who is you? Lawdy chile, you knows I know Mr. Pompy (my father). She laughed. "I'll tell you anything I knows.

"I was jes' 'bout ten years come slavery done. I was borned down on de Clayton place at Smith's Corners. My pappy he come from South Car'lina, where his pappy was sold. He name was Calop and my mammy was Hannah Clayton. There was eight of us chillun. Fred, Silas, Calop, Mary, Dolphus, Dora, Lula and me. Us all lived down in de quarters, which was five log houses, daubed wid mud. Dem logs was big ones, hand-hewed, and de fireplaces was big, too. Us went to de fiel's early in de morning and picked us a mess of young hick'ry and oak leaves to scald and cook in de pot wid meat. Dey made good greens and us had poke salad, too. (Made from the leaves of the pokeberry).

"When dey dried de fruit us would cook our kind of fruit cake. I don't recollect what went in it. Dere was plenty though. Mistis had de fruit dried on tins in de yard, and at twelve o'clock every day all hands went to de house and turned de fruit.

"Our beds was homemade, scaffold bedsteads wid ropes wove acrost de top what could tighten up. Sometimes us had homewove bedspreads on de beds most every day, but in gen'ally dat was for Sunday only.

"Our menfolks used to hunt possums and wild turkeys, but dey didn't mess 'roun' none wid rabbits. They didn't waste time on fishing either.

"Ev'y morning in May Mistis would call us little niggers to de house and ev'y other morning give us oil and turpentine. We made our own cloth for clothes. Our mammies wove us long drawers outen cotton. Dey bought wool and flannelet to make us pantalets. Us wore homemade homespun dresses. Some of hit was dyed and some checked. Us had shoes reg'lar in winter.

"Ole Marster Joe and Miss Rosa Clayton was good as gold. Dey had Sara, Jane, Henry, and Joe. De live in a big, two story house wid six rooms to hit and had a brick kitchen off from de house out in de yard. Ole Marster had a big plantation and his two aunties live dere, too. Dey was Miss Easter and Miss Charlotte.

"De slave women folks what had chilluns was 'lowed to go home half hour by de sun to wash ev'y day, and ev'y

Sunday morning all de little chillun had to be washed and carried to de Big House for de Mistis to inspect 'em.

"Us mostly stayed at home and didn't go 'bout none, and effen us went to Mt. Jefferson Church us had to have a pass or de paterollers would sho' git you. I did think dat 'Hark from the tomb in doleful sound, how careful, how careful den ought I to live, wid what religious fear' was de prettiest thing, and I sho' did love to hear dem sing hit. I never seed de baptising, 'ca'se I used to go to de 'Piscopal Church wid Mistis and open gates and hold de hosses. I sot in de foot of her carriage.

"Christmas dey'd give us provisions and de chillun some trash (meaning toys). Dey sho' had good times on moonlight nights at de cornshuckings. Dey would haul de corn from de fields and put it in a big ring, and as dey shucked dey would throw it in ring and den into de crib. Sometimes dey was so much corn it would stay on de ground 'twell it rotted.

"Mr. Dickey Williams' mother, Miss Emily, ma'ied while us was dere and my grandma cooked de cake. My daddy made de cake stand. Hit had three tiers, each one full of little cakes wid de big cake on top. Hit sho' was pretty.

"Dey let de little niggers have all de fun dey wanted. Us played jump rope and swung in de grapevine swings mostly. Den us had rag dolls. When any of us got sick, we was give hoarhound tea and rock candy. Sometimes effen dey wasn't looking and us got a chance us spit it out. Dey got de doctor effen us needed it.

"One of our Marsters was killed in de war and brought

home and buried. He was Mr. Joe. All de silver was hid out enduring de war but de sojers never did come to our house.

"One day my daddy says, 'Hannah, Marster said us is free now to do what we want to do.' But us stayed on two years mo'. In a few years I ma'ied Milton Heard and had a calico wedding dress and Judge Reed ma'ied us in Opelika in de ole plank court house. I didn't have no chillun and I lives now wid my niece, Sally Thomas.

"I don't know what I think 'bout Abraham Lincoln. I don't know nothing 'bout him. Slavery was all right in its place, I guess, 'ca'se some needed it to make 'em work.

"Folks get so sinful I thought I was safest in de church. I believe God intended for us all to be religious."

HATTIE ANNE NETTLES

Interview with Hattie Anne Nettles
—Preston Klein, Opelika, Alabama

DRUMS BEATING AND FIFES BLOWING

"Dey was sad times, honey; all de people was goin' to war wid de drums beatin' all aroun' and de fifes blowin.'"

Hattie Anne Nettles looks younger than her eighty years, but she remembers climbing a fence to watch gray-clad soldiers of the Confederacy marching toward the front. She also remembers a few details about slavery, although she was only a child at the time.

Hattie was born in Tallapoosa, Ga. Her father and mother were Archie and Matilda Benson. She had eight brothers and sisters; Charlie, George, Abraham, Mose, Lucinda, Mandy, Margaret and Queenie.

"Us had corded beds in dem times," she said, "an' dey was screwed in de corners to tighten 'em. Our cookin' was simple, too. Us used a griddle hoe to cook on de big fireplaces.

"Our dresses was homespun cloth dyed wid indigo, an' us didn't have very many clothes. But us kept plenty warm in de winter; an' in de hot summers us didn't need mor'n a thin li'l ol' dress."

Hattie called her master "a good Christian-hearted man who did de bes' he could for de niggers."

"I 'members," she said, "dat all de chilluns was good, too, 'ceptin' two of de boys. Dey was bad uns for sho' an' was arguin' an' fightin' all de time.

"Honey, Ol' Marster sho'ly did lak to sing, an' he was pretty good at dat. I 'members dat he useter git out in de back an' sing to de top of his voice: 'I'se Gwine Home to Die No More.'

"What I 'members most, dough, was de quiltin's an' spinnin' frolics dat de women-folks had. Den, on Sattidy nights, dere was Sattidy night suppers an' dances. All de peoples sho'ly did cut de high step at de dances."

Hattie beamed as the trend of conversation turned to Christmas on Southern plantations.

Hattie Anne Nettles, Opelika, Alabama

"Dat was a time!" she exclaimed. "Us had to go to mornin' prayer, but atter dat us went back to de cabins, dressed in our Sunday bes', an' went up to de 'Big House' fer some foolishness. An' it was sho'ly real foolishness, too.

"When I was growed up I married Bill Lockhart an' us had fifteen chilluns an' eight gran'chilluns. In de ol' days niggers axed de white marster for de bride an' no license was needed. Iffen dey lef' de plantation, de other white marster bought 'em so de girl could go wid her man.

"Our ol' marster was as good as he could be like I done tol' you. He looked atter de slaves when dey got sick an' sont for de doctor. In dem days dey would draw blood. Dey would draw almos' a quart from de body, an' you usually got well, too."

Hattie recalled one night of terror on the plantation when the Ku Klux Klan raided a prayer meeting where a large number of Negroes had congregated.

"De Klansmen beat up lots of dem," she said. "If a nigger didn't behave, dey'd nigh 'bout kill him."

Hattie lives in Opelika with a daughter. Flowers dot her clean yard and her old days are full of happiness.

W.E. NORTHCROSS

Autobiography of Reverend W.E. Northcross, 1897
—*Levi D. Shelby, Jr. (Colored), Tuscumbia, Alabama*

Chapter 1—How Reared

I was born a slave in 1840, in Colbert County, Alabama. Education was denied me, hence I grew up in ignorance. My mother and father were carried from me when I was only nine years old, but as soon as chance presented itself I ran away and went to them. My white people brought me back, and as they were not cruel to their slaves they did not "buck" me. I stayed with them until I was fifteen summers old. During this time my mistress made all the children, both girls and boys, come to her every Sunday, and she taught Sunday School. The book used was the old fashioned Catechism.

> Jesus keep me near the cross,
> There's a precious fountain,
> Free to all, a healing stream,
> Flows from Calvary's mountain.

It was against the law for them to learn to read and write, so she taught them the Lord's prayer and a few other things in the book. She said that she wanted them to know how to pray, how to tell the truth and not to steal, and always try to do right in the sight of everybody and in the sight of God. With these influences, I confessed a hope in Christ at the age of thirteen years.

> Am I a soldier of the cross,
> A follower of the lamb,
> And shall I fear to own his cause,
> Or blush to speak his name?

When she did not teach herself, she had an adopted girl to do the same. Finally the adopted girl married and moved to the farm where I was born, the farm from which I ran away. About this time, I was twenty years old. I felt that there was something for me to do. I began to lead prayer meetings. Still I felt that there was more for me to do.

Chapter 2—Entering The Ministry

I felt sure that I was called to preach, though "unlearned and ignorant." I trembled at the thought of preaching the gospel, but something seemed to push me forward in that direction. So I asked the people to let me preach. This request was granted. The people at that time had no place or house of worship. I began to fast and pray night and day. Being "unlearned and ignorant" (Acts 4:13) my heart silently murmured—

> Bread of heaven, bread of heaven,
> Feed me till I want no more.

This was the only school I attended, both day and night. At this time I did not know "A" from "B," but I met a man who could read a little. This man liked me and promised to teach me how to read, provided I would keep it a secret. This I gladly promised to do.

> I am weak, Thou art mighty,
> Hold me with Thy powerful hand.

I secured a blue-back speller and went out on the mountain every Sunday to meet this gentleman, to be taught. I would stay on the mountain all day Sunday without food. I continued this way for a year and succeeded well. I hired my own time and with my blue-back speller went to the mountain to have this man teach me. The mountain was the great school which I attended. I went from there to the blacksmith shop to work. From that place I was captured by the Yankees and carried to war. As I was crippled I was allowed to remain in the commissary department for about six months. While we were at camp at Athens, Alabama General Forest came upon us and defeated, captured, and killed until they were almost literally wiped out of existence. I had been kind to some little white children, by which I had won their love, and of course, the love of their parents, and stayed with them three days during the battle. I came to a river and turned aside to a farm from which all the people had gone to save themselves from the war, I got a man to help reach an island where I worked three days without anything to eat except grapes and muscadines. I preferred to die on the island than to be killed by the soldiers. Therefore, in time of danger, I rushed to this house and the good people hid me and changed my clothes. Hence, when I was found I was taken for one of the gentleman's slaves. When I was permitted by the man to try to return to LaGrange, and had gone some distance, I was caught by deserters from the Southern army, who voted to shoot me. They bound me and kept me overnight, intending to do away with me the next day. It was a lonely desert on the Tennessee river. I could not sleep, so all night I prayed to God, and the wives of the men prayed to God for the poor "nigger," and also prayed to their cruel husbands. Their prayers prevailed, and I was robbed and let go. I had vowed not to reveal their whereabouts. I left loving God and believing in his providence as I had never believed before.

> Earth has no sorrow that
> Heaven cannot heal.

I went home and got another spelling-book, although it was not allowed. Some of my own people told my master that I had a book trying to read. He sent for me to come to the house. I obeyed, though I dreaded to meet him, not knowing what the consequence would be. But his heart had been touched by Divine power and he simply told me that he heard that I had a book, and if I was caught with it I would be hung. So I thanked him and departed. Notwithstanding my master's counsel I thirsted for knowledge and got some old boards and carried them to my house to make a light by which I could see how to read. I would shut the doors, put one end of a board into the fire, and proceed to study; but whenever I heard the dogs barking I would throw my book under the bed and peep and listen to see what was up. If no one was near I would crawl under the bed, get my book, come out, lie flat on my stomach, and proceed to study until the dogs would again disturb me. I did this for many nights. I continued in this way to try to learn to spell and read as best I could.

> Blessed are they who hunger and thirst after righteousness,
> for they shall be filled.

I, like the Ethiopian, wanted a guide. I moved to Mrs. McReynold's. God bless her! She gave me a lesson every night for a period of four years. Then I went to my old master's brother, whose wife helped me every night as long as I would go to her for help. Rev. Shackleford (white) greatly aided me for a period of three years.

Boys and girls, grasp these golden opportunities which are now extended you from the school room. "Unlearned and ignorant" as I was I came along that way until the present time. My readers have better chances than I had. So I hope that they will make good use of their time and make my heart feel glad to see them setting their marks high and preparing themselves for the Great Beyond where all must go. Thither all nations will be called before the mighty judgment seat of the Ruler of the universe to give an account for the deeds done in this world. My prayer for the reader is, that they may make strong, useful, wise and Christian men and women, and at the end of time meet their God in peace.

Chapter 3—My Work

I will endeavor, in this chapter, to tell something about my works and whereabouts. I was ordained to the gospel ministry in 1867 by Rev. Mr. Slater (white), and Rev. Henry Bynum. Rev. Stephens Coleman and Rev. Henry Bynum, aided by Dr. Joseph Shackleford (white) laid down the foundation stones for the colored Baptist churches in Morgan, Franklin, Colbert, Lauderdale, and Lawrence counties, Alabama. I am now pastor of the First Baptist Church, at Tuscumbia, Alabama, which is the best Negro edifice in North Alabama. This church was organized thirty-five years ago, by me, with seventy-five members, but it now had a membership of nine hundred. I have pastored it for lo! these many years. This church is an excellent brick edifice. A few other brethren and myself organized the Muscle Shoals Baptist Association—one of the oldest and largest associations in Alabama. I have been Moderator for four years and its Treasurer for six years. I built the church at Russellville, Alabama, and pastored it for four years, and then ordained Bro. P. Jones and recommended him as pastor. I built the Barten church and pastored it for a period of fifteen years, after which I recommended Rev. James Hampton there as pastor. I pastored the Cherokee church five years, ordained Bro. Dennis Jackson and recommended him there as pastor. I pastored Liberty Baptist church for three years, ordained Bro. Alex Brown and recommended him there as pastor. I served Iuka, Mississippi for five years and then recommended a Brother from the West, who belonged to the Mt. Olive Association, to it. I built up the Sheffield church, pastored it three years and then recommended Bro. G.B. Johnson there as shepherd.

I also built up Mt. Moriah church at Prides, Alabama. I frequently uttered these words:

> Where Jesus leads me I will follow
> and his footsteps I'll pursue.

I organized St. Paul church (Colbert County) and pastored it for two years. Rev. E.C. White, who is now Assistant Moderator of the Muscle Shoals Association, was ordained by me. I have ordained more than twenty preachers to the gospel ministry, baptized six thousand persons, united in marriage five thousand couples, and buried about seven thousand persons. I have been faithful to every charge.

> Hark the voice of Jesus calling,
> Who will and work today?
> Fields are white and harvest waiting,
> Who will bear the sheaves away?

I have never left the old land mark. Not an one of the churches which I have pastored has brought a charge against me.

> The deepest secrets of our hearts
> shall shortly be made known.

I have been married three times and have known no woman but my wife, "though unlearned and ignorant." I have never had but one "fuss" with my wife. I told her at one time to hush and she failed to do so, then I slapped her, after which I went to the Lord in prayer and asked to be forgiven. I regret very much indeed to inform the world in print that I have been drunk from intoxicating liquors twice, which was before I professed religion. Notwithstanding I have ever held up temperance and aimed to keep it high until Shiloh comes to gather up his jewels. The following recommendation will show what the best people of Tuscumbia think of me:

Tuscumbia, Ala., March 13, 1897

To whom it may concern:—

We take pleasure in stating that we have known the bearer of this letter, Rev. Wilson Northcross for a number of years, and that he is a conscientious, intelligent colored man of good character. He has been pastor of the Missionary Baptist Church of this place since the war, having been instrumental in building the church, and always has made a good citizen. We believe him in every way worthy of the respect and confidence of his people.

Fox Delony, Judge of Probate
Jas. H. Simpson, Circuit Clerk
Chas. A. Simpson, Deputy Clerk
W.H. Sawtelle
Max Lueddemann

The following resolution was adopted by the church which I pastored thirty years:

Resolved, That Rev. W.E. Northcross, our pastor, is a good, moral, Christian man. He has been our pastor for thirty years, and we can truthfully say that he teaches in all things by example as well as by precept.

--TUSCUMBIA MISSIONARY BAPTIST CHURCH

The history of this church has undergone many changes, but they all worked for its betterment. At the close of the Civil war the few members went from brush arbor to brush arbor for three years. Then they held services in gin houses and under shelters for two years and six months. Then as the church was growing rapidly, they thought best to draw out, buy a lot, and build to themselves. So they bought a lot for what they paid fifty dollars ($50.) and erected a five hundred dollars ($500.) building thereon in which to worship the Lord. So the church continued to grow until it now has a membership of nine-hundred, a splendid brick edifice worth about six thousand dollars ($6,000.) and a thriving congregation. The church has never had but one pastor, and I have been as faithful as a clock. Through me (Rev. W.E. Northcross) the church was built, and I have ever since held high the Baptist doctrine throughout North Alabama.

WADE OWENS

Interview with Wade Owens
—Preston Klein, Opelika, Alabama

WADE OWENS HEARD ABE LINCOLN SPEAK

The Reverend Wade Owens of Opelika was born in Loachapoka, Alabama, in 1863 and just missed slavery, but he has heard his homefolks talk so much about freeing the Negroes, he feels as if he was grown then. His mother and father, Wade and Hannah Owens, came from Virginia and moved into "Jenks Quarters" on the Berry Owens place. They had several children, Wade, Nettie, Chance, Anderson and Iowa. Wade used to help drive up the cows. This cabin was of logs, mud and sticks with leaf and mud chimneys and slab floors. The beds fitted into the wall with plank sides, two posts with planks nailed on top, resembling tables. A box served as a dresser.

"All ash-cakes were cooked on poplar an' chestnut leaves, when dey roasted taters," Wade says. "Us chillun used to go early in de mornin' an' lick de honey offen de leaves for sweets den. Us didn't wear nothin' but our long shirts, an' us had homemade hats and brogans, hard as bricks with brass caps on de toes. I thought dey was de prettiest things I ever seed.

"Marsa Berry an' Miss Fanny Owens was good to us niggers. My daddy was de carriage driver for Miss Fanny, but take keer of dat man Ben Boddy, the overseer. He was de meanes' man God ever put life in. He wouldn't let us have no fire, matter not how cold, us had to work jes' de same or de nigger hounds 'ud sho' get you. Iffen not dog caught, dey would beat you to death nearly. He was so mean marsa run him off. Dey blew de risin' horn an' us worked from daylight 'twell dark or frum can to can't.

"Marsa had a pretty two-story log house, big columns an' big porch. He had 'bout two or three hundred acres an' worked 'bout three hundred slaves. Us had a jail an' locked runaways in hit. Brother Lockhart used to preach to us niggers in de white church at Lebanon an' us walked to hit.

"My daddy was sold fer $160. When dey put chains on de niggers dey was put 'roun' de legs and arms an' to a post. Dey took pains to ho'p my mammy an' pappy to learn. Dey would teach de Bible to 'em too. Marsa used to sing dem good ole songs, 'My heart frum de tomb, a doleful sound. My ears attend to cry,' and 'Amazing grace how sweet it sounds.'

"At baptising dey'd give de water invitation an' den go in water. An' didn't dey come out happy, shouting and praying? Ol' man Buck could hear dem two miles off, but hit was a glorious baptising.

"All de hands stopped when dey was a funeral an' didn't work no mo' 'till de body was buried. All de whites would go too. Dey would make de boxes, pour hot water over de plank to shape it up into a casket, den take turpentine an' smut to paint it. Den another big time, settin' up wid de dead, sing, shout an' holler an' try to preach.

"De patrollers would come to de colored frolic, an' one time a han' slipped off an', gentlemen, didn't he give 'em trouble to ketch him, an' dey didn't. When dey had dem Saddy night frolics an' dance all night long an' nearly day when hit was goin, dey would turn de pot upside down in de floor to hold de soun' in. My daddy pick de banjo. At de cornshuckings dey'd sing 'All 'Roun' de Corn Pile Sally,' an' dey had whiskey an' gin. Us had good time on Chris'mas, give us toys, syrup candy, light bread an' grape wine.

"My brother married up at de Big House an' dey giv' him a big dance an' marsa made me drunk. 'Twas fust one den t'other giv' it to me an' knocked me out. Dey had de preacher an' didn't jump de broom. Dey had de preacher so would be tied good. Dey would tell us chillun all kinds of ghos' stories 'bout witches gittin' outter dey skins. Us had free jumping grapevine ropes an' mumble peg. One night I was at Notasulga an' I heerd some singing. I stopped an' hit was right at my feet an' would go futher off. I took out wid hit an' hit kept stoppin' an' startin' off ag'in 'twell hit giv' out entirely. I looked to see where I was an' I was at de cemetery an' nothin' didn't bother me neither. I eased out an' shut de gate an' never foun' whut carried me dere.

"When us 'ud git sick, dey would bleed you, stick somp'n in your arm and draw de blood. Den dey would giv' us scurry grass and fever weed. Bone-set was use' as teas for colds an' fever to sweat you. An' hit sho' would sweat you, too. Marsa said war was comin' an' thought hit was to free us. Pappy went to war with young marsa an' stayed 'twell he got killed.

Rev. Wade Owens, Opelika, Alabama

"Dey hid de carriage horses, meat, silver an' plates. Yankees asked iffen marsa was good, an' us said yes. Dey searched de smokehouse an' some scraps no good an' nothin' but scrappy horses so dey didn't bother a thing.

Us stayed one year an' worked on one-eighth farm. The Ku Klux Klan was turrible. One John Lyons would cut off a woman's breast an' a man's ear or thumb.

"Atter I got growed I married Leila Benford at Mr. Lockhart's house, an' us had a nice little frolic, wid cake, syrup pudding an' wine. It was a fine night wid me, 'caze all kissed de bride. Us had fourteen children, jes' eight living, Minnie, Wade, Robert, Walter, Viola, Joe, Jim and Johnnie, an' ten grand-chilun.

"I heered Abraham Lincoln speak once at Chicaumaugee Mountain an' he said 'For people, by people, and through people.' I always 'membered dat. I jined de church 'caze I got converted."

United States. Work Projects Administration

MOLLY PARKER

Interview with Molly Parker
—Preston Klein, Opelika, Alabama

HE WAS A GOOD OVERSEER AND TREATED SLAVES RIGHT

Down in lower Lee County I found Molly Parker, an old acquaintance, ailing, and with the wandering mind of the aged. She could find answers to some of my questions, but some she couldn't get straight. She was just as clean and neat as she had always been, clad in an apron dress that she would call a "Mother Huggard."

Molly is eighty-five years old and lives with her sister Edna in a simple cabin, with a little patch of flowers between it and the field where Edna is still young enough to work. Molly was a housewife's treasure in the days gone by, but now she is too feeble to do more than work her little patch of flowers.

Molly Parker, Lee County, Alabama

She was born in Virginia but was brought to Alabama when a child and sold to a Mr. Dunn, near Salem. Her mother and father were John and Fanny, the parents of four children, Molly, Edna, Sam and Albert.

"I was a big size housegirl, but I sho' could work," Molly recalled. "Mr. Digby blowed a big bugle early every morning to get us all up and going by bright light. Mr. Digby was a good overseer and treated all de slaves de best he knew how.

"I married Dick Parker on a Sunday and dey fixed us a big dinner wid more good things to eat, but I was too happy to eat much myself. I ain't had no chillun of my own, but I ho'ped mammy with hern.

"De Yankees done camped nigh our house, and I had to help cook and tote de grub down to 'em. Us read in de free paper 'bout us being free. Massa didn't tell us nothing, but us stayed on for a long time atter dat. Massa had a passel of slaves.

"Yes'm, I'se a member of de church. Why I jined? Jest for protection, I reckon.

"I'd hate to see slavery time ag'in, 'cause hit sho' was bad for some of de niggers, but us fared good though."

LINDY PATTON

Interview with Lindy Patton
—Alice S. Barton, Eutaw, Alabama

FIFTY YEARS IN DE PO' HOUSE

"White folks," said Lindy Patton, from a chair in the Greene County Poor House. "I was born in 1841 an' it taken me fifty years to git to de po' house. Now I is got jus' fo' mo' years to make it an' even fifty dat I been dere. I hopes I makes de grade, caze dat would be some sorta rec'd wouldn't it? Fifty years in de po' house.

Lindy Patton, [TR: Eutaw], Alabama

"I wukked in de fiel's an' I worked hard all day long. De white folks useta gimme de clothes of de lil' white chilluns. I was born in Knoxville, Alabama, in Greene County, an' I belonged to Massa Bill Patton. I remembers a slave on our plantation dat was always arunnin' away. De Massa try beatin' him but dat didn't do no good. Dat nigger would run away in spite of nothin' they could do. One day de massa decided he was goin' to take de nigger to Mobile an' swap him for anudder one. De Misstis tol' him to leave de ole fool alone, said it warn't worth the trouble. Well, de massa started out to Mobile wid de nigger, an' when de got dere an' de train stop, de nigger, he lit out an' de massa runned right behine him. Dey musta runned a mile or mo' till finally de Massa he gib out an' let de nigger go. Two days later de massa he died f'm a-chasin' dat low down burr head.

"Nawsuh, de white folks didn't teach us to read or write. White folks, I can't hardly count none at all. We didn't have no church on dat place neither. We jus' went along wid de massa an' sot in de back. I ain't never ma'ied, an' I ain't never goin' to."

United States. Work Projects Administration

SIMON PHILLIPS

Interview with Simon Phillips
—J. Morgan Smith

EX-SLAVE LEADER RECALLS OLD DAYS

Simon Phillips, ex-slave, at 90 years is still as clear-thinking as a young man, and a leader among the oldsters of his race in Birmingham and Alabama. He has been for the past twenty-three years president of the union of ex-slaves which is composed of 1,500 Negroes scattered throughout Alabama. He is the only one of the Birmingham organizers of the society living today and though one of the oldest of his group, he shows but few signs of decrepitude. He walks with the aid of a hickory cane which has been in his possession for almost a half century, and his memory is not only accurate but vivid. His physical activity is shown by the fact that he had already spaded his garden and tiny stalks had pushed themselves above the ground on a plot of earth, covering approximately seventy-five yards square, on the Spring morning when he took "a little time off" to talk of the past.

Well does he recall the days when, under Alabama skies in the 1860's, he curried his master's fine carriage horses; the times old Aunt Hannah cured him of "achin's" with vegetable and root herbs; the nights he spent in the slave quarters singing spirituals with his family.

Simon Phillips was one of 300 Negroes belonging to Bryant Watkins, a planter of Greensboro, Alabama. He was a house man, which means that he mixed the drinks, opened the carriage doors, brought refreshments on the porch to guests, saw that the carriage was always in the best of condition and tended the front lawn. When asked about slave days, he gets a far-away expression in his eyes; an expression of tranquil joy.

"People," he says, "has the wrong idea of slave days. We was treated good. My massa never laid a hand on me durin' the whole time I was wid him. He scolded me once for not bringin' him a drink when I was supposed to, but he never whup me."

The old slave added that every plantation had a still and there was much brandy, but he rarely ever saw a drunk man. He says that when the men felt themselves becoming intoxicated, they would go home and lie down; now, he says, they go home and fall down.

The plantation on which Simon lived was seven miles long and three miles wide. When luncheon was served, the Negroes far off in the bottom lands had their food brought to them by the trash gang (boys and women) while those in the nearer cotton fields ate in a large mess hall. The food consisted of turnip greens, meat, peas, crackling bread and syrup, and plenty of it. "Not since those days," he states, "have I had such good food."

"What about the marriage situation, Simon?" he was asked. "How did you go about getting a wife?"

"Well, nigger jus' go to the massa and tell him that there's a gal over in Cap'n Smith's place that he want for a wife, if she happen to be there. Then the massa go to Cap'n Smith and offer to buy her. Maybe he do and maybe he don't. It depend on whether the Cap'n will sell her, and iffen she a good strong, healthy nigger. Niggers was bought mostly like hosses. I was too young to have me a wife when I was wid de massa, but I got me one later on after the war."

Simon Phillips, Birmingham, Alabama

During the War between the States, Simon served as body guard for John Edward Watkins, son of the plantation owner. Body guards went with their owners and cleaned the guns, kept the camp in order and did some cooking. Simon entered the war at the age of fourteen in Joe Wheeler's 51st cavalry. He distinctly recalls the time he stood within ten feet of the great general while he was making a speech.

Sometimes slaves were parted from their families, because when one planter bought a Negro from another planter, he did not necessarily buy his wife or children, or husband, as the case might be. The slaves were advertised around and put on a block to stand while they were auctioned. Women invariably brought more than men. He was asked, "about overseers, Simon. What sort of men were they?"

"Well," he answered, "some was mighty mean. When the massa be away, they tried to think up things to whup us for. But when the massa around, had he catch 'em gettin' ready for to beat a slave, he say, 'don't cut no blood from that Nigger!'"

Born in Hale County in 1847, Simon Phillips stayed with his master until 1886 at which time he went to live in Tuscaloosa to earn 17¢ a day, but he says he fared better on it than on three dollars now.

After the war many Negroes stayed with their masters and he remembers that some of the carpetbaggers came through his plantation and tried to make the ex-slaves stake off the land, saying that half of it belonged to them.

"One day," says Simon, "a few niggers was stickin' sticks in the ground when the massa come up.

"'What you Niggers doin'?' he asked.

"'We is stakin' off de land, massa. The Yankees say half of it is ourn.'

"The massa never got mad. He jus' look calm like.

"'Listen, niggers' he says, 'what's mine is mine, and what's yours is yours. You are just as free as I and the missus, but don't go foolin' around my land. I've tried to be a good master to you. I have never been unfair. Now if you wants to stay, you are welcome to work for me. I'll pay you one third the crops you raise. But if you wants to go, you sees the gate.'

"The massa never have no more trouble. Them niggers jus' stays right there and works. Sometime they loaned the massa money when he was hard pushed. Most of 'em died on the old grounds. I was the youngest of a family of sixteen and I has one sister still livin' on the old plantation. I'm going down to see her next week, 'cause I can never tell when the Great Master is goin' to call. We's gotta be ready when he does, and both us is gettin' mighty old. I wanta be sure and see her and the old place once more."

United States. Work Projects Administration

ROXY PITTS

Interview with Roxy Pitts
—Preston Klein, Opelika, Alabama

ROXY PITTS RECALLS CHILDHOOD

"I don't know 'zackly whar I was born," said Aunt Roxy Pitts, "but it was summuz 'roun Youngsboro, Alabama, en it was in 1855, fo' de wah started, dat Ole Marster said I was born. How ole dat make me? Eighty-two, gwine on eighty-t'ree? Dat's right, en I be eighty-t'ree year ole dis time nex' year, iffen I lives.

"Yassum, I goes to church putty reg'lar, iffen it don't rain; coz de rain makes de mizry in my hip en lays me up. I belongs to de Baptis' church en was baptize wid Jesus when I was twelve year ole. I'se a foot-washin' Baptis', I is, but dey ain't none of dem kind er Baptis' 'roun' here, en I jes goes wid de udder Baptis' en sets in de amen corner, en iffen I wants to shout, I shouts, en nobody ain't gonner stop me, bless the Lord!

"My fu'st marster was name Sam Jones, but I don't 'member him. My udder marster, de one what I 'members, was name Sam Peg, en us lived clost to a little town name Limekiln. My mammy was part Injun, en Ole marster cudden' keep her home ner workin' needer; she alluz runnin' off an stay out in de woods all night long. When I was a little gal, she runned off ag'in en lef' a teeny little baby, en nebber did come back no mo'. Dey said she gone whar de Injuns is. Dat was atter de wah, en pappy had to raise dat little bitsy baby hisse'f. He tuk it en me to de fiel' whar he workin', en kep' a bottle of sweeten water in he shirt to keep warm to gib de baby when it cry. Den Pappy he mai'ed Aunt Josie en dey had er whole passel er chilluns, en dey was my brudders en sisters.

"'Member 'bout de wah? Sho', I 'members 'bout de wah; but us don't hab no wah whar us was. Ole Marster got kilt in Virginny, dey said, en he didn't nebber come back home, en dem what did come back was all crippled up an hurt. Us didn't see no Yankees 'twel dey come along atter de wah was gone, en dey tuk Ole Mistis' good hosses en lef' some po' ole mules, en dey tuk all us's co'n en didn't lef' us nuddin' to eat in de smokehouse. Dey runned off all de chickens dey cudden ketch, en jes' fo' dey lef', de ole rooster flewed up on de fence 'hine de orchard en crow: 'IS-DE-YANKEES-G-O-N-E-E'? En de guinea settin' on de lot fence, say: 'Not Yit, Not Yit,' en de ole drake what was hid under de house, he say: 'Hush-h-h, Hush-h-h.'

"Us chilluns sho was misch'us. One time, atter a big rain, us foun' two hens swimmin' aroun' in de tater house, en us tuk en helt em under de water twel' dey's done drownded dead, en we tuk 'em to Mammy en she cooked 'em in a pot en shot de kitchen do'. When dem chickens got done, us went under de flo' en riz up a plank en got in de kitchen en stole one ob dem chickens outen de pot en et it smack up. When Mammy foun' dat chicken gone, she tuk er brush broom an wo' us plum out. But us didn't keer; de brush broom didn't hurt nigh lak de chickens taste good." Aunt Roxy nodded her head and rocked back and forth, as if she enjoyed recalling those youthful escapades.

"Yassum, I kin see plenty good enough to sew, cep'n' I can't tread de needle, en I has to keep atter dese triflin' chilluns to he'p me. You see dis quilt I'se piecin! Miss Lucy gwine gib me tree dollars fer it, coz she say it be made right, en dat's de way I makes em. Miss Lucy know she got er good quilt, when I gits t'ru wid it."

"Is yer got enny snuff, Missy? You don't dip snuff! No'me, I didn't tink you did."

United States. Work Projects Administration

CARRIE POLLARD

Interview with Carrie Pollard
—Ruby Pickens Tartt, Livingston, Alabama

A HUSBAND COULDN'T BE BOUGHT

Carrie Pollard was born in slavery time but she was never a slave. Her grandmother was a free woman who came to Tuscaloosa as a servant in the 1820's and was rescued from a man who claimed ownership, but whose claim was disallowed. The grandmother went to Gainesville, with her slave husband for whom she bought freedom.

One of her daughters, who was Carrie Pollard's Aunt Cynthia, was not so lucky. She couldn't buy her husband free. The story, told so often to Carrie when she was a child, is still a bright memory to the mulatto woman who was born in 1859 and still lives in Gainesville in the house of her birth.

Carrie Pollard, Gainesville, Alabama

"My Aunt Cynthy," said Carrie, "was free born in North Carolina. She come down here to Gainesville, an' though the deed sez you can't take a blue veined chile an' make a slave outa her, de man whut brought her made like he owned her or sump'in'. She lived on one plantation wid her guardian. Tom Dobbs, a slave nigger whut belonged to Mr. Dobbs here in Gainesville, he lived on another farm cross de road. An' dey couldn't marry, 'caze Mr. Dobbs wouldn't sell Tom an' Aunt Cynthy's white folks wouldn't let her marry, so dey jes' taken up an' went ahead. Her an' Tom had nine chillun, as fine looking mulattoes ez you'd wanta see. An' old Mr. Dobbs wanted 'em an' he couldn't get 'em.

"Aunt Cynthy was a good midwife, so a white lady sent fer her to come to Sumterville, Alabama, to nuss her an' she went. An' while she was dere, she dream't sump'in' done happened to her chillun an' dat dey was in trouble. So she tole de white lady she was nussin' 'bout whut she dream't an' she said, 'Mammy, iffen you is worried 'bout your chillun I'ze gwineter send you to a fortune teller an' see whut's de matter.'

"De fortune teller cut de cards, an' den she looked up en tole Aunt Cynthia 'All yo' chillun an' your husband done gone an' I can't tell you where dey's at.' So Aunt Cynthia run back an' tole de white lady. She called her husband an' he had one of his niggers saddle up two hosses an' ride wid Aunt Cynthy back to Gainesville. When she foun' her guardian, Mr. Steele, he met her wid de news dat dey was tuck to DeKalb, Mississippi.

"He got on his hoss an' tuck some other white men wid him, an' dey captured old man Dobbs right dere wid Tom an' de nine chillun. Dey done stopped an' camped an' was cookin' supper. So Mr. Steele tole him he could keep Tom, 'caze he was hissen, an' a slave, but Cynthy was free born an' he couldn't have her chillun. But Mr. Dobbs sez he didn't want Tom nohow, caze he was part Indian an' no 'count an' wouldn't work. So Mr. Steele bought Tom for Aunt Cynthy an' brought 'em all back to live wid him. An' he give Aunt Cynthy an' Tom an' de chillun a nice house right 'cross de branch here after surrender."

Carrie tells of how her grandmother used to send them to the mill in Gainesville with wheat, "jes' lack you do corn nowadays, to git flour. An' us git de grudgins an' de seconds an' have de bes' buckwheat cakes you ever et."

She says there are more black Negroes now in Gainesville than she has ever seen. She says, "Hit use to be a sight to see 'bout fifty bes' lookin' mulatto girls up in de public square here listenin' to de ban' an' nussen' de chillun, not five black ones in de bunch. An' dey had good sense, too. Us didn't have no clocks, so us white mistis would say, 'Yawl come home a hour by sun to do de night work,' an' us didn't hardly ever miss it." She says her grandmother sent her two daughters to school in Mobile, and they went down the river from Gainesville in a river boat called *Cremonia*.

IRENE POOLE

Interview with Irene Poole
—*Susie R. O'Brien, Uniontown, Alabama*

HUSH WATER FOR TALKATIVE WOMEN

Under the spreading branches of an enormous fig tree laden with ripe fruit "Aunt Irene" sat dreaming of old times. At her feet several chickens scratched and waited for the soft plop of an over ripe fig as it fell to the ground.

Aunt Irene's back is bent with age and rheumatism, but her two-room cabin is as clean and neat as a pin. Her small yard is a mass of color where marigolds, zinnias, verbena and cockscomb run riot, and over the roughly-made arch at the gate trailed cypress vine in full bloom. "Good morning Aunt Irene," I said. "A penny for your thoughts."

"Well honey, I don't know as dey is wo'th a penny; not to you anyhow. I was jes' stud'in' 'bout ole times an' 'bout mah ole marster. You know if he was livin' today he would be a hundred an' sixteen years ole."

"Who was your master Aunt Irene? Tell me about him."

"His name was Jeff Anderson Poole an' he was de bes' man in de world. Mah ole miss was name Mollie. I was born on his plantation three miles from Uniontown eighty five years ago.

"Mah pappy, Alfred Poole, b'longed to Marse Jeff an' he bought mah mammy, Palestine Kent, from another plantation 'cause mah pappy jes' couldn' do no work fer thinkin' 'bout her.

"Marse Jeff paid fifteen hunderd dollars for my mammy an' her three little chillun. Marse Jeff was rich, he owned three big plantations an' Lawd knows how many niggers. Dey was a hunderd head on our plantation. He lacked to race horses an' had a stable full o' fine racers. I spec' he made lots o' his money on dem horses. Miss Mollie say when he win he swell out his ches' an' stick his thum's in de armhole of his ves' an' talk 'bout it, but when he lose he don't say nothin'.

"Yas ma'am dere was always plenty to eat. A thousan' poun's o' meat wasn't nothin' to kill on our plantation. My mammy was de cook in de big house an' my pappy driv de carriage an' went 'roun' wid Marse Jeff when he tuck trips. I was a house servant too. When I wasn' nothin' mo' in a baby, de oberseer's wife tuck me to train, so I would know how to ac' in de big house.

"One day she started to give me a whuppin'. Us was out in de yard an' when she bent over to git a switch I runned under her hoopskirt. When she look 'roun' she didn't see me nowhar. After while she started on up to de house an' I runned along wid her under de hoopskirt, takin' little steps so I wouldn't trip her up, till I seed a chance to slip out." Irene threw back her head and laughed loud and long at this amusing memory.

Asked then about her mistress she said: "Yas ma'am she was good. She never punished me, she used to go 'roun' de quarters eve'y mornin' to see 'bout her sick niggers. She always had a little basket wid oil, teppentine an' number six in it. Number six was strong medicine. You had to take it by de drap. I always toted de basket. She gived me mah weddin' dress. It was white tarletan wid ban's o' blue ribbin. I sole de dress las' year but I can show you de pantalets she made me. I used to wear 'em to meetin' on Sunday when us had singin' an' de preacher said words." Aunt Irene brought out the deep ruffled pantalets carefully folded and yellow with age, she had treasured them for seventy-five years.

"No ma'am, Marse Jeff didn't go to de war, I don't know why. I guess it was 'cause he was so rich. Now don't you be thinkin' he was gun shy, 'cause he wasn't an' he done his part too 'cause he took keer o' five widders an' dey chillun when dey men got kilt in de war.

"My pappy lef de night de Yankees tuck Selma. It was on Sunday, an' I ain't seed him since.

"After de surrender us staid on with Marse Jeff. Us didn't keer nothin' 'bout bein' free 'cause us had good times on de plantation. On Sadday dey had corn shuckin's an' de niggers had a week at Chris'mas wid presents for eve'ybody. Camping at de big house an' mo' to eat in one day den I sees now in a year.

"Aunt Irene, do you remember anything about the conjurers in the old days?"

"I don't put much sto' by dem folks. Dey used to give you de han' so you could please yo' mistess an' dey would sell you hush water in a jug. Hush water was jes' plain water what dey fixed so if you drink it you would be quiet an' patient. De mens would git it to give to dey wives to make 'em hush up. I reckon some of de mens would be glad to git some now 'cause gals dese days is got too much mouf."

NICEY PUGH

Interview with Nicey Pugh
—*Ila B. Prine, [HW: Mobile]*

"I was bawn a slave, but I ain't neber been a slave", was Aunt Nicey's first remark to me as I came upon her pulling up potato draws in her garden in Prichard, Alabama. "Dere was 'leben chilluns in my family an' all 'em is daid ceptin' me an' one brother who is seventy-five year old at de present time. My pappy's name was Hamp West an' my mammy was Sarah West. All my folks belonged to Massa Jim Bettis, an' was born an' raised on his place.

"When I was a little pickaninny I worked in Massa Jim's house, sweepin' an' a-cleanin'. Us slaves had to be up at de house by sunup, build de fires an' git de cookin' started. Dey had big open fireplaces wid potracks to hang de pot on. Dat's whar us boiled de vegetables. An' honey, us sho had plenty somp'n' t'eat: greens, taters, peas, rosenyurs an' plenty of home killed meat. Sometimes my oldest brother, Joe West, an' Friday Davis, anudder nigger, went huntin' at night an' kotched mo' possums dan we could eat. Dey'd ketch lots of fish; 'nuf to las' us three days.

"I remembers one day when me an' anudder little nigger gal was agoin' atter de cows down in de fiel' an' us seed whut I reckon' was de Ku Klux Klan. Us was so skeered us didn't know whut to do. One of 'em walked up to us an' say: 'Niggers, whar you agoin'?'

"'Us is jus' atter de cows, Mr. Ku Klux,' us say. 'Us ain't up to no debilment.'

"'All right den,' dey say, 'jus' you be sho dat you don't git up to none.'

"Atter we got home us told de massa 'bout de 'sperience, an' he jus' laugh. He tol' us dat we warn't goin' to be hurt iffen we was good; he say dat it was only de bad niggers dat was goin' to be got atter by dem Ku Klux.

"When we was little we didn't hab no games to play, kaze Massa Jim an' Miss Marfa didn't hab no chilluns, an' I ain't neber had no speriences wid ha'nts or hoodoos. Dey neber teach us to read or write kaze when de niggers learn anything, dey would git upitty an' want to run away. We would hab Sad'day afternoons off, den us would sweep de yards, an' set aroun' on benches an' talk. It was on de benches dat mos' of us slaves set in warm weather. We et outen tin cups an' us used iron spoons to shovel de food in.

"At Christmas time, Massa would have a bunch of niggers to kill a hog an' barbecue him, an' de womens would make 'lasses cake, an' ole massa Jim had some kinda seed dat he made beer outen, an' we-alls drank beer 'roun' Christmas.

"But dere warn't no udder time such as New Years. Us all celebrated in a big way den. Most of dem no 'count niggers stayed drunk fo' three days.

"An' as fo' de funerals, I don't eber remember but three white folks dyin'. Dey jus' didn't seem to die in dem days, an' de ones dat did die was mostly kilt by somp'n'. One white gentman got hisself kilt in a gin 'chinery an' anudder was kilt a workin' on de big road. Den dere was a white 'oman who was kilt by a nigger boy kaze she beat him for sicking a dog on a fine milk cow. He was de meanest nigger boy I eber seed. I'll neber forgits de way dem white mens treated him atter he done had his trial. Dey drug him through de town behin' a hoss, an' made him walk ober sharp stones wid his bare feets, dat bled lak somebody done cut 'em wid a knife. Dey neber gib him no water all dat day an' kep' him out in de boilin' sun till dey got ready to hang him. When dey got ready to hang him dey put him up on a stand and chunked rocks at his naked body; dey thro gravel in his eyes and broke his ribs wid big rocks. Den dey put a rope around his neck an' strung him up till his eyes pop outen his head. I knowed it was a blessin' to him to die.

"But all and all, white folks, den was de really happy days for us niggers. Course we didn't hab de 'vantages dat we has now, but dere wus somp'n' back dere dat we ain't got now, an' dat's secu'aty. Yassuh, we had somebody to go to when we was in trouble. We had a Massa dat would fight fo' us an' help us an' laugh wid us an' cry wid us. We had a Mistis dat would nuss us when we was sick, an' comfort us when we hadda be punished. I sometimes wish I could be back on de ole place. I kin see de cool-house now packed wid fresh butter an' milk an' cream. I can see de spring down amongst de willows an' de water a trickling down between little rocks. I can hear de turkeys a gobblin' in de yard and de chickens a runnin' aroun' in de sun, an' shufflin' in de dus'. I can see de bend in de creek jus' below our house, an' de cows as dey come to drink in de shallow water an' gits dere feets cool.

Nicey Pugh, Prichard, Alabama

"Yassuh, white folks, you ain't neber seed nothin' lak it so you can't tell de joy you gits f'um lookin' for dewberries an' a-huntin' guinea pigs, an' settin' in de shade of a peach tree, reachin' up an' pullin' off a ripe peach and eatin' it slow. You ain't neber seed your people gathered 'bout an' singin' in de moonlight or heered de lark at de break of day. You ain't neber walked acrost a frosty fiel' in de early mornin', an' gone to de big house to build a fire for your Mistis, an' when she wake up slow have her say to you: 'Well, how's my little nigger today?'

"Nawsuh, jus' lak I told you at fus'. I was bawn a slave, but I ain't neber been one. I'se been a worker for good peoples. You wouldn't calls dat bein' a slave would you, white folks?"

United States. Work Projects Administration

SALLY REYNOLDS

Personal conversation with Sallie Reynolds
552 South Conception Street, Mobile, Alabama
—Compiled by Mary A. Poole

SATAN'S GOIN' 'ROUND WID HIS TAIL CURLED UP

Sally Reynolds, living at 552 South Conception street, was busy at the wash tub when the writer called to interview her on July 20, 1937, so it being a hot day we decided to continue our conversation out doors under the washshed amid a conglomeration of tubs, buckets, empty boxes, etc.

Sallie said she was born in Hiltown, Georgia, where her mother Margaret Owens was a slave and the cook on the plantation of Mr. Lit Albritton. When Sallie was about three years of age her mother gave her to Mrs. Becke Albritton, who lived at New Providence, near Rutledge in Crenshaw County, Alabama, to whom she was bound until 21 years of age. There was also a brother given by her mother to some folks in Florida and of whom Sallie never had any knowledge whatever.

Sallie said Mrs. Albritton was kind to her, taught her to spin and sew, and she tried to learn herself to weave, but, somehow, could never master it.

Mrs. Albritton had only a few slaves who were named, Mose, Dan, Charles, Sandy (the latter so called because he ate sand as a child), and two women, Hannah and Tene.

They had no regular quarters but just cabins out in a rear lot.

Sallie said all the whippings were given by either of the young Messrs. Albritton, they were high tempered, as their father was before them. She laughed and said she had Indian blood in her veins and sometimes she was sassy as she felt independent knowing Mrs. Albritton would always take her part.

She recalled the Yankee's coming through after the war, one remained at the Albritton home after the others had gone on, and she remembered hearing Mrs. Albritton telling friends who visited her, that after this soldier had left he wrote Mrs. Albritton a letter, telling her to look on the back of the bench on the gallery where he had sat and she would find his message. Sallie said she was a little girl sitting on the floor at her mistress feet, ready to fetch and carry for her and she often wondered but didn't dare ask what the message was; she did, however, hear some one say that the Yankees said, if they ever came again, they would take them from the cradle and that puzzled her, to know just what they meant.

Mrs. Albritton had a regular herb garden and Sallie helped her to gather the herbs, Pennyroil, Dock Sage, Tansy (single and double), Thyme, and Yarrow. They used Samson Snake Root in whiskey for cramps, and Butterfly weed for risings.

The writer asked Sallie about church and she said

they had no church but Mr. Albritton talked to her and impressed on her as a child to never touch anything that did not belong to her. "Ask for it and if not given to her, to let it alone and to never lie, or to carry tales, and she could always keep out of trouble." Sallie said she hated to see Sunday morning come, as the men folks were around the house and they would pick on her and somehow she would get a beating.

Sallie remained with Mrs. Albritton until she was 22 years, when she married John Russell, by whom she had three children. They all died as babies, later she married Gus Reynolds, (now dead) so Sallie just rents a room and lives alone.

Sallie says present generation knows too much and too little, that the "Old-time religion" was best for all, she thinks "Satan's goin' 'round wid his tail curled up, catching all he can devour"; and "folks should do like Christ did when Satan tried to tempt Him, and tell Satan to go get behind them, and they get behind Jesus they could not have sorrow run across their hearts and minds."

MARY RICE

Interview with Mary Rice
—*Gertha Couric, [HW: Eufaula]*

DESE UPPITY NIGGERS

Few of the ex-slaves will readily admit that they were mere field hands in the old days. Generally they prefer to leave the impression that they were house servants, or at least stable boys or dairy hands.

But "aunt" Mary Rice, age 92, who lives in Eufaula, holds no such view about the superior social position of house servants. She was a "big missy gal" ('teen age) during the War, and about her duties on the plantation of Dr. Cullen Battle near Tuskegee, where she was born, she said:

"Honey, I lived in de quahter. I was a fiel' nigger, but when I was a lil' gal, I helped around de milk-house, churnin', washing de pails and de lak, and den give all de little niggers milk.

Mary Rice, Eufaula, Alabama

"Massa Cullen and Mistis' Ma'y Jane was de bes' Marster and Mistis' in de worl'. Once when I was awful sick, Mistis' Ma'y Jane had me brung in de Big House and put me in a room dat sot on de 'tother side of the kitchen so she could take kere of me herself 'cause it was a right fur piece to de quahter and I had to be nussed day and night.

"Yassum, I was jes' as happy bein' a fiel' han' as I would'er been at de Big House; mebbe mo' so. De fiel' han's had a long spell when de crops was laid by in de summer and dat's when Massa Cullen 'lowed us to 'jubilate' (several days of idle celebration). I was happy all de time in slavery days, but dere ain't much to git happy over now, 'cep'n I's livin'—thank de Lawd. Massa Cullen was a rich man, and owned all de worl' from Chestnut Hill to de ribers, and us always had eberything us needed.

"Niggers dese days ain't neber knowed whut good times is. Mebbe dat's why dey ain't no 'count. And dey is so uppity, too, callin' dereselves 'cullud folks and havin' gold teeth. Dey sez de mo' gold teeth dey has, de higher up in chu'ch dey sets. Huh!"

CORNELIA ROBINSON

Interview with Cornelia Robinson
—*Preston Klein, Opelika, Alabama*

DE YANKEES WUZ A HARRICANE

"One time I 'members a storm us had. I calls it a harricane; but it was really de Yankees comin' through."

Quaint, little Cornelia Robinson was anxious to give all the facts she could remember about slavery days; but she was only about four years old during the latter days of that period, and must depend a great deal on what has been told her.

"Chile, dem Yankees come through an' cleaned out de smokehouse; even lef' de lard bucket as clean as yo' hand. Ol' Marster tuk his bes' horses an' mules to de big swamp, an' de Yankees couldn't fin' 'em. But dey tore up everything dey couldn't take wid dem. Dey poured all de syrup out an' it run down de road lak water.

"One pore little nigger boy was so skeered dat when he went out to git up de cows an' when he couldn't fin' some of 'em, he laid down in a hollow stump an' nearly froze to death. Dey had to thaw him out in de branch, but he was powerful sick. He war'nt no 'count for nothin' atter dat.

"I 'members dat Ol' Mistus saved all her jewels an' sech frum de Yankees. She brung 'em out to de nigger cabins an' hid 'em amongst us."

Cornelia, forever smiling, wears her gray hair in two short braids down the back. She says her father and mother were George and Harriett Yancey, who belonged first to a Mrs. Baugh and who were later sold to a Dr. Trammell, of near Lafayette. Her brothers and sisters were Charlie, Willie, Albert and Ann.

Cornelia Robinson, Opelika, Alabama

"I 'members de high, four-poster beds us useter sometimes sleep on," she said. "I was so little dat I had to crawl into 'em wid de help of a stool. I 'members dat de mud fireplaces of early times was far back, deep an' wide. All de little niggers was fed milk an' bread, wid de bread crumbled in. Us also had pot licker an' greens.

"Our clothes was muslin an' calico for de hot weather; an' den in winter us had linty cloth, part wool an' part cotton, homespun. Us raised de sheep, too, but us didn't wear no clothes hardly in hot weather.

"Us sho' did have a good marster an' mistis. Dey give us all de clothes an' food us needed an' gived us medicine. Us wore asafetida an' pennies aroun' our necks to help us not to git sick.

"Dey taught my mother to read an' write, too. Not many done dat. She'd read de Bible to us little niggers an' give prayers. Atter slavery, us had schools. I 'members dat George Hawkins an' his wife taught it."

Cornelia recalls some of the happenings of slavery times.

"If de slaves went off de plantation widout a pass, de patterollers would ketch 'em an' beat 'em powerful bad. If de niggers could outrun de patterollers an' git home fust dey couldn't be whupped. Dey had dogs called 'nigger hounds', same like dey had bird dogs, an' dey would track de slaves an' bring dem back home.

"I 'members my mother goin' to corn shuckin's. 'Course dey put us little niggers to bed 'fore dey went but dey sho' sounded lak dey was havin' a big time, hollerin' an' singin'. Us went to de white folks church in de afternoon, an' de Reverend Gardner was a mighty good preacher. When any of us niggers died, Marster was good to us an' let all de niggers quit an' attend de burial. Dey made de coffins at home an' would black dem wid soot.

"Us had a ol' quack herb doctor on de place. Some bad boys went up to his house one night an' poured a whole lot of de medicine down him. An honey, dat ol' man died de next day.

"Atter I got grown I married Robert Benson an' us had four chillun and several grandchillun."

Cornelia, beaming and apparently happy every minute of the day, lives with one of her grandchildren in Opelika.

GUS ROGERS

Interview with Gus Rogers
—Mary A. Poole, Mobile, Alabama

JABBO EXPLAINS HIS BLACK SKIN

Living on the Moffat road at Orchard, in western Mobile County, Alabama, on Mr. McIntyre's place is Gus Rogers, who is known better by the name of Jabbo. He claims to be over ninety years of age, but could give no proof. He claims the 26th of June as his birthday.

When asked how old he was, he replied with a smile:

"Miss, I don't know but I found everything here when I came along."

He was born at Salisbury, N.C. on the Rogers' plantation, and Mr. John and Mrs. Mary Rogers were his master and mistress. His parents were William and Lucy Rogers, who had five children, three girls and two boys.

Jabbo said the Rogers's home was built of boards of virgin timber and the slave quarters were some distance from the big house. Some of the cabins were built of logs and some of boards, all having clay chimneys and big open fireplaces equipped for cooking, as the slaves usually cooked their own meals, except during busy seasons, when meals were prepared in the house kitchen by the slave women too old to work in the fields.

Jabbo said one old man went around and rapped on the doors to wake up slaves to go to work. When asked how long they worked he laughed, and said:

"Just from sun to sun and then you went to bed, 'cause you knew that old man would sure be rapping before you were ready next morning."

When asked about earning any money, Jabbo said:

"Law, Miss we didn't even know what money was, and we didn't have no use for it. We had all we needed, plenty to eat and all the clothes necessary those days."

The Rogers raised lots of tobacco and wheat, and all the necessary farm products needed on the plantation. They had a large orchard and made all the cider they could drink.

Jabbo recalled driving many a refugee wagon during the War, and when they heard of the Yankees' coming, the Rogers family took all the horses and mules and hid them in the swamps and buried all the silver and other valuables.

After the devastation wrought by War, Mr. Rogers moved his family to Massey Station, Montgomery County, Alabama, intending to raise cotton. He brought Jabbo's father and mother and family with him, but meeting with little success he returned to Salisbury, N.C. Jabbo remained in Alabama.

Jabbo married and raised a family of five children.

There were two girls and three boys but he has no knowledge of their present whereabouts.

When asked if he was married more than once, Jabbo laughed and said:

"No, Miss I always had the price of a marriage license in my pocket, but somehow I never married."

In answer to inquiry as to religion, Jabbo replied:

"Miss, I am a Methodist, but there's only one religion. You have to be pure in heart to see Him, because He said so, and to do unto others as you desire others to do unto you."

Continuing about religion Jabbo said:

"God gave it to Adam and took it away from Adam and gave it to Noah, and you know, Miss, Noah had three sons, and when Noah got drunk on wine, one of his sons laughed at him, and the other two took a sheet and walked backwards and threw it over Noah. Noah told the one who laughed, 'you children will be hewers of wood and drawers of water for the other's two children, and they will be known by their hair and their skin being dark,' so, Miss, there we are, and that is the way God meant us to be. We have always had to follow the white folks and do what we saw them do, and that's all there is to it. You just can't get away from what the Lord said."

Jabbo said he would like "to go back to the good old days, 'though there was good folks and there was mean folks, then too, just like there is today."

Bibliography: Personal interview by the writer with Gus Rogers, ex-slave, better known as "Jabbo."

JANIE SCOTT

**Personal interview with Janie Scott
255 South Lawrence Street, Mobile, Alabama**
—*Mary A. Poole, Mobile, Alabama*

SLAVE CA'LINE SOLD FER A SACK O' SALT

Janie Scott, living in a cottage at 255 South Lawrence Street, was interviewed by the writer on July 14th, 1937. She claimed she was born April 10, 1867, but she appeared older than seventy years of age. She, of course, was unable to give any experiences of her own as a slave but recalled what had been told her by her mother, who was a slave on the Myers plantation at Tensaw, Alabama.

When asked how large was the plantation, Janie answered:

"Lordy, chile, many an acre an 'bout sixty slaves."

Her mother worked in the house, and when the field hands were working helped carry water out to them in buckets, each one getting a swallow or two a piece. Her father was Andy White, and was raised on the plantation of John Jewett at Stockton, Alabama.

Janie had heard her father say he was a coachman and drove the folks around, also came over in a boat with his master to Mobile to get supplies and groceries, and that they killed many a deer in neighborhoods just north of Bienville Square.

Jane said her mother's Master and Mistress didn't want her mother to marry Andy, because he was too light in color and light niggers Janie said folks didn't think as strong as a good black one, so her mother, Sarah Porter, and Andy White her father just borrowed a mule without the Master's consent and rode off and were married, anyhow.

Janie laughed and said she guessed it was all right after all because they had eleven children, two are now living, Janie and a sister Daisy.

When the writer asked if slaves ever earned any money, she replied:

"They didn't even know what money was." Then she continued: "Once when my mother was a little girl she asked her mistress to give her fifteen cents, and her Mistress wanted to know why she wanted fifteen cents. Her Mother replied: "I wants to see what money looks like."

Her Mistress thought she was trying to act smart and in place of fifteen cents she received a whipping.

The slaves wore homespun clothes, but her mother remembered having as her best dress one made of marino.

The slaves quarters were log cabins with clay chimneys, and they cooked in the open fireplaces in the winter and in the summer on what they called scaffolds, built out in the yard. These were made of clay foundations with iron rods across on which the pots hung.

Janie said her mother "was strong and could roll and cut logs like a man, and was much of a woman." Then they had a log rolling on a plantation the Negroes from the neighboring plantations came and worked together until all the jobs were completed.

After each log rolling they gave them molasses to make candy and have a big frolic.

During the Civil War when supplies were scarce, especially salt, Marster John rode off taking her mother's sister Ca'line with him, and when he returned alone his wife, Mrs. Meyers, wanted to know where was Ca'line, and Marster John replied: "I sold her for a sack of salt." At first they did not believe him, but Ca'line never returned and Sarah never saw her sister anymore.

After the Surrender the Yankees came through and the slaves hid under the house, but the soldiers made them come out and told them they were free, and gave the slaves everything on the place to eat. They all went down to the creek and praised God for what he had done for them.

Janie does not believe in charms, hoodoo or fortune-tellers, saying:

"Those folks can't tell you nothing. When Christ was risen He carried all prophets with Him and didn't leave any wise folks able to tell things going to happen here on earth—everything Christ wanted folks to know had already happened."

Janie did say the best charm she knew of was a bag of asafetida worn around the neck to ward off sickness or to take nine or ten drops in a little water would sure keep the worms down.

The slaves got plenty of coons, rabbits and bear meat, and could go fishing on Sundays, as well as turtle hunting.

The overseer on the Myers plantation was not a mean man, they had a calaboose or sweat box to punish unruly slaves in place of whipping them.

After the Surrender her father and mother moved to Mobile, Alabama, and her father continued to work for Mr. Jewett at his mill located at the foot of Palmetto Street on the Mobile river front.

MAUGAN SHEPHERD

Interview with Maugan Shepherd
—*Gertha Couric, [HW: Eufaula]*

SLAVERY COMING BACK? MAUGAN HOPES SO

"Mistus, I hears slavery times is comin' back."

Uncle Maugan Shepherd is past 80. He idled about the front of his tumble-down house in Eufaula, happily recalling the old plantation days. He has never learned to read, and therefore pins a great deal of dependence upon hearsay.

"Where did you hear about slavery coming back?" the interviewer asked him.

"Well, mam, 'pear lak I heard it somewhar. I don't rikolect jest now."

"Would you like to have the old times back again, Uncle Maugan?"

He studied a moment, beamed:

"Yassum, I would. I'se proud I was borned a slave. I'se too young to 'member much, but I knows I always had enough to eat and wear den, and I sho don't now.

Uncle Maugan said that he was "birthed" at Chestnut Hill; that he belonged to Marse and Mistus Rich Wiley, and that his father and mother were Bunk and Betsy Wiley, both "field niggers." Maugan had two brothers, Oliver and Monroe; but no sisters.

"I never seed ma and pa much 'cept on Sundays," he explained. "Dey was allus workin' in de fields an' I was out chasin' rabbits an' sech mos' of de time. At night I jest et my cornpone an' drink my buttermilk an' fell on de bed asleep."

Maugan remembers one overseer, scornfully referring to him as "po' white trash."

"Us slaves called him by his las' name behin' his back," the old darky explained, "'caze us hated to 'mister' dat white man."

Maugan remembers Reconstruction and a great deal about "atter de surrender," but says "rickolection ain't so good" on things that happened before.

"I 'members dat I was powerful scared of de Yankee soldiers," he said, "but dey never hurt nobody. Dey come through Eufaula an' all us niggers tried to hide; but dey jest come on by an' laughed at us fer bein' scared."

Maugan Shepherd, Eufaula, Alabama

More than fifty years ago, Maugan married Kitty. She is about 70 and makes her living washing clothes for "de white peoples." They never had any children.

Maugan says he never goes anywhere except to church on Sundays. His legs are not so strong anymore, he explains.

"My ol' 'oman, she sho' lak to go to funerals," he chuckled. "But in dese days day takes de body to have it vulcanized, so we can't have no settin' ups. Dis went hard on Kitty, 'caze she was a mourner; but it didn't do her no good, shoutin' an' amournin' all night. She would always come home wid her head tied up an' her eyes set back in her head."

Maugan still works. He is a good yardman, but says some day he is just "gwine ter drap out, lak his pa did."

ALLEN SIMS

Interview with Allen Sims
—*Preston Klein, Opelika*

PLENTY OF FOOD AND NO TRASH NEITHER

While interviewing former slaves in the rural sections of Lee County, I ran across Allen Sims, a sturdy old Negro, who proved to have an unusually clear recollection of slavery as the institution appeared to the small boy of that era. He was not old enough to make a work-hand at its close. He spoke slowly, but with evident positiveness as to the facts:

"I 'members lots 'bout slavery times; 'cause I was right dar. I don't 'member much 'bout de war, 'cause I was too little to know what war was, and de most I seed was when de Yankees come through and burnt up de Big House, de barns, de ginhouse and took all Old Marster's hosses and mules, and kilt de milk-cows for beef. They didn't leave us nothing to eat, and us lak to starve to death.

"Our folks, de Simses, dey come fum Virginny. My pappy and mammy was borned dere. Dey names was Allen Sims and Kitty Sims. My Old Marster was Marse Jimmie Sims, and my Old Mistis was Miss Creasie. Some of Pappy and Mammy's chillun was borned in Virginny, and some of 'em in Alabama. I was de baby chile, and I was borned right on dis very place whar us is now. Dey had a whole passel of chillun. Dere was Chaney, Becky, Judy, Sam, Phoebe, King, Alex, Jordan and Allen—dat's me.

"Us lived in a log house in de quarter, wid a board roof and a ol' rock fireplace wid a stick and dirt chimley. We had plenty wood, and could build jes' as big fire as we need, if de weather was cold. Mammy, she cook ash-cake in de fireplace, and it was de bes' bread I ever eat, better'n any dis store-bought bread. You ain't never eat no ash-cake? Umph, Missy, you don't know what good bread is lak!

"Old Marster was good to his niggers and all of 'em, big and little had plenty to eat, and it wa'n't trash neither. Us had ash-cake, hoe-cake, pone-bread, meat and gravy, peas, greens, roast-neers, pot-liquor, and sweet 'taters, I'ish taters, and goobers—I spec Old Marster's niggers live better dan lots of white folks lives now.

"Aunt Mandy, what was too old to work, looked atter all de little nigger chilluns, whilst dey mammys was working, and she whip us wid a brush, if we didn't mind her; but she fuss more dan she whip, and it didn't hurt much, but us cry lak she killing us.

"When us got sick, Old Mistis looked atter us herself, and she gin us oil and turpentine and lobelia and if dat didn't cure us, she sont for de doctor—de same doctor dat come to see her own fambly. Sometime a old nigger die, and Old Marster and Old Mistis dey cry jes' lak us did. Dey put 'em in a coffin and bury 'em in de graveyard, wid de white preacher dar and nobody didn't work none dat day, atter us come back fum de graveyard.

"Our beds was bunks in de corner of de room, nailed to de wall and jes' one post out in de flo'. De little chilluns slep' crosswise de big bed and it was plum' full in cold weather.

Allen Sims, Lee County, Alabama

"Our clothes was osnaburg, spun and weave' right at home, and it sho' did last a long time. De little niggers jes' wore a long shirt, 'twell dey got big 'nough to work in de field, and us had red shoes made at de tan-yard to wear in winter time; but us foots was tough and us went barefooted most all de winter too. Us played games too, ginerly, jumping de rope and base.

"De grown niggers had good times Sadday nights, wid dances, suppers and wras'lin. De corn-shuckings was de biggest time dey had, 'cause de neighbors come and dey laughed and hollered nearly all night.

"Old Marster and Old Mistis lived in a big two-story white house. Dey had ten chillun, five boys and five gals, and dey all growed up and married off. De old carriage-driver was name Clark, and he sho' was proud. De overseer was Tetter Roberson, and he was mean. He beat niggers a lot, and bimeby Old Marster turned him off. He used to blow de horn way befo' day to git de niggers up, and he work 'em 'tell smack dark.

"Atter de Yankees burned up everyt'ing 'cept de cabins, us jes' stayed right dar wid Old Marster when us freed. Old Marster built a new house for him and Old Mistis, but it wa'n't much better dan our cabin and dey lived dere 'tell dey died.

"When I growed up, I married Laura Frazier, and us had a big wedding and a preacher, and didn't jump over no broom lack some niggers did. Us had jes' two chillun dat lived to be grown. Dey is Filmore and Mary Lou, and us ain't got no gran'chillun.

"When I got grown, I j'ined de Baptist Church at Rough Neck, 'cause I felt I had done enough wrong, and I been a deacon forty year."

FRANK SMITH

Interview with Frank Smith
—D.A. Oden

"Yassuh, its jes' lak I tell yer. I was borned in Ole Virginny and my Ole Marster was Doctor Constable and he and us all lived out a piece fum Norfolk whar you kin see de whole ocean. I was writ down in de Bible, jes' lak Ole Marster's udder niggers, and Ole Mistis said hit was de six day of Jinnerwary in forty-eight when I was borned. How ole dat mek me now? Eighty-nine, gwine on ninety—dat's right.

"Ole Marster he died eight years fo' de Big War, and Ole Mistis 'refergeed' down to Alexandria, where her mammy and pappy lived and tuk me and Unker Dan and Aunt Melissy wid her; but she sole my mammy and my pappy and all de rest of de niggers ter de man what bought de plantation and us never did see 'em no mo'.

"I was de house-boy at Ole Mistis' pappy's house, I disremember his name; but, anyhow, I didn't wuck in de field lak de udder niggers. Wen de Big War started, Ole Mistis she tuck me and her chilluns and us 'refergeed', down somewhars dey was a co'thouse, whut dey called 'Culpepper', or sump'n lak dat, and us lived in town wid some mo' of Ole Mistis' kinfolks, but dey wan't her mammy and pappy. De so'jers marched right in front of our house, right by de front gate, and dey was gwine ter Ho'per's Ferry to kill Ole John Brown, whut was killin' white folks and freein' niggers fo' dey time. Dat was Mister Lincum's job, atter de war. And no niggers wan't ter be free tell den.

"We lived clos't ter de big hotel whar Gineral Lee and a whole passel of soldiers stayed, and dey had de shineyest clo's I ebber seed. Dey was fine gem'men and Ole Mistis she let me wait on 'em whilst she didn' need me ter wuck eround de house, and dey gimme a dime lots of times. I shined Gineral Lee's shoes sometimes—and he alluz gin me a dime and said: 'Dat looks nice.' Some of de ginerals jes' gimme de dime and didn't say nuthin' but dey wasn't big mens lak Gineral Lee and Ole Marster. He was straight and dignerfied and didn't talk much, but he'd walk up and down on de front gallery and de ord'lies brung him telegrafs from Bull Run, whar us and de Yankees was fightin'. Lawzy missy, I heard em talkin 'bout 'Bull Run' dat day and I 'lowed somebody's bull had got out and us and de Yankees was tryin' ter ketch him and git him back in de paster!

Frank Smith, Birmingham, Alabama

"Wen de war got too close to us, Ole Mistis tuck me and her little gal what was older'n me, and lef' Unker Dan and Aunt Melissa, and us went to Lynchburg, whar her mammy and pappy done move to, and us stayed wid dem ag'in, but Ole Mistis was gittin' worried over de war, and when I broke her iv'y-handled dinin' room knife and fergot ter tell her, she slap my head nearly off and got mad and sole me ter a man whut lived in Cleveland, Tennessee.

"Her pappy tried ter keep Mistis fum sellin' me. He said all I needed was a good brushin', but nobody couldn't do nothin' wid Ole Mistis wen she got good and mad!

"My new marster wan't lak my own whitefolks; so I up and runned way and jine de Yankee army and got a job workin' fer a cap'n name Esserton, or sump'n lak dat; him and a Lieutenant somebody. We followed General Sherman clear to Atlanta and ten mile fudder on, den dey turned back, and marched clear back to Chattanooga and den kep' on tell we got ter Nashville. I sho' was glad to git away fum Atlanta, cause dey was dead men eve'y way you looked atter dey quit fightin'. Dey gimme a uniform, but I didn't get no gun—I fought wid a fryin-pan.

"We stayed in Nashville a while and when de war was over, Cap'n Esserton wanted ter tek me to Illinois wid him and give me a job; but I didn't lak de Yankees. Dey wanted you to wuk all de time, and dat's sump'n I hadn't been brung up to do. Dey turned me free and I went wid a passel of Gineral Lee's so'jers, what come along goin' home and us went down and crossed de bigges' ribber I eber seed. I tuk up on fus' one farm and den anudder, tell I found one I lak and den dat was two years atter we lef' Nashville (1867) and I stayed dar close to Baton Rouge sixteen years. Lawd, de cotton and sugar cane us did mek on dat rich lan'. Its' richer'n de gwana dey sells out here in Alabama!

"I went to Memphis on a 'scursion and stayed dar, doin fus' one thing and den another, 'cep git in jail, and

I worked at a house painter's trade. I heered dey paid good wages fer paintin' in Bummin'ham and I come here de same year all dem niggers was killed in dat church stompede. I got a job wid Mr. Douglass, janitorin' at de Jefferson Theater and him and me stayed together three years. I bought a waggin and sold kerosene oil fer about a year, 'tell my money was all gone and den I got a job wid de Base Ball Association in de year 1913. I been wid 'em ever sence. I used ter meck fum $8 ter $15 a week, 'cordin' ter how times was, tell de 'pression come and I'se too ole ter wuk now, so I jes' totes de mail and does odd jobs and dey pays me $3 a week fer dat. I 'plied fer ole-age pension two years back, but it hain't come yit. I got one boy livin' in Bummin'ham. He's 40 year old, but he don't help me nary cent. My fus' wife died in Louisiana and I married a gal in Memphis, but she lef' me when I los' my job one time and went to Detroit wid a passel of niggers. She ain't nebber writ back to me and I done quit payin' her any mind.

"Cep'n de rheumatiz, I'se in good health and gits around pretty good. Ole Mistis showed me how to read print and I ain't never fergot how. De Yankees didn't know dat I could read, and I never did let on. I kin see pretty well but hafter put on my glasses to read de print. Sho! I'se gwine to live to be a hunded years old! How many mo' years I got to go? Ten. Dat's right. I know I'se good fer dis year, 'cause I alluz notice dat ef I live trough March, I lives all de rest ob de year!"

United States. Work Projects Administration

JOHN SMITH

Interview with John Smith
—Susie R. O'Brien, Uniontown, Alabama

"MAD 'BOUT SOMEPIN'"—SO THEY HAD A WAR

John Smith is 103 but he doesn't want to be tied down. "Effen I's free, I wants to 'joy it," John says, and he lives up to his desire. Though he is a "war veter'n" with bullets in his side and leg and his century of life has enfeebled him, he roams the countryside about Uniontown continually, "settin' a spell" with his acquaintances.

It was only after several trips I finally caught him "settin'," and he showed no inclination to move from his advantageous position near a watermelon patch. He was industriously working on a huge slice of melon, his face buried in the sweet fruit, as I drove up to the little cabin where he was visiting.

As the car came to a stop he raised his head and wiped his dripping chin on his sleeve. He called to a little Negro girl in the yard, "Gal, go bring de white lady a rockin' cheer", and turning to me he said, "You'll 'scuse me for not gittin' up lak I ain't got no manners, won't you Mistess? I got a misery in my laig; you know de one whar I got shot in de war."

The rocking chair was brought out and taking a seat nearby I said, "Uncle John, I want you to tell me all about yourself, were you in the war and are you really a hundred and three years old?"

"Glad to, glad to mistess, but fust don't you want a watermillon?" He pointed to a patch nearby where the melons glistened in the sun. "Dis July sun make de juice so sweet you'll smack yo' mouf for mo'," and searching the rind to see that he had left none of the juicy red meat, Uncle John began his story.

"Well, I been livin' 'roun' dese parts 'bout ninety year. I was born somewar in North Ca'lina, I don't 'member much 'bout my Mammy an' Pappy 'cause I was took 'way from dem by de speckerlaters when I was 'bout thirteen year ole. De speckerlaters raised Niggers to sell. Dey would feed 'em up an' git 'em fat and slick and make money on 'em. I was sold off de block in 'Speckerlater's Grove' in North Ca'lina. De fus' day I was put up I didn't sold, but de nex' day I brung a thousand dollars. Mr. Saddler Smith from Selma bought me. Dey called him Saddler Smith cause he was in de saddle business and made saddles for de army. Dey fotch us down on boats. I 'member de song de men on de boat singed. Hit go like dis:

> Up an' down de Mobile Ribber,
> Two speckerlaters for one po' lil nigger.

"My marster was de best in dis country. He didn't had many niggers, but he sho' tuck good keer o' dem what he did had. He didn't 'low nobody to hit 'em a lick. Sometime when I would git cotch up wid in some diverment de white folks would say, 'Whose nigger is you?" and I say, 'Marse Saddler Smith.' Den dey look at each oder an' say kinder low, 'Better not do nothin' to ole Smith's nigger. He'll raise de debil.'

"I didn't had no mistiss. My marster was a widder. He raised me up workin' 'roun' de saddle shop. I ain't never liked to work nowhow, but don't tell nobody dat. I was bout twenty seven year ole when de war broke out. De ole uns was called out fust and de young uns stayed home and practiced so dey could shoot straight an' kill a Yankee. Us practiced every Friday evenin'. Course I didn't know what dey fightin' 'bout. I jes' knowed dey was mad 'bout somepin'. Atter while Marster's son Jim j'ined de 'Federate sogers an' I went wid him for to tote his knapsack, canteen and sichlike and to look atter him. Dat's when I got dese here balls in my side and got a bullet in my laig, too. I was movin' de hawses to de back of de lines out de thick of de fight when, zipp, a minit ball cotch me right in de shoulder."

Proudly John displayed the balls in his side and the scar on his leg. The old woman, at whose cabin John was visiting, interrupted the story several times. Finally he got tired of it and said: "Shet yo' mouf 'oman, I don't need no ho'p, dis is grown folks talk, you don't know nothin' 'bout it, you wasn't even birthed tell two year 'fo' de Surrender. Now whar was I at? I slep' right by Marsa Jim's side. Sometime atter us done laid down and bofe of us be thinkin' 'bout home, Marse Jim say, 'John, I lak to have some chicken.' I don't say nothin' I jes' ease up an' pull my hat down over my eyes an' slip out. Atter while I come back wid a bunch o'chickens crost my shoulder. Nex' mornin' Marse Jim have nice brown chicken floatin' in graby what I done cook for him. Us was fightin' on Blue Mountain when Marse Jim got kilt. I looked and looked for him but I never did find him. Atter I lost my marster I didn't 'long to nobody and de Yankee's was takin' eve'y thing anyhow, so dey tuck me wid dem.

"I tuck keer of Gen'l Wilson's hawse, Gen'l Wilson was de head man in de Yankee army. But I didn't lak dey ways much. He wanted his hawse kep' spick and span. He would take his white pocket hankercher an' rub over de hawse and if it was dirty he had me whupped. I was wid Gen'l Wilson when he tuck Selma 'gins't Gen'l Forrest and sot fire to all dem things. I drive de artillery wagon sometime. Atter Surrender I was kinda puny wid de balls in my side."

"John," I asked, "why didn't they remove the balls at the time you were shot?"

"How could dey 'move de balls when I was runnin' fast as I could pick up my foots? I driv de stagecoach twixt Selma and Montgomery. I 'member my stops. Dey was Selma, Benton, Lown'esboro and Mon'gomery. I driv four hawses to it. Dere was a libbery stable at Benton and I changed hawses dere."

"Now John tell me about your wife and children," I said. "How many children did you have?"

"Gawd, I don't know mistess. Dey runnin' 'roun' de country like hawgs. Dey don't know me an' I don't know dem. I ain't never been mai'ed. Niggers didn't marry in dem days. I jes' tuk up wid one likely gal atter anoder. I ain't even mai'ed to de one I got now. I jes' ain't gwine tie myse'f down. Effen I's free, I's gwine to be free."

Uncle John sat for a time in deep thought, then said, "I wish I mought be back in dem days, 'cause I been seed de debil since I been free. Atter I was free I didn't had no marster to 'pend on and I was hongry a heap of times. I 'long to de 'Federate nation and always will 'long to y'all, but I reckon it's jes' as well we is free 'cause I don't b'lieve de white folks now days would make good marsters."

Uncle John had about talked out and as I rose to leave I said, "Thank you John, this will make a good story," to which he replied indignantly, "Hit ain't no story. Hit's de Gawd's trufe mistess."

ANNIE STANTON

Personal interview with "Aunt Annie" Stanton
Rylands Lane, Mobile, Alabama
—Ila B. Prine, Mobile, Alabama

Out on Ryland's Lane is an old negro woman 84 years of age who is totally blind, but whose mind is clear in regards to things pertaining to the long ago.

"Aunt Annie" says that things that happened when she was a child are much more vivid in her mind than are things of today. She said "Sumtimes I now starts tuh do dumpin' an' fogits what I wants tuh do, den I ahs tuh go bac' tuh de place whar I started from so I kin 'member whats I started tuh do".

"Aunt Annie" was born on Knight's Place on the Alabama River, June 2nd., 1853. This place is now known as Finchburg, in Monroe County, Alabama. Her mother's name was Mary Knight and her father's name was Atlas Williams, who had the same name as his owner, Mr. Offord Williams. "Aunt Annie's" mother's people were owned first by Mr. Cullen Knight and after his death, were owned by Mr. John Marshall.

"Aunt Annie" was seven years old then the Civil War

started, and that she had "nursed two cullered chillun afore de war."

When asked by the writer about nursing these children, so as to be sure she said colored children, she replied, "dat de slaves lived on de plantation, and dey had an overseer who libed on dis place, an' she neber seed de Marshall's place 'til after dey was freed. As I growed bigger into a big yearlin' gal I was tuk intuh de oversee'rs home to 'tend tuh de dinin' room table sich as settin' hit an' washin' de dishes an' cleanin' up, an' later on I was showed how to iron, spin thread, weave cloth, and make candles. Honey, folks talkin' 'bout depression now don't kno' nothin' 'bout hard times. In dem days folks didn't hab nothin' 'ceptin' what dey made. Eben if yo' had a mint ob money, dere was nothin' to buy. We made de candles to burn by tying strings on the stick and puttin' dem down in melted tallow in moulds. In dem times we had no matches, folks made fire by strikin' flint rocks together an' de fire droppin' on cotton. I don't know whether dese rocks were ones dat de Indians lef' or no, but day was dif'rent from other rocks. People usta carry dem an' de cotton roun' in boxes sumtin lak snuff boxes tuh keep de cotton dry. Sumtimes when dey could'nt get de fire no odder way, dey would put de cotton in de fireplace and shoot up in dere an' set hit on fire."

"Aunt Annie" said she never could start a fire with the flint rock and cotton, and she said, "de fust matches and lantern I'se eber seed was when de Yankees cum tuh dere place, I th'ot dey was two officers, 'couse dey had de matches and lantern. Two years a'ter I was freed, an' twar den I seed mah first lamp.

"De men did mos' ob de farm wurk, dey planted

cotton, corn, potatoes, cane, peas and pumpkins, an' dey ginned de cotton by hitching four horses tuh de gin, and dey run hit dat way."

When asked if they had plenty to eat when they were slaves, "Aunt Annie" said:

"Lor', yes I guess we had 'nough, but, 'tearn't much, c'ase I 'members when we was li'l chillun we had a big wooden tray dat dey put de food in and we all set 'round dat an' et like li'l pigs. De rations for a week was 3 lbs of meat a week, 1 peck ob meal, potatoes an' syrup. At Christmas times de overseer called all de men an' women in an' gib each woman a dress, a head handkerchief, an' tuh de men he gave a hat, knife, an' a bottle of whiskey. De overseer also gib tuh us flour and sugar fo' Christmas, an' I 'members one Christmas when I was a li'l gal, a'ter de overseer gib all de women a dress dere was a short piece ob cloth lef' an' he gib dat tuh me." "Aunt Annie" said "dat de slaves went tuh de white folks church, an' sot on de seats on de outside ob de church, an' dat church was a hewed log building. Atter de white folks got thro' preachin', den de cullered preacher would preach. Sumtimes de cullered folks would hab church when de white folks didn't an' den de slaves would hab tuh get a pass from his owner, 'ca'se dere would be some mean folks what would beat de niggers ef dey didn't hab a pass from dere owners or bosses."

"Aunt Annie" also said, "I'se neber hyeard of no hoodoo stuff 'til in late years, dey's mo' ob dat foolishness now dan I'se ebber hyeard of in mah life. Nowadays de hoodoos doctors, what is allus agoin' 'round foolin' folks out ob dey money, looks lack de dogs might ob and' dem, dey is so turrible lookin'. I don't believes in dem. Us folks a long time ago neber hab no money fo' dem to git. Us had tuh make own medicine. When de babies had de colic us wud tie soot up in a rag an' boil it, and den gib dem de water, an' tuh ease de prickly heat us used cotton wood powdered up fine, and fo' de yellow thrash us would boil de sheep thrash an' gib em de tea."

"Aunt Annie" has been married twice, her first husband left her years ago, when she married Louis Stanton and had five children by him. Louis was killed in a hailstorm, April 13, 1903, and all of her children are dead. She is now being cared for by friends, and she said, "that ef I's didn't git a li'l he'p from de Government tuh gib dis frien'" she didn't know what she would do as she has been totally blind for two years.

THEODORE FONTAINE STEWART

Interview with Theodore Fontaine Stewart
—Gertha Couric, [HW: Eufaula]

US GWINE 'ER WALK DEM GOLD STREETS

"De years are mighty long widout Lottie, Massa. She done gone on to de promise; but I knows she wid Jesus. And us gwine 'er walk dem golden streets together holdin' hands."

Uncle Theodore Fontaine Stewart lives alone in a weather-beaten, one-room Eufaula shanty. It is clean and surrounded by flowers. In the rear is a small garden; and there you will find Uncle Stewart when the dawn is fresh or the dusk is coolly approaching.

"Lottie been gone away nigh onto twenty-two year now, Massa. Her was a good woman; one of de best de Lord ever sont to de earth."

He paused to think when the interviewer asked his age.

"It hard fer me to tell 'bout dat," he said, "but I knows I'se well past de ninety mark. I guess I'se gwine on a hundred, caze I was borned 'fore de war an' was a right peart boy at de surrender."

"What about slavery times, Uncle Stewart?"

He mused a moment, his black fingers gently caressing the buttons on his rust-colored old vest.

"I 'members all 'bout dem times," he said, "an' de Lord know dey was better times den we got now, for white or black. Nobody was hongry den, Massa, and peoples didn't git in de devilment dey gits in now. Folks went to de church an' 'haved demselves in dose days.

"Who was my Ol' Marster?" He looked at the interviewer a moment, answered proudly, "Why, he was de riches' man in Georgy. I knows you has heard of Marse Theodore Fontaine. He had three big plantations and mo' niggers dan he could count. He moved clost to Florence, an' his three places was so big you couldn't see 'crost de littlest field.

"Ol' Marster he lib in a big house, bigger dan any meetin'-house in Eufaula. He had a gang of fine horses, an' when company was dar he had horse races on his own track. His horses could beat all de horses brought dar, an' dat's de direc' trufe."

Uncle Stewart filled a blackened old corncob pipe with tobacco, continued:

"Ol' Marster, he didn't go to de war. He too ol' to go, so he stay home an' make corn an' fodder an' oats an' sen' dem to de soldiers what killin' Yankees. One day de Yankees come along an' burnt up everything on de place, 'cept de nigger cabins. Dey took all de horses and everything us had to eat.

"Ol' Marster went off somewhar when dey come; I don't 'member where; an' when he come back he had to live in one of de nigger cabins 'twel he could build a house. But de new one wasn't big lak de old one.

"My pappy was a fiel' han' 'twel one time Ol' Marster put him on a horse to ride in a race, an' pappy beat de other horse so far Ol' Marster was tickled pink. He said a nigger what could ride lak dat had no bizness in de fiel', so he made a stable boy outen pappy.

Theodore Fontaine Stewart, Eufaula, Alabama

"Ol' Marster didn't have no Ol' Mistus. He say he so big all de little ladies look funny 'side of him. When company was dar his sisters, Mistus Mary an' Mistus Lucy, come an' kep' house; but dey lef' when de company did.

"My pappy was name Ed Stewart, caze Ol' Marster buy him from a Stewart. Atter de war dey call pappy's chilluns Stewart; but us is Fontaines by right, bet yo' life on dat.

"Ol' Marster was good to de niggers, but his overseers was mean. Ol' Marster fired dem atter awhile an' got some good overseers. He didn't 'low dem to whip a nigger 'cept when he say, an' he didn't say so much.

"My mammy was name' Sarah, an' her an' pappy stayed right wid Ol' Marster when de surrender come. Dey was right in de room when Ol' Marster died, an' dey cried something awful. Us all stayed dar 'twel pappy an' mammy die; den us chilluns split up an' went everywhere.

"Mammy an' pappy had ten head o' chilluns sides me, but I don' know whar dey at now. Mammy raise all her chilluns right, an', long as I knowed dem, none of dem ever got in a jailhouse.

"Mammy didn't 'low her chilluns to steal. Her was Ol' Marster's house cook, an' when she kotch any of us takin' things from de kitchen, she sho' did tan us hides wid a brush.

"Me an' Carlotta; us calls her Lottie; was married in de ol' Mount Maria church, whar all de niggers went to meetin' every Sunday. Us had fo' chillun, two gals an' two boys; but dey all dead now 'cept de las' boy, an I ain't heard frum him since 'fore his mammy died.

"Yes, Massa, her was a good woman. It won't be long now 'fore us will walk dem golden streets han' in han'."

United States. Work Projects Administration

GEORGE STRICKLAND

Interview with George Strickland
—*Preston Klein, Opelika, Alabama*

CORNSHUCKIN' WAS DE GREATES' THING

George Strickland, alert for all his ninety-one years but blinking in the bright sunlight as he laid his battered felt hat beside the rocking chair in front of his cabin in Opelika, Alabama, as he looked back down the decades and remembered the times when "cornshuckin' was de greates' thing." Though only a boy when the War between the States ended, he recalled days of slavery easily as he told the following story.

"I was nine years old when us niggers was sot free an' 'fo' dat time us refugeed from Mississippi to Mobile, den to Selma, den to Montgomery an' from dar to Uchie, near Columbus, Georgia, whar we stayed 'til us was freed.

"My mammy an' daddy come from Mississippi fust. Dey was Cleveland an' Eve Strickland an' dar was fo' of us chilluns, Will, Sam, Missouri an' me. Us quarters had dirt flo's an' was in two long rows wid a street between. On de east side of de settlement was de barns, shops an' sich like. De beds was boxed up an' nailed to de wall, den dey was filled wid pinestraw. Dey fed us li'l niggers in wood troughs made of poplar. De cook in de big house cooked pots of greens an' po'd potlikker an' all in de troughs. Us et hit wid mussel shells or wid usses han's or gourds. Our wimmin folks would bile de gourds to keep dem from being bitter. Usses had two acre paster dat usses would turn under in de fall an' plant hit in turnips. I 'clare fo' goodness dey growed nearly as big as a gallon bucket.

"Dey gived us clo'es ev'y Saddy night an' de winter clo'es had some cow hair in dem to make 'em warm.

"Ol' Marsa John Strickland was circuit preacher an' him an' Miss Polly lived up in a big log house. De logs was hewed an' split an' lined on each side. De logs stood on dey sides an' didn' lay flat. Dey chilluns was Mary, Laura, Sallie, Wiley, George an' Lougene.

"When Ol' marsa went off to preach, de overseer was mean an' whupped de niggers so bad Mistis runned him off. Dey had 'bout a hundred slaves an' would wake dem up by beating on a big piece of sheet ine (iron) wid a long piece of steel.

"De well didn' hab no windless but had a lever wid a bucket fastened on one end of hit, an' we would hold to de yuther end to dip de bucket in de water.

"When dey whupped de niggers dey would tie dem to a tree an' whup dem good. When dey was sold dey would put 'em on a stand or block, as dey called hit den, an' dey w'ud roll up dey sleeves to see de muscles. Den dey bid on dem an' bought 'em for 'bout $1,000 to $1,500 apiece. Us traveled in ox carts, an' I fust rid on a stage when I went to Uchie. When slaves would be ver' bad dey would chain dem out all night. You sho' had to stay at home an' wuk.

"Our chu'ch was nearby an' us sot nex' to de do'.

Mistis called up all de li'l niggers, talked to dem an' had pra'r. De yuthers had pra'r meetin' oncet a week.

"De wimmin folks had a big time quiltin's wid somebody aplayin' on ol' gourds wid horse hair strings, called old gourd, horse hair dance.

"Cornshuckin' was de greates' thing of all. Ol' Marsa tuck a jug of likker 'roun' an' got dem tight an' when dey got full dey would h'ist him up an' down, tote him 'roun' an' holler. Den de fun started an' dey would play de old gourd an' horse hair dance, de han'saw an' case knife. Dey could run dey han' up an' down de saw to change de tune an' de leader was on top of de pile of corn singin' whilst all de yuthers would follow.

"Us chilluns was 'sleep den, but us had our good times hidin' de switch an' playin' han'-over ball. Dey sho' skeer us nearly into fits wid tales of Rawhead and Bloody-bones.

"I'se never tuk a oath ner teched nothin' didn' b'long to me in all my life.

"Our med'cin' was Jerus'lem oak seed what was beat up to give de chilluns for worms.

"On Sund' mornin' dey giv' us biskits for breakfast, which was so rar' dat we would try to beat de yuthers outten dey'n.

"Oncet dey piled ev'ythin' on waggins an' put all us li'l niggers on top. Us rations, lak coffee, meal, meat an' mos' ev'ythin' was kivvered over wid sheets. Den dey tuk us off an' us stayed t'ree days an' nights.

"Ol' marsa tuk one of de fellers wid him to be on de

front line to help keep off de Injuns, so us chilluns b'lieves.

George Strickland, Opelika, Alabama

"Dat battle of Atlanta was de wust thing dat's ever been. All de houses for a fur piece jes' shuck from de big guns. De Yankees camped in a big hundred acre fiel' close by. Den dey rushed up to de house, kicked de gate down, tuk Mistiss trunk out an' bus' hit open huntin' money. But dey foun' none, so dey sot fire to de house an' ast, whar de horses? De niggers couldn' tell an' den dey burnt de house down.

"Atter dat, Ol' Marsa tell us, us is free from him but needn't leave iffen us didn' want to go, but could stay on wid him an' he'd treat us right an' give us half of what us made.

"In after years I ma'ed Josephine Bedell an' us had George, Phillip, Renza, Eldridge (de baby), May Willie an' Leila. I's got some gran-chillun, too, but kain't think of dey names.

"Hit was de plans of God to free us niggers an' not Abraham Lincoln's.

"I's allus tried to live under de correction of de Lord. Hit's my duty to try to do so."

United States. Work Projects Administration

CULL TAYLOR

Personal interview with Cull Taylor
364 N. Scott Street, Mobile, Alabama
—Ila B. Prine, Mobile, Alabama

A SLAVE IS GIVEN HIS YOUNG MISSY'S NAME

A tall, stoop-shouldered, black Negro man came trudging down the road with a hoe in his hand. Asked where Cull Taylor lived, the old man said, "Lady I'se Cull Taylor. Dis is mah house here. Does you want to see me?"

When told that his visitor was looking for old people who lived during slavery days Cull said:

"I were born a slave, but warn't very old when de niggers was freed. I were born March 5, 1859, in Augusta County, Alabama. Mah maw come from Richmond, Virginia and her name were Jane Hare. Mah paw's name were Willingham Hare, and he were brought to Alabama from North Carolina. I guess you'se wonderin' why mah name is Taylor when mah maws and paws name was Hare?

"You see when dey was fust brought here, a man name Tom Taylor bought 'em, an' when I were born, dey gib me to Miss Bennie Taylor. Ol' Marse Tom's girl. Miss

Bennie gib me de name Taylor an' I'se allus kept hit. She shorely was good to me. I neber had nothing much to do, I stayed wid her, 'til I was grown, atter she married Mr. Bob Alexander.

"'Bout de war, I does 'member how mah maw was a-weavin' cloth when de Yankees come through. An' atter de niggers was freed ol' Marse Tom gib mah maw de loom.

"Ol' Marse was a good man. He neber 'lowed no o'seer or anybody to mistreat his niggers. He had plenty of 'em, too, and a big plantation wid plenty to eat. Course de slaves had to work on de plantation an' raise de stuff to eat. His house was a big fine, white place, an' de cabins whar de slaves libed was built in rows, wid streets between dem, so you could drive 'tween 'em wid big double team wagons. De cabins was built out ob logs wid a notch out in de shoulders, an' laid on top ob one another an' when dey built de wall up as high as dey wanted hit, dey would bore a augor hole an' put a pin in hit to hold 'em together. Den dey put de roof on. Dey filled de cracks between de logs wid mortar, so as to keep de wind out, an' it sho' made de houses warm. Us had jes' wooden home-made beds, wid mattresses made of cotton, or moss, an' sometimes hay. Us neber hab no springs on de beds.

"As I said, Ol' Marse Tom was a good man, an' he was too old to go to de war, but he had two boys. De oldest one went to de war an' was killed. But de youngest warn't old enough to go. Ol' Marse Tom had de women sew, makin' clothes, an' had nurse women to look atter de little niggers while dere maws was in de fields. I 'members as a li'l boy how dey had one house whar de nurse kept de chillun an' it was as clean as a pin. Dere was wooden troughs different heights for de different age chillun, an' dose troughs was scrubbed as white as cotton mos'. When meal time come, dey would crumble up cornbread wid pot licker, or milk an' gib to de youngest ones. An' dey had plenty ob milk, I 'members de big milk dairy, an' smoke house on de place, an' when de Yankees come through dey went into de dairy an' drank all de milk dey wanted.

"I 'members mah paw was out in de woods hidin' de mules when dey come through an' dere was only one old horse on de place. Dem Yankees turn hit loose, but otherwise dey behaved very nice."

Cull said that they didn't know anything about dishes and spoons such as are used now, for they had wooden spoons for the slaves. He said that the usual rations for a week included a peck of meal, and six or seven pounds of meat to each man, and if he had a big family he was given more. They raised rice, sugar cane, pumpkins, watermelons, cushaws, peaches, pears, plums and grapes.

"Mah white folks not only tuk keer ob us durin' slavery times, but dey gib us things atter us was freed. You ax me 'bout de slaves clothes? Yas'm, lady, us had good, stout, clothes, made out ob de cloth dat de women wove. I can see mah maw throwing dat ol' shickle from one side to de other, weaving cloth on dat loom. Dey dyed de cloth wid red oaks an' dogwood bark, and Chinaberry bark, and had all kinds ob colors, sich as blue, red, brown, and black.

"Den dere was de big times, sich as de hog killin' time, an' corn shucking, an' 'specially cotton pickin' time. Sometimes de neighboring plantation would hab a regular cotton pickin' festival, an' all ob us would go and he'p pick de cotton, and de nigger what would pick de mos' would git a dress or de men would git a suit ob clothes. De suits was made out ob osnaburg, and sometimes bed tickin'. When a big crowd would come to dese cotton pickin's, dey would pick out three or four bales ob cotton.

"De li'l niggers had a good time playin' in de sand makin' frog houses, an' spinnin' tops. But, Lordy! when us got sick, dey gib us Jerusalem oak and sassafras tea. But neber was dere anything said 'bout hoo-doo stuf. I never heard ob hit, 'til dese later years.

"But us did hab church, an' prayer meetin', an' funerals! Lor', yes, dey don't bury folks now. In dose days dey started singin' at de house an' sung all de way to de graveyard; an' den dey put dem in de groun' good full six feet deep, dey jes' lays folks on top ob de groun' now-a-days. But times is different now, lady.

"I 'members how de men would go out nights an' hunt de possums an' de coons, and wild cats. Dey den would sometimes go deer an' rabbit huntin' in de daytime; an', too, dey would set traps to ketch other varmints. Dere was plenty ob squirrels too.

"But let me tell you, de bes' thing ob all, was de good locust beer, dey made from locust seeds. Dey also made 'simmon beer, an' wine out ob plums. Dem war good days den."

DANIEL TAYLOR

Interview with Daniel Taylor
Montgomery, Alabama
—*John Proctor Mills, Montgomery, Alabama*

Foreword:—In Uncle Daniel Taylor we find the unusual, fast disappearing type of negro ex-slave (it makes the sentimental white man feel a deep sadness in the passing of these gentle old souls, whose lives have been well spent in serving to the best of their ability.) Uncle Dan is a light complected mulatto (octoroon) with a high and broad forehead (a noble brow) devoid of all negroid features, a heavy suit of silk-like hair almost free of any kinks, a heavy suit of gray beard (it is in the short kinky hair next to his throat that the negro stands out most prominently) a fine moustache which matches the snowy silkiness of his hair up on his head. Deep set, dark blue-grey eyes which beam with kindliness, wide apart and far-searching. A voice well modulated and refined in timbre, of tenor quality. Uncle Dan has been so closely associated with the educated white man of the South until he uses no negro dialect, but his speech is that of one who has tried at all times to speak correctly and deliberately. He has served as janitor at nearly all of the Public Schools of the Montgomery City Schools system, and for fifteen years or more has been at the Baldwin High School; is janitor at this school at present (May 1937) where he is highly respected, and greatly beloved by the student body and members of the large faculty.

"Strange to say, I do not remember the name of my first master, nor of the second master to whom my Mother and myself were sold to in Alabama. I was born at Charleston, South Carolina, and at the age of two and a half years we landed at Luverne, Ala., where with my Mother I was sold for four-hundred dollars.

"I was fourteen years old at the time of the 'Surrender,' and was living at old 'Rocky Mount' in Crenshaw County, at the time of the 'Civil War.' Professor Mack Barnes of Highland Home, Alabama, was the first man I ever worked for, and he, as you know, was at the head of the large school located in Highland Home.

"The hottest moments of my life were the ones in which my Mother got tight in behind me with a hickory (switch) and I always took to the woods. I'll just bet that I knew and could tell more about the woods and the cane-brake than anyone in that section. Yes sir! I knew every varmint that crawled on its belly, and all the rest which went on four feet, that lived there. Believe me, I knew every one of them by name and right where they stayed.

"The hot moments just mentioned usually found me 'cooling off' in the creek in the old swimmin' hole.

Daniel Taylor, Montgomery, Alabama

"Among the thrilling moments of my life well do I remember the visits of President Jefferson Davis, (the first and only President of the Confederate States of America) to the home of my Master. Mr. Davis always gave me a quarter of a dollar for holding his horse, and up 'til lately I had one of those quarters as a highly valued keep-sake, but it suddenly disappeared, I know not where.

"The most exciting moments of my whole life was

when the Herron Street School (at present the Cottage Hill School) caught fire and burned to the ground. We had marched all of the children out of the building to safety (you see we had all had disciplined fire drills) but Professor Charles L. Floyd (Superintendent of the Montgomery Public Schools) was mindful lest there should still be one person left in the building, so hastened back into the rapidly burning building. He just wouldn't listen to the pleadings of Miss Jinny (Miss Virginia Hereford, who was the Principal of this school) nor to Miss Sophy (Miss Sophia Holmes) a teacher at the primary department, nor would he listen to my humble plea. The roof was already tumbling in, and the blazing rafters were falling in every direction. I could stand it no longer, so rushed right through the smoke and flames, finally I found Mr. Floyd and dragged him out to safety. My God! I loved that white man, he was one of the finest men I ever knew!

"No! Mister John, I have never sought a 'heroe's medal for bravery and for risking my life', my one great reward was in the saving of the life of my true friend Professor Charles L. Floyd."

GEORGE TAYLOR

>Personal interview with George Taylor
>409 South Hamilton Street, Mobile, Alabama
>—Ila B. Prine, Mobile, Alabama

CHILLUN WAS TAUGHT TO BE MANNERABLE

George Taylor, an old and very black man, who lives at 409 South Hamilton street in Mobile, says he is an ex-slave. He knows that he was born in Mobile on the corner of Cedar and Texas streets, but left Mobile, and was carried to Gosport, Alabama, when he was twelve years old. His father's name was Gus Taylor and his mother's Sarah Taylor, and they were owned by Mr. W.G. Herrin. There were twenty-one children in George's family, and he said he was the oldest one, and helped "nuss de odders."

"Mah grandfather's name was Mac Wilson an' mah grandmother's name was Ellen Wilson, an' de ol' Miss's name was Miss Mamie Herrin. All de colored folks' chillun called Mr. Herrin 'Cl' Marster, an' he sho' was a good marster, too. I 'members dat atter I got to be a big boy dey put me in de fiel's choppin' cotton, but I neber could pick cotton. I knows dat mah paw said I was too crazy 'bout de girls, so he tuk me an' made me plow.

"Ol' marster had a big place, I don't jes' exactly knows

how many acres dey was, but I knows us had plenty ob cotton, 'ca'se sometimes dey would pick four or five bales a day. An' den I knows durin' cotton time mah paw hauled cotton all day long to de gin whut was run by five or six mules.

"Durin' de busy season on de plantation ol' Marster had de older women cookin' an' sendin' de dinner to de fiel'. Dere was two big baskets, one to put de bread in, an' de odder basket to put de meat in. Every mornin' at three o'clock de women begun cookin' an' each han' brought his own meat an' bread to this cabin to be cooked. Every person's plate had their names on 'em. Ever'body had to be up by daylight an' ready to begin work. De men had to get up before daylight an' begin to harness de mules, an' soon as light dey was in de fiel's. Dere was two hundred and fifty head ob colored people, 'scusing chillun. Dey would raise four, five, and six hundred bales ob cotton, a year. Us worked den, dere warn't no walkin' 'bout den, not eben on Sat'day attermoons, but I believes I'd lack it betta dan I does now, 'cause de chillun was taught to be mannerable den, but now dey cuss if you say anything to dem.

"Us had a good place to stay, de ol' Marster's house was a big two-story house, an' our cabins was built ob boards an' was in a row. Us didn't hab no stoves, jes' cooked out in de yard ober a fire wid stakes on each side of hit, wid an' iron bar across 'em to hang de pots on. Ol' Marster rationed out de food, an' each man was 'lowed seven pounds ob meat, de women was 'lowed six pounds an' five pounds for each child. Den dey gib us a peck ob meal, five pounds of flour and some molasses.

"I neber did eat at home wid mah folks, 'ca'se I nussed

in de big house, an' ebery time dat de white chillun eat, I had to eat, too. Dere was plenty ob pecan, walnut, an' ches'nut trees on de place, an' us could eat all de nuts we wanted; and den de slaves had dere own gardens if dey wanted to.

"Den I 'members how dere was four men who put de hogs in de pens to fatten, sometimes, dey would put as many as a hundred or a hundred an' fifty at a time. Den hit was dere duty to tote feed from de fiel's to feed 'em.

"My! when I think ob dat big smoke house, mah mouth jes' waters. At hog killin' time, dere was certain men to kill, an' certain ones to cut 'em up. Dere warn't neber no special time to hog killin', jes' when de ol' Marster said do hit, we did hit.

"You see us was allus under his direction, 'ca'se if us wanted to go anywhere, us had to git a pass, eben to church. De white folks had Methodist church, an' de collored had de Baptist church.

"I also 'members de time I was put up on de block to be sold, an' when de man only offered five hundred dollars, fer me, an' Ol' Marster tole me to git down, dat I was de mos' valuable nigger he had, 'ca'se I was so strong, an' could do so muck work.

"Mah maw was de weaver, an' dere was a woman named Assella who did de dyeing. Mah paw gathered de bark, sich as red oak, elm, maple and juniper bark, an' dry hit an' den grin' hit up. Dey also used borax, alum and blue stone, to set de dye. De women made de clothes out ob dis cloth dat was woven on de place.

"You axed 'bout weddin's. Us didn't hab weddin's

lack us do now. De way us married would be to go to de big house, an' ol' Marster had us to jump over a broom stick, an' den us was considered married. But dere was one thing dat us warn't 'lowed to do, an' dat was to abuse or cuss our wives, an' you betta not strike 'em, ca'se hit would be jes' too bad.

"You know, Miss, I'se been here a long time. I 'members when dere was only one house 'tween St. Louis Street an' Frascati, an' dat was de Guard House. I also 'members de ole time remedies dat dey used in de ole days. Dey used red oak bark for fever an' colds, an' den dere was hoarhound, an' black snake root dat de ol' Marster put whiskey on. Ol' Marster made his own whiskey. An' oh! yes, de calomus root growed in de woods whar dey lived. I neber seed dem send to no store for medicine. I neber hyeard ob no hoodoo stuff, 'till I was grown, an' anudder thing folks didn't die of lack dey do now. When any one did die, dey allus had a big funeral, an' de men would sometimes hitch up a ox team or mule teams, an' as many as could git in would go. De coffins was home made an' stained. Dere was plenty ob han's to dig de graves, too.

"I'se tell you, Miss, folks is pretty much de same, if de white folks treat de niggers right, you couldn't get dem to leave dem. I 'members when de Yankees come through, I was standin' on de Ol' Marster's porch, an' I seed dem comming, an' Marster got up on his crutch an' go to de steps an' invite dem in, an' believe me dey come in, too. Dey jes' natcherly tore up ol' Marster's place; then de furniture all 'roun' an' broke heaps ob hit. I knows b'fore dey got dere ol' Marster had mah paw, an' Jerry Lee, an' Mace Pouncey, an' anudder man take four barrels ob money an' carry down to de spring an' put hit in de spring, an' I'se tellin' you, Miss, you couldn't any more git near dat spring, dan nothin', ca'se de quicksan' made dem barrels boil up, one at a time, an' de way dey had to git dem barrels, was to buil' a scaffold from de river, an' let a line down an' ketch aroun' dem barrels.

"Atter we was freed, Ol' Marster come out in de yard an' got in de middle ob all ob us, an' tole us dat de ones dat wants to stay wid him, to stan' on one side, an' de odders to stan' on de odder side. So mah paw got on de side wid dose who wanted to leave, an' us lef' Ol' Marster an' paddled down de river, in a paddlin' boat to Belle's Landing.

"As I'se said before, I'se been here a long time, I eben 'members seeing Jeff Davis. I knows I ain't here for long, but I'se ready, 'ca'se I'se been fightin' for Jesus twenty-nine years, an' I ain't tired ob fightin' yet. I'se a Deacon in de Baptist Church."

AMANDA TELLIS

Personal interview with Amanda Tellis
and her daughter Sarah Chastan
in Allenville, Mobile County, Alabama
—*Written by Ila B. Prine*

Amanda Tellis, a tall, thin, light lulatto woman, who was born a slave November 30, 1854, lives in Allenville, a negro settlement about four miles north of Mobile, Alabama.

Amanda's father was a spaniard, whose name was John Quick, and her mother's name was Sallie Pugh, her mother having the same name as the people who owned her. Sallie, Amanda's mother, was born a slave in Charleston South Carolina, and she and her mother were brought to Alabama and sold when Sallie was twelve years old. The mother was sold to someone in Demopolis, Alabama, while Sallie was sold to the Pugh family in Grove Hill, Alabama.

Amanda was born in Grove Hill, Alabama and Mr. Meredith Pugh was her master, and Mrs. Fannie Pugh was her mistress. Her young "Missus" was Miss Maria Pugh, a daughter, one of seven children in the Pugh family. Amanda said she willed to "Miss Maria" and she nursed and took care of her until the surrender. Many times when Amanda would be promised a whipping for not doing things as she should have, Miss Maria would save her from the whipping, by throwing herself back from the table and screaming for them not to touch Amanda, her nurse.

Aside from caring for "Miss Maria", Amanda said she spun three cuts of thread a day, and when the writer asked what a cut was, she said: "A cut was a broach full." During the war, (meaning the Civil War,) Amanda said she and her sister Nancy spun 160 yards of cloth, and they finished the last on the day of the Surrender, when the Cannons were fired at Fort Morgan, and they were mustering the men out.

Amanda's life was a very easy one in comparison to some of the other slaves. She said she had seen many of the slaves cruelly mistreated, but her people were fortunate in having a good master and mistress.

However, at the close of the war, Amanda was told to pretend she had a chill, and go to her mother's cabin, so she did as she was told. When she reached the cabin, her mother, brothers and sisters each had a pillow slip, filled with clothes and she was given hers and they ran away, and came to Mt. Vernon, Alabama. Amanda was only eleven years old then.

Her life has been varied since, having married three times. Her first husband was Scott Johnson, and was the father of all of her children, seven boys and one girl. Amanda lives with this girl now. Her second husband was Vance Stokes, and her third was S.T. Tellis, a negro Methodist preacher. Amanda said he was "no count and I did not stay with him long."

Amanda is now confined to her bed and has been for the past seven weeks, her body has wasted away, until she is skin and bones. Her eyes however are still bright and keen, her hair snow white and she still has a few teeth. Her mind seems to be clear, and her memory good, in fact the past is now a part of her, and she told the writer she was so happy because she had come to ask her about it, before it was too late.

United States. Work Projects Administration

ELLEN THOMAS

Interview with Ellen Thomas
—Mary A. Poole, Mobile

TABLE SERVICE AS TAUGHT TO AUNT ELLEN

In a little cottage at 310 Wienacker Avenue, in the western part of Mobile, lives Ellen Thomas, who claims to be 89 years old. She is small of stature, dark brown in color, with high cheek bones and small regular features. Although she wears the old-fashioned bandana handkerchief bound about her head, the story of 'Aunt' Ellen is unusual, in that having been raised as a house servant in a cultured Southern family, she absorbed or was trained in the use of correct speech, and does not employ the dialect common to Negroes of the slavery days.

'Aunt' Ellen was born in Mobile. Her mother, Emeline, was a dwarf who was brought from St. Louis to Mobile by a slave-trader. When put up for sale, her deformity enlisted the sympathy of Judge F.G. Kimball, who bought her and brought her to his home on Dauphin Street, between Hallett Street and Georgia Avenue. Later, Sam Brown, a free Negro from the West Indies, came to Mobile and, wanting Emeline for his wife, agreed to pay Judge Kimball for her, giving himself as security. Sam and Emeline had only two children, Pedro and Ellen, both born on Judge Kimball's place and raised in his home as house servants, having little contact with the field slaves.

In her childhood, Ellen had as her special mistress Miss Cornelia, one of the Kimball girls, who trained her in the arts of good housekeeping, including fine sewing, which was itself an art among the women of that period. Ellen relates with much pride, her ability to put in tucks and back-stitch them in the front of men's shirts, to equal the best machine work of the present day. Although hampered by failing eyesight in recent years, her work with the needle today is proof that her claims are not exaggerated.

In all her experience as a slave, she recalls but one whipping. This was with a small switch in the hands of Judge Kimball. The cause? She answered: "I ain't coming," when he called her; and at his second call, she said: "I shan't do it." She was seven years old at the time.

Judge Kimball insisted that the house servants use good English, she said. Thus brought up as a child among the Kimball children, and because of her duties as a house servant, she mingled little with the field hands and acquired none of their dialect. Even her long association with free Negroes since the war, has failed to eradicate early impressions and practices in the use of words, and she stresses this in conversation with educated white persons.

Because she was a house servant, Ellen was accorded many privileges not enjoyed by ordinary slaves. Good food, neat clothing and cleanliness of person were requirements rigidly enforced. As personal maid to young girls little older than herself, her lot was quiet and the association developed a devotion and friendship that was lifelong. Among the privileges that fell to her as a child, she recalls that of accompanying the family on carriage rides—usually seated beside the driver to the envy of her little mistress on the more dignified inside seat.

Ellen Thomas, Mobile, Alabama

Her training as a house servant was very broad and involved every feature of a well kept household of that period. She has especial pride in her ability to serve at table, particularly when there were guests present. A feature of the training given her and which Ellen says she never knew of anyone else receiving was, after being taught to set the dining table complete for guests, she would be blindfolded and then told to go through the motions of serving and so learn to do so without disturbing anything on the table. So proficient did she become in serving, that a few times when they had guests, Judge Kimball would for their amusement have Ellen blindfolded and direct her to serve the dinner. In passing dishes a small silver tray was used.

Ellen said that they tried to teach her brother Pedro to serve the table likewise; but his natural clumsiness prevented. He could never learn.

During the war, she said, her master had an immense pit dug near the house, put his cotton in the pit and built the woodpile over it. The Federal invaders never found it.

Judge Kimball owned extensive tracts of land above Mobile and used a large number of his slaves to cut timber for wood and lumber; hewn timber being largely used for house-building. He built a house for every one of his children, from his own timber, and even had his own coffin made from home-grown cedar. Ellen failed to follow this act of her master with approval, judging from her tone in speaking of it.

She remembers the Surrender and the incidents accompanying that event. She was seventeen years old. Thus she describes the first visit afterward of the enemy.

"I was helping to cook breakfast one morning, frying codfish and potatoes, when I heard a drum and ran to tell Master. He jumped up and said: 'It's the Yankees! Tell Pedro to get a sheet and hang it out in front.' Pedro was excited and, instead of getting a sheet, got one of Mistress' best table cloths and hung it from a big oak tree near the front gate. When the Yankees rode up, they dismounted and Master invited them in for breakfast."

One of the Yankee Lieutenants asked her name, and she told him: "Ellen Brown." He looked puzzled at her answer, knowing her master's name to be Kimball. (Since her father was a free man, 'Aunt' Ellen said that she and her brother, Pedro, always retained their own name, instead of "Kimball.") The lieutenant then said: "All right, Ellen, bring me a glass of milk at thirteen o'clock."

She went to her little mistress, and asked her "what that old lieutenant meant by 'thirteen o'clock.'" Miss Cornelia laughed and said he meant "one o'clock."

'Aunt' Ellen related how Judge Kimball was always teaching them and gave them regular lectures. She particularly remembers one of his sayings: "You can never swing on yellow pine tree, as it is tender and pliable."

She remained with the Kimballs three years after the war, worked for other families a short time and then married Amos Thomas when she was about twenty years old. They had a very large family, eleven girls and nine boys. She now has great-grandchildren who are married.

Although there is little doubt that her age is approximately what she claims, 'Aunt' Ellen is remarkably well preserved, physically and mentally. Her activity and industry would not be inappropriate to a woman a score of years younger. Unlike many persons of her years she does not constantly look forward to her time of departure, but takes life as it comes—caring more for today than for tomorrow.

ELIZABETH THOMAS

Interview with Elizabeth Thomas
—Montgomery

HID THINGS THEY AIN'T NEVER FOUND

Elizabeth Thomas who lives at 2 Eugene Street, Montgomery, Alabama stuck up one finger when asked her age. That meant 100 she said. She is typical the oldtime Negro with head rag tightly covering her hair, carrying a slick old walking-stick whose bark is worn in places because of constant use, and little old straightcut full apron. Her memory is not clear but her hearing is perfect.

She stated—

"I lived mighty fine in dem days, I tel' you. Mister Ben Martin Jones was my Marster, and I was born on de Red Bridge Road. I was a house servant. All our clo'es was made at de quarters. My Mammy made mine an' all I wanted, too. I useter hear my mammy say, de patteroles (patrols) would git us ef we done wrong but I didn't know nothin' 'bout patteroles, 'cause dey wasn't none on our place. Dey whipped you, too, but my Marster could control all his niggers so he didn't 'low none uv 'em on our place.

"I was 21 years ole when de Yankees come but I didn't run and dey didn't do nuthin' to me but folks was in such a hurry they hid things dat ain't never been foun' yet. I liked meetin' on Sundays an' sometime we never got outer church tell daylight. I wants to live jes' as long as Jesus say an' when he say go, I'se ready. At Christmas times we always had good dinners and heap o' company; plenty uv it. My Missus died and atter dat my mother raised ole Marster's chile, Tommy John, right 'long wid me. O, dem was happy days, I tell you."

MOLLIE TILLMAN

Interview with Mollie Tillman
—*Susie R. O'Brien, Uniontown, Alabama*

I WARN'T NO COMMON SLAVE

Aunt Mollie Tillman was fifteen years old when the Southern slaves were freed; but despite her advanced age, she is able to work every day in the cotton fields and admits that she is "purty peart."

She said, "Honey, I kin ricolleck all 'bout slavery time, 'caze I was a big ol' gal den. Why, I 'members when de 'mancipation come as if 't'was yestidy."

Aunt Mollie recalls that she was born on a plantation near Rome, Georgia, and that her owners were Dan and Lucy Phillips.

"Marse Dan was a Baptis' preacher," she explained, "an' he shorely was a good man. He was a chaplain in de big war and he didn't get hurt.

"Marster owned lots an' lots of slaves an' de plantation was jes' full o' niggers. He was a powerful important man.

"Honey, I warn't no common eve'yday slave, I ho'ped de white folks in de big house. Mistus Lucy wouldn't let 'em take me to de fiel'. Dem was good days, chile; might good days. I was happy den, but since 'mancipation I has jes' had to scuffle an' work an' do de bes' I kin."

Aunt Mollie's hair is snow white in sharp contrast to her ginger-cake skin.

"I 'members all 'bout when de Yankees come," she said. "Dey was jes' ruineration to de plantation. Dey tuck all de mules an' cows, den sont out an' got all de chickens an' eggs dey could fin'. Eatin' was kind o' slack wid us atter dey lef'."

Aunt Mollie's life has known romance. Let her tell it:

"I was ol' 'nough to be castin' my eyes 'roun' at de young bucks, an' dere was a nigger what lived on de plantation jinin' our'n whut tuck a shine to me. I lacked dat boy fine, too.

"He would come over to see me ever' time he git a chanct. One night he 'low he gwine'r ax his marster to buy me so's me an' him could git married. Well, atter dat he didn' come no mo'.

"I waited an' I watched, but I didn' hear nuffin of dat nigger. Atter 'while I got worried. I was 'fraid de patter-ollers done kotch him, or maybe he done foun' some gal he lak better dan he do me. So I begin to 'quire 'bout him an' foun' dat his marster done sol' him to a white man whut tuck him 'way down yonder to Alabama.

"Well ma'am, I grieved fo' dat nigger so dat my heart was heavy in my breas'. I knowed I never would see him no mo'. Soon atter dat, peace was 'clared an' de niggers was free to go whar dey pleased.

"My folks stayed on wid Marse Dan fer a year; den dey

'cided to go to Alabama an' farm. We hit it off to Alabama an' I begin to go 'bout some wid de young bucks. But somehow I couldn't git my min' off dat other nigger.

"Well ma'am, one day at a big meetin' I runned up on him. I was so happy I shouted all over dat meetin' house. We jes' tuck up whar we lef' off an' 'fo' long us got married."

And, Aunt Mollie continued, they lived happily until his death about 20 years ago.

She now lives in Uniontown, happy and contented. She has her garden and flowers; but emphasizes that "de ol' days was de bes' of all."

United States. Work Projects Administration

ALONZA FANTROY TOOMBS

Interview with Alonza Fantroy Toombs
—*Gertha Couric, [HW: Eufaula?]*

HE BELONGED TO BOB TOOMBS OF GEORGIA

"Missy," said Alonza Fantroy Toombs, "I'se de proudest nigger in de worl', 'caze I was a slave belonging to Marse Robert Toombs of Georgia; de grandest man dat ever lived, next to Jesus Christ. He was de bes' stump speaker in de State, an' he had mo' frien's dan a graveyard has ghosts. He was sho a kin' man, an' dere warn't no one livin' who loved his wife an' home mo' dan Marse Bob.

"Missy," Uncle Lon continued, "he was near 'bout de greates' man dat eber come outen de South. He were a good business man; he were straight as dey make 'em, an' he sho enjoy playin' a good joke on someone. I useta see him a-walkin' down de road in de early mornin' an' I knowed it were him f'um a long distance, 'caze he was so tall. I guess you knowed all 'bout his a-servin' in de State legislature an' in de United States Congress an' a-bein' a gen'l in de war an' him bein' de secretary of State in de 'federacy.

Alonza Fantroy Toombs, [TR: Eufaula?], Alabama

"I was bawn on Marse Bob's plantation in de Double Grade Quarters. My pappy's name was Sam Fantroy Toombs an' my mammy was Ida-Belle Toombs. In de slabery times I was too young to work in de fiel's, so my job was to hunt an' fish an' feed de stock in de evenin'. My pappy was a preacher an' Marse Bob learnt him to read and write, an' would let him go f'um plantation to plantation on de Sabbath Day a-preachin' de gospel. He was Marse Bob's carriage driver.

"Yas'm, white folks, Marse Bob was a good provider, too. Us niggers et at home on Sundays, an' us had fried chicken, pot pies, bacon, beef, pork, an' hot coffee. On de udder days, our meals was fixed for us so dat de time us got for res' could be spent dat way. On Sadday us stopped work at noon an' would come wid our vessels to git flour, sugar, lard an' udder supplies. My mammy's pots an' pans was so bright dat dey looked like silver, an' she was one of de bes' cooks in de lan'. She useta cook fine milk yeast bread an' cracklin' bread. All us slaves on Marse

Bob's place was cared for lak de white folks. We had de white folks doctor to treat us when we was sick. We had good clothes, good food an' we was treated fair. Dere warn't no mean peoples on our plantation.

"White lady, I 'members Marse Bob's smokehouse bes' of all. It had ever'thing in it f'um 'possum to deer; an' de wine cellar! Don't say nothin'! Dat was de place I longed to roam. But Marse Bob, he drink too much. Dat was his only fault. He hit de bottle too hard. I couldn't understand it neither, caze he lef' off smokin' in later years when he thought it warn't good for him; but he keppa drinkin'!

"I been ma'ied twice, Mistis. De fus' time to Ida Walker. She died at childbirth; de little fella died too. Den I ma'ied Alice James, an' she's been gone nigh on to twenty year now. My pappy, Rev. Sam Fantroy mai'ed me both times.

"Atter de S'render, nary a slave lef' Marse Bob. He gib eve'y nigger over twenty-one a mule, some lan' an' a house to start off wid. Yassum, Mistis, I kin read an' write; my pappy learnt me how. I'm eighty-six year' old now an' still goin' strong, ceptin' 'bout six years ago I had a stroke. But I come out all right. I lives here wid my sister an' she's good to me. De only thing lef' for me to do is to wish dat when I cross dat ribber I can slip back to de ole place to see some of my frien's."

United States. Work Projects Administration

WILLIAM HENRY TOWNS

Interview with William Henry Towns
—Levi D. Shelby, Jr., Tuscumbia, Alabama

DIS WAS DAT LONG AGO

"It's been so long sence, I don' 'member much," William Henry (Bill) Towns said talking of slavery days. Towns was only seven when the Civil War began and his memories are those of childhood, which he mixes with reminiscences and opinions of the older slaves with whom he came in contact immediately after the war. Towns knows the exact date of his birth. He says:

"I was born in Tuscumbia, Alabama, December 7, 1854. My mother was name Jane Smoots. She come from Baltimore, Maryland. My father's name was Joe Towns, and he come from Huntsville, Alabama.

"I had a passel of brudders an' sisters; Charlie and Bob was my brudders; Betty, Kate, Lula an' Nelie was my sisters. Dere wasn't but two of us endurin' slavery. Dat was me an' Nelie; de rest was born atter slavery. Me an' Nelie was Townses, the rest, Charlie, Kate, Lula, Bob and Betty was Joneses. How dat come 'bout was dis away. Endurin' slavery my father was sold to anudder slave owner. Atter de war my mother married Frank Jones; den dese yuther chillun was born.

"It done been so long sence all of dis was I disremembers most 'bout it. Anyway, the Big House was a two-story house; white like mos' houses endurin' dat time. On the north side of the Big House set a great, big barn, where all de stock an' stuff dat was raised was kep'. Off to de southwes' of de barn an' wes' of de Big House set 'bout five or six log houses. These house was built facin' a space of ground in de center of a squa'e what de houses made. Anybody could stan' in his front do' an' see in at the front of de yuther houses.

"Sometimes enduring' de week an' on Sunday, too, de people would git together out in dis squa'e an' talk 'fore goin' to bed. The chillun what was too young to work was always out in de front playin'. Jes' acrost from our place was anudder wid de quarters built 'mos' de same as ourn 'ceptin' dat dey had a picket fence 'roun' de quarters to pervent 'em from runnin' away. 'Course Mr. Young didn't have to worry 'bout his han's runnin' away, cause he wan't a mean man like some of de slave holders was. He never spoke harsh or whupped 'em, an' he didn't 'low nobody else to do it neither.

"I remember one day a fellow come from acrost on anudder farm an' spoke sumpin' 'bout Mr. Young bein' too easy wid his servants. He said, 'Them darn niggers will think they is good as you iffen you keep up de rate you goin' now, Young.' Mr. Young just up an' told him if he ever spoke like dat again he'd call his bluff. Mr. Young told him de he didn't work his people like dey was oxes.

"All of Mr. Young's hands liked him 'cause he didn't

make 'em sleep on corn shuck mattresses an' he didn't have dey meals cooked in a wash pot. A lot of de yuther slaves didn't know what it was to eat meat, lessen it was a holiday. Mr. Young 'lowed his people to eat just what he eat. I hear my mother tell a tale 'bout a man what took a meat skin an' whipped his chillun's mouth wid it to fool folks like dey had some meat for dinner. Ole Caleb told one a lil' bit bigger'n dat, though. He said one night him an' a feller was comin' from prayer meeting an' they runned 'crost a possum settin' in de root of a tree by de side of de road. He say he stopped to git him an' dis yuther feller told him he wouldn't bother wid him 'cause he wouldn't git none of him no how. Caleb ast him why he said that. He said, ''Cause your ole master is gwine take him jes' soon as you git home wid him.' Caleb told him dat Mr. Young wasn't dat kin'er man. De yuther feller ho'ped Caleb to ketch dat possum, an' he got a piece of him de nex' night when ever'body come in from de fiel'. Caleb said de ol' feller enj'yed de meat so much dat he wished he took him an' his family de 'hole possum.

"We didn't live so far from Big Spring Creek. 'Co'se, we didn't do no fishin', 'cause we younguns had to 'tend gaps to keep de cattle off'n de crops. De grownups had to go to de fiel'. Life was kin'er happy durin' slavery 'cause we never knowed nothing 'bout any yuther sort of life or freedom. All we knowed was work from one en' of de year to de yuther, 'ceptin' on holidays. Den we'd have to go to church or set around de fire an' lis'en to de old folks tell stories. The grownups would go to a dance or do sumpin' else for indertainment. Co'se us younguns got a heap of pleasure outten dem fairy tales dat was tol' us by de older ones. I know ma an' dem use to tell some of de awf'lest tales sometimes. I'd be 'fraid to go from one part of de house to de yuther widoutten somebody wid me. Us younguns would had to play some sort of a game for indertainment. Dere was a whole lot of games an' riddles to be played dem days. It have been so long sence I played any of 'em I'se mos' near disremembers de biggest part of 'em. I 'members a song or two an' a few riddles what ol' Caleb use to tell us. De song goes sumpin' like dis:

> Saturday night an' Sunday, too.
> Had a yaller gal on my mind.
> Monday mornin', break of day,
> White folks had me gwine.

"De riddles was like dis;

> Slick as a mole, black as a coal,
> Got a great long tail like a thunder hole.
> (Skillet)
>
> Crooked as a rainbow, teeth lak a cat,
> Guess all of your life but you can't guess dat.
> (black berry bush)
>
> Grows in de winter, dies in de spring,
> Lives wid de root stickin' straight up.
> (icicle)

"Dere was anudder song what Caleb use to sing. It goes like dis:

> Whar you gwine buzzard? Whar you gwine crow?
> Gwine down to de river to do jes' so.

"Dere was a whole lot more to dat song what I disremembers.

"Anudder song what comes to my min' is:

Hawk an' de buzzard went down to de law;
When de hawk got back he had a broken jaw.
Lady's pocketbook on de judge's bench
Haden' had no use for a pocketbook sence.

"Sometimes I visits wid ol' Mingo White an' me an' him talks over dem days dat me an' him was boys. We gits to talkin' an' 'fore you knows it ol' Mingo is cryin' lak a baby. 'Cordin' to what he says he is lucky ter be a-livin'. Dis is one thing I never likes ter talk 'bout. When slavery was goin' on it was all right for me 'cause I never had it hard, but it jes' wan't right to treat human bein's dat way. If we hadn't a-had to work an' slave for nothin' we might have somepin' to show for what we did do, an' wouldn't have to live from pillar to pos' now.

William Henry Towns, [TR: Tuscumbia?], Alabama

"Speakin' of clothin', everything that we wore back den was made by han'. Many a night my ma use' to set an' spin wid a spindle. I have set an' done the cardin' for her so she could git her tas' done. In de summer we would wear un'erwear what was made outten cotton. In de winter it was made outten flannel. De shoes was made of cowhide what was tanned right dere on de place. Dem was de hardes' shoes I ever seen. Sometimes dey'd wear out 'fore dey was any ways soft, an' den sometimes atter dey was wore out you couldn't hardly ben' 'em. Some of de han's would go bar'footed until de fall an' den wear shoes. Slippers wan't wore den. De fust pair of slippers I ever 'members havin' was de ones what I bought for my weddin'. Dey didn't cos' but a dollar an' six bits. My weddin' suit didn't cos' but eight dollars, an' a straw hat to match it cos' six bits.

"As I said afore, Massa Young an' ol' Mistis was mighty good folks on 'count of dey never whupped any of they han's. Iffen dere was one dat would give trouble dey would git rid of him. De overseers had to be kin' to de hands or else he was outten a job. De chillun was mighty nice, too. Ever' time dey went to town or to de sto' dey would bring us youngun s some candy or somepin'. Joinin' our farm was a farm whar de slaves fared lak dogs. Dey was always beatin' on some of dem.

"Ever'body worked hard enduring' dat time. Dat was all we thought we was 'spose' to do, but Abe Lincoln taught us better'n dat. Some say dat Abe wan't intrusted so much in freein' de slaves as he was in savin' de union. Don' make no diff'ence iffen he wan't intrusted in de black folks, he sho' done a big thing by tryin' to save de union. Some of de slaveholders would double de proportion of work so as to git to whip 'em when night come. I heard my ma say after slavery that dey jes' whipped de slaves so much to keep dem cowed down an' 'cause dey might have fought for freedom much sooner'n it did come.

"Caleb come from N'Orleans, Louiseanner. He say dat many a day ship loads of slaves was unloaded dere an' sold to de one offerin' de mos' money for dem. Dey had big chains an' shackles on dem to keep 'em from gittin' away. Sometime dey would have to go a long ways to git to de farm. Dey would go in a wagon or on hoss back.

"Talk 'bout learnin' to read an' 'rite—why, iffen we so much as spoke of learnin' to read an' 'rite we was scolded like de debil. Iffen we was caught lookin' in a book we was treated same as iffen we had killed somebody. A servant bett'nt be caught lookin' in a book; didn't make no diff'ence if you wan't doin' nothin' but lookin' at de pictures.

"Speakin' of church; we went to de same church as de white folks did; only thing was we had to go in de evenin' atter de white folks. De white folks would go along an' read de Bible for de preacher, an' to keep dem from talkin of things dat might help dem to git free. Dey would sing songs like 'Steal Away,' 'Been Toilin' at the Hill So Long,' an' 'Old-Time Religion.'

"Ever' once in a while slaves would run away to de North. Mos' times dey was caught an' brought back. Sometimes dey would git desp'rit an' would kill demse'ves 'fore dey would stand to be brought back. One time dat I heard of a slave that had 'scaped and when dey tried to ketch him he jumped in de creek an' drown hisse'f. He was brought from over in Geo'gia. He hadn't been in Alabama long 'fore him an' two more tried to 'scape; two of 'em was caught an' brought back but dis yuther one went to de lan' of sweet dreams.

"After de day's work was done an' all had eat, de slaves had to go to bed. Mos' slaves worked on Sat'day jes' lak dey did on Monday; that was from kin' to caught, or from sun to sun. Mr. Young never worked his slaves 'twell dark on Sat'day. He always let 'em quit 'roun' fo' 'clock. We would spen' dis time washin' an' bathin' to git ready for church on Sunday. Speakin' of holidays; de han's celebrated ever' holiday dat deir white folks celebrated. Dere wan't much to do for indertainment, 'ceptin' what I'se already said. Ever' Christmas we'd go to de Big House an' git our present, 'cause ol' Mistis always give us one.

"Slaves never got sick much, but when dey did dey got de bes'. Dere was always a nurse on de farm, and when a slave got sick dey was righ' dere to give dem treatments. Back in dose days dey used all sorts of roots and yarbs for medicine. Peach tree leaves was one of de mos' of'en. Sassafras was anudder what was used of'en; hit was used mostly in de spring made in tea. Asafetida was anudder what was use to keep you from havin' azma. Hit was wore 'round de neck in a lil bag. Prickler ash was anudder what was tooken in de spring. Hit was 'spose ter clean de blood. Some of de folks would use brass, copper an' dimes wid holes in 'em to keep from havin' their rumertiz.

"I was seben years old when de war commence. I 'members Mrs. Young said when de Yankees come dey was goin' to ast us iffen dey had been good to us. She said dat dey was goin' to ast us all 'bout how much money dey had; an' how many slaves what dey owned. She told us to say dey was po' folks an' dat dey didn't have no money.

I 'member my mother said dat she hoped Mr. Young and dem to hide deir money som'ers in a well dat wan't bein' used 'cause it gone dry. Dem Yankees sho' did clean up whar they went along. Dey would ketch chickens by de bunches and kill 'em an' den turn 'roun' an' make de ol' Mistis clean 'em an' cook 'em for dem. Dem Yankees set fire to bales an' bales of cotton. Dey took de white folks clo'se an' did away wid 'em. Sometimes dey would tear 'em up or give dem to de slaves to wear. De war ended in sixty-five an' I was eleben years ol' den.

"Jes' atter de war we was turned loose to go for ourse'f. What I mean by dat, we was free. I didn't mean that we lef' Mr. Young's 'cause we stayed wid him for de longest atter slavery was over.

"My fust work was in a blacksmith shop down on West Six Street. I worked for fifty cents a day den until I learned de trade. Atter I worked at de blacksmith shop for about two years I took up carpenter work. I served apprentice for three years. I followed carpent'ing the res' of my life.

"I married Lizzie Anderson when I was twenty-one years ol'. She wan't but seventeen years ol'. We didn't have no big weddin', we jes' had de fambly dere. I raised ten chillun up until April de twenty fourth. That's when William Henry died. My chilluns doin' pretty well in life. Dere's two of my sons what's doctors; one is a carpenter. The other one is Grand Orator of the Shriners. My gals is doin' fine, too. Three of 'em is been school teachers, one a beauty cult'ist an' de other one a nurse. I feels sati'fied 'bout my chillun now. Dey seems to be able to make a livin' for they se'ves pretty well.

"I thinks that Abe Lincoln was a mighty fine man even if he was tryin' to save their union. I don't like to talk 'bout this that have done happened. It done passed so I don't say much 'bout it, specially de Presidents, 'cause it might cause a 'sturbance right now. All men means well, but some of 'em ain't broadminded 'nough to do anythin' for nobody but themse'fs. Any man that tries to help humanity is a good man."

STEPNEY UNDERWOOD

Interview with Stepney Underwood
—*John Morgan Smith*

THE COURT JESTER

"Yassuh, I was a slave. I was tin year' old whin de war begin." Uncle Stepney spoke the words between intermittent jerks of an uncontrollable voice. The nervousness which resulted from hard work and a long struggle for existence had not only given him palsy, but had left him with an upheaving diaphragm. Thus he shook and shivered while stuttering so constantly as to be almost unintelligible.

"My mammy belonged to the Johnstons and my pappy was owned by the Underwoods," he continued; "dey lived next to each other on two big plantations in Lowndes County. Dey was good peoples—dem Underwoods. I remembers dat dey use to think I was as funny as a little monkey. De massa usta laugh his head off at me, and when dere was parties, de guestes would always say: 'Whar Stepney? We wants to see Stepney dance.' I usta cut many a [...] pigeon wing fur 'em.

"One day atter I finish' my chores, I slip off an go across de line to see my mammy. When I was a-comin' back th'ough de woods, I met up wid two pattyrollers. Dey stop me and say: 'Nigger, who you belong to?'

"'Massa Jim Johns'on,' I answers.

"'Whut you a doin' out here, den?' dey say, all de time a slippin' a little closer so's to grab me.

"I don't take time to gib 'em no mo' answers kaze I knowd dat dis meant a beatin'. I starts my legs a-flyin' an' I runs through de fores' lak a scar't rabbit wid dem pattyrollers right behin' me. My bare feets flew over dem stones an' I jus' hit de high spots in de groun'. I knowed dem two mens didn't have no chance to kotch me, but dis sho meant a whuppin' when I got home.

Stepney Underwood, [TR: Birmingham], Alabama

"But I didn't go home dat night. I stay out in de woods and buil' me a little fiah. I laid down under a sycamo' tree a-tryin' ter make up my min' ter go an' take dat beatin'. I heered de panthers a screamin' a way off in de fores' an' de wildcats a howlin', an' how I wished I coulda been wid my mammy. Eve'y now and den, I could see eyes a shinin' in de darkness an' rustlin's in de bushes. Warn't no use of me a-cryin' kaze I was a long way fum home an' dere warn't no one to could hear me. Eve'y thing seem to be agin' me. Far off across de ridge I heered a screech owl a-callin', an' I knowd dat meant death. I was glad I had my overalls on so's I could turn my pockets inside out'ards to stop him. Atter I done dis, he sho-nuf stopped. Den my lef' ear it commence to ichin', and I knowd dat someone was a-sayin' somethin' mean about me. Probably dat oberseer dat was a-goin' to whup me when I got home. Soon I fell slap to sleep on a bed of moss. De nex' day I was awful hongry, an' long 'bout de time de sun was a-comin' ober de ridge, I heerd some mens a-comin' through de brush. It was de massa, de oberseer an' some mo' mens. I runs toward de massa and I calls as loud as I could: 'Massa Jim, here I is.'

"He come up wid an awful frown on his face and de oberseer, he had a big whup in his han'.

"'You little bur-head Nigger debil', de massa say, 'I teach you ter run away fum yo' place. Come on home; I'se gwine give you a good breakfast an' fix you up in some decent clothes. I'se got visitors a-comin' an' heah you is out in de woods when I needs you to dance.' Den de massa, he smile lak I ain't done nothin' wrong. 'I guess you wants yo mammy, you little lonesome pickaninny.

Well, I s'pose I hadda go ober and buy her. You little debil you—now git on home.'"

CHARLIE VAN DYKE

Personal conversation with Charlie Van Dyke
713 S. Lawrence street, Mobile, Ala.
—Written by Mary A. Poole

IT TOOK $50.00 TO PUT UNCLE CHARLIE ON DE FLOOR!

An old colored man, named Charlie Van Dyke, living at 713 S. Lawrence street, Mobile, Ala. claims to be 107 years old, but he has no authentic record of his birth. He told the writer he was born in North Carolina, and when he was ten years old, Mr. William Martee King, who owned his mother, "Nellie Drish", moved to Tuscaloosa, Ala., where the King family remained about a year, moving then from Tuscaloosa down into Dallas County, near Selma, Ala.

While Mr. and Mrs. King and their family remained in Tuscaloosa, Charlies mother Nellie Drish met and married William Van Dyke, who belonged to the Van Dykes, who owned the neighboring plantation.

Charlie assumed his step-father's name, but knew little of him, or of the Van Dykes to whom his step-father belonged, because, as Charlie explained to the writer, after the Kings moved down in Dallas County, (as Charlie always referred to his home in Alabama) and brought his mother Nellie and her family with them, his stepfather could only visit them once a year, and that privilege was given him on Christmas Day. He had to start back the next day, as he had to make the trip to and fro on horse back.

Uncle Charlie said the Kings owned about a thousand acres in Dallas County and had about a hundred head of slaves, but with all their riches they lived in a plain plank house.

He smiled and said, "Now-a-days folks passing such a house, would say 'Colored folks live there.'"

The slave quarters were the regular log wood cabins, said Uncle Charlie, with space between each row and a little plot of ground to separate each cabin to itself.

Uncle Charlie said his mother cooked for the white folks, and sometimes she didn't get down to their cabin but on Sunday afternoon, that he being the oldest had to look after the younger children, and that he was never required to do heavy work as he broke his leg when a boy, so the folks let him just work around the yard and look after his sisters and brothers and also the other slave children.

Uncle Charlie said Mr. King traveled a lot, went to France once, that took almost a year and the overseer had full charge and he was mean and made everybody stand around. He even made the slaves shuck corn on Sundays, each had their allotted amount to shuck before they could stop.

When the writer asked about church on the plantation, Uncle Charlie replied: "Church was what they called it but all that preacher talked about was for us slaves to obey our masters and not to lie and steal. Nothing about Jesus was ever said, and the overseer stood there to see the preacher talked as he wanted him to talk."

The only day that Uncle Charlie said they were given any real holiday was Christmas, everybody got his drink of whiskey on Christmas, and not another drink until next Christmas, "it sure seemed a long time between drinks", added Charlie with a smile.

Uncle Charlie said they did let you have a funeral when some one died, they made the coffin on the plantation and carried it by hand to the graveyard, singing as they went along. He tried to recall the hymns, but all he could chant in a sing-song way was,

> Last word he said was about Jerusalem
> And he traveled along to the grave!

When asked about war days, Uncle Charlie was first on the Confederate side, then on the Northern side, and he seemed somewhat bewildered about it all, he said he saw a stockade, as he called it, in Selma, Ala., and he remembered food stuff being sent to the soldiers, and also recalled the Yankees coming, and a Captain coming up the road and telling them the soldiers were coming. Uncle Charlie said the colored folks thought the Captain had to go back North before they came back, but in a flash like lightening there they were, hundreds of them, and they scared folks so bad some of them jumped in the river and tried to swim across and those that couldn't, they just drowned.

When the writer tried to check up on Uncle Charlie's age, asking him how old he was when the war started, he replied:

"I dont know but I was a man long afore it all started, lady, and I was thirty-three years old when I married 'bout a year after the surrender."

When asked why he waited so long to get married, Uncle Charlie said:

"Didn't you know in slavery days they wouldn't alow a man to marry unless he could split a hundred rails a day?"

The writer smiled and said:

"Now, Uncle Charlie," and then he chuckled, and said:

"Well, I guess the right one didn't come 'long till I met her."

When asked if he had a regular wedding feast, he replied.

"Yes, lady, it took $50.00 to put me on the floor."

Charlie and Theresa had "five head of children", as Uncle Charlie expressed it, of which three are dead and two living, but he claims his children do not look after him, but his church folks and friends give him the helping hand. He is a member of the St. Luke Missionary Baptist Church, of Mobile.

Uncle Charlie says he has his religion from the foregone prophets, that he "don't understand this day religion", that he came along when people were serving Daniel's God, and when people had to be born again, now they serve a sanctified God and jump from one religion to another.

Uncle Charlie finished the interview by saying, "Lord teach me how to pray, And teach me to love it woo."

United States. Work Projects Administration

LILAH WALKER

Interview with Lilah Walker
—William B. Strickland, Carbon Hill

I HEAR DE WHIRRIN' OF QUARE WINGS

I walked through a small glade overshadowed by large oak trees, near Carbon Hill in Walker County, Alabama. A weird little cabin confronted me; its porch and steps loosely held to the main part of the structure by a few weak boards. Lilah Walker, an old Negro woman, squatted on the steps with her chin resting in her black hands, in an attitude of deep reverie. As the old woman heard me approaching she raised her head in cordial greeting.

"Come in, young marster," she said. "How is you today?"

"Fine, Aunt Lilah," I answered. 'How's the world treating you?"

"Oh, I can't complain," she replied.

The old woman continued.

"It mought be safer to set inside, 'case dey says when de sun swing low lak dis dat de miassahs whut make you sick 'gin to rise outten yon' swamp." Then she chuckled:

"I bin here since 'fo' de wah, an' I ain't neber seen no miassahs rise outten dat swamp yit. Yassuh, dat sho is so, but from whut I seed rise outten it my 'pinion is dat dey done lef' long 'fo' dis. But I seed quare wings whirrin' outten dat swamp jus' 'fo' days atter de surrender, an' I seed 'em near 'bout eve'y day since. I seed 'em an' I heered 'em jus' a whirrin'!

"Nawsuh, I sho can't 'splain de wings, but I is got my 'pinion how come dey is. When I tells you whut took place here durin' dem dark ole days, den maybe you'll hab yourn. Ole Mistis died 'fo de war, an' ole Massa, he too ole to go. He didn't do nothin' but set aroun' an' read de books an' papers. 'Peer lak to me he jus' plum forgit 'bout young Mistis after her mammy died, an' de little gal jus' growed up lak a wild flower in de woods, cep'n for a handsome young boy on de nex' plantation. Dey was nearly always together.

"By an' by de boy got ole enough to go to de wah. It was jus' a little fo' de close. Den young Mistis, she droop an' she droop. 'Reckley she 'gin to swoon, long jus' anywheres she would. One day she swoon an' nothin' I could do would bring her back to her senses. I jus' couldn't fetch her to. I call ole Massa an' he git a doctor. Dey putt me outten de room an' I ain't neber heared whut dat doctor said till yit, but ole Massa, he go stark wild. He holla an' carry on in his sleep all de night; an' de nex' day he druv' de young Mistis away. Dere was a cabin den in de swamp, an' she went dar to live. I snuk out dar an' tote her vittles to her fo' days an' days. She always grab me an' say: 'Don't you love me an' don't you believe in me, mammy?'

"'Co'se I does, honey chile, 'ca'se I useta sing to you

'bout de good ole lan' of promise.' Den I says to her: 'Dese times is powerful triflin', an' maybe 'fo' long I's gwine home an' de white folks will miss me 'ca'se dey can't raise chilluns.' Den she cry an' I cry.

"'Bout dat time de word come of de surrender. Ole Massa seem to come to his wits den an' he kep' a close watch on me so's I can't leave de house to carry de food. On de fo'th day, I cotch a chance an' I snuck off. When I come close to de cabin I call, but young Mistis neber answer. Den I went to de do', but I neber go in de do', 'ca'se millions of black wings come a-whirrin' outten de house. I run an' run an' I pray too, but de big black wings still follow me. Sometimes in de early mornin' I still hears an' sees two pairs of wings, sometimes white, sometimes black.

"Yassuh, I is aimin' to tell you 'bout ole Massa; whut 'come of him. One evenin' I ventured to de aidge of dat swamp, an' somep'n cracked under my feets. I is jus' about to run when I sees it's jus' a piece of paper. I sees it has writin' on it so I taken it to ole Massa. Den when he read dat he sho 'nough go plum crazy. 'Bout dat time dey open what dey called a 'sane 'slylum in Tusaloosy an' dey taken ole Massa dar an' a little later he died.

"De young boy who went to wah, whut about him? Dey say he was killed in de las' battle of Appomatox. Dat piece o' paper? Yassuh. It was a paper sayin' dat young Mistis and de young boy on de nex' plantation was 'nited in ma'iage. Listen, young Massa. I hears dem quare wings a-whirrin'."

United States. Work Projects Administration

SIMON WALKER

Interview with Simon Walker
—*Ira S. Jordan*

Softly mumbling to himself and gravely shaking a bare, shiny head that had only a fringe of white, closely-kinked wooly hair about the ears, the old Negro shuffled out of the crowded courtroom into the corridor.

Turning clear, quizzical eyes toward a group of white men loitering near the doorway and addressing no one in particular, with a final emphatic shake of his head he said:

"Hit do beat all, de way dese young niggers is allus in trouble wid de law. Now, whin Ah was a young buck de only law mongst us niggers was de word uv ole Massa. Mebbe you all's heerd tell o' him—Cun'l Hugh Walker?

"Ef de Cun'l wasn't de richest man anywhar 'round Forsyth, Georgy, den mah name ain't Simon Walker. Yassuh! Dat's mah name too. Ah belonged to de Cun'l 'long wid more'n er hundderd mo' slaves, an' my mammy an' pappy befo' me belonged to de Walkers.

"All uv 'em gone now—gone to Glory, an dis ole nigger heah all by hisself—de las' one er de fambly. De

Cun'l, he had eight boys, an all 'cept de least un jined de Confederits.

"'Twas a turrible sad day when young Maas Chap was brung home wid one of his laigs shot plumb off by de Yankees; an me settin' dar by him a-fannin' erway de flies endurin' all de long hot days whilst he was layin' dar on de aige o' Kingdom Come. An' all de time Ah was thankin' de Lawd dat mah lil' Maas Jim was too young to go to de wawh—(all de Cun'l's sons dey had body servants, an Ah was Maas Jim's boy). Ah useter look atter him, go to school wid him an play in de woods 'tell school was out, an ef he had 'er gone to de wawh, dis nigger would er been right dar wid him.

"Nawsuh, Maas Jim an me never did go to de wawh, but us seed de Yankees whin' Gen'l Sherman come marchin through our plantation. An ef Ah live fur thousand yeahs Ah'd never fergit dat day! Ah ain't nivver seed so many men in one crowd befo' er since, an de las' one uv 'em wearin' de same kind of clo'es. Dey come right up in de yahd, an a passel of 'em tromped right into de Big House, jist lak it was dare'n. Dey turned ebrything wrong side out'ards a-lookin' fer de silver an de jewl'ry, but Ole Missis, she done had news dey was comin' an all de stuff was hid in de woods. Whin dey couldn't fin' de plate an' jewl'ry, dey was hoppin mad, an atter takin' all de hams an rations dey could tote off dey sot fire to de smoke-house, an' de bahn an' all de cotton dat was piled around de ginhouse, to keep de Confederits frum gittin it, dey said. Dey took all de good houses an' mules an' lef' dere ole hongry, broke-down nags dat won't fittin' fer nothin' 'cept fert'lize. But dey didn't hu't nobody, not eben Cookie whin she tuck er broom atter em in de kitchin."

Simon Walker, Birmingham, Alabama

"Ah reckon dem soldiers thought de Cun'l was plumb ruint whin dey lef, but Ah says, Cun'l Walker was er rich man, an' 'fo' long us done bought fresh rations, en drive up de hargs frum de swamp an kilt mo' meat. Den de Cun'l he sont off fer mo' mules, an whin dey come de wu'k went on ergin.

"Come de day whin all de niggers was sot free. Cun'l Walker call all de slaves up to de Big House, an standin dere on de verandah he told 'em dey was now all free niggers—free to go whar dey pleased. But, ef anybody wanted to stay on de plantation to hole up dare hans. Mos' all de hans stayed on de plantation 'tell de Cun'l died, an de fambly sorter broke up. Dat was fo' yeahs atter de Surrender.

"Well, atter dat, Ah jist drifted eroun', an fin'ly landed heah in Bummin'ham in 1888. Wont nothin' much heah den but muddy roads an swamps, but Ah got er job totein' mortar whar dey was buildin' de fust brick sto', an' den er long time atterwards Ah wo'ked fer de 'T.C. and I.' fer twenty-five yeahs.

"But de ole nigger ain't no mo' good fer hahd labor. All dah white folks done gone on, an heah I is on de Welfare, jist waitin' fer de good Lawd to call me up dare fer de Great Reunion—Amen."

LUCINDIA WASHINGTON

Interview with Lucindia Washington
—Alice S. Barton

Little black Cindy skipped along the narrow path that led to the Spring House. In her hand she swung an empty cedar pail that she was soon to fill with cool, fresh milk. She entered the small glade overhung with willow trees and spread with soft grass, and gazed at the sparkling water of the spring as it caught the beams of sunlight coming through the trees and reflected them in myriads of little points. Shadows of the waving leaves danced over the ground and up the side of the stone Spring House. How cool and nice it was here, she thought. Gentle breezes rustled the limbs of small saplings and quietly stirred the long grass along the upper part of the branch.

A young rabbit hopped from a little clump of bushes and Cindy watched him as the small creature drank thirstily from the crystal water. Occasionally, the bunny would lift his head as if warned by a slight sound, but in a moment she saw him fold back his delicate ears and once more dip his small mouth into the babbling water.

After quenching his thirst, the rabbit hopped a few feet away and nibbled on a wisp of tender grass. Cindy was as still as a statue as she watched the procedure. "Dat's de cutest little bunny I ever seed," she said to herself. "I wish I could ketch him." But Cindy knew that she could not catch a rabbit, so she was content to stand in the shadow of a sycamore and gaze eagerly at the animal, nibbling the grass.

Suddenly, without warning, Cindy's eyes protruded from their sockets with an expression of fear. Slipping noiselessly through the green undergrowth she saw a giant rattler gliding slowly toward the young rabbit. She wanted to cry out, but she was afraid; afraid of attracting the rattler's attention toward her. She was deathly afraid of snakes. Since babyhood, she had harbored a growing fear of them. If Cindy had been still before this time, she now became a frozen image. It would not have been apparent that she was even breathing. So frightened was she of the snake that her whole body broke out in a profuse perspiration. Her eyes were glued to the tremendous brown monster which, without the slightest sound, oozed deftly toward its victim. Cindy was hypnotized! The snake seemed to hold her in a strange spell. Slowly, inexorably he moved entirely out of the undergrowth and was now weaving on the clear ground. He approached the rabbit within a distance of three feet and began to carefully form himself in a deadly coil. Cindy saw every movement. She saw each diamond on its brown back; each scale of its crawling skin; each lash and point of its tongue; the whiteness of its breast, the large track that it had made in the sand. She watched its eyes gleam, expressionless and ominous. She gazed at the deadly mouth as it slowly began to open. She was aware of the first appearance of the two death-like fangs pointing downward. She saw the ten-buttoned rattle stand erect. She saw it quiver; shake; sound. She saw the rabbit turn with fear. She saw the strike; the sinking of the fangs into the soft, brown fur. She watched the rabbit give an ephemeral struggle; witnessed the brief pitiful look in the bunny's eyes and at last saw the mouth sink into the small belly and draw the last breath of life away.

The experience was more than the little girl could stand. Cindy was now in a state of frenzy. She could not move, nor speak, nor turn her eyes. She could only stare! At what?

The monstrous snake then girded himself for further onslaught. After being sure his victim was dead, he loosed his grip and stretched at full length upon the ground; drew the rabbit out until it too was stretched carefully out with its hind feet together and its head pointing in the opposite direction. Then followed an experience that to Cindy seemed entirely impossible. The snake took the hind feet of the rabbit in his mouth, until gradually they had disappeared. Then came what seemed to 'Cindy an agonized struggle. The snake's mouth stretched almost to the breaking point as it began slowly to close over the rest of the rabbit's rear quarter. With fits and starts and jerks and stretches, the rattler reeled and squirmed; contorted and wreathed and sucked until the rabbit had half gone. With the last great effort the serpent threw himself into another series of bodily contortions that seemed to 'Cindy positively agonizing to him, until at last the rabbit had entirely disappeared from the earth. For several minutes 'Cindy apparently watched the tremendous hump in the snake move slowly backward. With gradually diminishing intermittent jerks, the snake finally got the small animal to his digestive tract. The monster then crawled to a hot sandy section and went to sleep.

Two hours later it was twilight. An overseer was walking along the path to the Spring House. He paused for a moment beneath a sycamore tree to rest and cool himself. As his eyes roamed the shadowy little glade they came to rest on the body of a little Negro girl, lying inert upon the soft grass with the handle of a cedar bucket clutched in a death grip. He lifted the small black form into his arms and carried her to the house. He saw in her face an expression of mingled agony and fear.

"Yassuh, white folks, dat was me," Aunt 'Cindy smiled as she told me of the experience, 80 years later. "Dat was de biggest snake I ever seed. He musta been seven feet long."

Cindy Washington, [TR: Eutaw], Alabama

"All dis happen in Sumter County whar I was bawn. Us had a pretty place dere. I'll never forgits how de niggers worked dere gardens in de moonlight. Dere warn't no time in de day. De white folks work tuk dat time. De oberseer rung a big bell for us to git up by in de mawnin' at fo' o'clock, an' de fus' thing we done was to feed de stock."

"You axe was we punished?" Yassuh, we was punished for something: most of all for stealin'.

"Yassuh, we was taught to read an' write, but mos' of

de slaves didn't want to learn. Us little niggers would hide our books under de steps to keep f'um havin' to study. Us'd go to church wid de white folks on Sunday and sit in de back, an' den we go home an' eat a big Sunday meal. When we got sick f'um eatin' too much or somp'n, Massa Jim Godfrey was a doctor an' he'd ten' to us. Den when new nigger babies came, nine little black bugs was tied up in rags 'roun' dere necks for to make de babies teethe easy. When I was ma'ied, white folks, at de age of thirteen, Alex Washington, my husband an me had a forty-dollar weddin'. My mistis baked me a cake, an' a white school-master named Henry Hindron spoke de ceremony. Me an' dat ole husband had twenty-two chilluns.

"Yas ma'm. I sho does believe in ghosties. We's got one good spirit an' one bad un. One goes to heaben an' de udder stays on earth. Ghosties sho does lak whiskey, caze dey'll follow you iffen you got any. Iffen you po' it on de groun' beside you, dough, dey'll lose track of you. Always give a gos' de raght han' side of de road, white folks, an' he won't bother you.

"Yes my chile, I is got religion. I seed Jesus a hanging f'um de cross. He give his blood so dat us could live. I knows I is goin' to heaben."

ELIZA WHITE

Interview with Eliza White, age around 80
Opelika, Alabama
—Preston Klein, Opelika, Alabama

SHE SEED A HA'NT

Eliza White lives by the Central of Georgia Railroad tracks in Opelika. The passing of many years has not dulled her mind, and so she was able to tell of many things which happened "befo' de wah."

"Yas, suh, I was a slave. Ole Massa was name' Billy Jones, and Ole Mistis was name' Angeline. Dey lived in Harris County, Georgia, close to Columbus. My pappy and mammy was Peter and Frances Jones, and I had a brother, Dennis, and a sister, Georgianne.

"Massa was a good man, and I did love Ole Mistis. Dey was mighty good to us niggers; fed us out dey own garden. We had checked homespun clothes foh eve'yday, and purty calico and dyed osnaburg ones foh Sunday. I went to church wid de white folks, settin' in de foot of de carriage. I 'members well de Sunday I fust seen a shoutin'. It was two white ladies.

"Massa and Mistis had four chillun. Two of dem, Dave and Quit, was bad fighting kids. I seen Massa make dem strip to dey waist, and whip 'em, den make dem go in and bathe.

"Massa lived in a big, fine white house. He had two or three hundred slaves, and de quarters was in two long rows, runnin' up near 'bout to de big house on de hill. Dey even raised deer on de place. De houses in de quarters was two-room log houses wid a shed room to cook in. My mammy was de cook at de big house, and granny was de weaver. Pappy was de bedmaker; he made most of de beds outen poplar. I had a little chair in de corner where I sot and kept de flies offen Mistis wid a green twig brush.

"Whenever Massa sont any de slaves offen de place he had to gib 'em passes so de patterollers wouldn't ketch 'em and whip 'em foh runnin' away. De patterollers was a good thing foh de lazy ones. When daylight come we had to get up, else we'd be whipped. Massa didn't have his slaves whipped much; just when dey was lazy and wouldn't work.

"Ev'ey now and den we would have some good frolics, mostly on Sattiday nights. Somebody would play de fiddle and we all danced to de music. De folks sure had some big times at de cornshuckin's, too. De men would work two or three days, haulin' de corn and pilin' it near de crib. Den dey would invite folks from other quarters to come and help wid de shuckin'. While dey shucked dey would holler and sing:

> You jumped and I jumped;
> Swear, by God you out jumped me.
> Huh! Huh! Round de corn, Sally.

"Granny used to give us tea made outen sage roots, mullen, pine, hoarhound—dat sho' was bitter stuff. We had purty beads made wid corn. And I still 'members de Christmas I got my fust shoes. I just hugged dem tight and went to sleep holdin' 'em. Dey was button shoes.

"When we heard de Yankees was comin' we hid all de meat and rations and de silver in de big swamp, and turned de horses loose, and all us kids hid in de bedticks (mattresses). De Yankees stayed around two or three days and would pull de hands out of dere beds by dey toes.

"But I really seed a ha'nt one time. I knowed it was. De was one old man been havin' de toothache all de time; he used to keep he jaw tied up. I was gwine over to see him day time. Well, 'fore I got dere I seen what look like him comin'. When I got nearer he turned to a man riding a mule and wearing a big hat. Den, 'fore he got to de house he was plum gone. Dat's how I knowed it was a ha'nt."

MINGO WHITE

Interview with Mingo White
—Levi D. Shelby, Jr., Tuscumbia, Alabama

JEFF DAVIS USED TO CAMOUFLAGE HIS HORSE

Mingo White lives at Burleson in Franklin County, Alabama, and though he doesn't know his age he remembers that he was a big boy when the War between the States began. His reminiscences of slavery days, when he was a field hand, are an incongruous combination of stories of severe cruelty and free Saturday afternoons, Sunday holidays and happy festivals of cornshucking and community cotton picking. He talks of punishments visited on recalcitrant slaves beyond human endurance and of tasks saddled on one person that would take half a dozen to accomplish. Mingled with these perhaps fogged memories of the nonagenarian are interesting sidelights of "drivers," paterollers," Ku Kluxers and share-cropping in reconstruction days.

"I was born in Chester, South Carolina, but I was mos'ly raised in Alabama," Mingo said. "When I was 'bout fo' or five years old, I was loaded in a wagon wid a lot mo' people in 'hit. Whar I was boun' I don't know.

Whatever become of my mammy an' pappy I don' know for a long time.

"I was tol' there was a lot of slave speculators in Chester to buy some slaves for some folks in Alabama. I 'members dat I was took up on a stan' an' a lot of people come 'roun' an' felt my arms an' legs an' chist, an' ast me a lot of questions. Befo' we slaves was took to de tradin' post Ol' Marsa Crawford tol' us to tell eve'ybody what ast us if we'd ever been sick to tell 'em dat us'd never been sick in our life. Us had to tell 'em all sorts of lies for our Marsa or else take a beatin'.

"I was jes' a li'l thang; tooked away from my mammy an' pappy, jes' when I needed 'em mos'. The only caren' that I had or ever knowed anything 'bout was give to me by a frein' of my pappy. His name was John White. My pappy tol' him to take care of me for him. John was a fiddler an' many a night I woke up to find myse'f 'sleep 'twix' his legs whilst he was playin' for a dance for de white folks. My pappy an' mammy was sold from each yuther too, de same time as I was sold. I use' to wonder if I had any brothers or sisters, as I had always wanted some. A few years later I foun' out I didn't have none.

"I'll never forgit de trip from Chester to Burleson. I wouldn't 'member so well I don't guess, 'cepin' I had a big ol' sheep dog name Trailer. He followed right in back of de wagon dat I was in. Us had to cross a wide stream what I tuk to be a ribber. When we started 'crost, ol' Trailer never stop followin'. I was watchin' him clost so if he gived out I was goin' to try to git him. He didn't giv' out, he didn't even hab to swim. He jes' walked 'long an' lapped de water lack a dog will.

"John took me an' kep' me in de cabin wid him. De cabin didn' hab no furniture in hit lack we has now 'days. De bed was a one-legged, hit was made in de corner of de room, wid de leg settin' out in de middle of de flo'. A plank was runned 'twix' de logs of de cabin an' nailed to de post on de front of de bed. Across de foot an' udder plank was runned into de logs an' nail' to de leg. Den some straw or cornshucks was piled on for a mattress. Us used anythang what we could git for kivver. De table had two legs, de legs set out to de front whilst de back part was nail' to de wall. Us didn't hab no stove. Thar was a great big fireplace whar de cookin' was done. Us didn't hab to cook, though, lessen us got hungry after supper been served at de house.

"I warn't nothin' but a chile endurin' slavery, but I had to wuk de same as any man. I went to de fiel' and hosed cotton, pulled fodder and picked cotton wid de res' of de han's. I kep' up too, to keep from gittin' any lashes dat night when us got home. In de winter I went to de woods wid de men folks to ho'p git wood or to git sap from de trees to make turpentine an' tar. Iffen us didn't do dat we made charcoal to run de blacksmif shop wid.

"De white folks was hard on us. Dey would whup us 'bout de leas' li'l thang. Hit wouldn't a been so bad iffen us had a had comforts, but to live lack us did was 'nouf to make anybody soon as be dead. De white folks tol' us dat us born to work for 'em an' dat us was doin' fine at dat.

"De nex' time dat I saw my mammy I was a great big boy. Dere was a 'oman on de place what ever'body called mammy, Selina White. One day mammy called me an' said, Mingo, your mammy is comin'.' I said, 'I thought dat you was my mammy.' She said 'No I ain't your mammy, yer mammy is 'way way from here. I couldn't believe dat I had anudder mammy and I never thought 'bout hit any mo'. One day I was settin' down at de barn when a wagon come up de lane. I stood 'roun' lack a chile will. When de wagon got to de house, my mammy got out an' broke and run to me an' th'owed her arms 'roun' my neck an' hug an' kiss me. I never even put my arms 'roun' her or nothin' of de sort. I jes' stood dar lookin' at her. She said, 'Son ain't you glad to see your mammy?' I looked at her an' walked off. Mammy Selina call me an' tol' me dat I had hurt my mammy's feelin's, and dat dis 'oman was my mammy. I went off an' studied and I begins to 'member thangs. I went to Selina an' ast her how long it been sence I seen my mammy. She tol' me dat I had been 'way from her sence I was jes' a li'l chile. I went to my mammy an' tol' her dat I was sorry I done what I did an' dat I would lack fer her to fergit an' forgive me for de way I act when I fust saw her. After I had talked wid my real mammy, she told me of how de family had been broke up an' dat she hadn't seed my pappy sence he was sold. My mammy never would of seen me no mo' if de Lawd hadn' a been in de plan. Tom White's daughter married one of Mr. Crawford's sons. Dey lived in Virginia. Back den it was de custom for women to come home whenever dey husbands died or quit 'em. Mr. Crawford's son died an' dat th'owed her to hab to come home. My mammy had been her maid, so when she got ready to come home she brung my mammy wid her.

"Hit was hard back in dem days. Ever' mornin' fo' day break you had to be up an' ready to git to de fiel'. Hit was de same ever' day in de year 'cep' on Sunday, an' den we was gittin' up earlier dan the folks do now on Monday. De drivers was hard too. Dey could say what ever dey wanted to an' you couldn't say nothin' for yourse'f. Somehow or yuther us had a instinct dat we was goin' to be free. In de even't when de day's wuk was done de slaves would be foun' lock' in dere cabins prayin' for de Lawd to free dem lack he did de chillun of Is'ael. Iffen dey didn' lock up, de Marsa or de driver would of heard 'em an' whupped 'em. De slaves had a way of puttin' a wash pot in de do' of de cabin to keep de soun' in de house. I 'members once ol' Ned White was caught prayin'. De drivers took him de nex' day an' carried him to de pegs, what was fo' stakes drove in de groun'. Ned was made to pull off ever'thang but his pants an' lay on his stomach 'tween de pegs whilst somebody stropped his legs an' arms to de pegs. Den dey whupped him 'twell de blood run from him lack he was a hog. Dey made all of de han's come an' see it, an' dey said us'd git de same thang if us was cotched. Dey don't 'low a man to whup a horse lack dey whupped us in dem days.

"After my mammy come whar I was I ho'ped her wid her work. Her tas' was too hard for any one person. She had to serve as maid to Mr. White's daughter, cook for all of de han's, spin an' card four cuts of thread a day an' den wash. Dere was one hundred an' forty-four threads to de cut. If she didn't git all of dis done she got fifty lashes dat night. Many a night me an' her would spin an' card so she could git her task de nex' day. No matter whut she had to do de nex' day she would have to git dem fo' cuts of thread, even on wash day. Wash day was on Wednesday. My mammy would have to take de clo's 'bout three quarters of a mile to de branch whar de washin' was to be done. She didn't have no wash board lack dey have now 'days. She had a paddle what she beat de clo's wid. Ever'body knowed when wash day was 'case dey could hear de paddle for 'bout three or four miles.

"Pow-pow-pow," dat's how it sound. She had to iron de clo's de same day dat she washed an' den git dem four cuts of thread. Lots of times she failed to git 'em an' got de fifty lashes. One day when Tom White was whuppin' her she said, 'Lay it on Marsa White 'case I'm goin' to tell de Yankees when dey come.' When mammy got through spinnin' de cloth she had to dye it. She used shumake berries, indigo, bark from some trees, and dar was some kind of rock (probably iron ore) what she got red dye from. De clo's wouldn't fade neither.

"De white folks didn't learn us to do nothin' but wuk. Dey said dat us warn't 'spose' to know how to read an' write. Dar was one feller name E.C. White what learned to read an' write endurin' slavery. He had to carry de chillun's books to school fer 'em an' go back atter dem. His young marsa taught him to read an' write unbeknowance' to his father an' de res' of de slaves. Us didn' have nowhar to go 'cep' church an' we didn' git no pleasure outten it 'case we warn't 'lowed to talk from de time we lef' home 'twell us got back. If us went to church de drivers went wid us. Us didn't have no church 'cep' de white folks church.

"After ol' Ned got sech a terrible beatin' fer prayin' for freedom he slipped off an' went to de North to jine de Union Army. After he got in de army he wrote to Marsa Tom. In his letter he had dose words:

"'I am layin' down, marsa, and gittin' up, marsa;' meaning dat he went to bed when he felt like it an' got up when he pleased to. He told Tom White dat iffen he wanted him he was in the army an' dat he could come after him. After ol' Ned had got to de North, de yuther han's begin to watch for a chance to slip off. Many a one was cotched an' brung back. Dey knowed de penalty what dey would have to pay, an' dis cause some of 'em to git desp'rite. Druther dan to take a beatin' dey would choose to fight hit out 'twell dey was able to git away or die befo' dey would take de beatin'.

"Lots of times when de patterollers would git after de slaves dey would have de worse' fight an' sometimes de patterollers would git killed. After de war I saw Ned, an' he tol' me de night he lef' the patterollers runned him for fo' days. He say de way he did to keep dem frum ketchin' him was he went by de woods. De patterollers come in de woods lookin' for him, so he jes' got a tree on 'em an' den followed. Dey figured dat he was headin' fer de free states, so dey headed dat way too, and Ned jes' followed dem for as dey could go. Den he clumb a tree and hid whilst dey turned 'roun' an' come back. Ned went on widout any trouble much. De patterollers use ter be bad. Dey would run de folks iffen dey was caught out after eight o'clock in de night, iffen dey didn' have no pass from de marsa.

"After de day's wuk was done there warn't anything for de slaves to do but go to bed. Wednesday night they went to prayer meetin'. We had to be in de bed by nine o'clock. Ever' night de drivers come 'roun' ter make sho' dat we was in de bed. I heerd tell of folks goin' to bed an' den gittin' up an' goin' to yuther plantation. On Sat'day de han's wukked 'twell noon. Dey had de res' of de time to wuk dey gardens. Ever' fambly had a garden of dere own. On Sat'day nights the slaves could frolic for a while. Dey would have parties sometimes an' whiskey and home-brew for de servants. On Sundays we didn't do anything but lay 'roun' an' sleep, 'case we didn' lack to go to church. On Christmas we didn't have to do no wuk: no more'n feed de stock an' do de li'l wuk 'roun' de house. When we got through wid dat we had de res' of de day to run 'roun' wharever we wanted to go. 'Co'se we had to git permission from de marsa.

"De owners of slaves use to giv' cornshuckin' parties, an' invite slaves from yuther plantations. Dey would have plenty of whiskey an' other stuff to eat. De slaves would shuck corn an' eat an' drink. Dey use'to giv' cotton pickin's de same way. All of dis went on at night. Dey had jack-lights in de cotton patch for us to see by. De lights was made on a forked stick an' moved from place to place whilst we picked. De corn shuckin' was done at de barn, an' dey didn' have to have de lights so dey could move dem frum place to place.

"De only games dat I played when I was young was marbles an' ball. I use to sing a few songs dat I heard de older folks sing lak:

> Cecess ladies thank they mighty grand,
> Settin' at de table, coffee pot of rye,
> O' ye Rebel union band, have these ladies understan'
> We leave our country to meet you, Uncle Sam.

"Dese songs was 'bout de soldiers an' de war. There was one 'bout ol' General Wise what went:

> Ol' General Wise was a mighty man,
> And not a wise man either,
> It took forty yards of cloth to make a uniform,
> To march in de happy land of Canaan.

> Chorus:

> Ha-ha, ha-ha, de south light is comin',

Charge boys, charge, dis battle we mus' have,
To march us in the happy land of Canaan.

"There was a song 'bout General Roddy too:

Run ol' Roddy through Tuscumbia, through Tuscumbia,
We go marchin' on.

Chorus:

Glory, glory hallelujah, glory, glory hallelujah,
Glory, glory hallelujah as we go marchin' on.

Ol' Roddy's coat was flyin', ol' Roddy's coat flyin' high,
Twell it almost touch de sky, we go marchin' on.

"I was a pretty big boy when de war broke out. I 'member seein' the Yankees cross Big Bear creek bridge one day. All of de sojars crossed de bridge but one. He stayed on de yuther side 'twell all de res' had got 'crost, den he got down offen his horse an' took a bottle of somp'in' an' strowed it all over de bridge. Den he lighted a match to it an' followed de res'. In a few minutes the Rebel sojars come to de bridge to cross but it was on fire an' dey had to swim 'crost to de yuther side. I went home an' tol' my mammy dat de Rebels was chasin' de Union sojars, an' dat one of de Unions had poured some water on de bridge an' sot it afire. She laugh' an' say: 'Son, don't you know dat water don't make a fire? Dat musta been turpentine or oil?' I 'member one day Mr. Tom was havin' a big barbecue for de Rebel soldiers in our yard. Come a big roarin' down de military road, an' three men in blue coats rode up to de gate an' come on in. Jes' as soon as de Rebels saw 'em de all run to de woods. In 'bout five minutes de yard was full of blue coats. Dey et up all de grub what de Rebels had been eatin'. Tom White had to run 'way to keep de Yankees from gittin' him. 'Fo de Yankees come, de white folks took all dey clo's an' hung 'em in de cabins. Dey tol' de colored folks to tell de Yankees dat de clo's was dere'n. Dey tol' us to tell 'em how good dey been to us an' dat we lacked to live wid 'em.

"All day dat we got news dat we was free, Mr. White called us niggers to the house. He said: 'You are all free, jes' as free as I am. Now go an' git yerse'f somewhar to stick your heads.' Jes' as soon as he say dat, my mammy hollered out: 'Dat's 'nough for a yearlin'. She struck out 'crost de fiel' to Mr. Lee Osborn's to git a place for me an' her to stay. He paid us seventy-five cents a day, fifty cents to her an' two bits for me. He gave us our dinner along wid de wages. After the crop was gathered fer that year, me an' my mammy cut an' hauled wood for Mr. Osborn. Us lef' Mr. Osborn dat fall an' went to Mr. John Rawlins. Us made a share crop wid him. Us'd pick two rows of cotton an' he'd pick two rows. Us'd pull two rows of corn an' he'd pull two rows. He furnished us wid rations an' a place to stay. Us'd sell our cotton an' open corn an' pay Mr. John Rawlins for feedin' us. Den we moved wid Mr. Hugh Nelson an' made a share crop wid him. We kep' movin' an' makin' share crops 'twell us saved up 'nough money to rent us a place an' make a crop fer ourse'ves. Us did right well at dis until de Ku Klux got so bad, us had to move back wid Mr. Nelson for protection. De mens that took us in was union men. Dey lived here in the south but dey tooken us part in de slave business. De Ku Klux threat to whup Mr. Nelson 'case he took up fer de niggers. Heap uv nights we would hear of the Ku Klux comin' an' leave home. Sometimes us was scared not to go an' scared to go 'way from home.

"One day I borrowed a gun frum Ed Davis to go squ'el huntin'. When I taken de gun back I didn't unload hit lack I allus been doin'. Dat night de Ku Klux called on Ed to whup him. When dey tol' him to open de do', he heard one of 'em say, 'Shoot him time he gits de do' open. 'Well, he says to 'em,' wait 'twell I kin light de lamp.' Den he got de gun what I had lef' loaded, got down on his knees an' stuck hit th'ough a log an' pull de trigger. He hit Newt Dobbs in de stomach an' kilt him. He couldn't stay 'roun' Burleson any mo', so he come to Mr. Nelson an' got 'nough money to git to Pine Bluff, Arkansas. The Ku Klux got bad sho' 'nough den and went to killin' niggers an' white folks, too.

"I ma'ied Kizi Drumgoole. Reverend W.C. Northcross perform' de ceremony. Dere warn't nobody dere but de witness an' me an' Kizi. I had three sons, but all of 'em is dead 'cepin' one an' dat's Hugh. He get seven chilluns. He wuks on de relief.

"Abe Lincoln was as nobler man as ever walked. Jeff Davis was as smart man as you ever wan' to see. Endurin' de war he sheared his horse in sich a way dat he looked lack he was goin' one way when he'd gwine de de yuther. Booker T. Washington did one of de greates' things when he fix it for nigger boys an' girls to learn how to git on in de worl'.

"Slavery wouldn't a been so bad, but folks made it so by selling us for high prices, an' of co'se folks had to try to git dey money's worth out of 'em. The chillun of Is'ael was in bondage one time an' God sent Moses to 'liver 'em. Well I 'spose dat God sent Abe Lincoln to 'liver us."

ABE WHITESS

Interview with Abe Whitess
—*David Holt*

"MAYOR OF DOUGLASVILLE"

When the sunshine is warm, Abe Whitess, "Mayor of Douglasville," sits outside his cabin door near Bay Minette, Alabama, and watches the stream of traffic on US 31 just beyond his bare feet, "a' restin'" in the soothing sand. More than 90 years ago he was born not many miles from this same cabin over in Mississippi as a slave of Col. Rupert, who owned plantations in Alabama and Mississippi.

"I come over to Alabama after the surrender," Abe Whitess told his interviewer after he had retired with dignity to put on shoes before he permitted his photograph to be taken. "I went to a plantation in Butler County fust and then came on down here to Bay Minette.

"Slavery wasn't so bad. Col. Rupert was a good marster, but he lived way over in Mobile and us was at his Scooby (Scooba) plantation. That was in Kemper County and his overseer there sho was handy with a whup. I was a cotton hand and spent most of my time totin' water for the other hands. When Mr. Lincoln 'mancipated us we was free and I didn't carry any more water. It wasn't 'twell after the surrender I went to Butler County, where Colonel Rupert had him another plantation.

"I come down here to Bay Minette a long time ago. I us'ta be chairman of the Republican party in Baldwin County here, but when the Republicans got in they made the white gem'mun what took my job postmaster. Then the bank I had my money in went busted in another Republican time and I loses $658.05. I votes for Mr. Roosevelt now."

Abe Whitess stopped to take a chew of his favorite tobacco and admitted that he lived alone in his one-room cabin by preference. He doesn't want women "botherin' 'round his place and ain't had no truckin' with 'em for years." He cooks on the hearth just as his mammy did before him decades ago in the slave quarters of Colonel Rupert's plantation.

Abe Whitess, Bay Minette, Alabama

Despite his years, he is well able to take care of himself. He carries his nine decades lightly, and his kindly face is topped by a wealth of snow white hair. Though he lost money in the bank failure that made him a Democrat in politics, Abe owns 14 acres of land, part of which he farms. He has cleared a portion of it for a baseball diamond which is rented to Negro teams, who play there frequently. The fee is always collected before a ball is thrown.

Several years ago he donated a part of the acreage to be used for a public road which opened up a portion of Douglasville, the suburb in which he lives, where a number of Negroes had developed a residential section. His people named him then and since "Mayor of Douglasville," without office or emolument, but Abe wears the title with a dignified content for his remaining years.

United States. Work Projects Administration

CALLIE WILLIAMS

Interview with Callie Williams
—*Mary A. Poole, Mobile*

PATTEROLLERS USED SHACKLES, SAYS CALLIE

Callie Williams was only four years old at the time of the surrender, but stories told to her by her mother are vividly remembered, and the fact that she has had the same environment continously throughout the years imprinted these happenings permanently on her mind. She lives at 504 Eslava Street, Mobile.

"My mammy and pappy was brought to Alabama by specalators who sold 'em to Mr. Hiram McLemore at Newport Landing, on de Alabama ribber," Callie said. "Mammy's name was Vicey and she was born in Virginia, but my pappy was born in Kentucky. His name was Harry. Mr. McLemore had about three hundred head of slaves, some of 'em on one plantation of about two thousand acres an' de res' on another place of about five hundred acres. He sho' did have a pretty house. It was all white and ramblin-like and had big trees aroun' it. Dere was a cool well and a big dairy right close by it and den de cabins was all in a row in de back, some of 'em made out of planks, but mos' of 'em was made wid logs. Dey was all named after whoever lived in 'em."

Aunt Callie needed little urging to tell of the old days, and she claims to vividly remember her master's family.

"His wife was named Axie Bethea and he had seven children," she said.

"One of 'em I never will forget, Miss Julia, 'case she gimme de first calico dress I ever had and I was proud as a peacock wid it. Miss Julia was de oldest little girl and dey give me to her.

"My mammy say dat dey waked up in de mornin' when dey heard de sweep. Dat was a piece of iron hangin' by a string and it made a loud noise when it was banged wid another piece of iron. Dey had to get up at four o'clock and be at work by sunup. To do dis, dey mos' all de time cook breakfast de night befo'.

"Pappy was a driver under de overseer, but mammy say dat she stay at de little nursery cabin and look after all de little babies. Dey had a cabin fixed up with homemade cradles and things where dey put all de babies. Der mammies would come in from de field about ten o'clock to nurse 'em and den later in de day, my mammy would feed de youngest on pot-licker and de older ones on greens and pot-licker. Dey had skimmed milk and mush, too, and all of 'em stayed as fat as a butter balls, me among 'em. Mammy saw dat I always got my share.

"De slaves got rations every Monday night. Dere would be three pounds of meat and a peck of meal. Dere was a big garden dat all of 'em worked and dey had all de vegetables dey needed and dere was always plenty of skimmed milk. Dey cooked de meals on open fireplaces in de big iron 'spiders.' Dem was big pots hangin' over the fire from a hook. Dey do de cookin' at night and den warm it over the nex' day if dey wanted it dat way.

"While mammy was tendin' de babies she had to spin cotton and she was supposed to spin two 'cuts' a day. Four 'cuts' was a hard day's work. What was a cut? You oughta' know dat! Dey had a reel and when it had spun three hundred yards it popped. Dat was a "cut." When it had been spun, den another woman took it to de loom to make cloth for de slaves. Dey always took Saturday afternoon to clean up de clothes and cabins, 'case dey always had to start work on Monday mornin' clean as a pin. If dey didn't, dey got whupped for bein' dirty.

"Some of de niggers, after dey'd been beat, would try to run away and some of 'em got loose, but de patterollers caught a lot of 'em and den dey'd get it harder dan ever befo' and have shackles out on dere feet wid jes' enough slack for 'em to walk so dey could work.

"If dey wanted to go 'possum huntin' or fishin', dey could get passes from de overseer. Two things dey really loved to eat was 'possum and fish. Dey'd eat and eat 'till dey'd get sick and den dey'd have to boil up a dose of Boneset tea to work 'em out. If dat didn't make 'em feel better, dey'd go to Marster. He always kept calomel, bluemas and quinine on hand. If dey got too bad off sick, den marster would call de doctor. De children wasn't bothered with nothin' much but worms and dey'd take Jerusalem oak. It was de seed of a weed dat cook' and mix' 'lasses to make it taste like candy. Boneset was a bush and dey'd boil de leaves to get boneset tea.

"Mos' of de time de slaves would be too tired to do anything but go to bed at night, but sometimes dey would set around and sing after supper and dey would sing and pray on Sunday. One of de songs dat was used mos' was 'Yon Comes Old Marster Jesus.' If I remembers rightly, it went somp'n' like dis:

> I really believe Christ is comin' again
> He's comin' in de mornin'
> He's comin' in de mornin'
> He's comin' wid a rainbow on his shoulder
> He's comin' again bye and bye.

"Dey tried to make 'em stop singin' and prayin' durin' de war, 'case all dey'd ask for was to be sot free, but de slaves would get in de cabins and turn a big wash pot upside down and sing into dat, and de noise couldn't get out. I don't remember nothin' about dis ceptin' what mammy say.

"When de Surrender come, she say dat a whole regiment of soldiers rode up to de house yellin' to de niggers dat dey was free. Den de soldiers took de meat out of de smokehouse and got all de 'lasses and meal and give it all to de niggers. Dey robbed de bees and den dey eat dinner and go on to de nex' place, takin' de menfolks wid 'em, all 'ceptin' de ones too old, my pappy among 'em.

"After it was all over my pappy rented land on Mr. McLemore's place and he and mammy stayed dere till dey died. Dey was buried in de same graveyard dat Mr. McLemore had set aside for his slaves. I married Frank Williams in Montgomery, Alabama, but our marriage was nothin' like mammy say her and pappy's was. She say dey 'jumped de broom stick.' When any of de slaves wanted to get married dey would go to de big house and tell marster and he'd get his broomstick and say, 'Harry, does you want Vicey?' And Harry would say 'yes.' Den Marster would say, 'Vicey, does you want Harry?', and she say 'yes.' Den marster say, 'Jine hands and jump de broomstick and you is married. De ceremony wasn't much but dey stuck lots closer den, and you didn't hear about so many divorces and such as dat.

"All my children is dead but two. I had five. One is livin' in Atlantic City, N.J., and I live here wid de other one. I 'spects I'll jes' go on livin' here 'till I die, serving Ole Marster as bes' I can. If all de peoples on dis here earth would do dat, we wouldn't be pestered wid all dese here troubles like we is nowadays.

United States. Work Projects Administration

SILVIA WITHERSPOON

Interview with Silvia Witherspoon
—*Susie R. O'Brien, Uniontown, Alabama*

FOOTS GETS TIRED FROM CHOPPIN' COTTON

Aunt Silvia Witherspoon sat dozing on the steps of her small cabin, her bare feet stretched out in the dry dust of the yard. A large horsefly settled upon her broad nose and after a moment Aunt Silvia's composure was disturbed to such an extent that she waved it off with her hand. On doing so her eyes opened and she saw me approaching the steps. She straightened. "Mawnin', Mistis. Jus' settin' heah coolin' off my foots. I'se plum wo' out f'um choppin' cotton.

"Yassmam," she continued, after I had asked a few questions, "I remembers some things 'bout de slavery days. 'Co'se I can't remember jus' 'zactly how old I is, but I mus' be mought nigh on to ninety, 'ca'se I was a raght sizable gal when war ended. I was bawn on a plantation in Jackson, Mississippi, dat belonged to my Massa, Dr. Minto Witherspoon. My Pappy an' Mammy was name Lum an' Phyllis Witherspoon. De white folks lived in a big, white house made outten logs. Honey, Massa an' Mistis Witherspoon was quality! Yassmam, dey was quality. Us slaves was treated lak we was somp'n round dat place. Massa didn't 'low no oberseer to tote no strop 'hine his niggers. Besides dat we was fed good an' had good clothes. He useta done had brogans sont out in boxfuls f'um Mobile. My job was to do little things aroun' de white folks' house, but befo' dat I stayed in de quarters an' nussed my mammy's chilluns, while she worked in de fiel's. She would tie de smalles' baby on my back so's I could play widout no inconvenience. I laked to stay at de big house, dough, an' fan de flies offen de white folks while dey et. Dat was de bes' job I eber had. Mistis gived me a dress dat de white chilluns done out-growed an' on Sunday I was de dressed-upest nigger in de quarter.

"Massa 'longed to de Presbyterian chu'ch, so all us niggers was Presbyterians too. We all went to our own chu'ch dat was on de place dar.

"Massa kep' a pack of blood hounds but it warn't often dat he had to use 'em 'ca'se none of our niggers eber runned away. One day, dough, a nigger named Joe did run away. Believe me Mistis, dem blood hounds cotch dat nigger 'fo' he got to de creek good. It makes me laugh till yit de way dat nigger jumped in de creek when he couldn't swim a lick jus' 'ca'se dem houn's was atter him. He sho made a splash, but dey managed to git him out 'fo he drowned.

"I ma'ied about a year atter de war, an' Mistis, I didn't have no pretty dress to git ma'ied in. I ma'ied dat ole nigger in a dirty work dress an' my feets was bare jus' lak dey is now. I figured dat iffen he loved me, he loved me jus' as well in my bare feets as he would wid my shoes on.

"Does I believe in ghosties? Sho I does. I don't suppose you was bawn wid a veil on yo' face lak I was, 'ca'se I can see dem ghosties as plain as dey was here raght now. I'll tell you 'bout one dat comes out de white folks chu'ch yard. On dark rainy nights, I sees him, tall wid long white robes drappin f'um him. He carries a big light so bright dat you can't see his face, but he looks jus' lak a man. It don't bother me none, 'ca'se I don't bother it.

"I keeps a flour sifter an' a fork by my bed to keep de witches f'um ridin' me. How come I knows dey rides me? Honey, I bees so tired in de mawnin' I kin scarcely git outten my bed, an' its all on account of dem witches ridin' me, so I putt de sifter dere to cotch 'em. Sometimes I wears dis dime wid de hole in it aroun' my ankle to keep off de conjure, but since Monroe King tuk an' died us ain't had much conjerin' 'roun' here. You know dat ole nigger would putt a conjure on somebody for jus' a little sum of money. He sold conjure bags to keep de sickness away. He could conjure de grass an' de birds, an' anything he wanted to. De niggers 'roun' useta give him chickens an' things so's he wouldn't conjure 'em, but its a funny thing Mistis, I ain't never understood it, he got tuk off to jail for stealin' a mule, an' us niggers waited 'roun' many a day for him to conjure hisself out, but he never did. I guess he jus' didn't have quite enough conjurin' material to git hisself th'ough dat stone wall. I ain't never understood it, dough."

GEORGE YOUNG

Interview with George Young
—Ruby Pickens Tartt, Livingston, Alabama

PETER HAD NO KEYS 'CEPIN' HIS'N

"De Lawd wouldn' trusted Peter wid no keys to Heaven," in the opinion of George Young, of Livingston, Alabama, born into slavery ninety-one years ago. George knew the rigors of slavery under an absentee landlord and brutal overseers, according to the story he tells.

"I was born on what was knowed as de Chapman Place, five miles nor'wes' of Livingston, on August 10th, 1846," George began his tale. My name was George Chapman an' I had five brothers, Anderson, Harrison, William, Henry an' Sam, an' three Sisters, Phoebe, Frances and Amelia. My mother's name was Mary Ann Chapman an' my father's name was Sam Young, but he b'longed to Mr. Chapman. Us all belonged to Governor Reuben Chapman of Alabama.

"The overseer's name was Mr. John Smith, an' anudder's name was Mr. Lawler. He was dere de year I was born, an' dey called hit "Lawler year." Bofe of 'em was mean, but Lawler, I hear tell, was de meanes'. Dey had over three hund'ed slaves, caze dey had three plantations, one at Bodke, one in Huntsville and dis yere one. I can't say Marsa Chapman wasn't good to us, caze he was all de time in Huntsville an' jes' come now an' den an' bring his family to see 'bouten' things. But de overseers was sho' mean.

"I seed slaves plenty times wid iron ban's 'roun' dey ankles an' a hole in de ban' an' a iron rod fasten to hit what went up de outside of dey leg to de wais' an' fasten to another iron ban' 'roun' de waist. Dis yere was to keep 'em from bendin' dey legs an' runnin' away. Dey call hit puttin' de stiff knee on you, an' hit sho' made 'em stiff! Sometimes hit made 'em sick, too, caze dey had dem iron ban's so tight roun' de ankles, dat when dey tuck 'em off live things was under 'em, an' dat's whut give 'em fever, dey say. Us had to go out in de woods an' git May-apple root an' mullen weed an' all sich to bile for to cyore de fever. Miss, whar was de Lord in dem days? Whut was He doin'?

"But some of 'em runned away, anyhow. My brother Harrison was one, an' dey sot de "nigger dogs" on him lack fox houn's run a fox today. Dey didn't run him down till 'bout night but finely dey cotched him, an' de hunters feched him to de do' an' say: "Mary Ann, here' Harrison." Den dey turned de dogs loose on him ag'in, an' sich a screamin' you never hyared. He was all bloody an' Mammy was a-hollerin', 'Save him, Lord, save my chile, an' don' let dem dogs eat him up.' Mr. Lawler said, 'De Lord ain't got nothin' do wid dis here, an' hit sho' look lack He didn't, 'caze dem dogs nigh 'bout chewed Harrison up. Dem was hard times, sho'.

"Dey didn't l'arn us nothin' an' didn't 'low us to l'arn nothin'. Iffen dey ketch us l'arnin' to read an' write, dey cut us han' off. Dey didn't 'low us to go to church, neither. Sometimes us slip off an' have a little prayer meetin' by usse'ves in a ole house wid a dirt flo'. Dey'd git happy an' shout an' couldn't nobody hyar 'em, 'caze dey didn't make no fuss on de dirt flo', an' one stan' in de do' an' watch. Some folks put dey head in de wash pot to pray, an' pray easy, an' somebody be watchin' for de overseer. Us git whupped fer ev'ything iffen hit was public knowed.

"Us wasn't 'lowed visit nobody from place to place, an' I seed Jim Dawson, dis here same Iverson Dawson' daddy; I seed him stobbed out wid fo' stobs. Dey laid him down on his belly an' stretch his han's out on bofe sides an' tie one to one stob, an' one to de yuther. Bofe his feet was stretch out an' tied to dem stobs. Den dey whupped him wid a whole board whut you kiver a house wid. De darkies had to go dere in de night an' take him up in a sheet an' carry him home, but he didn't die. He was 'cused of gwine over to de neighbor's plantation at night. Nine o'clock was de las' hour us had to be closed in. Head man come out an' holler, "Oh, yes! Oh, yes! Ev'ybody in an' do's locked." An' iffen you wan't, you got whupped.

"Wan't nobody 'lowed to co't. Us jes' taken up together an' go ahead, an' dat thing wan't fixed 'twel atter S'render.

"De Patterolles come frum diffe'nt places, an' de Tank'sleys, de Potts, de Cock'ells an' de Greg'rys was neighbors. I may of went to dey house an' dey claim to pertec' me playin' wid dey little nigger chillun, but iffen de Patterollers ketch me, dey claim dey wan't 'sponsible. One day, dey tuck out atter me an' I come right here in Livingston, but I was gwiner run away anyhow, 'caze I had seed ole Uncle Thornton dat mornin'. See, I was de ca'f nusser an' soon as I lef' de house I met him, an' here come de overseer, Mr. Smith. He sent atter me an' he said, 'I seed six niggers in de woods whut run away,' an' asked did I see ole man Thornton. I said, 'No, I ain't seed nobody.' He said, 'Nev' mine, I make you tell a better tale'n dat in de mawnin'.' So when I went wid de slop to dem ca'ves I got to thinkin' 'bout dat whupping so I come right here.

"Mr. Norville had a wood-shop right 'crost de road dere by de white folks Baptis' church an' I hid in de back of hit dat night. But dey foun' me an' tuck me back. Den dey stop me from ca'f nussin' an' put me in de fiel' under de head man. I was glad of dat, 'caze I wanted to be wid de other han's, but when I foun' out how 'twas, I wanted to be back. Hit was a harder tas' den when I was nussin' ca'ves an' keepin' 'em from breakin' in de fiel' an' eatin' up de crop.

"I was a good han' an' obeyed de owners an' de head man an' never had no 'fuse 'bout work. I went one time to Bennet's Station, ten miles b'low here, wid jes' seven mo' niggers from de Chapman place, an' us driv' over a thousan' head of cattle to Atlanta, Ga., an' never had no trouble. I was easy pleased. Give me a piece of candy an' I'd lick hit 'twel my mouf was so'. I reckon hit was all right, but I dunno. All de nations couldn't rule. Jes' lack hit is now, de stronges' people mus' rule.

George Young, Livingston, Alabama

"Atter S'render, dey tuck a darky for de probit jedge, but dat nigger didn't know nothin' an' he couldn't rule. So den dey tuck a white man name Sanders, an' he done all right. We was under hard task-masters an' I'm glad dey sot me free, 'caze I was under burden an' boun'. But ignerrancy can't rule, hit sho' can't. We is darkies, an' white folks ought to be favorable. Some speaks better words'n others, but ev'ybody ain't got de same heart, an' dat's all I knows.

"No'm, I dunno nuthin' 'bout no spirits, either, but Christ 'peered to de 'postles, didn't He, atter he been dead? An' I'se seed folks done been dead jes' as na'chel in de day as you is now. One day me an' my wife was pickin' cotton right out yonder on Mr. White's place, an' I looked up an' seed a man all dressed in black, wid a white shirt bosom, his hat a-sittin' on one side, ridin' a black hoss.

"I stoop down to pick some cotton, den look up an' he was gone. I said to my wife—I call her Glover but she go by two names—I said, Glover, wonder whar dat man went what was ridin' long yonder on dat pacin' hoss?' She say, 'What pacin' hoss an' what man?' I said, 'He was comin' down dat bank by dat ditch. Dey ain't no bridge dere, an' no hoss could jump hit.' Glover said, 'Well, I'm gwine in de house 'caze I don' feel lack pickin' cotton today.'

"But I ain't skeered of 'em. I gets out de path plenty times to let 'em by, an' iffen you kin see'em, walk 'roun' 'em. Iffen you can't see 'em, den dey'll walk 'roun' you. Iffen dey gets too plentiful, I jes' hangs a hoss shoe upside down over de do', an' don' have no mo' trouble. But ev'ybody oughter have dat kinder min', to honor God. He 'peered to de 'ciples atter He died, an' he said also, 'Peter, I'll give you de keys to de kingdom'. But Peter didn't have nobody's keys 'cep'in' his'n. Don't you know iffen he'd of give Peter all dem keys, dey's a heap of folks Peter gwineter keep out of dere jes' for spite? God ain't gwineter do nothin' dat foolish. Peter didn't have nobody's key 'cepin' Peter's!"

Transcriber's Note

Original spelling has been maintained; e.g. "*stob*—a short straight piece of wood, such as a stake" (American Heritage Dictionary).—The Works Progress Administration was renamed during 1939 as the Work Projects Administration (WPA).